I0576807

James Spedding

Reviews and Discussions

Literary, political, and historical not relating to Bacon

James Spedding

Reviews and Discussions
Literary, political, and historical not relating to Bacon

ISBN/EAN: 9783337068790

Printed in Europe, USA, Canada, Australia, Japan

Cover: Foto ©ninafisch / pixelio.de

More available books at **www.hansebooks.com**

REVIEWS AND DISCUSSIONS

LITERARY, POLITICAL, AND HISTORICAL,

NOT RELATING TO BACON.

BY

JAMES SPEDDING.

LONDON:

C. KEGAN PAUL & CO., 1, PATERNOSTER SQUARE.

1879.

PREFACE.

ALMOST all these papers were written, not because I wanted a subject for an article, but because an article on the subject was wanted at the time. The occasions have passed away, and the particular value which they then possessed has passed away with them. But the subjects—whether notable books, or characters of interesting men, or disputable questions in policy or literature—are for the most part still open for discussion, and liable to reappear on the stage from time to time. Now, when I have had to study a question myself, I have always wished to know something of its history, and what was thought and written about it in its former stages. Each of these Essays may be regarded as a chapter or section in the history of the question it deals with; and as they were all written carefully, and upon good information, and with no other object than to represent the case truly as it then appeared to me, it has been thought worth while to collect them into a volume, where they may be found by those whom they concern.

Taken as representing the opinions of an individual inquirer, and not of a judicial board, they may carry less weight in the reader's estimation, but he can judge better what weight is due to them.

I have reprinted them without other alteration than the correction of misprints or awkward sentences, the omission of one or two passages which I do not now altogether approve, and the restoration of the original text where alterations, which I did not think improvements, had been made by the editor.

CONTENTS.

I.

HENRY TAYLOR'S STATESMAN.

A REVIEW.*

This is a book full of excellent matter, on a subject which has hitherto occupied very little attention. It consists of Essays on various points connected with the administration of Government; written, it would seem, at different times and in different moods, as the sundry experiences of a life occupied in public business have happened to suggest them. Its more immediate and especial importance lies in its bearing upon our present system of Executive Government; the manifold defects of which, both in theory and in practice, are well held up to the public view, and a plan of reform suggested and urged with earnest eloquence upon the general attention, which needs nothing but a strong call from without to be introduced with the greatest ease and advantage. It is in the hope, we imagine, of awaking such a call, that the book has been published in its present somewhat immature and undigested state. The essays, though composed with the intention of working them up afterwards into a complete body of doctrine, have been hurried into the world almost as they were originally written, for the professed purpose of " diverting the attention of thoughtful men from the forms of government to the business of governing ; "—with a view (we may add) to such a reconstitution of our executive establishment as may ensure for the public service both a more plentiful supply of able men and a fairer scope for the exercise of their abilities. But although, to those who are capable of entering fully into the author's views, this will form

* *Edinburgh Review*, October, 1836.

the point of main and central interest, it is not by any means the only point of interest which the book possesses. Though the questions discussed in it relate especially to government and persons governing, the manner in which they are discussed is pregnant with instruction for all persons, and applicable to a great variety of occasions; and everybody who cares about the government of life, or takes a serious interest in the philosophical knowledge of men and manners, will find his account in a diligent study of it.

·Much wanted, however, and well timed as the book appears to us to be, it is in danger, we fear, of falling into temporary neglect; and we could almost wish it had been aimed more to catch immediate attention, though at the risk of detracting something from its permanent value. It is written in a tone of subdued earnestness, with an almost total abstinence from false effects and exaggerated expressions; and its leading characteristic is unqualified, uncompromising good sense, brought to the consideration of all matters, great and small; with a steady resolution to treat no subject as unworthy to be gravely written about, which is worthy to be seriously entertained by a wise man with a view to conduct and action. These qualities, while they stamp it unequivocally as a sterling and standard work, must at the same time prevent it from being immediately appreciated as it deserves, except by those who may be disposed to read it with a kind of interest which is rarely felt by contemporary readers in any work which is not posthumous. By the generality, the work of a living author will always be read carelessly and inadvertently; for they always expect to find everything done to their hands by him; and if they miss any of his meanings, they are satisfied with thinking, not only that it is his fault—which it may or may not be,—but that he is the loser, which, if the meanings be worth anything, he certainly is not. We have endeavoured, for our own part, to keep clear of this delusion, and to read the book as if it were our business, not to deal out critical judgments for the sake of the author and his publisher, but to understand its value for our own benefit, and to proclaim it for the benefit of the public.

The task of pointing out defects we would willingly dispense with altogether; knowing how much healthier it is for the mind to be engaged in feeding freely on what is good than in pointing out what is bad. But it sometimes happens that the detection of one error is the removal of many. A defect in one part will often, by placing the reader in a false position, make other parts appear defective likewise; which are not so in reality. And few persons will be at the pains of correcting the fault and re-adjusting their position for themselves. The principal faults which we have observed in this book are of this kind ; and do in fact, as it appears to us, throw more difficulties in the way of ordinary readers than they can be reasonably expected to overcome.

In the first place, the title (which is not so unimportant a thing as it may be thought, for it gives the first direction to the reader's expectation) seems to us ill chosen ; as tending to raise anticipations which the work itself is neither calculated nor intended to fulfil. The name seems to promise a finished portrait of a Statesman, ideal or actual,—or at least a finished sketch, more or less roughly executed, but made out in all its parts, and exhibiting all his proportions; whereas we are presented only with the *disjecta membra*, thrown together with little regard to their completeness, and with no attempt at all to show how they will compose into a consistent figure. We cannot regard this as a trifle. On all subjects which do not admit of exact treatment it is necessary to have a constant reference to the *purpose* of the writer in order to interpret his meanings rightly. If we set out with a wrong notion of this purpose, we are less likely to correct that notion as we proceed, than to misinterpret everything else with reference to it. " The Statesman " must look to suffer much irrelevant criticism from this cause. People will perplex themselves with attempting to discover in each paragraph a more direct bearing on the character of *the* Statesman, than it was meant to have. Hence the meaning of some passages will be distorted ; that of others overstretched ; detached observations will be mis · construed with reference to what goes before ; what are meant merely for remarks will be taken for precepts ; qualities and practices which are only described will be understood as 'recommended.

The difficulty is increased by the division of the book into chapters, and still further by the orderly arrangement of the first five or six of them; in which the education, the fortunes, and the duties of a statesman are treated of, if not with completeness, yet with a coherency which prolongs the promise of the title-page.

It must at the same time be observed, that this fault, whatever it be, is entirely confined to the title and the typographical arrangement. The preface and the conclusion warn us what to look for. But as it is usual to skip the preface, and at least not to begin with the conclusion, we suspect that the original misdirection will send more people the wrong way than the warning will set right again. Otherwise we should have had nothing to object; for we cannot better describe the real nature, purposes, and pretensions of the book, than in Mr. Taylor's own words. In the preface, after speaking of the want of some coherent body of doctrine on administrative government, as it ought to be exercised in a free state, he proceeds—

"I should be much indeed misunderstood, if, in pointing to this want in our literature, I were supposed to advance, on the part of the volume thus introduced, the slightest pretension to supply it. Amongst the dreams of juvenile presumption, it had, I acknowledge, at one time entered into my fancy, that if life should be long continued to me, and leisure should by any happy accident accrue upon it, I might, in the course of years, undertake such an enterprise. When this vision lost some of its original brightness, I still conceived that I might be enabled to blot from Bacon's note of 'deficients' so much of the doctrine 'De Negotiis' as belongs to the division which he has entitled 'De Occasionibus Sparsis.' But the colours of this exhalation also faded in due season; and when the scheme came to be chilled and condensed, the contents of the following volume were the only result that, for the present at least, I could hope to realize."—Preface, p. x.

On reviewing these contents, he speaks in his Conclusion thus—

"I close these dissertations with a full sense of the incoherent manner in which they have been brought together,—shaping themselves into no system, falling into no methodized sequence, and holding to each other by hardly anything beyond their relevancy to one subject. My apology for so offering them is, that if I had applied myself to devise a system, or even a connected succession, I must necessarily have written more from speculative meditation, less from knowledge. What I knew practically, or by reflection flowing from circumstances, must have been connected by what I might persuade myself that I knew inventively, or by reflection flowing from reflection. I am well aware of the weight and value which is given to a work by a just and harmonious incorporation of its parts. But I may be permitted to say, that there is also a value currently and not unduly attached to what men are prompted to think concerning matters within their knowledge. Perceiving that I was not in a condition to undertake such a work as might combine both values, the alternative which I have chosen is that of treating the topics severally, as they were thrown up by the sundry suggestion of experience.

"It is possible, indeed, that by postponing my work to a future period, a further accumulation of experience might have enabled me to improve it in the matter of connection and completeness, without derogating from the other claim. But it has appeared to me that there are considerations which render the present time seasonable for the publication of a book even thus imperfect upon this theme."—P. 261.

That the work does not possess that double value which Mr. Taylor distinctly disclaims for it, we have certainly no right to complain, even if we were otherwise disposed to regret it. But we do in fact rate so highly that kind of value which it does possess, that we are glad he did not risk the loss of that in an attempt to combine the other with it. Where the object is general instruction, inquiry, or illumination, and not to prove some specific point or recommend some specific act, dispersed and aphoristic writing is on many accounts the best. Dispersed observations can be better depended on for sincerity than those which are made to complete a treatise or to support a theory; for in the latter case, if they do not fit their place naturally, there is a strong temptation to *adapt* them to it. And, if not insincere, they will often be found to be empty. Thoughts called forth by the passing occasion, or strongly suggested by present experience are always valuable so far as they go—for they represent something in nature. Those suggested only by general theory and speculation have often no value at all, and represent nothing. Moreover the former, if written down as occasion presses them from the mind, are certain to be not only more sincere and substantial in themselves, but more just and forcible in the expression. Like notes made on the spot, or sketches taken from nature, they are better left as they are. Every attempt to retouch them from imagination or from memory diminishes their force and truth. Add to this, that as knowledge, when conveyed in a dispersed manner, is handled with more soundness and vigour in the writing, so it is commonly better digested in the reading. When presented in a complete and systematic form, it is generally either swallowed whole or dismissed altogether. The particular truths which build up and vivify the system—if not corrupted to give a show of support to it—pass alike untasted by those who accept and by those who reject the whole. By the one they are indolently received as true; by the other they are not less indolently set aside as false or from the purpose. In neither case is the reader induced to turn his own mind loose upon the matter presented to it, to work upon and digest it for itself and derive its own conclusion; which is the only just and reasonable process by which mind acts upon mind, and knowledge is increased and multiplied.

There is something, no doubt, very noble and imposing in a complete and comprehensive system, made out in all its features, and supported by the coherency of its parts. But such systems are rarely without some mixture of falsehood, and the falsehood passes current with the rest. These are the false gods that steal away men's worship from the truth. Not only is the mind of the reader dazzled and won by their beauty, their pretensions, and the final rest to inquiry which they seem to promise; but the patient and laborious circumspection with which the inventor himself sets out is not unfrequently exhausted in the construction of them, and turns into mere devotion before they are completed. Of all the systems invented to provide a final solution for the doubts and difficulties which perplex an intricate question, where is that one which does not contain, in one part or another, some prodigious assumption?

> " We figure to ourselves
> The thing we like; and then we build it up,
> As chance will have it, on the rock or sand;
> For Thought is tired of wandering through the world,
> And homebound Fancy runs her lark ashore;"—*

Words which we would almost venture to fix as a motto to every book that ever professed to contain a system.

For his own personal reputation, indeed, Mr. Taylor might have done better had he given to his book that appearance of absoluteness and pretension which is fitted to catch indolent attentions, and to make men think less of the quality of the

* Philip van Artevelde.

matter and more of the authority of the writer. But his object being not to provide men with opinions on administrative government, but to set their minds freely at work about it; "to ring a bell to call other wits together—which is the meaner office;" to draw attention to the subject rather than to himself; to excite inquiry rather than satisfy it;—he has on all accounts, we think, judged wisely in choosing the dispersed manner of discussion.

At any rate, whatever may be thought about the mode of treatment which Mr. Taylor has thought fit to adopt, the book must be taken for what it is. It distinctly professes to be in its nature fragmentary. We are not, therefore, to look for completeness in its several parts; we are not to fancy that questions which are not discussed are thereby represented as unimportant; that duties which are not urged are meant to be considered unessential; that distinctions not dwelt on have been therefore overlooked. The reader must fill up the picture for himself. He is not to inquire whether the writer has said everything in the way of qualification and explanation which is necessary to prevent his judgments and precepts from being misunderstood; but whether they are capable of being so explained and qualified as to be free from objection. Obvious however as this is, it is not less obvious that such a task requires more candour and a more simple and serious spirit than is usually brought to the perusal of a "new work, by the author of," etc., and more trouble than the generality of readers will think fit to impose upon themselves; and that much misconception and some offence will arise in consequence. We certainly wish that Mr. Taylor had provided against this more carefully; which he might have done, without endangering the freshness of his matter, by merely adopting a different arrangement of topics and interposing a few sentences here and there to keep the reader in company with him.

It occasionally happens that in the pursuit of his argument he just crosses the border of some neighbouring question of great extent and importance, and passes out again, not only without surveying it, but without any apparent notice of its existence. In consequence of this, some readers will not be aware that anything lies beyond; and of those who are, the greater number will suppose that Mr. Taylor is ignorant of it himself. A simple sentence of warning, conveying some general idea, however dim and undefined, of the direction, the nature, and the extent of the inquiry which it did not suit him to pursue, would have prevented both these misapprehensions. To take the first example which offers itself. Speaking in the second page of the course of education which parents should provide for those sons whom they design for political life, he says, "At the age of sixteen, or thereabouts, the general education of the boy should be for the most part completed; and whether or not it be completed, at that age, or but little later, the specific should begin." He then goes on to recommend a variety of studies and exercises in which the boy should be worked,—all with a view to his efficiency as a practical statesman,—not to the integrity and expansion of his character as a man. Now Mr. Taylor cannot mean that, by the age of sixteen, the character can (generally speaking) have had room and time to expand freely in all directions; still less can he recommend such an education as would cripple or neglect one half of the character, in order to give greater intensity and effect to the other. But his expressions do not preclude such an interpretation; and we the rather mention it, because it is the tendency of these times to run headlong into the very error which he has omitted to guard against. If he were himself charged with assenting to this doctrine, he would probably say that, by the "general education of the boy," he meant only that elementary education, which has no reference to any specific career, and furnishes no preparation for the performance of any specific duty; that, by the commencement of the specific education at the age of sixteen, he meant only that it should then begin to *mix* with the general; that, at that age, such a direction should be given to the general education as might gradually take in more and more of the peculiar studies requisite for the after career, and without interfering with the development of the other faculties, might call gradually into more especial activity those which would be more especially wanted for the business of life; not that the *education* should cease, but that the *apprenticeship** should

---

* We borrow this expression from a book which has attracted less attention than, considering its attractive qualities, we can well account for,—Mr. Hartley Coleridge's "Biographia Borealis;" a book which has every title to be popular, which a

begin. And certainly looking to the large field of a statesman's operations, the variety of powers and knowledge which he should

light and entertaining subject, a masterly treatment, singular fulness and variety of interesting m itter, and a playful brilliancy of execution, can give. There are few subjects of much interest either to men or philosophers, in which something may not be found in it either wise or witty, generally both. The passage to which we have adverted in the text, is so valuable in itself, and so much to our present purpose, that we take leave to extract it entire.

" The position is simply this—*a mere apprenticeship is not a good education.*

" Whatever system of tuition is solely adapted to enable the pupil to play a certain part in the world's drama, whether for his own earthly advantage, or for that of any other man or community of men, is a mere apprenticeship. It matters not whether that part be high or low—the hero or the fool.

" *A good education,* on the other hand, looks primarily to the right formation of the Man in man, and its final cause is the well-being of the pupil, as he is a moral, responsible, or immortal being.

" But, because to every man there is appointed a certain ministry and service, a path prescribed to duty, a work to perform, and a race to run, an office in the economy of Providence,—a good education always provides a good apprenticeship; for usefulness is a necessary property of goodness.

" The moral culture of man, and so much of intellectual culture as is conducive thereto, is essential to education. Whatever of intellectual culture is beyond this should be regarded as pertaining to apprenticeship, and should be apportioned to the demands of the vocation for which that apprenticeship is designed to qual fy.

" A man whose education is without apprenticeship will be useless; a man whose education is all apprenticeship will be bad, and therefore pernicious, and the more pernicious in proportion as his function is high, noble, or influential.

" Most of the systems of tuition provided for the subordinate classes have been defective; as aiming either solely to qualify the pupil for his station, or to give him a chance and hope of rising above that station; either to make the man a mere labourer, or to turn the labourer into a gentleman,—the discipline or improvement of the man being too often postponed or omitted. The tuition of the higher castes is equally defective, when it forms gentlemen to be mere gentlemen; where it refers the primary duties to the rank, not to universal obligation. Secondly, when it inculcates the acquirement of mental or personal accomplishments as ultimate ends, without reference either to practical utility or to self-edification. Thirdly, when all apprenticeship is omitted, or an apprenticeship given wholly alien from the peculiar, individual, and functionary duties; as *e.g.*, when a scion of nobility is crammed with the arbitrary technicals of professional scholarship, or wastes his time in learning to do for himself what his steward, his gamekeeper, or his chaplain could do better for him. Fourthly, where the whole education is subservient to the apprenticeship. This is perhaps the commonest fault of all, especially with that unfortunate class whose education is to be their portion and means of advancement. It bears a creditable semblance of steadiness and industry, it wins the applause of parents and tutors, it makes shining and rising young men, and sometimes judges, chancellors, ambassadors, and ministers of State. But it does not make good men or wise men either. Even if it leave the heart uninjured, it keeps the mind unnaturally ignorant; for, viewing all things in an artificial relation to one object, it sees, and therefore knows, nothing in its true relations to man and the universe. The more their knowledge the greater their errors. The greater their command of

possess, the variety of interests which he should enlarge his
understanding to comprehend and his heart to sympathize with ;
and looking also to the neglected state in which the whole region
of this power and knowledge is left by the ordinary liberal
education of these times ; he might well urge that the early
intermixture of such studies as he recommends ought to be considered not as a crippling of any other faculties or a usurpation of
the time due to them, but as an essential element in the education,
not of the statesman only, but of the man ; indispensable to the
harmonious development of the entire character—to the accomplishment of the mind in one of the three graces which constitute
its perfection. "For as the good of the body is divided into
health, beauty, strength, and pleasure ; so the good of the mind,
inquired in rational and moral knowledges, tendeth to this—to
make the mind sound and without perturbation ; beautiful and
graced with decency ; and *strong and agile for all duties of life.*"

There is evidence elsewhere in the volume that Mr. Taylor
does by no means overlook or underestimate these considerations.
We doubt not that in speaking of the specific education he saw it
in its due subordination to that which has for its object the
formation of a manly character. What we complain of is, that
he has not taken care that his reader shall see it in the same
relation, and from the same point of view.

As another example of the same defect, we may mention the
omission, in the earlier part of the book, of any reference to the
ends which a statesman should propose, and the spirit in which
he should enter his career. Yet is this the most important thing
of all ; for it is the constant pursuit of a good end which can
alone guide a man safely through the more perplexed paths and
difficult dilemmas of duty : the end which each action proposes
not only determines its direction, so that it can rarely be erroneous,
but imparts its savour, so that it can never be corrupt,—a security
this, which doctrine cannot teach ; for there is no precept for the
politic government of a man's actions, which may not be used or

facts the more perilously false their inferences. They may, indeed, be wise in their
own craft, but they are pitiful blunderers when they step beyond it. Be it recol-
tected that we are not speaking of that devotion of time to a professional study
which may be a duty, but of that perversion of self-government which makes the
profession all in all."—Life of Roscoe, *Note.*

construed basely, unless each action be tested by the only true criterion of its fitness—its conformity to a noble purpose.

The very familiarity of this contemplation to Mr. Taylor's own mind, may be one reason why he has not thought it necessary to dilate upon it. His own imagination is filled, as we shall presently have occasion to show, with an august conception of the ends to which a statesman ought to dedicate himself, and the faith in which he ought to live. To him therefore it did not seem necessary to introduce cautions and qualifications of this kind; for to a mind so occupied every precept presents itself at once corrected and justified by a silent reference to this standard: base actions are base *of course;* misapplied precepts stand detected beyond the necessity of exposure. But here again he has forgotten to carry his reader along with him, which he might and should have done. It was not necessary to discuss the subject; perhaps it was judicious to avoid it. But it ought not to have been silently dismissed. Something should have been said to raise the reader to the same point of view, and fill his imagination, if not with the same idea, at least with some vague conception of noble aims to be accomplished, towards the accomplishment of which every action which does not directly or indirectly work is understood to be condemned.

There is another defect of a somewhat different kind, but which will equally give rise to misconceptions and interfere with the just impression which the work is otherwise calculated to produce. In treating of the several qualifications which a statesman should possess and the rules which he should observe, there is no attempt to mark their *relative* importance as compared one with another. Questions, not indeed unworthy of consideration, but certainly of no vital interest, are introduced with as much formality, and discussed as gravely, as minutely, and as earnestly as others with which his gravest duties and permanent wellbeing are intimately connected. Matters so unlike in their relative importance that they ought not, in the popular phrase, to be mentioned in the same day, are handled, one after another, with no difference in the manner of treatment, and no pause between to mark the transition. As many pages of grave advice and sound argument are devoted to the arrangement of the statesman's drawing-room, as to the management of his office;—to the regulation of his diet, as to that of his conscience. The background (so to speak) and the distance are not less distinct in their forms and bright in their colours than the foreground, and are thus brought too close to the eye. Hence the book is out of perspective, and the first impression is one of disproportion and incongruity,—a thing to be avoided at any rate, because it is ludicrous; but more especially to be avoided here, because most readers, not feeling a real interest in the subject, will exert themselves rather to enjoy the impression than to overcome it; and such readers, whatever other claims to respect they may want, will have at least the respectability of numbers, and due allowance should have been made for their infirmity. This might have been done, either by simply throwing all these lesser matters together into one section; with a few words of introduction, explaining their real bearing on the statesman's character and the space which they might justly occupy in his thoughts; or, which is better, by a more careless and disengaged way of handling them,—by treading, as it were, more lightly over the ground, and playing a little with the argument. This latter method demands however for its execution a peculiar genius, and not a common one, which Mr. Taylor either does not possess or does not think it honest to indulge. If so, we disagree with him; for as a truth is not the less deep and touching for being presented in a ludicrous aspect, so the discussion of it need not be the less grave and earnest for mixing a little laughter with its gravity.

We beg it at the same time to be understood, that it is to the *manner* of these discussions, and to the manner only, that we object. The habit of earnestly investigating and meditating upon ordinary matters we strongly approve. There is scarcely anything so trivial, but a wise man will be wiser for knowing exactly how and what it is; and that, not so much because it is always worth while to do in the best way possible whatever must be done in one way or another, as for the sake of the *principles* which the inquiry is sure to disclose. It may be said of the human as truly as of the physical world, that "they be not the highest instances which give the securest information;" and that "mean and small things can discover great, better than great can discover the small." For the knowledge of human nature, and the government of human conduct, more light is gained by watching a man in his ordinary and familiar concerns, in which he is most true to himself, and least an actor to the world, than in the execution of his more ambitious and agonistic duties. The principle of the action is developed as perfectly in the small as in the great; but the case being simpler, of more common occurrence, and taking less hold on the imagination and affections, it is much more open to a steady examination.

We would therefore recommend every man to cultivate this habit of philosophical meditation on "familiar matters of to-day" —on the ordinary life and conversation both of himself and of other men; and only to beware of announcing the result of his meditations with too much pomp and circumstance ;—remembering that they who hear him will compare the tone of announcement with the *instance*, which is trivial; not with the principle involved, which in its wider and remoter applications may be of infinite importance.

It may be thought that we have insisted more on this want of keeping and proportion than we had any right to do, considering that the book does not profess to be a complete and harmonious whole. But the fact is, that whatever the book may profess to be, people reading a volume consecutively will always regard it more or less as one thing, and its several parts as belonging to each other; and they will not the less *feel* the effect of any disproportion, for being warned, however distinctly, that proportion is not meant to be preserved.

Perhaps it is worth while to show in an example how the same kind of speculation looks, when drawn, as it were, in its proper perspective; and we select the example by an obvious preference from Mr. Taylor's own writings. In "Philip van Artevelde" there are several passages in which a few hasty words serve to inform us that the thoughts of the hero have been gravely occupied on matters no less trivial than dress and diet ; and that he could, if necessary, have given a great deal of detailed advice to statesmen on these subjects, which they might have followed with great advantage. Yet we will venture to assert that these passages have struck nobody as ludicrous; because in that finished work the picture is complete, and every lesser matter in due subordination to the greater. The following soliloquy, for instance, is the fruit of a meditation on the importance which a statesman should attach to eating and sleeping. Artevelde is on the tower at daybreak, overlooking the town, then suffering under the double misery of plague and famine. After a while it occurs to him that he has been watching all night—

> " I have not slept; I am to blame for that;
> Long vigils, joined with scant and meagre food,
> Must needs impair that promptitude of mind
> And cheerfulness of spirit, which, in him
> Who leads a multitude, is past all price.
> I think I might redeem an hour's repose
> Out of the night that I have squandered yet.
> The breezes launched upon their early voyage
> Play with a pleasing freshness on my face.
> I will enfold my cloak about my limbs
> And lie where I may front them—here, I think—
>   (*He lies down.*)
>
> *If this were over,*—blessed be the calm
> Which comes on me at last—a friend in need
> Is Nature to us—that when all is spent,
> Brings slumber—bountifully—whereupon
> We give her sleepy welcome—*If all this*
> *Were honourably over—Adriana——* "

He then sleeps for a moment, but starts up again suddenly at the sound of the horse's foot; and this little "Chapter concerning Sleep" (most skilfully subdued, while it lasts, by the intermingling of deeper interests) passes away altogether; absorbed in "the cares and mighty troubles of the times," from which it has afforded, like sleep itself, a brief recess.

Our meaning will be better understood if we add, that the *substance* of those chapters in the "Statesman" which relate to ordinary matters—as chairs, tables, candles, or dessert—is as proper and pertinent as the reflections above quoted; but that the manner in which they are introduced produces something of the effect which would have been felt, if Artevelde had been introduced addressing Van den Bosch in a formal speech on the propriety of not forgetting to go to bed.

Having said thus much by way of preparation, we beg to indulge our readers with the following sketch of the statesman's drawing-room, which, we think, deserves attention, if not for its importance to his Majesty's Government, at least for its beauty as an *interior* :—

"But as there will not always be life enough in the society of books to afford enjoyment to a statesman, let him step from the library to the drawing-room. A small society should not infrequently be formed there, consisting for the most part—but not wholly—of intimate acquaintances, and they should be persons of lively conversation—but above all, of easy natures. Knowledge and wit will naturally be found in sufficient proportions in the society of a man of talents occupying an eminent position; but if knowledge be argumentative and wit *agonistic*, the society becomes an arena, and loses all merit as a mode of relaxation. An adequate proportion of women will slacken the tone of conversation in these particulars, and yet tend to animate it also. And there is this advantage in the company of women—especially if some of them be beautiful and innocent—that breaks in conversation are not felt to be blanks; for the sense of such a presence will serve to fill up voids and interstices. But though knowledge, wit, wisdom, and beauty should be found in this circle, there should be no sedulous exclusion of such persons not possessed of these recommendations, as would otherwise naturally find a place there. For unless the statesman between the business and the pleasures of the world have lost sight of its charities, he will not find his society the less of a relaxation for mixing some of the duties and benevolences of life with its enjoyments, and he will count amongst its amenities, if not amongst its charms, some proportion of attentions to the aged, and kindness to the dull and unattractive. It may also be observed that dulness, like a drab ground, serves to give an enhanced effect to the livelier colours of society.

"It will be perhaps equally desirable for the statesman whose business exhausts his excitability, and for him whose excitement, beginning in business, pursues him in his social hours, that the society which they cultivate should be *quietly* gay. Exuberant noisy gaiety will overbear the spirits of the exhausted man, and over-stimulate those of the other. Some reference should be had to this object in the lighting of his rooms, for the loud or low talking of a company, together with the tone of mind belonging to the tone of voice, very much depends upon that,—as any canary-bird will teach us when a handkerchief is thrown over his cage.

"Music is an excellent mode of relaxation to those who possess—I will not say an *ear* for it, because that seems a shallow expression—but a faculty of the mind for it. Yet unless a man's susceptibility in this kind be very peculiar, he will generally prefer music which mixes itself with conversation, or alternates with it by brief returns, to music which sets it aside. Instrumental music, exciting without engrossing the mind, will often rather stimulate and inspire conversation than suppress it; though to take this advantage of it, the company must break up into retired groups or couples, speaking low in corners. But the singing of ladies is a thing which, in courtesy if not for enjoyment, must be heard in silence; unless (which is best) it be heard from an adjoining room,

through an open door, so that they who' desire to listen to the song closely may
pass in, and they who would listen more loosely and talk the while, may stay
out. But under all circumstances, and not for the sake of the talk only, but for
the sake of the songs, it is well that there should be some pause and space
between one and another of them—filled up with instrumental music, if you
will. For a song which has a wholeness in itself should be suffered to stand by
itself, and then to die away in the mind of the hearer, time being allowed for the
effect of a preceding song to get out of the way of the effect of one which is to
follow. It would be well therefore if ladies, who are often slow to begin their
songs, would not be, when once begun, unknowing to intermit them."

A third fault produced by this defective method of arrangement
is of a more serious kind. We allude to the mixing up of two
subjects which ought to be kept distinct,—the doctrine which
teaches a man to do well for himself, with that which teaches
him to do his duty. There is a chapter on the "Arts of Rising;"
another on "Manners;" and a few paragraphs here and there
occurring, in which gentlemen whose object it is to get on in the
world are informed how they may best secure a reputation with
the world for abilities and virtues which they do not possess.
These chapters are so grave in their tone, so reasonable in many
of their suggestions, and come in company with so many earnest
appeals to the sense of duty and serious precepts for the government of life, that it is not at once obvious in what character they
are presented to us. They have no mark on their forehead to
distinguish them from their betters. One of them, to be sure, is
introduced with the following paragraph: "The arts of rising,
properly so called, *have commonly some mixture of baseness,*—more
or less according as the aid from natural endowments is less or
more." And the other concludes with an admonition that these
are the "mere *tricks* of statesmanship, *which it may be quite as well
to despise as to practise.*" But this is not enough to consign them
to their proper rank—to brand them as belonging to a different
class of doctrines;—a class which cannot be safely approached
by any one without great caution and without a mind strongly
.preoccupied with the *primum quærite.* Lord Bacon saw this so
clearly that he took care doubly and trebly to guard against
misapplication his elaborate and masterly treatise on the raising of
a man's fortune. He separated it from the rest of his book, "*De
Negotiis,*" under a distinct head,—"*De Ambitu Vitæ.*" He introduced

it with an elaborate apology and explanation; and concluded it with a solemn denunciation of all practices for the pressing of fortune, which should either lead a man to violate the laws of charity and integrity, or engage him in an "incessant and sabbathless pursuit." We certainly wish Mr. Taylor had followed this example; for we cannot but think that in assuming the base nature of the practices described to be too obvious to need denouncing, he pays a greater compliment to his readers than many of them will deserve. If they all felt as natural a contempt for whatever "has some mixture of baseness," as it is obvious from other parts of the book that he himself feels, there would be no danger of a misapprehension. But he should have remembered that the many highly respectable persons who know by precept, but do not feel in their hearts, the baseness of selfish cunning, will not perceive that these practices are spoken of with scorn.

Due allowance being made, however, for this objection, these chapters are heartily welcome to us on a double account. While they detect and put to shame the tricks of selfish ambition—and he who practices to gain favour in men's eyes for no end which he can justify, and in no spirit which he can honourably avow, will always be put to shame by detection—they at the same time contain much useful instruction for the man who seeks worldly honour and advancement in the spirit of duty. For it must never be forgotten that he who would not only keep his vessel pure but use it for the benefit of mankind, especially if his functions be of that kind which can only be exercised by working on and through the opinions and affections of other men, must stand well with the world no less than with his own conscience. For this end the simple possession of integrity is not enough. To the harmlessness of the dove he must unite the wisdom of the serpent. He must not despise the lesson which the unjust steward could teach him; for the children of light are not so wise but that they may learn something from the children of this world, who are in their generation wiser.

To what extent this wisdom may be *safely* practised—what kinds of artifice in this way are lawful—to what practices a man may bend himself without compromising his integrity—how low he may stoop to raise his neighbour without falling himself—how

C

unclean materials he may with clean hands work upon—how coarse may be the texture of his honour;—these are hard and dangerous questions, which can be adequately solved only by the fine sense of an honourable nature seeking a purpose purely honest with a resolution truly moral.* It is better therefore that they be not reduced to precept, nor discussed till they present themselves for practical decision ; but left to be decided in each case as it arises, and for that case only, by the individual conscience.

The same defect of arrangement has led to a fourth fault of a kind exactly opposite to the last ; which may be almost described as the mixing up of sacred with profane. As in the cases there referred to the tone of discussion sinks, or seems to sink, suddenly below the general level of the work, so in some other parts it rises as suddenly above it. There, in the midst of grave admonitions of what wise and good men ought to do, we stumble upon a description of what base men do. Here, in the midst of practical precepts and discussions addressed to the plain business-like understanding, we pass with imaginations unawakened and affections unprepared to strains of higher mood and far other interest, —vocal only to the purged ear and softened heart. We all know the effect of a pathetic speech on a mind not capable of, or not prepared for, the pathos. Such will be the effect of two or three chapters in this volume, which have reference to deeper interests, and point to perils and deliverances more intimate and spiritual, than the reader's mind has been instructed or his imagination raised to understand. The course of our criticisms may perhaps conduct us into this region before we conclude ; but for the present we are in too profane a mood to approach it nearer.

We have now pretty well exhausted our stock of objections ; and it is time to present our readers with a sample of the work itself—its substance and main import.

We have already said that it is chiefly important from its bearing on our system of executive government. The " Reform of the Executive " is treated in two successive chapters, which form together the most complete disquisition in the book. The

* " Whereas the resolution of men truly moral ought to be such as the same Consalvo said the honour of a soldier should be, e tela crassiore, and not so fine as that everything should catch in it, and endanger it."—Adv. of Learning.

subject is discussed from beginning to end,—the disease exposed, and the remedy prescribed. The remedy might be readily and safely applied ; but they from whom it should proceed are not at leisure; and even if they were, would doubtless wait, as the appeal is addressed to the public, till the public shall take up the cry. We wish these chapters had stood more in the front of the book; for the public is busy with novels and newspapers, and will not hear unless loudly addressed. The interior workings of Government, the slow processes by which measures are conceived, digested, and matured, are of necessity so reserved and noiseless and removed from public observation,—have so little in them of the interest which attaches to personal and party warfare, —that popular attention can never be naturally attracted towards those silent operations. Yet it might be thought that the magnitude of the results dependent upon them, together with a certain mystery which hangs about them, might be sufficient to awaken some passing interest, and draw away the public curiosity occasionally, and for a while, from the election, the elopement, or the last new novel. Consider how many things the Government has to attend to—the complication of affairs which it has to control—the enormous magnitude and variety of interests of which it is (nominally at least) the guardian, and which are, in fact, continually appealing to its protection. Where is the eye that watches, the head that comprehends, the hand that manages these many and conflicting matters ? "The Providence," says Ulysses—being in office, and speaking officially—

"The Providence that's in a watchful state
Knows almost every grain of Plutus' gold ;
Finds bottom in the uncomprehensive deep ;
Keeps pace with thought ; and almost, like the gods,
Does thoughts unveil in their dumb cradles.
There is a mystery (with which relation
Durst never meddle) in the soul of state,
Which hath an operation more divine
Than breath or pen can give expressure to."

Now, without daring to meddle with the deeper mystery which is here pointed at, we shall have mystery enough on our hands for the present, if we say that all this is done (so far as it is done) by human heads—by men with Christian names and surnames,

who may be seen in the flesh. Does anybody know who these
are, or where they come from? The heads of departments indeed
we know, and their under-secretaries; but we know also how
insecure is their official existence—how rapidly Tories give place
to Whigs, and Whigs to Tories—how incessantly they are occupied
during their short career—and what kinds of business their heads
and hands are full of during the parliamentary session. They
are responsible to Parliament for all that is done; but it is
obviously impossible that they can effectually superintend in
person any considerable proportion of the matters which are transacted in their name. Duties of vast extent and importance must
be devolved upon others. Can any one tell us who these persons
are? Whence they are supplied? How they have been educated?
What are their qualifications? We believe, that so far from being
provided with an answer to these questions, most persons will
have to pause before they perceive the difficulty at which they
point. Ask why it is that, whenever an able and accomplished
physician, lawyer, or clergyman is wanted, the difficulty is not
to find but to choose—the answer is ready. They have their
colleges, lecturers, tutors, professors; high prizes are offered;
into one or other of these professions almost everybody is drawn
who has his fortune to make, or any natural gifts to make it with.
Year after year we see multitudes venturing their hopes and
talents on those seas, and of those multitudes there are always
some who prevail and prosper. But how are we supplied with
able and accomplished statesmen? It cannot be said that abilities
and accomplishments are unnecessary, or that those which are
will come of themselves. Their duties are not less wide, less
complicated, or less important than those which belong to the
liberal professions. They stand in need of qualifications, certainly
not inferior, nor to be acquired by a less engrossing application;
nor can the number of those who try to acquire them and fail be
smaller in proportion. Yet where is the stream and succession of
candidates from whom, as in the other case, the most eminent
may be chosen for the highest offices? Of the few stragglers
who, being independent by inheritance, are nevertheless not
indisposed to do their work in the world, those who enter public
life are for the most part drawn away at once by one or other of

the noisy questions which happen to be agitating the public
mind at home from the multitude of pregnant interests—certainly
more numerous and often far more important—which call from
distant lands or from remote times. A few more there are who
being, though not independent, yet enterprising and ambitious,
also enter the public service; but they enter it as political
adventurers, and, if not narrowed in their moral character by that
most dangerous trade, are at least shut up in the creed and hopes
of a political party. But these (such as they are) are before the
public eye. Where are those whose operation is behind the
scenes, and for whose ability to discharge their duties a more
careful security ought to be taken in proportion as they are less
watched in the exercise of it? We do not pretend to answer this
question ourselves; but beg instead to call attention to the
following extract, which we are unable either to enlarge upon
with advantage, or to abridge without injury. It will probably
suggest the answer which Mr. Taylor (who professes to speak
" concerning matters within his own knowledge ") would give.
We do not venture to pronounce it to be the true one; but we
have not any better to suggest.

" The minister being thus relieved during the whole year, and his parliamentary assistant during the session of Parliament, it remains to inquire how
the office business (setting aside the mere routine and mechanical part) is to be
done without their help. The theory says, by one permanent and experienced
officer. Whether we admit that the theory speaks the truth, depends entirely
upon the view which we take of what the duties are, and of the manner in which
they ought to be executed.

"Descriptive and authenticated estimates of such duties are manifestly impossible to be given; but let some considerations be deemed worthy to be well
weighed.

" The far greater proportion of the duties which are performed in the office of
a minister are and must be performed under no effective responsibility. Where
politics and parties are not affected by the matter in question, and so long as
there is no flagrant neglect or glaring injustice to individuals, which a party can
take hold of, the responsibility to Parliament is merely nominal, or falls otherwise
only through casualty, caprice, and a misemployment of the time due from Parliament to legislative affairs. Thus the business of the office may be reduced
within a very manageable compass without creating public scandal. By evading
decisions wherever they can be evaded; by shifting them on other departments
or authorities, where by any possibility they can be shifted; by giving decisions
upon superficial examinations, categorically, so as not to expose the superficiality
in propounding the reasons; by deferring questions till, as Lord Bacon says,

'they resolve of themselves;' by undertaking nothing for the public good which the public voice does not call for; by conciliating loud and energetic individuals at the expense of such public interests as are dumb or do not attract attention; by sacrificing everywhere what is feeble and obscure to what is influential and cognizable; by such means and shifts as these, the single functionary granted by the theory may reduce his business within his powers, and perhaps obtain for himself the most valuable of all reputations in this line of life, that of 'a safe man;' and if his business even thus reduced strains, as it well may, his powers and industry to the utmost, then (whatever may be said of the theory) the man may be without reproach; without other reproach at least than that which belongs to men placing themselves in a way to have their understandings abused and debased, their sense of justice corrupted, their public spirit and appreciation of public objects undermined.

"Turning (I would almost say revolting) from this to another view of what these duties are, and of the manner in which they ought to be performed, I would in the first place earnestly insist upon this,—that in all cases concerning points of conduct and quarrels of subordinate officers, in all cases of individual claims upon the public and public claims upon individuals, in short, in all cases (and such commonly constitute the bulk of a minister's unpolitical business) wherein the minister is called upon to deliver a quasi-judicial decision, he should on no consideration permit himself to pronounce such decision unaccompanied by a detailed statement of all the material facts and reasons upon which his judgment proceeds. I know well the inconveniencies of this course; I know that authority is most imposing without reason alleged; I know that the reasons will rarely satisfy, and will sometimes tend to irritate the losing party, who would be better content to think himself overborne than convicted; I am aware that the minister may be sometimes by this course inevitably drawn into protracted argumentation with parties whose whole time and understanding is devoted to getting advantages over him; and with a full appreciation of these difficulties I am still of opinion, that for the sake of justice they ought to be encountered and dealt with. One who delivers awards from which there is no appeal, for which no one can call him to account (and such, as has been said, is practically his exemption), if he do not subject himself to this discipline, if he do not render himself amenable to confutation, will inevitably contract careless and precipitate habits of judgment; and the case which is not to be openly expounded will seldom be searchingly investigated. In various cases, also, which concern public measures as well as those which are questions of justice, ample written and recorded discussion is desirable. Few questions are well considered till they are largely written about; and the minds and judgments of great functionaries transacting business *inter mœnia* labour under a deficiency of bold checks from oppugnant minds.

"Again, in the view of those duties to which I would point, let this be included, that the department of the highest authority in the state should always be ready to take the lion's share of responsibility and labour where the importance of the affair invites it. Where there is hazard and difficulty the inclination on the part of the superior authority should be that of the stronger nature, rather to assume than to devolve. For it is in this harmony between official power and natural strength that the state is justified.

" Further, it is one business to do what must be done, another to devise what ought to be done. It is in the spirit of the British government as hitherto existing, to transact only the former business, and the reform which it requires is to enlarge that spirit so as to include the latter. Of and from amongst those measures which are forced upon him, to choose that which will bring him the most credit with the least trouble, has hitherto been the sole care of a statesman in office ; and as a statesman's official establishment has been heretofore constituted, it is care enough for any man. Every day, every hour, has its exigencies, its immediate demands ; and he who has hardly time to eat his meals, cannot be expected to occupy himself in devising good for mankind. 'I am,' says Mr. Landor's statesman, 'a waiter at a tavern, where every hour is dinner-time, and pick a bone upon a silver dish.' The current compulsory business he gets through as he may ; some is undone, some is ill-done, but at least to get it done is an object which he proposes to himself. But as to the inventive and suggestive portions of a statesman's functions, he would think himself a Utopian dreamer if he undertook them ; and such he would be if he undertook them in any other way than through a reconstitution and reform of his establishment.

" And what then is the field for these inventive and self-suggested operations ; and if practicable, would they be less important than those which are called for by the obstreperous voices of to-day and to-morrow ?

" I am aware that under popular institutions there are many measures of exceeding advantage to the people, which it would be in vain for a Minister to project, until the people, or an influential portion of the people, should become apprised of the advantage, and ask for it ; many which can only be carried by overcoming resistance, much resistance only to be overcome with the support of popular opinion and general solicitude for the object. And, looking no further, it might seem that what is not immediately called for by the public voice was not within the sphere of practical dealing. But I am also aware, that in the incalculable extent and multifarious nature of the public interests which lie open to the operations of a statesman in this country, one whose faculties should be adequate, would find (in every month that he should devote to the search) measures of great value and magnitude, which time and thought only were wanting to render practicable. He would find them, not certainly by shutting himself up in his closet and inventing what had not been thought of before, but by holding himself on the alert ; by listening with all his ears (and he should have many ears abroad in the world) for the suggestions of circumstance ; by catching the first moment of public complaint against real evil, encouraging it and turning it to account ; by devising how to throw valuable measures that do not excite popular interest into one boat with those that do ; by knowing (as a statesman who is competent to operations on a large scale may know) how to carry a measure by enlargement, such as shall merge specific objections that would be insurmountable in general ones that can be met : in short, by a thousand means and projects lying in the region between absolute spontaneous invention on the one hand, and mere slavish adoption on the other ; such means and projects as will suggest themselves to one who meditates the good of mankind— 'sagacious of his quarry from afar,'—but not to a Minister whose whole soul is, and must be, in the ' notices of motions,' and the order-book of the House of

Commons, and who has no one behind to prompt him to other enterprise, no
closet or office-statesman for him to fall back upon as upon an inner mind.

"This then is the great evil and want—that there is not within the pale of
our Government any adequately numerous body of efficient statesmen, some to
be more externally active and answer the demands of the day, others to be somewhat more retired and meditative, in order that they may take thought for the
morrow. How great the evil of this want is, it may require peculiar opportunities of observation fully to understand and feel; but one who with competent
knowledge should consider well the number and magnitude of those measures
which are postponed for years, or totally pretermitted, not for want of practicability, but for want of time and thought; one who should proceed with such
knowledge to consider the great means and appliances of wisdom which lie
scattered through this intellectual country,—squandered upon individual purposes, not for the want of applicability to national ones, but for want of being
brought together and directed; one who, surveying these things with a heart
capable of a people's joys and sorrows, their happy virtue or miserable guilt on
these things dependent, should duly estimate the abundant means unemployed,
the exalted ends unaccomplished, could not choose, I think, but say within himself, that there must be something fatally amiss in the very idea of statesmanship
on which our system of administration is based, or that there must be some
mortal apathy at what should be the very centre and seat of life in a country,
that the golden bowl must be broken at the fountain, and the wheel broken at
the cistern.

"How this state of things is to be amended, it may be hard to teach, at least
to minds which are fluttering in the perpetual agitation of current politics, or to
those who have stiffened in established customs. But to a free and balanced
understanding, I would freely say, that whatever other things be necessary (and
they are many), it is in the first place indispensable to a reform of the Executive
Government of this country, that every Minister of State charged with a particular department of public business, should be provided with four or six permanent under-secretaries instead of one;—that all of those four or six should be
efficient closet-statesmen, and two of them at the least be endowed, in addition
to their practical abilities, with some gifts of philosophy and speculation well
cultivated, disciplined, and prepared for use.

"Yet such is the prevalent insensibility to that which constitutes the real
treasure and resources of the country—its serviceable and statesmanlike minds—
and so far are men in power from searching the country through for such minds,
or men in Parliament from promoting or permitting the search, that I hardly
know if that Minister has existed in the present generation who, if such a mind
were casually presented to him, would not forego the use of it rather than hazard
a debate in the House of Commons upon an additional item in his estimates.

"Till the Government of the country shall become a nucleus at which the
best wisdom in the country contained shall be perpetually forming itself in
deposit, it will be, except as regards the shuffling of power from hand to hand,
and class to class, little better than a government of fetches, shifts, and hand-to-
mouth expedients. Till a wise and constant instrumentality at work upon
administrative measures (distinguished as they might be from measures of
political parties) shall be understood to be essential to the government of a

country, that country can be considered to enjoy nothing more than the embryo
of a government,—a means towards producing, through changes in its own
structure and constitution, and in the political elements acting upon it, something worthy to be called a government at some future time. For governing a
country is a very different thing from upholding a government. 'Alia res
sceptrum, alia plectrum.' "

Mr. Taylor then proceeds to consider in detail the establishment which a minister of state, according to the foregoing estimate
of his duties, ought to command; the functions which should be
assigned to his clerks; and the principles which should be observed
in selecting, in remunerating, and in promoting them. We have
not time to accompany him through this discussion; but we may
briefly state the practical suggestions to which it conducts him.
In the first place, he would have the mechanical part of the
office-business entirely separated from the intellectual, and
assigned to a separate class of persons, whose views and prospects
should be confined within their own sphere;—all the copying—
which is often of great importance in the transaction of business
—to be performed by hired writers, attached to the office, but
paid by the job; allowing only " a small class of salaried clerks
for the despatch of such part of it as requires secrecy." In the
second place, in order to secure a fit selection from among the
candidates for the intellectual department, he recommends that
there should be probationary appointments as well as confirmed
ones; and that for each vacant clerkship, not less than three
probationers should compete; and for each vacancy among the
probationers, not less than three candidates.

With respect to remuneration, Mr. Taylor decides that, on the
whole, " what is most conducive to good appointments in the first
instance, and thenceforward to deriving benefit from them, is to
offer a small remuneration to the beginner, with successive ex-
pectancies proportioned to the merits which he shall manifest,
and of such increasing amount as shall be calculated to keep easy,
through the progressive wants of single and married life, the
mind of a prudent man. Upon such a system, if unfit men belonging to influential families shall make good an entrance into the
service, they will be more easily got rid of; since, finding that
they have got but little in hand, and have but little more to
look to, they will hardly be desirous to continue in a career in

which they must expect to see their competitors shoot ahead of them."

But remuneration in money will not be enough to keep long in a state of contentment men gifted with the energy and ability which is requisite for this kind of work. "Active and intelligent men will, by the common ordinances of nature become discontented, and gather some rust upon the edge of their serviceable quality, if, whilst they find themselves going with large steps down the vale of years, they do not fancy themselves to be at the same time making proportionate approximations to some summit of fortune, which they shall have proposed to themselves to attain." Mr. Taylor is therefore of opinion, that the system should be so contrived that a "meritorious man may find some advancement accrue to him at least once in every ten years;" and that, wherever there is a marked distinction of merit, prefer-ment should invariably go by that, not by seniority. The security against abusive patronage would, he thinks, be adequate in the main; because "it is in the nature of industrious ability, acting through various methods and upon various motives, to vindicate its own claims under any system in which those claims are recognized; and the system which shall conform to this natural tendency, and be so framed as to *legitimate the rising of what is buoyant*, will be found to work the best."

There can be no doubt, we think, as to the wisdom of these suggestions, and the very great superiority which such a consti-tution of the Executive would have over the present system. The improvement, so far as we can judge, would be both immediate and unmixed.

It may still, however, be doubted whether this department of the public service, excluding as it does all political and parlia-mentary distinction, would, even thus constituted, be rich enough in worldly advantages and temptations to attract candidates of the best quality in sufficient numbers. The advantages which it holds out to young men of ability and enterprise are attended with some material drawbacks. The remuneration, though cer-tain, is small; the higher prizes are few and far between; the labour and confinement, sometimes the anxiety, not inconsider-able; and all the reputation which can be acquired is confined within the walls of the office. But there is yet a more serious disadvantage, which will be most felt by the best men. The life is essentially a subordinate, and may almost be termed an *unreal* one. Everything the clerk does must be done in the name, and subject to the approval, and (nominally, at least) under the direction of another. Thus he is always working on another man's ground, and seems to have no property in what he does. This want of something felt and recognized as proceeding from himself —of something for which he may claim credit, and which he may be called on to answer for—this privation, as it were, of a personal existence, we cannot but regard as a very serious evil in this kind of life; and as very likely not only to make a man dissatisfied, but to induce habits of indifference, to damp the spirit of energy and enterprise, and to enfeeble the sense of duty. To separate the man from his business is bad for both.

To a certain extent, indeed, the evil is inseparable from the thing, for somebody must be master; but we think it might be considerably alleviated, with great advantage to all parties concerned. The business, be it remembered, of the "indoor statesman" is not to execute only, but to consider, to devise, to suggest, to do everything but direct and decide. Many matters, therefore, must be trusted to him of great importance, and requiring the full weight and application of his mind. This he will rarely lend, unless he feel either that the whole transaction is to proceed from himself; or, at least, that in all which does proceed from him his own character is implicated. It appears to us, therefore, that those persons who are trusted for suggesting what is to be done, ought to be made publicly and personally responsible for all that they suggest; not, of course, that their names should ordinarily appear, but that they should be *liable* to appear, in case any transactions in which they have had a hand should be called in question. There would be no difficulty in effecting this. The under-secretary, we will suppose, or the clerk, draws up a paper for the information of the Secretary of State, recommending a decision. That decision is either adopted entirely, or adopted only in part, or set aside altogether. If adopted, let the paper on which it is founded remain as an official document,— producible, should the matter be inquired into, in the name, and

as the production of the author;—so he will be answerable for all
that is his own. If partly set aside, let the original paper remain
as before, with a note of the points overruled, and the reasons for
overruling them—so he will be answerable for nothing which is
not his own. If set aside altogether,—that is, if the matter be
taken entirely out of his hands,—his paper may be cancelled at
once. Under such a regulation his heart would be in his business.
But a man can hardly be expected to apply the full force of his
mind and conscience to the consideration of a question, when (as
under the present system) he knows that he is thinking only for
another,—that his opinion may very likely be overruled,—and
that he is in no way responsible for the ultimate decision. It
must often happen that an inferior functionary drawing up a
paper for the approval of his superior, entertains a different
opinion on the *principle* of the question at issue from that which
his superior is known to entertain. In that case, the best he can
do is to argue as well as he can on principles to which his own
mind does not assent,—generally a lame operation; adding,
perhaps, if he be solicitous to absolve himself from all responsibility, that in his private opinon the decision is an unjust one,
but with that he has nothing to do. It is more probable, however,
that he will not think it necessary to interpose such protest; and
then, in addition to the lameness of the operation, the responsibility
of the unjust decision falling between the two, is felt by neither.
If he knew himself liable to be called on to stand father to all
his own recommendations, he would take more care to keep the
breed pure.

We submit that this plan would be of advantage to all parties:
to the minister, because his position would be less false—he would
have less to avow of what he did not perform; to the clerk,
because he would have more to avow of what he did perform; to
the service generally, both because it would nourish a deeper
sincerity in devising, a bolder integrity in urging, and a more
hearty activity in executing; and because, by opening a new path
to ambition—an ambition humble indeed, but of the most wholesome kind—the ambition to enjoy a reputation for doing good
service in obscurity—it would increase the dignity of the profession, and tempt more aspirants into its ranks.

If the public service held out to young men of aspiring natures yet too poor or too wise to trust themselves in the hazardous game of party politics, such temptations as might enable it to compete with the liberal professions, able men would never be' wanted for it : they would present themselves unsought. As it is, a man can hardly be recommended to enter the public service, who has reasonable prospect of success in any other career; and while it remains thus, the selection of able men must be left to chance, or to the watchfulness and zeal of public men on behalf of the public ; which (if we may trust the spirit of Mr. Taylor's censures) is not much more to be depended on.

We have dwelt thus largely on this part of the book, not only because of its immediate practical importance, and because the Reform proposed is one of those towards which no step will be taken by those within, except through the influence of importunacy from without ;—but because, in order to understand the full value and meaning of the book, it is necessary that this question should be prominent in the reader's mind. An indifferent and inexperienced person will not readily appreciate the case and the importance of it ; but in reading these scattered essays (in which the subject is touched and crossed and approached in a variety of ways and moods), with a constant reference, direct or indirect, to the practical question, an impression will gradually work itself on the mind, of the great abilities, natural and acquired, which are requisite for the competent discharge of the public service; of the cultivation necessary to endow a man with such abilities; of the absence of any attempt in this country to provide a systematic education for that end; of the consequent " solitude of able men " to serve in affairs of state; and of the manifold duties undischarged or ill discharged, from the mere want of strength and spirit to guide the councils and execute the decisions of the Government;—an adequate appreciation of all which things cannot but inspire him with a zealous interest in the question concerning the remedy.

We had intended to enter at some length into Mr. Taylor's more miscellaneous disquisitions ; and to endeavour, by gathering up and arranging his scattered notices and precepts, to put together a Statesman, such as he would approve, out of the materials which

he has supplied to our hands. But we must be content with
recommending our readers to attempt this for themselves. Such
an exercise will at once disperse those misapprehensions which we
have pointed out as likely to mislead careless perusers. It will
keep their minds at that elevation, and in that state of activity,
which may enable them to fill up or allow for the breaks and
gaps; to entertain with a light attention the lighter matters; to
mark strongly whatever is essential and important; and so to see
the whole picture in proportion and perspective. Nor will the
study which this may require be otherwise thrown away; for the
reflections which they will meet with at every step (though so
just as to seem obvious, and to be actually barren to an inattentive
observer) will be found, by one who gives them time to unfold,
pregnant with meanings, and must be tasted curiously and digested
leisurely that their full virtue may be felt. We must be satisfied
with a single extract taken almost at random, which we submit
both as a sample of the work and as a theme for meditation. It
relates to "a statesman's most pregnant function—the choice and
use of instruments."

" It is less desirable to be surrounded and served by men of a shallow clever-
ness and slight character, than by men of even less talent who are of sound and
stable character.

*   *   *   *   *   *   *

" But if there be in the character not only sense and soundness, but virtue of
a high order, then, however little appearance there may be of *talent*, a certain
portion of *wisdom* may be relied upon almost implicitly. For the correspondences of wisdom and goodness are manifold; and that they will accompany each
other is to be inferred, not only because men's wisdom makes them good, but
also because their goodness makes them wise. Questions of right and wrong are
a perpetual exercise of the faculties of those who are solicitous as to the right
and wrong of what they do and see; and a deep interest of the heart in these
questions carries with it a deeper cultivation of the understanding than can be
easily effected by any other excitement to intellectual activity. Although, therefore, simple goodness does not imply every sort of wisdom, it unerringly implies
some essential conditions of wisdom; it implies a negative on folly, and an
exercised judgment within such limits as Nature shall have prescribed to the
capacity. And where virtue and extent of capacity are combined, there is
implied the highest wisdom, being that which includes the worldly wisdom with
the spiritual.

" A statesman who numbers the wise and good amongst his political friends,
men of sense and respectability among his adherents; who demeans himself in a
spirit of liberal but disengaged good-will towards his ordinary partisans, and

holds himself towards his tools in no reciprocity of that relation; who enlists in the public service all the capable men he can find, and renders them available to the extent of their capabilities, all other men's jealousies notwithstanding, and any jealousy of his own out of the question;—such a statesman has already, in the commonwealth of his own nature, given to the nobler functions the higher place; and as a minister, therefore, he is one whom his country may be satisfied to trust, and its best men be glad to serve. He, on the other hand, who sees in the party he forms only the pedestal of his own statue, or the plinth of a column to be erected to his honour, may, by inferior means and lower service, accomplish his purposes, such as they are; but he must be content with vulgar admiration, and lay out of account the respect of those who will reserve that tribute from what is merely powerful, and render it only to what is great. 'He that seeketh to be eminent amongst able men,' says Lord Bacon, 'hath a great task; but that is ever good for the public. But he that plots to be the only figure amongst ciphers, is the decay of a whole age.'"

The part of the book which is least satisfactory to us is the chapter "on the Ethics of Politics." We have not time to enter at large into the subject, and only mention it for the sake of keeping it in agitation; for there is no subject which needs agitating more.

The evils resulting from the unsettled state of this science as at present existing, and the perplexities which beset the path of a public man, whether he adopt the stricter or the looser creed, Mr. Taylor seems to us to estimate very justly. Those who would apply to political transactions the recognized rules of private morality cannot act up to their principle; those who deny their applicability "are often unable to find footing on any principle whatever."

We do not, however, think him happy either in the examples which he gives of the dilemma or in the solution which he offers. He attempts to find footing for himself on a distinction in principle between political and private ethics; and proposes to permit the statesman to set aside any precept of private morals, when he thinks that less harm will be done by the violation of the rule than by the action which the rule would prescribe.

The distinction, we think, is not a sound one; and is, in fact, a step the wrong way. To say that the violation of a *principle* of morality, whether in public or private life, can ever be morally justifiable, is little better than a contradiction in terms. To say that cases may occur in which the *rules* of morality must be violated in order to preserve the *principles* inviolate, is as true in private as in political matters. No doubt the cases are so very different, that the same principle applied to both prescribes a different set of rules for each ; and for want of observing this, the recognized code of political morality (so far as any code is recognized) is miserably defective; as appears from the number of doubtful actions which everybody pronounces wrong, yet everybody admits must be done " under existing circumstances." That the authorized bounds of morality, public or private, should be so strictly defined, that *every* action which they include may be set down as lawful, every action which they exclude as unlawful, is not perhaps to be wished ; for the conscience can perceive subtler distinctions than any words can define. But they should be made to include all actions to which a man will *ordinarily* have to consent; leaving a few doubtful ones outside, that they may not be assumed on general authority to be allowable, but explicitly sanctioned in each case by the individual conscience, duly exercised and awakened by the peril of responsibility. So far is our code of political morals from hitting the just boundary, that everybody actively engaged in politics is of necessity, with regard to that code, a truant and a vagabond ;—what he *must do* leaves out of sight what he must profess to approve of doing.

Fully conceding, however, to Mr. Taylor, that our creed stands in these respects grievously in need of revision, we cannot but think that the disease lies far deeper than any revision of the creed can reach ; and that the cure must be effected not by drawing the distinctions, but by pressing the *analogies*, between public and private duty. The root of the disease is this—there is no genuine sense of obligation towards the public. Among the motives to action of a sane man, mere public spirit is hardly recognized as one. In all dealings with the public, every man is assumed to be acting from motives of private interest. If any selfish motive be apparent, his conduct is accounted for at once and nobody wonders ; if none can be assigned, he is suspected of some *sinister* object, and people like him the worse ; if he persevere in a consistent course of action to his manifest disadvantage, he is pitied and forgiven as an enthusiast. Till of late years this state of feeling manifested itself in shameless dissoluteness. We are now more refined, and though our hearts are not better our conversation and professions are much more virtuous. Though we do not "appreciate in feeling" the importance of public duties, we at least "magnify them in words." From strumpets we are turned prudes. This is an improvement, no doubt, so far as it goes; for in all the ordinary duties which can be learned by rote prudery will go along with virtue. But as soon as a question presents itself which is not set down in the book, and requires for its solution the living and thinking principles of virtue and the delicate sense of honour, it is at once thrown out and lost.

How is this to be reformed? How is a vital principle of duty to be substituted for this heartless form of words? A manly consistency of action, for the mere movement in a straight line? We answer,—not by relaxing the code (for it is not by unlacing a prude that you can make modesty sit easily on her), but by teaching men to feel the same interest and sense of obligation in their dealings with the public which they do feel in their daily dealings with each other, and then to carry whole into the wider sphere the same principles of action which their heart and conscience have prescribed and sanctioned in the narrower. Nobody could execute this task better than Mr. Taylor, and we earnestly hope that he may hereafter apply himself to it.

When all is done, however, the principle of public obligation will in most men be comparatively weak—the rules intricate and difficult of application—the path of duty slippery and surrounded by temptations. The statesman must still "be engaged in a field of action which is one of great danger to truthfulness and sincerity," —his conscience must still "walk too like the ghost of a conscience, in darkness or twilight." In all these perils he must look for light to show him the way, and strength to carry him through, to the experiences and exercises of his private life in the duties between man and man. For this reason it is more peculiarly incumbent on him to preserve that side of his character sound and healthy; and to endeavour in all ways and at all times—by a stricter performance of all private duties—a deeper appreciation of private virtues—by exercising and enlarging his heart in domestic affections and neighbourly charities—to guard on all sides his private conscience from assault, and keep that vessel

D

pure; that his political conscience, parched with restless anxieties and exhausted by incessant attention to duties which it has not leisure to feel, may draw from it continually fresh supplies of health and nourishment.

To this division of the subject three chapters must be referred, —which we have already alluded to as likely to provoke a laugh, —because likely to be read in a different spirit from that in which they were written; the chapters on Marriage, on Order, and on the "Statesman out of Office." We have already transgressed our limits, or we should be tempted to quote them here, for the benefit of all those who are capable of appreciating the peril and the deliverance;—of all who can be made sad by the thought how easily the *man* may be absorbed in the *Statesman*,—may learn to know *himself* only as the controller of public interests, or the leader of a political party;—of all into whose imagination it has entered to conceive the dismal possibility of a man, through long practice in official transactions, official manners, and official forms of speech, acquiring in the end an *official heart!*

But we must content ouselves with recommending the book itself; and so break off. The peculiar conciseness and pregnancy of the style requires that it should be read slowly and every sentence tasted.

II.

THE WORKING OF NEGRO APPRENTICESHIP IN 1838.*

THE quantity of talking and writing which goes on under the sun has grown of late years into a practical inconvenience, towards the diminution of which every man ought, we think, to do something. Accordingly, having nothing conclusive to make known, we have been silent for some years on the condition of the negroes in the West Indies. Soon after we last addressed our readers on this subject, the object which we had so long laboured without ceasing to bring about was taken up in the true spirit by those to whom it especially belonged, and put in a way to be speedily and satisfactorily accomplished. The old language of argument and admonition, which had been vainly persevered in till it had become little better than a mockery and pretext for delay, was at length abandoned; and a new language was adopted which the Colonial Assemblies could hear. On the 28th of August, 1833, their consent to the ABOLITION OF SLAVERY was secured by an Act of Parliament, declaring that, whether they consented or not, within twelve months SLAVERY SHOULD POSITIVELY BE ABOLISHED; and they were invited to anticipate the operation of that law by making one in the meantime for themselves. For the loss of property thence accruing, ample compensation in sterling money was provided; and by withholding the payment of that compensation until effectual measures should be passed for the protection of the newly emancipated population, a further security

* 1. "Report of the Select Committee appointed to enquire into the working of the Negro Apprenticeship" London: 1837. 2. "Papers relative to the Abolition of Slavery." Parts I., II., III. London: 1837. (*Edinburgh Review*, January, 1838.)

was taken for their co-operation in that work also. The enactment of proper laws being thus secured, it remained only to secure the proper administration of them. This was effected by intrusting it to a body of magistrates sent out from England, paid by Government, independent of all local authorities, unconnected with all local interests, and, above all, "unacquainted with the negro character;"—capable, that is, of believing that black men are born not merely to raise sugar for white men, but to die and rise again for themselves.

Since the change was thus fairly set on foot, and the conduct of it was placed in willing and trustworthy hands, we have been content to watch its progress in silence; and though we have seen many things to deplore and some things to disapprove, we are bound to confess that our predominant feeling has been one of triumphant satisfaction. Many things we have seen to remind us how grievously the nature of a man may be defaced and degraded by the tyranny of his brother; but more to assure us how much will remain undestroyed, after all that tyranny can do;—how safely we may trust that good will be called forth by good, and that the place on which mercy drops will never long be barren; to teach us, not indeed for the first time, but by the largest and most striking example which has yet been given to the world, that neither complexion, nor climate, nor oppression itself, can make the condition of a man desperate, or exclude him from the great brotherhood of humanity. In watching the progress of this, —the newest and the noblest experiment in this kind,—we have seen the most sanguine hopes which in the confidence of our common humanity we venture to entertain, fulfilled one by one even beyond our expectations and taking their place among established truths; while the predictions of those who in the confidence of an exclusive acquaintance with the negro as distinguished from the human character so scornfully rejected them, we have seen one by one pass onwards to the proof, burst, and be forgotten. Already have the original disasters, announced for twenty years as unavoidable if ever slavery should be abolished, yet as more to be avoided than sin itself, been left in the secure distance. The cheerful augurs have forgotten their own presage. Other new forebodings have bubbled up in their place to meet the shifting occasion, and to vanish along with it, each swallowed by its practical refutation faster than we can pursue them; and so chasing each other to the place whither all false things go. The experiment has not yet reached its close. The prophetic soul of the planting interest has yet many things to dream of which are not to come. Many a fatal fear has to be engendered, announced, and forgotten, within the next few years. Such fears requiring no ground to stand on, and taking up no room in the mind, are not to be counted for their number; nor will they be all set at rest until the new system shall have had time to adjust itself, and the account of hopes and fears shall be finally closed. We have no wish to anticipate that natural consummation. Why should they die before their time? That the matter will finally issue in a state of enduring good, which will leave room for only one opinion with regard to the abolition of slavery,—namely, that it was in every view expedient and ought not to have been delayed a day longer;—for only one regret, namely, that it was not done sooner and done more boldly; that in the framing of the new law, the negroes were not trusted more and their masters less;—all this we seem to foresee so clearly, that we would willingly wait in silence for the due arrival of that day, rather than vex the subject with premature and needless disputation. Till that day arrives, the closing chapter in the history of the ABOLITION OF SLAVERY —perhaps the most instructive of all human histories—will be wanting, and it will be too soon to take a final review of it.

But though we have no wish to pursue a fruitless triumph in honour of ourselves, or to interfere with the progress of the measure which is going on, if not in all respects as well as we could wish, at least as well as we could hope to make it; and though to those who have watched it like ourselves we have in fact nothing of importance to say, yet for the benefit of others who, being unacquainted with the real state of the case, are likely, from representations recently put forth, to take a very false impression of it, we have thought that we might now perform a useful service by exhibiting the actual results of the measure so far as it has yet proceeded;—giving, as far as may be, distinct references to the facts on which we rest our conclusions and the sources from which we draw our information.

Purely good those results cannot well be. A single Act of
Parliament may release all slaves from their servitude, and deprive
all slave-owners of their authority; but to change a slavish
multitude into an orderly and happy peasantry, a slave-driving
oligarchy, deformed and made fierce by their false attitude, into a
natural upper class, must be the slow work of time. In order to
judge how well the experiment has succeeded, we must endeavour
to remember the position in which we stood before, and the difficulties and perils which seemed to beset us whichever way we
turned. The evils of slavery were, indeed, pretty generally
admitted, and were becoming more and more obvious every day.
Slave property, from being an object of greedy, gambling speculation, in pursuit of which so many fortunes had been lost and won,
had become valueless in the market :—ruined, as some said, by
the interference of the mother country—dying, as we say, of its
own inherent sinfulness, the wages of which is death. Gangs of
slaves could be bought for almost any thing. Estates could not
be sold at all. The slave proprietors themselves had begun to
feel that they would gladly escape from their position, if they
knew how to do it, without putting themselves in a worse. But
how to get rid of slavery, without drawing down some very serious
calamity on one side or the other—either by the sudden ruin, not
of the proprietors alone, but of all those whose incomes were
derived directly or indirectly from the many millions annually
paid for the exported produce of the West Indies, or from the
inroads on social peace and security which could not but be apprehended from a mass of slaves suddenly let loose—was at that time
a problem by which the wisest as well as the most sanguine
abolitionists were perplexed. The sudden cessation of sugar
cultivation in our slave colonies would be a lighter calamity than
the perpetuation of slavery. Still it would be a serious and substantial disaster, which it was most desirable to avoid. The
relapse of the slave population, sudden or gradual, into a primitive
condition of society, without effective civil government or organization; without any principle of order within, or any power to
impose order from without; without any securities for the weak
and simple against the tyranny of the strong and cunning; and,
above all, inaccessible to the influence of teachers and preachers—

their relapse into such a state would be a lighter evil than a continuance in their former condition, by just so much as such a state of society would be better than slavery. Still it would be an evil of great magnitude; and if they could be made to pass from bondage to freedom without overthrowing the existing apparatus of social order in the passage, a considerable sacrifice might well be made by all parties, themselves not excluded, for the sake of so bringing the matter about.

To devise a measure, then, which should secure the immediate extinction of slavery, and some immediate relief to the slaves, without involving any of the evils above mentioned, was the problem to be solved; and the measure, into the success of which we are about to inquire, is to be regarded as an experiment towards the solution of it—a measure which, at the time of its introduction, was attended with more anxiety, and involved in more uncertainty as to its immediate issue, than it is easy to remember now that the issue is known.

To discuss the *à priori* probabilities of success would be beside our purpose. Enough that it has succeeded. But in order to judge how far that success ought to be considered as a matter of congratulation, it is essential that we should call to mind what we thought ourselves entitled *beforehand* to expect—how we stood, and what we looked for five years ago. Five years ago controversy was cut short. It was finally resolved that, come what might, slavery should be abolished without delay; and we were left to anticipate the issue in silence.

Now, endeavouring to recall our own feelings at that crisis,—our confusion of hopes and fears,—we well remember, predominant above all other feelings, an unshaken conviction that nothing permanently bad could come of it; and, at all events, that, come of it good or bad, it was *right* that it should be done; but, as to the *immediate* issue, we remember some strange misgivings. That so inveterate a sin could be purged away, and no penalty exacted; —that nature had no revenge to take for the long violation which she had suffered; that the transition from an unnatural to a natural state would be itself natural and easy, and society restored to health without passing through some painful discipline;—it was almost impossible to hope. Eight hundred thousand human

beings, from whom all instruction had been withheld, in whom all
exercise in the duties between man and man had been discouraged,
all sense of responsibility repressed—who had never been asked
for love or pity—who *owed* no love or pity—who had rather been
taught that love, pity, forbearance, fellowship in human rights
and duties, were not *for them*—who had been taught to fear
nothing but the lash, to hope for nothing but exemption from
animal pain—to whom industry had been made odious, obedience
a blind necessity, mercy itself a thankless and degrading boon—
eight hundred thousand human beings, in whom all the gentler
and more ennobling sentiments of humanity, "self-reverence, self-
knowledge, and self-power," had been thus checked in their growth,
while the lower passions and instincts must have been, under that
very discipline, growing stronger — eight hundred thousand
human beings, so trained and taught, were to be told to come
forth and be free ; to go where they would, seek their food where
they could find it, to be henceforth their own masters ; still however holding themselves subject to the necessary regulations of
society—subject, that is, to a life of labour and privation, and all
the hard conditions attaching to ignorance and poverty in lands
where rich men rule.   To these conditions (hard surely, though,
it may be, inevitable) they were to be told to submit cheerfully.
From what motive, or on what consideration ?   Not as being a
powerless minority, who might understand the necessity if not the
justice of the case ; they formed everywhere a large majority—a
majority conscious of their strength and numbers, and wearing an
indelible badge, which, while it divided them from the overruling
minority, united them to each other by the assurance of sympathy
and a common cause.   Not because their minds had been subdued
into apathy : on the contrary, their discontents had but just before
broken out in open insurrection, and their hearts were still
inflamed and agitated by the fierce passions which had been
generated in the struggle.   Not because they would have nothing
more to wish for : they would wish to find in freedom that golden
state which they had dreamed of.   For their submission to the
necessary regulations of society we could trust to none of these
things, but only to their respect for the laws of the world—a world
which had never been their friend—for obligations, the sense of

which had never been called forth in them—for the mutual
charities of a society from which they had been scornfully
excluded—for personal interests which they had never been
qualified to understand—for common duties which they had never
been allowed the opportunity to practise, involved in common
rights which had never before been recognized.

Such, and no less, would have been the experiment of an
emancipation, immediate and unqualified, of the slaves in the
West Indies. Could it have been safely made? Seen from the
position in which we stood then, we should say it was scarcely
reasonable to hope so. Seen from the position in which we stand
now, we should still say it was impossible to be confident of it.
Knowing now all that we did not know then, we are still disposed
to think that, had the slaves in all our colonies, as in the very
favourable case of Antigua, been emancipated at once and absolutely, though it is very possible that no great disaster would
have followed, it is scarcely to be affirmed that no great *risk*
would have been run. Where there is on one side ignorance,
excitability, natural causes of discontent, and overpowering
numbers; on the other, violence, intemperance and a disposition
to provoke; there are the elements of an explosion. And though
the explosion may not come for years or for ages, still there is
every day a danger of its coming, and at the end of each day it is
impossible to say how many times a mere breath may have
averted it. That state of things is not safe, on the stability of
which, or at least on its speedy restoration in case of disturbance,
it is impossible to *calculate*. That community could not have
been safe, the peace of which depended in any considerable degree
upon a population of slaves newly emancipated not proving
inflammable—a magistracy of managers and overseers newly dis-
whipped not scattering fire—a colonial police newly organized
being able promptly to extinguish the flame—or a colonial militia
not making more mischief than it found.

Smoothly, therefore, as this critical time has passed; few and
trifling as are the disturbances which have occurred and the
dangers which we have seen; and secure as the rest of the way
now appears to be; we are far from believing that unqualified
emancipation, especially if forced on the colonial legislatures

against their will, would have been either politic or justifiable. At all events, without pretending to say that the probationary state of Apprenticeship could not have been safely spared, we can at least say this—that under this probationary state much has been done: uncertainty and alarm have vanished; many dangers, which seemed to lie in the path, have been passed over safely and without risk; some advances have been made in civilization; some hearty co-operation has been secured towards a further advance; nothing as yet has gone backward. And very sure we are, that if among the numerous plans for the abolition of slavery, sudden or gradual, which were rife in 1832, any one could have been *ensured* to work as well as this has done,—as well and no better—it would have been eagerly accepted by all parties.

Before we proceed to examine how far the objects of the measure have been attained, we must state briefly what we conceive them to have been. The main ends proposed were, as it appears to us,—

1st. The immediate and absolute extinction of the *essential principle* of slavery,—that principle which recognized the slave only as a *chattel*, subject not to the law but to the mere will of his master, and capable of legal protection only as horses and cats are protected by Mr. Martin's Act. From the hour when the Abolition Act came into operation, the slave became in all respects a *person;* having his rights and duties defined by law; entitled for any infringement of the former to a definite legal remedy, and liable for any infringement of the latter to a definite legal penalty. The show of conferring and protecting such rights which had been previously made by inoperative meliorating laws, was to be now realized by the operation of laws revised by the Crown, and administered by the Crown's paid servants.

2ndly. The immediate extinction not only of the principle of slavery, but of every remnant of the servile relation, in respect of all persons not yet involved in it;—every child born within the six years previous to the passing of the Act being placed at once on the same footing with other British subjects.

3rdly. Some immediate relief in the physical condition of those who were not to be immediately released from all their existing obligations;—one-fourth of the time which had previously been at their masters' disposal being at once placed at their own.

4thly. The immediate removal of the more important impediments to the civilisation of the existing servile population; by admitting their evidence in courts of justice, by encouraging them to make contracts and receive wages; by recognizing the validity of their marriages; by introducing new facilities for education; by removing all restraints upon the free communication of religious knowledge; by qualifying them to demand their entire freedom on tendering the fair value of their remaining services; by exempting females from the lash; and by some other provisions of the same nature.

5thly. The maintenance, in the meantime, of the existing order and framework of society; the protection of the proprietors against the sudden paralyzation of the immense capital invested in West Indian property,—of commerce against the sudden stoppage of a most fruitful source of productive industry, the failure of which would leave a hundred channels dry,—of the community generally (the labouring population not excluded) against that dissolution of all social polity which the subversion of the existing order would carry with it. This was to be effected by upholding the former barriers of society, confining labour within its former channels, and enforcing the performance of certain mutual obligations between the master and the slave, similar to those formerly subsisting, though curtailed in extent and under a new sanction,—for such limited period as might allow each party to feel their way through the change, gradually to adjust themselves to their new position, and to prepare their minds and fortunes for whatever might befall.

Such we take to have been the main ends of the new law, the attainment of which was essential to its successful operation.

The next point was to contrive that they should be carried into effect according to the design, by the enactment in the several colonies of laws adequate for that purpose. This was a point which could of course be only partially attained. There was never yet a law so well devised and so faithfully administered, as altogether to defy encroachment, evasion, violation, or defeat; scarcely one (always excepting laws made for the protection of the law-makers or lawyers) under which the injured party could be secure of a remedy adequate to the injury sustained. Murderers, robbers, seducers, slanderers, may be made to suffer, but not to restore what they have taken; the debtor may be made to pay his debt, but cannot repay the cost, the time, or the anxiety of the prosecution: in cases of disputed property the ruinous effects of "going to law" have passed into a proverb. And if this be the case in England, with her impartial judges, her learned lawyers, her competent juries, her magistrates, if not always learned and impartial, yet with every chance of being so which general education and a jealous public opinion can secure; how much more so in the West Indies, where for so many years all the education, and with it all the making, administering, and interpreting of the law, and all the public opinion which can make itself heard, has been confined to a small minority,—interested, as all ruling minorities must be, *against* justice,—and as if by a common conspiracy of legislature, judges, grand jurymen, petit jurymen, magistrates, and journalists, deliberately set to defeat its ends. Moreover, in the legislative colonies, this difficulty was formidably increased by a condition conceded to the legislature as the price of their cordial co-operation; namely, that they should be permitted to make these laws themselves. The Government might disallow all acts containing improper provisions, and withhold the compensation until proper ones should be substituted: but was not at liberty to dictate the terms. How hard it must have been in the hurry of that time to overcome this disadvantage altogether, may be readily conceived. In such a society, indeed, and under such conditions, to contrive that laws should be passed within twelve months, not only faithfully declaring the new rights of the emancipated population, but so framed as to preclude the possibility of any violation of them, was a thing not to be expected. Though the colonial legislatures might have every wish to pass a perfect law, they had scarcely the skill. Though the Government might be perfectly acute and vigilant, it could hardly clear away all loose phraseology and all objectionable provisions, without tendering more assistance than the Assemblies would accept. Even though a perfect law were passed, it would be impossible to secure for it a perfect administration; or to ensure it against misinterpretation by the colonial courts. Difficulties and obstructions would rise at every step. First there were the Assemblies, above dictation, but not above blunders, and with their hearts not in their work :—They were to frame the law. Then there were the attorneys, managers, overseers, and book-keepers, interested in every way—by old prejudices, by fresh mortifications, by the thirst of gain—in trenching upon the new rights of the negro and defeating the law framed for his protection :—They were to be kept from encroaching. Next there were the negroes themselves, with all the taint of their former condition upon them,—suspicious, cunning, deceitful, ignorant, callous to shame, and too much used to the lash to be reclaimable by light correction :—They were to be made to work their forty-five hours weekly. Then again there were the special magistrates, a miscellaneous body with heavy duties and light pay ; called suddenly to a most critical and laborious office, with no precedents to guide them ; unpractised in the kind of duty, and exposed to a variety of vexations and obstructions in the performance of it :—They were to administer the law. Lastly, there were the colonial courts, filled by persons deeply interested in West Indian property, swelling with West Indian prejudices, exasperated against the special magistrates as being trusted with an authority from which their own class was jealously excluded :—In cases of appeal or prosecution they were to interpret the law.

Here were traces of slavery which it was beyond the power of Parliament to abolish. The natural effects of these it was impossible altogether to escape or overcome. That in many individual instances the negroes would not be perfectly protected against hardship, oppression, or cruelty, and that their duties could not be always enforced without a degree of severity shocking to those who measure severity by an English standard, might as surely have been predicted beforehand as it is loudly proclaimed now ; and might be better used as an argument for immediately setting about the abolition of slavery wherever it exists, than as a proof that the measure adopted with that view in this instance has not worked well.

We have dwelt on this part of the subject longer than we should have done—longer perhaps than our limits justify—because we perceive that some persons have conceived great disappointment and indignation at finding that the negroes are still liable to frauds and injuries;—are still exposed to some hardships, and may still, in case of misbehaviour, be flogged or sent to the tread-mill. And this unreasonable disappointment we believe to have arisen simply from their not adverting to the inevitable conditions of the case. It is not that they have neglected to make honest inquiries; nor that in pursuing them they have indulged in a partial credulity; still less that they have endeavoured to miscolour the facts; but simply that it has never occurred to them to view the subject in this its proper and natural light.

Assuming, then, that we are not to look for results *purely* satisfactory, but only for successive states of improvement, and a new condition of society good only as compared with that which went before, we shall now proceed to trace briefly the stages of this great progress. Brief our statement must be; and more of it than we could wish must rest, we fear, upon our own credit; for to produce all the evidence from which we have drawn our conclusions and guard it with the necessary qualifications, explanations, and discussions, would require such another volume as those in which it is contained.

In this inquiry we shall confine ourselves chiefly to Jamaica; partly because it is the most important of all our West Indian colonies in extent and population; partly because it is probably the *least* favourable instance—as the one in which public opinion is in the most diseased state, in which faction is most rife and virulent, in which the whites and blacks were on the worst terms to begin with—the slaves most inflamed with discontent, and the masters (as shown in 1831) most prone to reckless acts of oppression—in which the superintendence of the governor, by reason of the multitude of duties and the extent of surface, was likely to be least effectual; and in which (we must add) the law itself, which was permitted to take effect, was the least adequate for its purposes; but chiefly because we have fuller and completer information about this than about any of the other colonies. It is, in fact, the only one concerning the state of which all parties have had an opportunity of giving evidence, and the evidence of each has been submitted to a rigid cross-examination. In relation to Jamaica, we have, in the first place, Lord Sligo's *Despatches,*—showing proof of unwearied vigilance which avoids no labour and blinks no difficulty,—written in a tone of frank and careless candour, the sincerity of which it is impossible for a moment to doubt,—clearly and faithfully reflecting all his impressions with regard to the internal state of the island from the very beginning, each as it arose in his mind, and (which is of great importance) reflecting his confused and half-formed impressions not less faithfully than his deliberate and grounded conclusions. In the second place, we have a multitude of *Reports* from the special magistrates, weekly, monthly, and quarterly, fresh as they were written, and evidently representing what they thought, saw, and did;—their value of course varying with the various powers of thinking, seeing, and acting, with which the writers were gifted. Lastly, we have the *Evidence* published by the Apprenticeship Committee of the House of Commons, before which a variety of witnesses were examined, comprising representatives of each interest concerned, from Mr. Beaumont, the hot and hotly persecuted Jamaica abolitionist, to Mr. Burge, the professional advocate of the slaveowners. And thus we have altogether a body of various and conflicting evidence, from which the true state of the case, in its main features, may be faithfully enough inferred by any one who really desires to find it.

With respect to the progress of the measure in the remaining colonies, our information is much less ample. But, judging by the broad results, we should infer that the general success has been of the same kind, and the general movement in the same direction; though more or less smooth and rapid according to accidental circumstances; and, upon the whole, that the conclusions suggested by the case of Jamaica may be transferred to the others without any material error.

The first announcement of the Abolition Act in Jamaica seems to have produced nothing of great note. The dismay spread by Lord Stanley's original Resolutions of the 14th of May, in which the only compensation proposed was a loan of fifteen millions, had been allayed by the grant of twenty millions, which was announced about a month after. And when, on the 8th of October, Lord Mulgrave, in fair, firm words, commended the measure to the attention of the assembled legislature, as a thing that was to be;—reminding them of the danger of delay and agitation, and cheering them with the promise of better times to come, and "the prolific expansion of hitherto unexplored resources;"—they seem to have received the message with a kind of sullen tranquillity. They were willing that it should be so; they had never advocated slavery as a good thing in itself, but only as a thing profitable to them; no Englishman could desire the improvement of the negro population more sincerely than they,—let but the proof of this cost them nothing, and they would be proud to prove it; they would do their best to secure all the good that could, to avert all the evil that might, arise from an experiment in legislation, of which the history of the world furnished no parallel; nor were they without hope, so ably had Lord Mulgrave disposed the forces at his command, that the island might, after all, be preserved in peace;—that the perilous condition of the colony would ever settle into permanent prosperity, they were less sanguine—but at that also, should the period ever arrive, they would be ready to rejoice.*

To the work, however, which was assigned them, they applied in earnest; and by the middle of December an Auxiliary Act had passed through all its stages, and was sent home for Lord Stanley's approval. Lord Stanley had promised to construe any such act candidly and liberally, according to the desire rather than the performance; and most liberally did he redeem his pledge. The Act in question was in its supplemental parts extremely deficient, as he seems to have perceived; though we cannot think that he perceived the whole length and breadth of the deficiency. Many necessary clauses were omitted, some objectionable ones inserted, from which much inconvenience has been already felt, and more is to be felt yet. The offences which might be committed by apprenticed labourers, and the penalties attached to them, were very loosely defined; the obligations of the master towards the apprentice more loosely still. The supplies of food, clothing, medicine, etc., were not defined at all—they were to be "customary" or "sufficient"—and how much was to be considered "sufficient" was left to the decision of the parish vestry; that is, of the masters themselves. No security was taken against the

---

* See Parliamentary Papers, I., p. 26. It is proper to state that we give the *meaning* only, not the *words*, of the address.

use of improper whips, or improper places of confinement. Worst of all, one mode of arbitrary punishment, and that no light one, was still left in the masters' hands. If he had a complaint against an apprentice, and the special magistrate were not by, he might order him into confinement till the magistrate could be sent for ; provided only that the complaint was to be preferred when he did come, and that if he did not come within twenty-four hours the apprentice was to be released. The pretext for this clause was safe custody—a thing not wanted in one case out of a hundred—but its practical operation would obviously be to leave a punishment of undefined severity in the hands of the master; with no better security against the abuse of it than a small fine in case the complaint should be adjudged frivolous. Moreover, the Act contained no adequate provision for determining the *class* to which each apprentice belonged; and the regulations for compulsory manumissions were in many material points defective. Some other objections, of less practical importance, we pass over ; but Mr. Jeremie has made the worst of them in his evidence before the Apprenticeship Committee, which the curious may consult.

All these defects were, however, regarded by Lord Stanley (perhaps justly enough) as oversights, rather than intentional departures from the spirit of the British Act;—as entitled, therefore, to the promised indulgence. Accordingly, while he drew the attention of the legislature to several of them as requiring amendment, he at the same time declared that the Act was " adequate and satisfactory," and that Jamaica was entitled to her share of the compensation; in the romantic assurance that they would appreciate and respond to a style of dealing so "frank and unreserved," and would make their Act *really* " adequate and satisfactory," not for money but for love.*

This, it seems to us, was a mistake ; and, to say the truth, it is much easier to understand and sympathize with the feelings under which Lord Stanley acted, than to justify his yielding to them. We cannot but think that, instead of encouraging the Assembly and indulging his own courteous impulses with promises of liberal dealing and constructions of law according to the presumed intention rather than the actual effect, he would have done

* Parliamentary Papers, I. p. 33.

E

better had he reminded them that all liberal dealing was forbidden him by the public duty he was charged with ; that he was bound to the most jealous and rigid construction of all their enactments ; that the intentions of one Assembly were no security for the intentions of another ; and that even if they were, the construction which the law would bear in Courts of Justice had nothing to do with the construction which its makers intended it to bear. Neither was the promptitude of the Assembly, however laudable in itself and however beneficial as an example, in passing their imperfect law, any good reason for granting them this indulgence.* If the promptitude was catching, so was the imperfection. If speedy legislation in one colony was likely to speed legislation in others, it should have been remembered that one imperfect Act approved was likely to entail its imperfections on the rest. Whatever was accepted as adequate in the first, could not be rejected as inadequate in those which followed. Neither can the event be pleaded in justification. If it was an error at all, it has certainly not proved a lucky one. To this original mistake most of the imperfections which we shall have to notice in the working of the new system may be distinctly traced. Of the very inconsiderable portion of truth which, by the admixture of some unnamed ingredient, has on certain recent occasions made itself appear so terrible ; which has filled the capacious lungs of Mr. O'Connell, expanded to the full dimensions of Exeter Hall, and after forcing conviction like a shock through a thousand hearts, has been condensed into six columns of the *Times ;*—of the very inconsiderable number of facts which were swelled into so considerable a manifestation, we believe that the greater number would never have happened, if all the objectionable provisions in the first Jamaica Act had been resisted as they ought to have been, and the compensation withheld until every defect, whether in design or execution, had been removed,—until really adequate and satisfactory provision had been *made* for giving *effect* to the British Act.

However, the deed was done—the money was paid. Thenceforth, whatever amendments the Assembly might think it right in delicacy to pass, must in prudence be accepted, as so much better than nothing.

* Parliamentary Papers, I. p. 29-36.

Meantime, Lord Mulgrave prorogued the Assembly in a speech of just congratulation, in which they could hardly join, mixed with good advice, which they do not seem to have generally followed ; and the members returned home to assist in allaying any excitement or misapprehensions which the agitation of the great news might have excited among their slaves, and which might possibly break out during the licence and relaxed discipline of the Christmas holidays in some disturbance. At the same time the number of troops was doubled ; the militia was warned to be in immediate readiness ; and Lord Mulgrave himself went round the island diffusing confidence and tranquillity. But there was nothing to fear,—the news had only excited in the negroes a greater content, cheerfulness, and alacrity.

The preparations for the 1st of August went on slowly. Special magistrates began to arrive by twos and threes—here and there a planter might be seen modifying his system and sloping the way to the change—and measures were in progress for the organization of an efficient police : in the midst of which Lord Mulgrave quitted the government on account of failing health. He was succeeded in March by Lord Sligo, himself an owner of property in Jamaica, and at one time, we believe, an opponent of emancipation ; but really a noble lord ; humane and earnest in his purposes —clear and frank in his dealings ; teeming with unwearied activities ; plunging boldly into the middle of all businesses in the confidence of a just intention, and writing like a man. The interval between his arrival and the 1st of August seems to have passed in inquiries and observations, in tours of inspection, in distributing proclamations to be read among the slaves, in receiving, disposing, and instructing the special magistrates. On the 26th of June the Assembly met again, and having passed the Police bill, proceeded to take into consideration the suggested amendments in the Abolition Act. Several of them they adopted in a new act passed on the 4th of July ; taking care, however (with a caution which Lord Stanley had probably not permitted himself* to anticipate), that it should expire at the end of 1835. This Act Lord Aberdeen accepted † as a satisfactory compliance with Lord Stanley's suggestions—as indeed what else could he

---

* Parliamentary Papers, I. p. 36.　　　　　† Ibid. p. 41.

do?—objecting only to the period of its expiration, which he left them to alter if they would.

Thus the time wore on to the 1st of August—the eventful day, big with the fate of planters and their prophecies, which was to settle the long-disputed question, whether the driver's whip could indeed be laid down without blood. Here is Lord Sligo's Report, written on the 13th:

" In all parts of the island with the exception alone of Saint Ann's parish, the transition from slavery to apprenticeship has been effected in the most satisfactory manner. It is a remarkable feature in the progress of that transition, that the first of August was devoted in most parts of the island to devotional exercises. In the sectarian chapels the service was performed several times in the course of the day; in fact, as long as a fresh succession of auditors presented themselves. It has been generally remarked, that hardly a drunken man was seen in the streets on that day ; the Saturday was divided between business and pleasure ; they were fully aware that the next day's market would be abolished, and in consequence of this, being a holiday besides, the markets on that day have been remarked everywhere to have been unusually large. Towards evening the streets were crowded with parties of John-Canoe Men and their usual noisy accompaniments. At night in some of the towns there were fancy balls, in which the authorities of the island, past and present, were represented. Several individuals in the towns had given dinners to their new apprentices on the previous day, and on very many of the estates steers were killed by the proprietors and given to the negroes, besides their usual holiday allowances of sugar, rum, and salt-fish; so that both in the country and in the towns 'the apprentices had their due share of amusements. On Sunday, the places of worship were again unusually crowded, and the day passed over in the most orderly and quiet manner. My reports from all parts of the island, with the exception of St. Ann's alone, state that on Monday the apprentices turned out to their work with even more than usual readiness, in some places with alacrity, and all with good humour."—P. 44.

It appeared afterwards that in four or five parishes some petty disturbances had taken place, owing chiefly to the indiscretion of overseers and managers, who had withdrawn the nurses and field-cooks, had stopped the paths leading from the negro huts to their provision grounds, or had refused to the mothers the time necessary for suckling their children ; * but all of these had been easily quelled. In one instance, there had been an obstinate *strike* of work, which was not overcome without some severe punishments, and some show of military force. In another, an attempt was made to rescue some apprentices from punishment, and in the confusion a trash-house was set on fire ; but it was found that

* Parliamentary Papers, p. 45.

only two men had been concerned in it, and order was very soon
restored without resorting to any farther severity.* The rest of the
island appears to have been perfectly tranquil, and so the terror
of that day passed by. The driver's whip had been resigned to the
magistrate; sudden destruction had not come to man or beast.

But though a negro could be quiet without whipping, it did
not follow that he would work. All practical men knew that he
would not, and now the time was come to prove it. August,
September, October passed on, and the new system was still
struggling doubtfully. It had not yet got under way. The
practical men sate inactive,—waiting for the fulfilment of their
prediction. The number of special magistrates was insufficient.
The cane-pieces were growing foul. Crop time was approaching;
and how was the crop to be taken off? All parties agreed that,
in the forty-five hours a-week allowed by law, it could not be done;
and Reports were coming in to Lord Sligo from all quarters, that
"the apprentices were most unwilling to work for hire." † It
was time for the Assembly to interfere: a case could now be
made out against the new system.‡ Three committees were
appointed to inquire how it was working, and how it could be
made to work better. The greater part of November was spent
in taking the opinions of practical men. Thirty-two persons
connected with the management of sugar estates were examined;
of these twenty-seven agreed that the system was working ill, and
anticipated a ruinous deficiency of produce;—nine of them estimating the probable falling off at not less than one-half; twelve
at not less than one-third; a twenty-eighth thought the system
was working pretty well, and the produce would not fall off more
than one-fourth. The remaining four reported favourably, and
anticipated no great difference.§ On the 13th of November, the
first of these committees arrived at the following conclusion,—not
an unimportant one in the history of West Indian prophecy:

"That the new system is not succeeding; that forty and a half hours of
labour in the week are inadequate to enable the cultivation of the country to be
continued; that the negroes are performing no fair proportion of work, even
during that limited number of hours, and that during their own time very few

---

* Parliamentary Papers, I. p. 47.   † Ib. I. p. 48.
‡ pp. 75, 108.   § p. 49.

of them will work for such rate of wages as sugar cultivation can afford to pay ; that idleness and contempt of authority are daily becoming more apparent and alarming; that the pimento crop, the only article that has come to maturity since the 1st of August, has been, to a great extent, lost to the proprietors, from the impossibility of getting it gathered in; that the coffee crop, now commencing, is likely to share a similar fate; and that the prospect to the proprietors of sugar estates is still more desperate, *in the certainty that their canes must rot upon the ground*, from the absolute impossibility of manufacturing the juice into sugar during the limited number of hours which the factories can be kept in operation."—p. 49.

Divers recommendations followed; and the Report having been discussed in the Council and Assembly, was forwarded to Lord Sligo on the 26th of November, with an Address, requesting him, as the only chance of averting all this ruin, to invest forthwith a sufficient number of local magistrates with the special commission. He replied, that he could not do that, but that more special magistrates were already on their way from England ; that he would make the system work well enough if they would but lend him their hearty co-operation ; and that, if they would not, they must take the consequences themselves.*

In the mean time, the special magistrates had not been idle. While the Assembly was busy in proving that the system worked ill, they were occupied in making it work well ; and by the time that the Assembly had got all their proofs in order, the case was altogether altered. The jealousies and misapprehensions which clouded the minds of the apprentices had been cleared away. And scarcely had Lord Sligo replied to the Address when letters began to come in from all quarters, reporting that arrangements had been made for taking off the crops, with every prospect of success ; and that there was no difficulty in inducing the negroes to do extra work for such wages as the estates might very well afford. On the 9th of December he writes :—

"I am happy, however, at being able in conclusion to state, that in spite of all the obstacles which I have met with, matters are, up to this date, hourly coming into a more healthy state. The masters are becoming more reconciled to the new system, and the apprentices more reasonable. The consequence is, that the negroes are falling by degrees into a steady system, advantageous alike to themselves and the proprietors. I cannot help thinking that the managers will now, when the important season of crop is arrived, feel that their interests are too important to be trifled with ; that ruin must follow their want of success ;

---

* p. 49.

that all chance of recovering their lost power of punishment is passed by ; will really co-operate, and each in their own interior adopt their only resource, a humane but energetic system, which will produce the best effects on the minds of the apprentices. In that confidence, I look now with much less apprehension on the result of the present crop, than I did some few weeks ago, although I have no certainty on the subject.

" I have not the slightest apprehension of any disturbance at Christmas ; but at the same time I think it expedient to send out the usual detachments, which will move on the 17th, and, I trust, return home on the 10th January. I do hope that after this occasion there will no longer be found any necessity for the adoption of this expensive measure."—p. 63.

The new system was now fairly under way. Each succeeding report was more favourable than its forerunner. The planters were growing daily more reconciled ; all alarms of disturbance and insurrection had vanished ; and doubts began to arise whether, after all, the canes would really rot in the ground. The Christmas holidays came, were spent merrily, and passed off quietly ; the negroes returned cheerfully to their work. On the 1st of January, Lord Sligo sent extracts from all the letters which he had received on the subject,—showing that all over the island they were behaving as well as need be. The rest of that month and the next was occupied in receiving more Reports to the same effect. " On all the estates, where hard labour had gone on for two or three weeks, and *wages were regularly paid* on Saturday night, any extent of work might be performed." *

Thus the first chapter of the experiment was closing, to the surprise of practical men. But one thing was yet wanting to wind it up ; to clench the conclusions which it pointed at ; and finally to dismiss into oblivion the Evidence, the Report, and the Recommendations of the November committee. The special magistrates had indeed *said* that the crop could be taken off ; but they might be partial, or ignorant ; whatever they might know of the new negro character, they knew nothing about the raising of sugar ; what had been *done?* This last refuge of destitute discontent Lord Sligo, who shuns no inquiry and fears the face of no fact in the world, determined to overthrow. He called for as many returns as could be procured from the managers, of the quantity of sugar which had been actually made up to the latest

* Parliamentary Papers, p. 115.

period, as compared with the quantity made up to a corresponding
period the year before. These returns may be found at pages 20
and 36 of the second part of the Parliamentary papers, in the
state in which be received them. The result may be best seen in
the following summary, which we have made by our own private
arithmetic.

SUMMARY OF RETURNS showing the number of hogsheads of sugar made on
    several estates in Jamaica up to the 28th of February, 1834, and up to the
    same date 1835; amounting to something less than one-fifth of the whole.

Parishes.	1834.	1835.	Increase.	Decrease.	Per Cent.	
St. Andrews . .	357	318		39	10·9	
St. Catherine . .	25	18		7	28	
Clarendon . .	854	849		5	0·5	
St. David's . .	551	377		174	31·5	
St. Dorothy's . .	184	248	64		3·4	Incr.
St. George's . .	12	17	5		41·6	do.
Hanover . . .	774	616		158	20·3	
St. James's . .	1861	1332		529	38·4	
St. John's . .	118	128	10		8·4	do.
St. Mary's . .	204	147		57	27·9	
St. Thomas in East .	1851	1602		249	13·3	
St. Thomas in Vale .	376	305		71	18·8	
Trelawney . .	1660	1572		88	5·3	
Vere . . .	1066	1171	105		9·8	
Westmoreland . .	5820	5051		769	13·2	do.
Totals · .	15713	13751	184	2146	12·5	Dec.

Thus we see that at the end of February the produce had
fallen below that of the preceding year by not more than twelve
per cent.; though, only three months before, a falling off of at
least thirty-three per cent. had been confidently predicted by
twenty-seven planters out of thirty-two. And this comparatively
trifling deficiency was afterwards reduced by about a third. The
whole crop of 1835 fell below that of 1834 by about 8·5 per cent.

It was now therefore clear, even to experienced persons, that
the crop then on the ground would be got off, and got off without
difficulty or ruinous expense. Thus far the visionaries had proved
the truer prophets. The predictions of the November committee
might be put by. All alarms on that score fled from the minds
of men, and took refuge in the newspapers—the last refuge which
false things find on earth before they take their final departure to
the place appointed for them.

But what matter? Experience was not yet exhausted; other predictions might yet be made. The negroes might work in taking off the crop; it was a kind of work which they had always liked.* But would they work in digging the ground? Experience answered NO. Ruin, then, would come in 1836 instead of 1835. In a Memorial drawn up in May, 1835, by the proprietors, planters, and other persons connected with the management of plantations in Trelawney, this new prophecy found fit utterance. The Memorial showed that the apprenticeship system " had, after nine months' trial, confirmed the anticipations of all practical men of its ruinous consequenc. s; " the present sugar crop, for want of the requisite labour, did not promise to be " even an average one; " such as it was, it had been purchased at the expense of the necessary preparations for the next; the falling off next year would be more serious, the year after more serious still, and so on till the system terminated in the gradual throwing up of sugar estates; thus " they had the miserable prospect before them, that in a short period the cultivation of the staple productions in the island must cease: " the only chance left was a large emigration of whites at the expense of the mother country.†

This Memorial was signed by seventy-three persons, and at their request was immediately forwarded by Lord Sligo to the Secretary of State. Close upon its heels followed letters from each of the special magistrates whose districts lay in that parish, written of their own accord,‡ denying, on the authority of the overseers themselves, that the statements were true as regarded that immediate neighbourhood; § and about a month afterwards came a host of Reports from all parts of the island relative to the state of cultivation and the prospects of next year's crop;‖—the sum of which was, that on 224 out of 762 estates, the cultivation was from various causes more or less backward; a result more favourable than Lord Sligo had anticipated, and readily enough accounted for without adopting the conclusion of that melancholy Memorial.

But crop was now over, or nearly so; and this last best

* See the evidence given before the Committee of 1832.
† Parliamentary Papers, II. p. 44.   ‡ p. 215.
§ p. 45-47.   ‖ Parliamentary Papers, 224 -239, 270.

prediction was coming, like its predecessors, to the proof. That it was not confirmed by the event does not appear to have been the fault of the planters. The interval which was yet theirs seems to have been used in a strange manner—used in devising new modes of vexation, in reviving a system of opppression not the less o.lious because it was now altogether ineffectual, in spreading discontent and distrust all around them. Before the last crop commenced they had done simply nothing; when it came on, and they found that "their interests were not to be trifled with," they had adopted a more liberal and conciliatory system with complete success; but now that the pressure and alarm were over, their hearts were hardened, and they would fain recover what they had lost. Such instruments of arbitrary annoyance as were still unhappily within their reach they eagerly grasped at. Indulgences, which custom had made necessaries, were withdrawn, or extra labour exacted in return for them. Old and feeble persons, mothers of many children,—"sitting down people," as they were called,—were employed in labours which the customs of slavery had spared them. Women in the latter stages of pregnancy, or soon after confinement, were ordered to work in the field. The "eight hour system" *—an arrangement, of which the object, and apparently the only object, was to deprive the negroes of their half holiday on Friday—was generally adopted. Though it was visibly spreading discontent all over the island, it became so favourite an object with many of the planters, that meetings were got up in various places to bring it into fashion, and remonstrances only made them the more determined to have their way.†

By such devices as these, a considerable number of the planters seem to have hoped, in spite of all reason and all experience,— experience so plentiful that it might be had for the picking up,— to make the negroes work freely in the kind of work which was least agreeable to them. That there was much positive cruelty in their proceedings,—that in physical comfort, indeed, the negroes were much the worse for them,—we see no reason to

---

* The system under which the apprenticed labourers were made to work eight hours for the first five days in the week: instead of nine for the first four, and four and a half on the fifth. The law admitted either arrangement.

† See Mr. Bravo's Letter, III. p. 87.

believe. But morally and politically, the effect must have been extremely bad ; worse, probably, than the planters themselves can be made to understand. It was a most false step at a most critical conjuncture. How many hearts willing and ready to learn that a master might be a friend,—how many confiding dispositions then timidly venturing forth—shrunk back corrected by those most foolish proceedings and relapsed into their former not unreasonable jealousy, must be for ever left to conjecture.

With all these exertions, however, they did not succeed in bringing to pass the evils which they had predicted. From this time Lord Sligo's Despatches come thicker and thicker. The special magistrates' Reports grow longer and more numerous. Every successive packet brings in a cloud of anecdotes, facts, opinions, and anticipations, of various tendency, credibility, and weight; but carrying with them altogether indubitable evidence of a general advance on the part of the negroes both forwards and upwards;—offences less frequent ; their new position and obligations better understood ; instances of mutual confidence more common; marriages coming into fashion; more wages paid ; more work done ; cultivation recovering its proper forwardness, in some instances extending itself; the digging of cane holes becoming the favourite, because the most profitable, kind of work ; * here and there a plough taking place of the hoe gang—it being found " that even negroes could guide and manage it; that they could see straight enough; which till of late seems to have been generally disbelieved ; " †—in a word, the last best prediction of the practical men not coming true.‡ The Trelawney Memorialists may cheer up. Their Memorial may be put by.

* Mr. Price's Letter, III. p. 374.
† Mr. Daughtry's Letter, II. p. 264.
‡ It is of course impossible to make distinct references in support of a general statement like this. The better, however, to assure ourselves that it is the result of no vague impression made up of what is most agreeable in the evidence, but of a fair judgment upon the whole, we have thought it worth while carefully to analyze the entire series of Reports for October, 1835, and we have noted the following conclusions, as distinctly deducible from them :—

1. Throughout the island, without exception, the apprentices showed no disposition to be insubordinate as a body.

2. In every district, without exception, they are represented as improving.

3. In every district except two (Jones and Harris, St. Thomas in the Vale), in

From this time to the end of June, when the correspondence
terminates, the tenor of these Reports continues much the same,
so far as the general working of the Apprenticeship is concerned.
Crimes continued to grow less frequent; complaints between
master and apprentice fewer; corporal punishment was more
rarely inflicted. In the early part of December "an extraordinary revolution all over the island" * was announced by Lord
Sligo in the feeling between master and apprentice. The planters
" appeared to be aware of the perilous consequences of harshness.
And (with a few obstinate exceptions) a totally. different manner
of treatment had been adopted, which promised the happiest
results."† It was observed also that the Christmas holidays had
passed over more rationally than was ever before known; that
there had been less "John Canoeing" than usual; and that
Christmas-day and Sunday had been spent in a remarkably
serious manner. In the meantime, the cry of ruin was no longer

which they are described as sullen and obstinate, their behaviour to their masters
was proper and respectful.

4. In every district except six (Hulme, Hanover; Jones and Harris, St. Thomas
in the Vale; Dawson, Willis, and T. Baines, St. Thomas in the East), they were
doing a fair proportion of work in their masters' time.

5. During crop they had in almost every instance laboured in their own time for
wages willingly and well.

6. Both in and out of crop, where high enough wages were offered (i.e., more
than they could make by working on their own grounds), they were in the great
majority of cases willing to work for hire.

7. During the hours of labour they were doing at least as much work as they did
during slavery—generally much more.

8. In working by the task, they had in all cases shown unusual energy and
activity.

9. Of the six properties on which the apprentices were described as not doing
their fair work, there was only one on which the cultivation was said to be backward, or the prospect of the ensuing crop unpromising. Wherever else the cultivation was backward, it was ascribed to weather, mismanagement, scarcity of hands,
or other causes; but not to any misconduct on the part of the negroes.

10. In the cultivation of sugar, much labour and expense might be saved by
using the plough. Where it had been tried, it had been perfectly successful.

11. The planters themselves were beginning to be of opinion, that during the
apprenticeship the staple articles might still be successfully cultivated. This
appeared, in some cases, by their own confession ;—in others, by their more extensive
preparations for ensuing crops.

12. In general a better feeling was growing up between master and apprentice.

13. Crimes of a serious kind were rare.

* P. 150.   † Parliamentary Papers, p. 161.

heard. Silence, more significant than speech, had fallen upon the planting interest. A severe drought during October and November had blighted the promise of the ensuing crop; heavy rains during the following summer had retarded the gathering; it was the shortest that had been for many years; yet the planters did not despair. Their hopes had risen with the price of sugar. Ruin was not to come till 1840 at least. Instead of preparing themselves for "the gradual throwing up of sugar estates," they began to enlarge their cane-pieces; to pay higher wages; in many instances to restore old indulgences which had been withdrawn; and, in short, to bid boldly for their share in the *expected profits of the apprenticeship.*

The foregoing pages contain, we believe, a fair picture of the progress of the Apprenticeship in Jamaica, in its broad and general features. For the truth of it we appeal with confidence to the testimony of the special magistrates;—a confidence not shaken by the scorn with which some persons—who would be thought to know what they are speaking of—have set aside that testimony as worthless. We are not unaware of the light in which these gentlemen have been held up in pamphlets and at public meetings, nor of the plausibility of the arguments and anecdotes which have been advanced in illustration. Stories have been told, many of which we can well believe to be true, of secret oppressions passing undetected by them, or detected too late for redress; of piteous tales summarily set aside as frivolous; of lashes inflicted for offences apparently slight; of stinted allowances and medical neglect; of pieces of plate presented by the planters to magistrates dismissed for misconduct. Stories like these, told confidently one after another, without any allusion to the countless stories of exactly opposite tendency which *might* be told, will naturally make a deep impression on persons unprepared by an acquaintance with the whole matter to assign to them their proper place and *comparative* importance. They may even seem to countenance the opinion that the special magistrates are the mere agents of the overseers and managers, and their reports worthless, as excluding everything which is either disagreeable to the planters or discreditable to themselves. We, however, who have been led in pursuit of the truth to peruse the Reports in question—stretching as they do over many scores of closely-printed folio pages,— to read them all through, and to scrutinize many of them very closely,—are bound to say that the opinion is most unjust and injurious, and altogether destitute of plausibility. We will venture to add, that no reasonable person who has read any considerable proportion of the Reports contained in these volumes can believe it to be true. There is nothing for which these compositions are more remarkable than the distinct impress which they bear of the temper and spirit in which·they are written. We almost feel personally acquainted with the greater number of the writers. We could almost point out by their styles the good, the bad, and the indifferent. One writes himself down a feeble magistrate; another harsh; another careless; another pompous. One or two we place no faith in; and there are a few who give us little or no information. But taking them as a miscellaneous body of men,—who have to ride two or three hundred miles and dispose of five or six hundred complaints every month, and to receive only £450 a year,—we must say that they have discharged their most important, but at the same time most difficult, laborious, harassing, and thankless duties, with a degree of zeal, ability, and integrity which deserves some other reward than these idle aspersions. That they have not succeeded in protecting all apprentices against all injustice, is most true. That they have not even detected all the injuries to which the apprentices have been exposed, is most probable. That where they have detected the injury, they have in some cases been unable to afford redress, we are not prepared to deny. But that complaints have been preferred and not listened to—abuses and oppressions detected and passed over—injuries proved and not redressed, so far as redress was practicable—we have yet to learn. That such things have happened in any considerable number of instances we should find it very hard to believe; and, to say the truth, we could well wish that those who are so dissatisfied with the measure of justice which the negroes obtain under the Apprenticeship system, would suggest the means of securing for them as fair a measure when the Apprenticeship shall be over. As far as we can make out, the worst injuries to which the apprentices are exposed have been inflicted by the overseers and managers, acquiesced in by the local justices, brought to light by the special magistrates, prosecuted by the Attorney-General, and finally secured from punishment by the Grand Jury throwing out the bill.* We fear that all this indicates an inveterate disease which will hardly yield to the simple specific proposed by Mr. Beaumont—an extension to them of the elective franchise.† Elect who will, be returned who may, summary justice there must still be ; and it will be but Jamaica justice when all is done.

What, then, after all, has been the effect of the change upon the interests of the two parties more immediately concerned—the Planters and the Apprentices?

That the effect upon the planters has been less injurious than they expected, will hardly be denied. Ruin was to have met them at every step. First, the negroes would never be restrained from violence ; then they would never be compelled to work without the driver and his whip ; then they would never do extra work in crop-time for wages ; then they would never do extra work out of crop-time for wages, and so on. All these fears are blown away. It is quite clear that the planters are not yet ruined. But there is yet room for one fear more. Though they can get as much labour as they want, it does not follow that they can afford to pay for it. Though sugar cultivation be carried on, it may be carried on at a loss, or at a profit so much reduced that the planter may have a right to complain.

Let us now inquire how the matter really stands. Unfortunately, our information on this head is very partial and incomplete. The few cases, however, on which we have sufficient data for comparing the present with the former profits of sugar estates will perhaps, if rightly weighed, justify a pretty large conjecture as to the rest. Or though they may not help us to a knowledge of the profits which have been actually made by the Jamaica proprietors since the Apprenticeship began, they will at least enable us to judge with some accuracy what might have been made by a judicious management.

* See " Correspondence relative to Maltreatment of Prisoners in the House of Correction," etc. Printed for the House of Lords, 15th July, 1837.

† See Evidence taken before the Apprenticeship Committee, 4294, *seq.*

It must be remembered that besides the gratuitous labour of each apprentice for forty hours and a half during the week, which the proprietor still retains, he has received, in compensation for what was taken away, a sum of money, of which the annual interest amounts, in Jamaica, to about £1 sterling for each apprentice.* This he may do what he likes with. He may throw it into the Thames or the Mersey in disgust; he may keep it in a napkin, to show how much less it is than what he has lost by the diminished produce of his estates; he may place it in the Funds, as so much saved from the wreck; he may invest it in land or railroad shares at home, or send it abroad on other adventures. But unless he spends it upon his estates in Jamaica, he has no right to complain that the produce of those estates is falling off.

Now, though we know how much sugar has been annually made by the apprentices, at what prices it has sold, and what is the amount of compensation, we cannot ascertain generally what has been the additional cost of production. We cannot therefore represent in figures how much the Jamaica proprietors have gained or lost by the change; or how much of the diminution of produce is to be charged upon themselves, as not having laid out in wages all the money which was given them for that purpose. We have little doubt that if the truth could be known, nearly the whole deficiency of the sugar crops of 1835 and 1836 might be accounted for in this way. We believe that a very small portion of the interest of the compensation has been applied to this purpose; and that much even of that has been applied injudiciously in hiring jobbers at an enormous price, when the apprentices might have been induced to do all the work that was wanted by a comparatively trifling advance in the rate of wages. This, however, without having access to the estates' books, we cannot prove. We can only prove that the evidence we have, so far as it goes, points that way.

This evidence was given before the Apprenticeship Committee, in 1836, by four different planters, all sensible and liberal men, each of whom adopted a different style of management with answerable results.

First, there was Mr. Maurice Jones, with about 6000 negroes

* See Mr. Shirley's evidence before the Apprenticeship Committee, 5050, *seq.*

under his management,* who set out with an unfavourable opinion
of the Apprenticeship, which has not been altogether removed,
and is now anxious (solely, he says, in consequence of the abolition
of slavery) to separate himself altogether from Jamaica.† This
gentleman began by assuming that sufficient labour to keep up
his former cultivation would not be procurable, and at once threw
up one-third.‡ He did not, however, reduce his former expenses.
He continued all the old allowances and indulgences,§ and paid
wages for all the extra labour which was wanted for the cultivation
of the remaining two-thirds of his estates.‖ This extra labour
cost him £336 currency, where formerly it used to cost him only
£200.¶ The issue was, that two-thirds of an average crop were
produced. The two estates used to produce three hundred hogsheads. One-third being abandoned, they produced only two
hundred.**

Now, the interest of the compensation money would have
enabled Mr. Jones to lay out £500 sterling in extra labour, in
addition to his usual outlay; whereas he only laid out £136
currency, or about £80 sterling. The remaining £420 remained
idle. Had this sum been employed in cultivating the abandoned
portion of the property, it is not impossible (as Mr. Jones does
not seem to have found any difficulty in procuring labour) that
the other hundred hogsheads might have been made.

Next comes Mr. Miller, who also began with a bad opinion of
the Apprenticeship,†† though he now entertains a better. He
had several estates under his management, and did not manage
them all alike; but he has furnished full particulars of the
expenses connected with one of them, which may be taken, we
presume, as a fair specimen.

He also, in common with all the large attorneys, continued
the old allowances and indulgences as usual,‡‡ but abandoned no
part of his cultivation. During the first four months of the
Apprenticeship he paid no wages—appears, indeed, to have made
no attempt to obtain extra work;§§ but in December he made

---

* See App. Com., 5316.   † 5489-90.   ‡ 5369.   § 5354.
‖ 5318, 5324, 5431-6.   ¶ 5397-8.   ** 5383.
†† See his evidence before the Jamaica Committee of November, 1834. Parliamentary Papers, I. p. 98.
‡‡ 3651-5.   §§ Parliamentary Papers, I. p. 98.

arrangements for taking off the crop. The estate in question contained 320 apprentices. To these, during the eighteen weeks of crop, he paid wages for extra work at the rate of about £13 currency a-week.* His whole additional expense, therefore, amounted to £234 currency—about £137 sterling; and the result was, that the produce of the estate fell off by not more than one-tenth; † and that falling-off was owing, he says, to " want of labour."

Now, supposing the interest of the compensation to have been about £320 sterling, we find that Mr. Miller could have afforded to pay £183 sterling more than he did; and that would have enabled him to keep up the same quantity of extra labour for five or six months longer,—which labour, judiciously applied, would have probably ensured not only an average crop that year, but adequate preparations for the next.

Next comes Mr. Oldham, a proprietor and attorney, with 4000 negroes under his charge,‡ who entertains a favourable opinion of the Apprenticeship,§ and thinks Jamaica property a good speculation.

He also continued all the usual indulgences and allowances,‖ and paid liberal wages. In return, he found no difficulty in getting as much work as he wanted,¶ except on Saturdays, when he was obliged to hire jobbers.

His extra expenses amounted in twenty-two months to about £2000 currency for wages, and about £8000 currency paid to jobbers.**

Now, the interest of the compensation during the same period amounted to about £10,728 currency. Nearly the whole of this, therefore, he had spent in the proper way. And what was the result? That the crops produced were about equal to those produced during slavery,†† or rather more.‡‡

Lastly, we come to the plan adopted by Mr. Shirley, apparently the most judicious of all. It was he who gave it as his opinion,§§ before the Jamaica Committee, in November, 1834, that the

---

* 3556, *seq.*   † 3591.   ‡ 4581-4.   § 4818-9.
‖ 4664-70.   ¶ 4743-8.   ** 4802-36, 4865, 4900-17.
†† 4812.   ‡‡ Letter to Lord Sligo; Parliamentary Papers, III. p. 378.
          §§ Parliamentary Papers, I. p. 61.

Apprenticeship would do very well; and was taunted* in return with his short residence in the island and his unacquaintance with the negro character.

He seems to have been the only proprietor whose plans extended beyond the term of Apprenticeship. Most of them seem to have thought only of geting off the current crop. Others looked forward to the year beyond, and laid out money in the necessary cultivation. Others again went farther, and, by general kindness and liberality, by promoting education, and encouraging the negroes to work for wages, endeavoured to secure their lasting confidence and goodwill. But Mr. Shirley alone seems to have aimed at altering and elevating their position;—at making them feel less like apprentices, and more like hired labourers;—and thus at giving them a foretaste of independence, and of that feeling of responsibility to themselves for their own actions which goes along with it.

He began by explaining† to them how much labour he had a right to require from them—40½ hours weekly, at a rate of not more than nine hours a day. This was an hour less than their accustomed day's work, and might possibly give rise to disputes. To avoid this, he proposed (it appears to us most judiciously), that they should go on as they had been used to do,—working ten hours a day for the first four days in the week; and then, if they would agree to work the fifth day also, he would allow them for that day's work the highest wages which he could afford to pay; and this arrangement should extend to the whole gang, and continue the whole year round.‡ To this they assented readily; and it was settled that they were to work for him in the ordinary way for five days in the week, receiving wages every fifth day.

But this was not all. It was desirable to accustom them not only to receive wages regularly, but to look to them as a part of their ordinary means of subsistence, instead of a mere matter of extra luxury; §—to accustom them, in short, to labour for their daily bread. With this view, he immediately withdrew such usual supplies and allowances as he could withdraw legally; on

---

* Parliamentary Papers, I. p. 5099. † Parliamentary Papers, 5037, *seq.*
‡ 5092.   § 5090, 5102, 5106.

the understanding that the value of them was to be added to their Friday's wages. By adding the sum thus saved to the interest of the compensation, he found that he could afford to pay them for their fifth day's work a sum equal to the highest sum paid to jobbers. The whole arrangement appears to have been fully understood by them, and cheerfully assented to.

In this way, having laid out the entire interest of the compensation and the entire value of the withdrawn allowances in wages for extra work to the whole gang the whole year round, Mr. Shirley found that he had made as much sugar as he could have made if slavery had been continued; * that his preparations for the succeeding crop were just as forward as usual; and, in addition to all this, that he had put his Apprentices in the fairest way to understand the duties and appreciate the position of the free labourers which they were shortly to become.

It may, perhaps, be suspected that these cases have been selected for show, out of many others which would have given a different result. This, however, is not true. These four cases are all that we have been able to find, in which particulars enough are given for comparing the present with the former position of the Jamaica proprietors. So far as they go, they appear to justify the inference, that if any planter be a loser under the new system, it is only because he has not used his capital judiciously. To say positively that no instance has occurred in which the whole interest of the compensation has been laid out on the property, and yet the produce has fallen off, is of course impossible. We can only say, that, if any such case has been brought forward, we have not succeeded in discovering it.†

* 5084.

† A case of increase in the value of property since the Apprenticeship, is mentioned by Mr. Pennel, a special justice; Par. Papers, III. p. 207. "An estate in my district was rented at the commencement of the apprenticeship system by Mr. Walcott of this parish, from Mr. Lyons of London, on the following terms :—Forty hhds. to be given yearly, and everything replaced at the end of the apprenticeship that may be deficient. I am given to understand that, for many years past, this estate has not paid one fraction to the proprietor, and that Mr. Walcott has, notwithstanding, been so fortunate as to clear £1200 on the last crop, and will probably continue to do so (if not even better) to the end of the time."

It is to be regretted that the mode of management adopted by Mr. Walcott is not mentioned. A case somewhat similar is related by Mr. Innes, in Antigua.

If our inference be correct—and we claim for it no more authority than appears in the premises—it is one of considerable importance; because we cannot find any other statistical information from which a safe conclusion can be drawn as to the prospects of the planters, and the work that may be looked for from the apprenticed labourers.

For indications of the value of Jamaica property in the market, we have searched in vain. Some large assertions have been made about it, but they appear to rest on the credit of the asserters. Captain Oldrey, in his evidence before the Apprenticeship Committee, said he could prove that it had risen from 30 to 50 per cent;[*] and Mr. Beaumont declared that it had risen at least 25 per cent.[†] But no proof was offered in support of these opinions; and the truth seems to be, that, though notoriously more valuable than it has been, it has not yet acquired any settled price in the market; and therefore no accurate estimate of its comparative value can be formed. Some estates have been sold, others offered for sale; but they were valued according to the returns which they might be expected to make during the remaining years of the Apprenticeship, without reference to their value afterwards.[‡] Mr. Miller[§] and Mr. Oldham[||] both agree that they would not give more than four years' purchase for an estate; though the former admits that "it is a matter of feeling," and that "persons disposed to speculate might give more;" and the latter confessedly does not share in the general anticipation of "a total failure after 1840."[¶] It would appear, therefore, that the remaining term of Apprenticeship has a value in the market, though the land itself has not; not because it is worth nothing, but because people are waiting to see what it is worth. It is clear that it is worth something, in Mr. Oldham's eyes; for he is himself a buyer;[**] though he will not say, and very likely does not know, how much. In fact, from the tenor of his evidence on this subject (which is not quite consistent), it may be inferred that he has made no very definite calculations as to the probable profits of sugar cultivation in future; but has certain general

---

[*] Parl. Papers, 3142.   [†] 4469.
[‡] See Miller's evidence, 3798, et seq.; and Oldham's, 4851.
[§] 3728.   [||] 4815.   [¶] Parl. Papers, 4837.
[**] See Letter to Lord Sligo, Parliamentary Papers, III. p. 378.

favourable anticipations which induce him to speculate in West Indian property himself, but not to overpraise the thing which he wishes to buy. And the general result of the inquiry appears to be (as might have been anticipated), that there is nothing in the state of the market from which any inference can be drawn as to the value of property in Jamaica, one way or other. Each person must be left to form his own anticipations.

Neither does the amount of produce, actually made since the Apprenticeship began, afford a fair criterion of the state of productive industry in Jamaica. Each of the crops has been affected by a variety of accidental causes, which will account for a temporary diminution; and by one permanent cause from which a constant diminution must always be expected and allowed for. We allude to the number of poor weak-handed estates which have hitherto been kept up in profitable cultivation, by over-working the slaves in a way which ought never to have been permitted, and therefore for the prevention of which no compensation is due; as well as to the number of properties which have been already worked out, which are naturally producing less and less every year, and are to be considered as having already paid their owners.

Independently of this, the crop of 1835 was subject to disturbing causes in two ways. First, the amount of the crop (as observed by Mr. Shirley) depends chiefly upon the quantity of plants put in, and the state of cultivation in the previous year. All that was to be done in that year, was to take off, by apprenticed labour, the crop which had been reared under the whip. Had the crop of 1835, therefore, been a plentiful one, it would only have proved that, under the apprenticeship a plentiful crop could be *taken off*,—not that it could be raised. As it was, it only proved that a short crop could be taken off. But then again the shortness of the crop may have been owing neither to the weather, nor to the want of work, but to the distrust of the proprietors; of whom it is probable that many besides Mr. Maurice Jones, abandoned a considerable portion of their cultivation, on the assumption that labour for getting off an average crop would not be procurable.

All that can be said is this,—that though several planters talk of the falling off of this crop as owing entirely to "want of labour," and the difficulty of obtaining extra work for hire (evidently meaning a difficulty created by the new system), it has not been stated any where, so far as our recollection serves us, that any part of the crop of 1835 was *lost* for want of labour. Nothing has been stated from which it can be inferred that—if, at the commencement of crop, the old system had been restored and the masters reinvested with all the power they ever had, and all the rest they ever wished for,—one hogshead more of sugar could have been made. Upon the whole, the only safe inference which can be drawn from the amount of produce made in 1835 appears to be this—that the negroes had worked better than the majority of planters expected,—for that they did get off the whole crop, of which it was predicted by the Jamaica Committee that a considerable portion was to rot in the ground.

The crop of 1836, however, was raised entirely by apprentices; and it may be thought that whatever falling off there was in that, must be ascribed to the want of labour consequent upon emancipation. But here again considerable deductions must be made on account, not only of injudicious management, but of the difficulties in getting the new system under way.

1*st*. It was impossible to prevent many of the negroes from expecting more than they were to get. It was impossible also to inspire them at once with confidence in the fair dealing of their masters,—to whose proposals they were afraid of acceding, lest they should be falling into some trap, and committing themselves to some new mode of servitude. They feared, likewise, that the wages liberally offered would not be faithfully paid. And other misapprehensions there were which obstructed the operation of the new system;—misapprehensions very natural and reasonable;—the fruit and just recompense of the unnatural and unreasonable position in which they had been placed. These misapprehensions and jealousies were indeed rapidly removed. Being trusted, the negroes were not slow to trust again; being treated with consideration, they could be considerate in return; being paid for their labour, they were not unwilling to labour for pay. But, at the same time, there can be no doubt that some time was necessary to learn these lessons,—and that so much time was lost to the estate.

Hence an undue proportion of the labour procurable was spent in getting off the current crop; to the neglect of the necessary preparation for the next.

2ndly. Independently of the real difficulty which did at first exist in procuring labour for wages, there was a good deal of imaginary difficulty. Many of the planters made up their minds that the necessary labour was not to be obtained at all, and therefore did not take the necessary steps to obtain it. Up to November 1835, there were as many as 237 estates on which wages had not even been offered.* On many of those on which they had been offered and accepted, it was only during crop. Mr. Shirley predicted a considerable falling off in the crops in Trelawney, owing entirely to this cause. (See 5086—93.) Whereas on his own estates, on which extra labour had been employed all the year round, he looked for an increase instead of a decrease in 1836. Again, of those who did offer wages out of crop, as well as during crop, many did not bid high enough. The negroes could make more than the wages by raising provisions on their own grounds. Some abandoned part of the cultivation in despair; others kept up the quantity of plant, but from want of the necessary labour (that is, from not laying out enough money in wages) neglected the cleaning.†

In March, 1835, Lord Sligo predicted a falling off generally throughout the island from these causes; ‡ and, in June 1835, he sent home a set of Reports on the actual state of cultivation in all the properties concerning which he could obtain the information. The result was, that out of 762 estates, the cultivation was more or less backward on 224.

3rdly. Another cause of diminution of crop must be added, in which certainly the negroes are not concerned; and of which we have the following timely and emphatic notice by Lord Sligo.

* Apprent. Com. App. p. 134.   † Mr. Shirley's Evidence, 5092.

‡ "That the crop of next year will be somewhat deficient I have reason to fear. Such has been the dread of not getting off this crop, that all the exertion which was formerly applied to the double object of taking the year's crop and preparing for the next year's, has been devoted to this year's service. That there may have been good and sound reasons, etc. etc., but I think the apprentice has, in most places, now acquired such an avidity for money, as to remove from my mind the apprehension that any falling off in the crop of the year after next will be experienced."— March 27, 1835, Parl. II. p. 19.

In a Despatch, dated 13th December, 1835, he says, "The communication I have to lament is the fact reported to me by almost all the special magistrates in their weekly journals, that owing to the unusual absence of the October seasons, the canes in most parts of the island have begun to arrow; the canes never grow after this has taken place, and as they were much stunted before, in consequence of the drought, I fear that the crop will be very short this year. It is, however, well that this should be known before the crop commences, in order that those who are anxious to misrepresent matters, if such there be, may not attribute to the misconduct of the apprentices what is the act of God."*

Before, therefore, we can safely draw inferences from the amount of produce in 1836, as to the work that may be expected from the Apprentices, we must make allowance for these things :—

1. The unsettled state of their minds for the first three or four months after they were made free. Hardly any extra work was done till the beginning of December, when crop began.

2. When extra labour was procured, the absorption of the whole of it in the taking off of the crop, to the neglect of the next year's preparations.

3. The voluntary and probably unnecessary abandonment of a considerable quantity of cultivation, in despair of obtaining extra labour to keep it up.

4. The number of exhausted properties which (slavery or no slavery) must every year yield less and less produce in proportion to the labour spent on them.

5. The number of short-handed estates which have hitherto kept up their cultivation and got off their crops by working the slaves more severely than they had any right to do.†

6. The early arrowing of the canes, which prevented that portion of the land which was still planted, and kept in good order, from yielding its fair quantity of sugar.

---

* Parliamentary Papers, I. p. 150.

† "But this [diminution] may be principally owing to the short-handed estates being obliged to be thrown up, for these estates only made sugar out of the very heart's-gore of the former slave."—GREGG, June, 1835, p. 241.

7. The fact that some of the produce was sent to America, and does not therefore appear in the returns of produce imported into Great Britain, from which all these calculations are taken.*

The result was, that the crop of 1836 fell below that of 1835 by about one-twelfth—below the average of 1833 and 1834 by about one-sixth—and below the average of the six years previous to emancipation by about one-fourth—a deficiency which, after making the above-mentioned allowances, will scarcely appear sufficient to justify any inference against the general prospects of the island, or the industrious dispositions of the negroes.

The produce of 1837 should have been a fairer instance. After the experience of the past year, the minds of the negroes were more settled; liberal wages were more generally offered; cultivation, which had been thrown up, was again extended; and thus the first three disadvantages, noted in the preceding list, were in great part removed. The official returns of the amount of produce imported during this year have not yet been published. It is known, however, that Jamaica has been visited during the last year with one of the severest droughts ever known; and it is understood that, owing to that cause and to it alone, the crop of 1837 is still shorter than that of 1836.

It appears then, upon the whole, that we have as yet no statistical data for an inference with regard to the future prospects of Jamaica; and that we must look for the promise of other years in the general progress and struggle from bad to good, and from good to better, which in the foregoing pages we have endeavoured to trace.

In the meantime, we believe it will be found, that in spite of the diminution of produce, the actual income of the proprietary body has been increased and not diminished by the change;—as will appear from the following calculation, which, though not pretending to exactitude, is probably exact enough for the purpose.

For the six years immediately preceding the abolition of slavery, the average sugar crop in Jamaica was 1,362,748 cwt., and the

---

* "The total failure of the sugar crop in the slave states of America, has raised the price here so enormously, that when estates are unembarrassed, most advantageous sales have been made in this is'and for the American market."—Lord Sligo's Desp. 24th May, 1836. Parliamentary Papers, III. p. 375.

average price about £1 6s. per cwt.   For the years 1835 and 1836
the average crop has been 1,101,400 cwt., and the price about
£1 17s. 7d.

Hence the value of a year's produce since the abolition would

be	£2,069,794
Before	1,839,779
	£230,015

And thus (assuming that the additional cost of production was
not more than the interest of the compensation) we have a balance
in favour of the Jamaica proprietors of more than £230,000
sterling.

Our limits forbid us to follow our inquiry through the remaining colonies.   Due allowance being made for the circumstances
pointed out in the first part of this article, as distinguishing the
case of Jamaica from the rest, the main features of the progress
seem to have been much alike in all;—the same trifling agitations and misunderstandings at the outset, giving way with the
same readiness before the friendly interference of the special
magistrates or the governors, and subsiding with the same rapidity
into tranquil, orderly, and not uncheerful industry.   The various
degrees of prosperity attained, and of ease in the attainment, may
be, for the most part, accounted for by varieties of soil, climate,
laws, or customs, into the consideration of which it is impossible to
enter.   A view of the general results in each colony (so far as the
quantity of sugar made can be taken to represent them), will be
found in the subjoined table.   The first column gives the average
proportion which the quantity of sugar annually raised bore to
the numbers of the slave population, for the six years immediately
preceding the abolition of slavery.   It is intended as a kind of
scale (a very rough one, it must be owned, but the best we have
been able to invent), by which the comparative *productiveness* of
the several colonies may be measured.   According to this scale
we arranged them, expecting to find that as in Jamaica the most
niggardly management seems to have been the least prosperous,
so the falling off of produce in the several colonies would bear
some sort of proportion to their comparative wealth.   The result

has answered our expectations about as well as so rude an operation could admit; and if some necessary qualifications and corrections were introduced, it would answer much better.*

This table does not otherwise present any result so striking as to call for explanation; unless it be the unexampled prosperity of British Guiana; which, under the. threefold. advantage of an exhaustless soil, a most intelligent and energetic governor, and *no* independent legislature, has been, from the very beginning, making uninterrupted advances in every direction.

	Average proportion of Sugar to Population.	Average Sugar Crop from 1829 to 1834, in cwts.	Average Sugar Crop in 1835 and 1836.	Difference per cent.
Virgin Islands † . .	3·4	17,763	13,615	23·4 dec.
Montserrat . .	3·5	22,835	14,206	33·4 do.
Dominica . . .	3·8	55,539	30,113	45·7 do.
Barbadoes . . .	4·1	343,513	359,058	4·5 inc.
Jamaica † . .	4·3	1,362,798	1,101,400	19·3 dec.
St. Lucia † . .	4·9	66,828	46,413	30·5 do.
St. Kitts † . . •	5	104,809	76,015	27·4 do.
Nevis . . .	5·7	49,647	32,180	35·1 do.
Antigua . . .	5·9	173,947	157,149	9·6 do.
Tobago . . .	8·1	93,157	97,450	4·5 inc.
Grenada . . .	8·5	200,708	163,295	18·6 dec.
St. Vincents † . .	9·6	222,732	190,770	14·3 do.
B. Guiana . . .	10·2	874,347	1,032,342	18·0 inc.
Trinidad . . .	13·4	310,797	300,766	3·2 dec.

· Thus much for the working of the Apprenticeship as it regards the Planters. Let us now inquire how it has worked for the Negroes.

We have already explained the relief which was designed for them; the causes, inherent or accidental, which were likely to interfere with the operation of that design; and the manner in which it has in some instances been actually thwarted. We have endeavoured to represent the matter faithfully; and we do not believe that in the picture which we have drawn, we have given to the exceptions less prominence than they deserved. But for the sake of presenting in a clearer light the amount of benefit

* The points in which the test fails with regard to the thickly inhabited Barbadoes are obvious enough.

† In these colonies the crops had been gradually falling off before 1834,

which the Apprenticeship, with all its restrictions, drawbacks, and inconveniences, has already conferred upon the negroes, we must briefly recur to the subject.

We shall not pause again to inquire whether a probationary term of restricted liberty was really necessary; nor to explain why it is that liberty with every restriction is preferable to slavery with every indulgence,—the reign of justice, however armed with terror, to the reign of terror, however administered with justice. Enough that it was so decided. A certain quantity of labour was still to be enforced by law; certain powers of coercion were still necessary to enforce it. So far the condition of the apprentice was still to resemble that of the slave. But if the labour required of the apprentice is lighter than that exacted from the slave and the means of enforcing it less painful or less terrible, by so much is his condition improved, even though the moral elevation which has come to him—the possession of duties, rights, and hopes,—be thrown aside as weightless in the scale.

Now, before the 1st of August, 1834, the great body of slaves in Jamaica were required, during seven months of the year, to work upwards of sixty hours weekly; during the remaining five, upwards of seventy. To make them work their best, the driver followed them with his cart-whip; which he used at his own and the overseer's discretion; either as a simple persuasive and stimulant to quicken their exertions; or as a summary punishment in case of negligence, insolence, or obstinacy; or as a ready instrument of passion and revenge in case of displeasure. Nor was this all. Where the whip was not terrible enough, there was the terror of the chain-gang, the chain and collar, the loathsome plantation dungeon, with its filth, darkness, solitude, and starvation. All these instruments of coercion were at the master's absolute disposal; guarded only by some professed restrictions which notoriously came to nothing. This, then, is what slavery was,— these the alternatives to which every slave, man or woman, was daily liable to be reduced. Let us now turn to what Apprenticeship is.

In the first place, no apprentice is required to work, in or out of crop, for more than forty-five hours in the week; nor to work harder during these forty-five hours than the special magistrate, a disinterested English gentleman, shall think reasonable. In the second place, for refusing or neglecting to do such reasonable proportion of work, he cannot be punished without the express authority in writing of the special magistrate, who is sworn to use his authority justly, and liable to be deprived of it on the first proof of abuse. In the third place, even with that authority, he cannot be punished for such offence with more than twenty lashes. In the fourth place, no female apprentice can be punished with flogging at all. In the fifth place, no apprentice, male or female, can be made, for any offence whatever, to work beyond the ordinary time for more than fifteen hours during any one week ; so that the full amount of labour which can be exacted as a punishment from the apprentice, is not more than the ordinary portion of the slave. In the sixth place, the worst offence which an apprentice can commit against the abolition law cannot be punished, on any authority whatever, with more than fifty lashes.

These, however, are the extreme limits of legal coercion ; the worst that an apprentice can possibly suffer. The question is what he does actually suffer as compared with what he used to suffer in his former condition. This indeed cannot be exactly determined. How much use was made during slavery of the whip, the chain, and the dungeon, we can never know. Nor have we access to any records, though such records exist, from which the amount of punishment by imprisonment and hard labour which has been inflicted since the apprenticeship began, can be ascertained. Judging, however, from the reason of the case, and from such information as we do possess, we can have no doubt that the practical amelioration quite corresponds to the theoretical.

That the cart-whip was very freely used during slavery may be inferred from the opinion then universal among slave-drivers, that nothing less could make the negroes work ;—an opinion since proved to be so merely and absolutely groundless, that its prevalence can only be accounted for by supposing that it had never before been put to the test. As for the other instruments of terror or torture, what use was made of them will not be known till every secret thing shall be brought to light. In the mean-

time, let us hope that they were only resorted to when "necessary;"
—that is, when the sixty or seventy hours of weekly labour could
not be obtained without them.

Now, on the 1st of August, 1834, upwards of 300,000 slaves
exchanged the coercion at will for the coercion according to law;
—the overseer's mercy for the special magistrate's justice. Ever
since, the number of punishments inflicted during each month
has been steadily decreasing. By reference to a return annexed
to the Jamaica Correspondence,* it will be seen that within the
ten months ending in May, 1836, punishments of all kinds had
been reduced by about one-fourth; corporal punishments by not
less than two-thirds. In taking, therefore, the general average
on the whole of that period, we do the Apprenticeship less than
justice; because we do not get any measure of its improving
tendency. But let this pass. The monthly average of floggings
inflicted during these ten months was not more than 364; of
punishments generally (including the lightest with the heaviest),
not more than 3302:—a dreadful amount indeed when compared
with happier communities;—a degree of severity which, to those
who have passionately pitied the negro till they have learned to
regard him as an object of no feeling but pity,—who have hated
his wrongs till they have forgotten what his wrongs have made
him,—may well seem intolerable—may well make 630,000 British
ladies cry "shame, shame," and demand the repeal of the law
which sanctioned it. We also can sympathize with the emotion,
though we may not yield to it. In our zeal against slavery, we
have urged its brutalizing effect upon the character of the slave.
In pleading the cause of the slave, we must not forget that therein
we spoke the truth. The slave *is*—that which we have made him.
In every community of slaves there must be a larger proportion
than elsewhere of such characters as in this country are marked
for the tread-mill or the hulks. Let us not, however, mistake the
exception for the rule; let us look at the face of the picture; let
us learn the meaning of the result by comparing it, not with what
England is, but with what Jamaica was.† If during each month

* Parliamentary Papers, III. p. 408.

† In British Guiana, a Crown colony, with the advantage of a slave protector, and
an enforced return of all punishments inflicted on each estate,—therefore, probably,

many apprentices have been punished, have not a hundred times
as many gone unpunished? If many have been flogged, have
not a thousand times as many gone unflogged? and have not all
been relieved from one-fourth of their former labours? Can it be
said that before the 1st of August, 1834, a single month ever
passed in Jamaica, at the end of which 299,636 slaves could say,
that not one of them had worked more than 180 hours *—yet not
one had felt the lash; and 296,698 of them could add, that they
had not suffered any punishment of any kind, not even the terror
of it?

But, it will be said, though these severities be all we hear
of, who knows what goes on in secret? Who knows how many
apprentices are daily robbed of their time, their food, their liberty,
—assaulted, terrified, overworked,—and yet never complain; either
because they do not know their rights or because they dare not
claim them? True, indeed; who does know? Such things
must no doubt have occurred. This law, like others, cannot have

not so bad a case as Jamaica,—we have the following progressive decrease of corporal
punishments:—

Period.		Average Floggings per Month.	Period.		Average Floggings per Month.
1831	July to December	1039	1835	November ...	55
1832	January to June	860	——	December ...	21
1832–3	July to September	734	1836	January	47
1833–4	October to April	484	——	February ...	34
1834–5	August to August	181	——	March	46
1835	August	88	——	April	19
——	September ...	79	——	May	25
——	October	77			

Since that time, we believe that flogging has been almost entirely discontinued in
this well-governed colony.

In the Bahamas, it has been for some time abolished by law, owing to the
excellent exertions of Sir William Colebroke. We are truly glad to find that the
mild activity and earnest persuasive humanity of this gentleman have now been
transferred to the wider sphere of the Leeward Islands, of which he is Governor-in-
Chief.

* Strictly speaking, we should have excepted the *non prædials*, whose weekly
amount of labour has not been reduced. The nature of their occupations made this
impracticable; but their period of apprenticeship was shortened in proportion, and
they become absolutely free in August, 1838. The distinction, it will be seen, does
not affect the argument.

been carried perfectly into effect. Where a brutal overseer has met with a feeble magistrate, it is impossible to say how much advantage may have been taken of the ignorance of the negroes. Violence we know is occasionally committed; the twenty-four hours' confinement we know has been occasionally abused; sometimes hospitals have been made prisons under pretence of sanitary regulations. In the absence of clocks and watches, gangs may have been here and there worked beyond the legal hours. Special magistrates have been obstructed in their attempts to detect these offences. Indictments against detected offenders have been thrown out with contumely. But though it must be admitted that great *injustice* may have been extensively committed in these ways, it may be confidently asserted that great *cruelty* cannot.* Cruelties may have been inflicted in individual cases, more than we dream of. Many we know have been brought to light by the merest accident. But had any considerable degree of cruelty . been extensively or systematically carried on, it is hardly to be believed that complaints *could* have been effectually stifled. It is well known, in every district, that scarce a month passes in which some overseer is not punished on a complaint brought by some apprentice. The special magistrate is, generally speaking, studiously accessible to complaints. Even if the injured party wants the wit or the courage to complain himself, he has friends, missionaries or others, who will be glad to complain for him. Even if the special magistrate's ears should be closed (and among

* Mr. O'Connell will not agree with us here. He believes that it is the interest of the planters to "work the negro out of his existence" before the end of the apprenticeship; that they are accordingly now about it; and that such necessary cruelty must therefore be now going on in Jamaica as may end in the death of the whole apprenticed population by the 1st of August, 1840. "Already," he says, "the negro's life is counted by the hour—but before the expiration of the apprenticeship, it will be counted by the minute." (See the proceedings of the Anti-Slavery meeting in Exeter Hall, on the 23rd of November, as reported in the *Times*.) This is one of those prodigious assertions which that large nature seems to generate without an effort. If Mr. O'Connell had considered for a moment, he must have seen that no single case of this kind can by possibility occur. How can an apprentice be worked to death unless he wishes it? Though this was the biggest thing of the kind, it was not the only one uttered on that occasion. In fact, all the arguments derived their force from a single figure of speech;—that of representing whatever is not impossible as having been done, and whatever has been done once as having been done generally;—and of assuming that wherever any discretion has been permitted to a special magistrate it has been carefully abused.

G

the seventy or eighty gentlemen who have filled that office some must have been harder of hearing than others), the governor's at least are open. And in spite of some idle speeches which have been tossed about, we believe that both Lord Sligo and Sir Lionel Smith may frankly challenge all Aldermanbury to produce a single instance of a complaint made against a special magistrate and not inquired into, or of a magistrate convicted of misconduct and not either sharply reprimanded or shortly dismissed.

That the abuses practised in houses of correction have not been of an intolerable kind, we unfortunately have not a like assurance. There the local magistracy—the parish vestry—rules supreme. The regulations are at their entire disposal; and under that name lie cart-whips, chains, collars, and solitary cells, to which all prisoners, male and female, apprenticed and free, are alike exposed. The special magistrate's authority is set at nought; the governor himself cannot interfere; and all appeals to the Grand Court of Jamaica justice are voted nuisances. We are glad to find that an officer has been sent out specially to inspect these places. It is quite clear that some law is wanted here, and that the Jamaica constitution must again be violated unless the Assembly think fit to pass one without delay.

In the meantime it must be remembered that grievous as such things are, they are not to be taken as a measure of the working of the Apprenticeship; because the great mass of apprentices are, in fact, scarcely affected by them. Every effort has been made to detect abuses of this kind in which apprentices have been the sufferers; and the number of those which have been brought to light, though very large considered by itself, bears no proportion to the body of the apprenticed population, and can hardly interrupt their ease or retard their progress. And since these secrets have been revealed, the special magistrates have been instructed to abstain from committing apprentices to any house of correction where such atrocities can occur.*

Here we must for the present take leave of Jamaica; we wait with interest, but without anxiety, for the sequel of the correspondence, which is shortly to appear. Meanwhile we leave the interests of the apprentices in hands that may be trusted. Lord

* See Lord Glenelg's Despatch, 14th June, 1836.—*Parl. Papers*, III. p. 306.

Sligo is indeed gone; but his place has been taken by Sir Lionel Smith; as different a man in many respects as could have been found; but one whose character for general zeal in the cause of humanity, for clearness of purpose, and plain vigour of execution, is above suspicion or reproach. We perceive by his last opening speech that he is still on courteous terms with the Assembly. So much the better. He is not a man to persevere in refreshing that parched land with idle compliments, if he shall see that no fruit is to come of it. The Assembly may before this hour have discerned and redeemed the time. If not, the hour has come when they may properly be assisted.

The condition of the Apprentices in the other colonies we cannot now discuss. Our readers will readily spare us an inquiry which from the incompleteness of our information could not be conducted within any reasonable limits to any profitable result. In its general aspect, their condition is undoubtedly not less favourable,—for the most part we should say much more favourable,—than in Jamaica. But as the same labourers have not been at work there, it is impossible to say how many individual cases of hardship might not be raked up from the bottom, nor how the general aspect might be changed if all these cases were carefully placed at the top.

Neither can we venture, in the short space which is left us, to penetrate the cloud which still hangs over the period beyond 1840, and which the experience of the last three years has not done much to clear away. Antigua, it is true, keeps up its crops nearly to the same extent as before; though at what increase of cost we are unable to ascertain. But there are very few of the colonies in which the labouring class, when free, will continue so dependent on the proprietors for their subsistence as they are in Antigua. It is also true that the apprentices almost everywhere work freely for hire: but because a labouring man bound to work for forty-five hours during the week is willing for two or three shillings to work a few hours more, it cannot safely be concluded that he will continue to live the life of a labouring man, when he finds that he can exchange it for a better. On the other hand, however, if we cannot say how much scarcer or dearer labour may become after 1840, neither can we say how much more may be made of it. It is easy to believe that half the number of hands now employed might be made to produce more sugar than is now raised. Till now, the total want of any free circulation of social interests and energies has rendered every attempt to economize labour both objectless and ineffectual. The amount of waste and refuse is therefore enormous. With the breaking up of the old system this will be changed. The command over industry will be lost, but its limbs will be unbound. After 1840 every new invention by which one pair of hands may be enabled to do the work of two, every new division of employments by which two pair may be enabled to do the work of three, will have its separate value. In this field hope may range at will, for everything is yet to be done. It must however be admitted that those colonies which have been forcing the cultivation of sugar against natural disadvantages may in the end have partly to give it up. How far this is to be deprecated is a question which we cannot stay to consider. For the present we would only refer to the example of the Bahama Islands, which, barren and scattered as they are, appear to be rapidly covering themselves with flourishing townships, and a contented peasantry, as suggesting a hope that, even where the present field of production must be deserted, other sources of social prosperity may discover themselves;—that the reduction of commercial importance may not leave the land naked, but may be silently replaced by new undergrowths of industry, humbler perhaps, but more natural, wholesome, and enduring.

In the meantime we shall content ourselves with repeating our conviction, that the results of this measure, so far as it has yet proceeded, are matter of just and earnest congratulation; and with expressing a hope that all parties will exert themselves to make the best of it, and not the worst. The planters, to judge by their silence, have hope; let them show it in liberality and enterprise. Why should they fold their hands together and eat their own flesh? The Friends and the Ladies are disappointed. Be it so. It spurs them to labours, which upon the whole are good. We do not desire that Aldermanbury should sleep. Humanity, even when it runs wild, is a noble passion; and the best Government will be the better for being troubled. One thing however we do desire of them—to be a little nicer as to what they believe, a little more cautious as to what they infer; and above all not to labour to persuade the world that the greatest work which has been done in these times, and at the noblest sacrifice, has been done in vain ; that the cause of human nature, which has borne all else, has not borne the test of success; that this, perhaps the noblest example ever set to the nations, is one to be shunned, not followed. They may be well assured that such will be the tendency, how far soever from the intention, of their labours. *They* indeed would have it inferred that as slavery cannot be mitigated, it ought to be abolished. But the inference which will in fact be drawn by less sanguine or more interested men will be that since slavery cannot be abolished suddenly without ruin to the planter, and since it now appears that slavery cannot be modified without injury to the apprentice, it must be left as it is.

NOTE.

THE inquiry into the management of the Jamaica prisons (see above, p. 82) led to the "Abolition Act Amendment Bill," which transferred the authority in all cases concerning apprenticed labourers from the parish vestry to the Governor in Council. The passing of this Bill by Parliament led to a resolution by the Jamaica Assembly to put an end to the apprenticeship at once. The announcement in England that the apprentices would all be free labourers on the 1st of August 1840 (whereby they would again come under the control of the parish vestries) led to the "Jamaica Prisons Act." The Prisons Act led to a declaration by the Assembly that they would do no more work, and that declaration (repeated by a new house elected after a dissolution) led the Ministry to bring in a Bill for a suspension of their legislative functions, and the temporary substitution of government by Governor in Council, as in a Crown colony.

The previous measures had been passed with general consent both of Parliament and people. The House of Commons understood the wrongs of the negro, and were ready in any particular case where he was concerned to overrule the legislation of the Jamaica Assembly. But to suspend their legislative functions altogether was to violate a popular constitution; for which they were the less prepared, because the history of the relations of that Assembly with the Crown ever since the Home Government took action against the slave trade and in defence of the slave, was very little known to our representatives in 1838.

The Bill was carried by so small a majority that the Ministers did not think themselves strong enough to proceed with it. They resigned; but Sir Robert Peel (who as the leader of the opposition against the bill was invited to take their place) not thinking his own party strong enough to govern, Lord John Russell consented to return; substituted a less stringent measure; and addressed himself to make the best of the business with such powers as it put into his hands.

It was at this crisis that the following article was written, to the argument of which later events have added a fresh significance and a conspicuous illustration.

III

BILL FOR THE SUSPENSION OF THE JAMAICA CONSTITUTION, 1839.*

THE events which followed the defeat of the Bill for the temporary government of Jamaica, though they have somewhat damped the interest, have not diminished the importance, of that question. The new measure which the anomalous position of the Ministry, on their return to office, compelled them to introduce, must be regarded as a temporary expedient at best. Should it be carried, it will prevent some very serious evils, but it will not stop the source out of which all evils flow. The quarrel between the Assembly of Jamaica, and the Government and Parliament of Great Britain, springs from an incompatibility of feeling, an opposition of purposes, and an unhappy divorce betwen constitutional privilege and natural right, which no forms of speech can remove, and which *occasional* exertions of power rather aggravate than allay. It must therefore be expected that the original question (which by the original Bill would have been set finally and happily at rest) will rise again; in what precise shape it would be rash to predict; but certainly in some shape or other more difficult to deal with than the present. In whatever form it may present itself, however, it is of the highest importance that the Public should be prepared, by a knowledge of what the thing itself is, to resist impressions which are due only to the names by which it may be called. In what motives the opposition to the dropped Bill originated, we do not pretend to say ; nor would we hastily presume that the leaders of it were incapable of being

* *Edinburgh Review,* July, 1839.

imposed on by their own arguments; but of this we are sure, that if the real nature of the question had been generally understood, those arguments could never have prevailed with half the House of Commons. By a review of the debate, it would be easy to remove all the grounds of objection which were then urged; but this would be hardly worth while; for the stock of bad objections is inexhaustible. We prefer to present a plain statement of the circumstances which made the measure necessary; leaving all objections, past and future, to fall away of themselves.

The knowledge of the question with which gentlemen came away from the debate, does not appear to have been considerable. That an Act for the regulation of Prisons in Jamaica was hurried through Parliament, towards the close of last session, with unusual rapidity, attracting little notice and meeting with no opposition; that this Act interfered with certain privileges of the local Legislature; that the Assembly took offence at it, and refused to proceed with their business until some reparation should be made; that the reparation which they desired could not be conceded; that the Ministry proposed, therefore, to suspend their functions at once; but that Sir Robert Peel thought it better to give them a *locus pœnitentiæ*, and try whether they would not resume their functions when duly warned of the consequences of continuing refractory;—such, we conceive, would be the best account of the question which an ordinary member of the Opposition could give. Some may know a little more, and some a little less; but this we take to be the average acquaintance with the subject, in virtue of which the two hundred and eighty-nine gentlemen who voted against the Jamaica Bill, thought it their duty to take the management of the business upon themselves.

Now, if this were all;—if it were the first time the Jamaica Assembly had taken offence at an Act of Parliament; if their dispositions and intentions were to be interpreted from this particular act alone; if there were no points in their past career from which their present direction and future course might be determined; if the circumstances of the time were ordinary, and could be trusted to regulate themselves;—in short, if neither the past, nor the present, nor the future, had any bearing upon the question, we should ourselves be inclined to agree with Sir Robert, that the effect of a warning ought to be tried in the first instance. But when we know that this is not the first, nor the second, nor the third time, that they have become refractory upon this very same quarrel;—that the *locus pœnitentiæ*, in all its shapes, has been already resorted to rather than bring it to a final issue; that reasoning, entreaty, admonition, intimidation, promises, and large sums of money, have in turn been tried for the chance of avoiding a rupture; that they have still persisted in their original demand, and shown a fixed determination to be neither begged off, nor reasoned off, nor bought off, from the assertion of what they deem their rights; that the daring step which they have now taken has not been taken in ignorance or momentary passion, but with the deliberate purpose of cutting short all further evasion, and forcing Parliament to decide the question at once, yes or no; when we know that the quarrel is not accidental, but inherent in the relation in which the bodies permanently stand towards each other;—when we remember all this, we cannot consent with Sir Robert Peel, with Lord Stanley, even (strange to say) with Mr. Gladstone, to argue the question without reference to anything which has gone before. We need make no apology, therefore, for entering upon a history of past transactions, which will be thought irrelevant by those persons alone, who care for nothing in the present question beyond its bearing upon the interests of political parties in this country.

The constitution of Jamaica was framed upon the model of our own—very much as the "High life below Stairs" was framed upon the model of the high life above; only that, in the latter case, together with the names of the original, something of its intrinsic properties and relations is retained in the copy; whereas, in the other, they are entirely wanting. The privileges and forms of the House of Commons are transferred to an Assembly representing a constituency of 2000, in a community of nearly 400,000; those of the House of Lords are entrusted to a Council appointed by the Governor, and removable at his pleasure; the prerogatives of the Crown are vested in a Governor, who has no natural influence or authority in the colony—whose name commands no reverence, whose powers are sufficient to make him obnoxious, without procuring for him either fear or respect; who represents nothing but the policy of the British Government, which, for the last fifty years, the dominant classes in Jamaica have always hated. Such is the parody of the Three Estates, which is now extant in the local constitution of Jamaica. Upon the laws passed by these powers, the Crown has a veto, and Parliament has its transcendental authority over all—an authority not confinable within definite limits, but the exercise of which is generally understood to be an awful thing, not to be resorted to except in extremity.

Now, so long as these several powers were of the same mind on all important questions, they might proceed together harmoniously enough. But it must have been obvious from the beginning, that so soon as a difference of policy should arise between the Assembly and the Home Government, a war of legislation must follow, in which the latter must either give way or call in the aid of Parliament; and that a direct collision must then take place between the local and the imperial Legislature. Accordingly we find, from the Journals of the Jamaica Assembly, that altercations between them and the Government commenced at a very early period, and were renewed from time to time; but that, the matters at issue attracting no national interest, they always succeeded in carrying their point; to their own great profit and triumph, and to the serious inconvenience of the public. But as soon as the agitation of the Slave Trade question, towards the close of the last century, roused the people of England to take a part in the quarrel, it assumed at once a different aspect; and discerning men soon saw that it could end only in one way, and the sooner the better. It soon became apparent that the prospect of inducing the Assembly to conform its policy to that of the mother country was quite hopeless. All the arts of encouragement were tried in vain. Every step, every pretence of a step, in the right direction, was hailed with delight as a pledge of future progress; everything was conceded which could be conceded, without abandoning the cause; nothing was insisted on which was not essential; whatever it was necessary to urge, was urged in the tenderest manner, with anxious professions of respect and deference —with unweariable confidence in their good intentions—with patient reasoning. But all was worse than fruitless. Everything turned into bitterness. The whole conciliatory process served only to fill them with false ideas of their own importance; to render them more obstinate in their prejudices, more tenacious of their rights, more reckless in their actions;—to aggravate the original difference into an abiding system of hostility, which drew away the attention of the Legislature from all public objects, bred nothing but altercation, and made the hopes of a final reconciliation more distant every session. This tendency was so evident from the first, that the process ought to have been cut short long ago. The authority which, it was plain, must be resorted to at last, should have been used at once. So, the disease would not have settled into the constitution, and the civilization of Jamaica might have commenced half a century the sooner. But distant evils, of which, though we know the magnitude, we do not feel the smart, are most easily dealt with by hoping that they will abate; and there is probably no hope which will outlive so many disappointments. Thus we have gone on for more than forty years—grieving that each successive effort to secure the cordial co-operation of the Jamaica Assembly had only exasperated their hostility, but still hoping that the next effort would be successful; and now, in 1839, we are as ready to hope as ever that a few fair words, and a *locus pœnitentiæ*, will really turn their hearts towards us.

Now, patience is a great virtue; but, when cultivated at other people's expense, it is apt to be abused; and hope, indulged beyond a certain point, may become criminal as well as foolish. Let us review the history of our attempts to conciliate the co-operation of the Jamaica Assembly, since the beginning of the great quarrel; with what forlorn prospects they were commenced; with what patient perseverance, under what manifold discouragements, they were renewed; in what mere failure they have all ended; and let us then ask, whether we have any right to persist in the same course still.

The temper in which a proposal to co-operate for the extinction of the Slave Trade, in 1797, would probably be entertained by the Assembly of Jamaica, might have been inferred from a variety of reports and protests which they had been putting forth during the ten years preceding. Mr. Wilberforce's Bill was denounced, not merely as an invasion of their constitutional privileges, but as an act of spoliation;—"an absolute breach of the solemn assurances held forth by repeated proclamations and Acts of Parliament, to supply the sugar colonies with labourers from Africa, which must ultimately alienate the minds of his Majesty's subjects in those colonies."* But when the hoping faculty is strong, protests like this only act as stimulants. And when, in 1797, the question of immediate abolition was revived, it was suggested by persons friendly to the object, that the Colonial Assemblies would be best able to bring it about. Certain preliminary measures were necessary to prepare the way;—the condition of the slaves must be improved, and the annual decrease of their numbers checked, and then the trade would come to a natural end, to the general benefit of all. But these measures must be left to the local legislatures. The Jamaica Assembly had said, indeed, that the abolition of the trade would certainly ruin them, and that they would resist it by all constitutional means; but they only meant to protest against its being done by the Imperial Parliament:—let them be requested to do it themselves, and those "who were best acquainted with their feelings" undertook for them that they would cheerfully set about it. The experiment was not a very hopeful one; but, perhaps, it was worth trying for once. And so it was resolved to try it. A recommendation from the King was laid before the Jamaica Assembly, in August, 1797, that they should adopt "such measures as might appear to them best calculated gradually to diminish the necessity of the slave trade, and ultimately to lead to its final extinction."† In December they sent their answer. They had already passed two Bills for the benefit of the negroes; one to increase the efficiency of the clergy, the other to prohibit the importation of Africans above twenty-five years old; they would do more as they saw occasion; but they "must at the same time declare that they were actuated by feelings of humanity only, and not with any view to the abolition of the slave trade:" the right of obtaining labourers from Africa, was an essential right, "which they

* Resolution of Assembly, 8th November, 1792. See Journals, x. p. 130.
† See debate on Mr. C. R. Ellis's motion. Hansard, vol. xxxiii. p. 252.

could never give up, nor do any thing that might render it doubtful."*

Such was the result of the first experiment towards securing the cordial co-operation of the Jamaica Assembly by conciliation. It might have been thought sufficient to extinguish for ever so young and so forlorn a hope. But no! Gentlemen who were acquainted with their feelings assured the House of Commons that their meaning had been misunderstood: when they said they would never give up the slave trade, they only meant that they would not give it up *for fear of Mr. Wilberforce.*† So conciliation was still to be the order of the day. What they had done was accepted as a pledge of their good intentions; for what they said they meant to do, they were liberally thanked; what they said they meant *not* to do, was overlooked. A year or two was allowed to pass, that the first wound might have time to heal; and then, by way of a gentle stimulant, a series of suggestions was laid before them, concerning the best means of carrying their intentions into effect. They were proposed in the most delicate manner—rather as inquiries for the information of Government, than as hints for their own guidance. But they drew forth nothing except a Report on the general state of the island, declaring that everything which could be done for the benefit of the slaves, "consistently with their reasonable services, and with the safety of the white inhabitants," had been done already;— that on this point they alone were competent to form an opinion; that the policy of Ministers was unwise, unjust, and cruel; that "the being supplied with labourers from Africa, for supporting, improving, and extending settlements already made, and also for making new settlements," was a sacred right, in the defence of which it was their duty to resort to every constitutional measure; and concluding with an intimation that, should the present course be persevered in, they would not be able to raise the taxes from which alone their engagements with the British Government could be made good.‡

Here was another extinguisher. If hope could be defeated by

---

* Journals, vol. x. p. 99.

† Mr. Sewell's speech, Parl. Hist. vol. xxxiv. p. 531.

‡ Journals, vol. x. p. 416.

words alone, this should have been enough. But no: they were only words—the outbreak of a natural irritation: only let them alone, and see what they would do. It was plain that nothing could be *said* which would not provoke hostility, but they might perhaps be moved by silence. Silence, however, did not answer. For two years they did nothing which even an agent could represent as tending to follow out the recommendations of the Government; and in the third they did worse. In 1802 they passed an Act to prevent unlicensed preaching ; the intention and practical effect of which was to silence the missionaries ;—to cut off all the moral and religious instruction which could really find its way to the heart of the slave. The system of saying nothing, therefore, proved the greatest failure of all: bad deeds were worse than bad words. It was next determined to try the effect of a definite recommendation, backed by the show of authority. In signifying the disallowance of the Act in question, as contrary to all principles of toleration, Lord Camden forwarded, for the information of the Assembly, the draft of a Bill which, if passed in Jamaica, would be confirmed by the Crown. If the recommendations of Government were to have any influence with them whatever, such a communication would at least be entertained with respect. But it only called forth a resolution, that the proposition was an unconstitutional interference with the appropriate functions of the House, " which it was their bounden duty never to submit to."*

This at last appears to have been decisive. When their friends in England found that seven years' conciliation had procured no measure affecting the condition of the slaves, except one to their disadvantage; when they found that the Slave Trade was going on with greater activity than ever, and was as far as ever from its termination; when they found that general intimations of the wishes of Parliament produced nothing but flat refusals to comply with them; that specific inquiries were treated with neglect, specific recommendations rejected as dictation—they do seem to have inferred that cordial co-operation for the suppression of the Slave Trade was not to be obtained by that process. They agreed therefore to abolish it at once.

* Journals, vol. xii. p. 153.

Such was the grand result of the first series of attempts at conciliation. The trade was abolished in 1807. Why should it not have been abolished in 1792? The slave population was not worse prepared for it; the Colonial Assemblies could not have been worse disposed to co-operate; fifteen years would not have been lost; hundred of thousands of Africans would not have been imported into the West Indies; the difference between the Jamaica Assembly and the Government would not have been fretted into a never-ending quarrel, which has now become a parcel of its constitution.

The immediate result of the Act was, of course, a furious protest, with threats of resistance. Unless their grievances were redressed (that is, unless the Act were repealed, full compensation granted for all losses and disappointments, military protection provided at the expense of the mother country, and all pretensions to interfere with their internal government and affairs abandoned by Parliament), they could not again vote the usual provisions for the troops; and in the meantime all grants for public buildings, barracks, etc., would be suspended.* All this was very properly received in silence. It was hoped that the cause of quarrel was now removed. The supply of slaves being stopped, the planters must, for their own sake, improve the condition of the existing stock; and their interests might be safely left to the Assembly and to time. This new hope seemed more reasonable than the last; but that it was not the less to be disappointed, the very next proceeding of the Assembly plainly showed. A Bill for the prevention of unlicensed preaching (framed, we presume, on the model of Lord Camden's draft), was brought in and rejected. They had not given up their own measure yet; and they were resolved that, by fair means or by foul, the disallowed law should still be the law of Jamaica. They therefore passed an Act, such as it had been usual to pass from time to time, consolidating in one all former laws for the order and government of slaves; and in the middle of this Act they silently inserted a proviso which had never been inserted before, —namely, "that no methodist missionary, or other sectary, or preacher, should presume to instruct the slaves, or to receive them

* Journals, vol. xi. p. 287.

in their houses, chapels, or conventicles of any sort or description." This Act became law in Jamaica in November, 1807, but was not forwarded to England in the usual course. As soon as it did arrive, it was of course disallowed, and (the better to provide against the repetition of such an act of treachery) the Governor was forbidden to sanction any Bill touching on religious liberty, unless it contained a clause making it inoperative until specially confirmed by the Crown.*

Here, again, was a case from which the hopelessness of getting any good out of the Assembly might have been learned. If the wishes and recommendations of the Government, acting in accordance with the known views of Parliament, were to have any weight with them, this surely should have been decisive. Yet mark the result! They promptly resolved that this new instruction was " a violation of their birthrights ;"—they had an indefeasible right to enjoy the immediate operation of such acts, " without the same being suppressed in their progress to his Majesty by the arbitrary fiat of a minister," (meaning the Governor's veto)—they would not submit to this—they would grant the usual provision for the troops for one quarter more; but after that, unless their grievances were redressed (i. e. unless the instruction were withdrawn), they would refuse it.† This was a little too much, and that Assembly was dissolved. It would appear, however, that nothing is gained by dissolutions in Jamaica. The new Assembly, indeed—so decidedly did Lord Liverpool refuse to withdraw the instruction—durst not openly re-affirm the original resolution. They intimated their dissatisfaction, and re-asserted their right; but said nothing about the supplies.‡ They had, however, one trick left; and they were silently resolved not to be beaten. They passed a new Bill for the prevention of unlicensed preaching, containing the same forbidden and now twice-rejected provisions; on the 14th of November (by what art we cannot learn) they obtained the Governor's assent to it ;§ and on the 15th they consented to vote the supplies for the troops! ‖

Such are the manœuvres by which a legislature " co-operating " on the spot, may defeat a policy which it disapproves. During

* Journals, vol. xii. p. 153.
‡ Ibid. p. 251. § Ibid. p. 275.
† Ibid. p. 241.
‖ Ibid. p. 277.

the fourteen years which had now elapsed since the Jamaica Assembly was first invited to assist in devising measures for the benefit of the negro population, they had so far prevailed against the direct, the repeated, the strictly constitutional resistance of a strong Government, backed, if necessary, by an overwhelming majority in the House of Commons, that this obnoxious law had actually been in force in Jamaica for separate periods amounting in all to five years. Yet we are still called upon to seek the accomplishment of our hated purposes, by trusting it to them!

It is perhaps to be regretted that this last act of contumacy did not lead at once to an open and final rupture. But such a quarrel was not forced upon the Government, and they did not choose to seek it. The Assembly, knowing that the law would be disallowed as soon as it reached England, had enacted it for one year only, and it expired a few weeks before the disallowance reached Jamaica. They did not venture to renew it. They had found by this time that a fresh season of patience had set in upon the people of England; and they could best effect their own purposes by avoiding any further collision. The missionaries might be silenced by other means than legal ones. The matter therefore was permitted to drop. Session after session the people waited, and the slave code remained unaltered. At last they became sensible that something more must be done. Eight years had elapsed since the passing of the Abolition Act, and not one of those measures had been adopted by the Jamaica Assembly which their friends had promised, in 1797, that they would adopt at once if they were but asked to do so. In 1815 therefore Mr. Wilberforce proposed his Slave Registry Bill; and the revived threat of Parliamentary interference reminded them of the expediency of seeming to be doing something for the amelioration of the condition of the negroes. The subject was dealt with in an elaborate Report drawn up towards the close of that year; which is interesting as giving their own account of what they had done for that object since the matter was first agitated in Parliament. By their own showing they had done *nothing*. To prove the charge of inattention to the welfare of the negroes groundless, they appeal—to what?—to a succession of Acts for humanizing their condition, raising their morals, enlightening their minds, securing them more effectually against oppression? By no means: no such Acts existed. They appeal to an Act for their better order and government, passed in 1784! to that Act of which Burke spoke in 1792, when he said—"I have seen what has been done by the West Indian Assemblies. It is arrant trifling. They have done little; and what they have done is good for nothing, for it is totally destitute of an *executory* principle."* To this Act they appeal in 1815, as containing everything needful for the good of the servile population! †

Mr. Wilberforce's Bill was of course denounced with the usual epithets. But the passion for conciliation had not yet abated. Gentlemen who understood the feelings of the Colonial Assemblies were as ready as ever with assurances, which Ministers were as ready as ever to confide in, that in their hearts they were anxious to pass such a Bill. In virtue of these promises the measure was withdrawn, and the subject was recommended to the consideration of the Assembly, with a warning which, since the Abolition Act, had acquired some significance;— namely, "that should the recommendation be wholly disregarded, or should some measure be adopted altogether nugatory, however much, in the present agitated state of the population in the West Indies, the interference of the British Parliament was to be deprecated on a question of this description, his Majesty's Ministers were persuaded that this interference could not be effectually resisted." ‡ This was to the purpose. To avoid this dreaded interference, and put off for an indefinite period the adoption of effectual measures, they must at least pretend to be doing something. And let us now enquire how they sped in so novel an enterprise.

First, they passed a Slave Registry Bill, which, though not perfect, was eagerly hailed as a pledge of the best intentions in the world—as the commencement of a new era of justice and liberality. In fact, it was so far from perfect, that it might almost have been described as nugatory. The object was to

* Burke's Works, vol. ix. p. 283.   † Journals, vol. xii. p. 791.
‡ Minutes of Assembly, 1816, p. 18.

prevent the smuggling of slaves into the island : it was to be effected by compelling every owner to send in periodically a return of the names and descriptions of all the slaves in his possession. Of course the efficacy of the measure depended upon the accuracy of these returns. But this Bill provided no sufficient regulations for identifying the *persons* named in the return ; nor any security against the falsification of their *numbers*. A slave-owner, therefore, who intended to increase his stock, could escape detection by simply returning the names of as many slaves as he *expected* to have before the next census. For the purpose in view, this bill was worth little or nothing. Secondly, they passed a revised Slave Act, containing little new except a clause prohibiting the purchase of slaves by middlemen—a real improvement, though a slight one ; and another, enlarging the powers of vestries, as a council of protection for negroes wronged by their masters—a clause practically worthless, because the vestries consisted of masters. Thirdly, they passed an Act for appointing twelve additional curates, making the number of clergy in the island twenty-four—about one clergyman to every 14,000 slaves ;—an improvement certainly, but so utterly inadequate, that it could hardly make itself felt as a practical benefit : an admirable *show* measure, but not a working one. Altogether the improvement was not considerable. Still they were all steps in the right direction, and were hailed with applause as promising marvellous things. The defects in the Registry Bill were ascribed to inadvertence ; the *animus* was inferred from the rest. The age of liberality and justice was setting in in earnest, and the people need only wait to hear of the good things that were coming to the negroes. So they waited for seven years more ; and then they inquired whether anything had been done ; and the answer was, in this as in all former cases, *nothing*.

Now came the question, How long was this to last ?—Was Slavery, or was it not, to continue for ever ? Fifteen years had now passed since by the abolition of the Slave Trade it was supposed to have become the interest of the planters to adopt such measures as might gradually prepare the slave population for freedom ; and, in Jamaica at least, no such measures had been taken. In 1823 the prospect of ultimate emancipation seemed no nearer than in 1807. Such being the history of former hopes, what mere mockery to renew them now! Surely now at least Parliament would assume another tone, and insist upon the preparatory measures being passed at once. But it was not to be so. After so many trials, all ending in disappointment, it was yet determined to try once more. General resolutions were passed by Parliament; specific measures were to be proposed by Government; the Colonial legislatures were to be recommended to adopt them: should they refuse contumaciously, it would be then time to take further measures. Such was the result of Mr. Buxton's motion in 1823. Once more the co-operation of Jamaica was to be sought by conciliation; once more her friends in England came forward with liberal promises on her behalf; once more let us ask what was the result?

The result was not long in coming. The resolutions of the House of Commons, indicating the general wishes and views of Parliament, were laid before the Assembly, and were answered by an angry protest and a flat refusal to comply. "*So long as the right of unqualified legislation was denied*, the House could not yield to any measure proposed for their consideration, however specious the object might be, or however high the authority from which it emanated."* Was not this enough? Simple admonition had always been unavailing; to give the admonition weight, you accompany it with a menace; and now you are told that, until that menace be withdrawn, your suggestions cannot even be taken into consideration. Surely if authority is to be used at all, it should be used now.

But no: not yet! That would be to unveil the transcendental majesty—to take the *arcanum* out of the *penetralia*. Gentler methods were not yet exhausted. It was true that argument and persuasion had been tried in vain; true that suggestions had been rejected as dictation; advice resented as unjustifiable interference; the declared wishes of the Parliament and the people of England entertained with contumely; their resolutions and deliberate determinations answered with defiance;— true that the show of compliance which the dread of Parliamen-

---

* Parliamentary Papers, 1824, No. 2, p. 7.

tary interference had extorted was too plainly a mere pretence; true that year after year had passed away since our eyes were opened to the iniquity of the system, leaving us still burdened with the sin, the shame, and the growing danger involved in it— a burden which a word would relieve us from;—but all was not done yet: one course yet remained, "the *slow* and steady course of temperate but authoritative admonition."* Here, then, was a new experiment, or series of experiments, to be entered on, which certainly could not be tried out within any assignable period, and might easily be made to last for ever. With a view to the question before us, the results of this experiment (though we have not room to trace them in detail), are well worth a careful study; for they show us what is to be expected from a body like the Jamaica Assembly, in circumstances very closely resembling those in which it has recently been proposed to place them. The system of conciliation was to be partly abandoned; a series of specific measures was to be proposed to them for adoption, with a fair warning that, in case of refusal, those measures would be forced upon them by the supreme authority of Parliament. The issue of this policy can only lead, we think, to one conclusion— that it ought never to be tried again;—a policy which, under pretence of avoiding an appeal to the transcendental powers of Parliament, escaped none of the evils of such an appeal, while it missed almost all the good; which, under pretence of forbearance and conciliation, bred nothing but controversy the most irritating, and agitation the most dangerous; which, under pretence of securing the co-operation of the Assembly in a work of great moment, urgency, and necessity, did in fact only postpone the commencement of that work for many years; which, after all, left the original evil unsurmounted and unabated;—for the transcendental powers of Parliament had to be appealed to in the end, in circumstances much less favourable than before. We must content ourselves with a hasty review of the principal stages of the controversy.

, A copy of a law framed for the Crown Colonies was sent to Jamaica in 1824. The Governor, having called the attention of the Assembly to it in two successive sessions, reported (22nd

* Mr. Canning's speech in 1824.

December 1825), that "there was no hope of persuading that House to do anything effectual for the relief of the slaves."* On the 13th of March following, he was instructed by Lord Bathurst to dissolve them. For the information of the new House, eight separate Bills were drawn up, embodying the measures proposed by the Government for their adoption. The new House replied (November, 1826), that such measures, "if adopted in that island in their present shape, would not only endanger their lives and properties, but would ultimately terminate in the ruin and destruction of the colony."† They felt, however, that something must be done: another flat refusal to do anything would be beyond the patience of Parliament. They would, therefore, do something:—"sincerely actuated by that ardent desire, which had long distinguished the Assembly of Jamaica, to embrace every opportunity of improving the condition of the slave population," they passed an Act, "to alter and amend the slave laws of the island." We have now to see what sort of things these gentlemen do when they can no longer persist in doing nothing. Into this new Slave Act, which (though falling far short of what was wanted, and still subject to Burke's censure—worthless, because destitute of an executory principle) did certainly contain many plausible appearances of improvement upon the old one, they introduced restraints upon the free communication of religious instruction, which would unquestionably have operated as a great hindrance everywhere, and might easily be abused into a total and absolute stoppage of all those sources of instruction from which the slaves drew real benefit. But this was to be the price of their approaches—their distant and ineffectual approaches—to a compliance with the wishes of Parliament. Only let the planters have the benefit of the preaching clauses, and the slaves were welcome to all the benefit they could get out of the others. This would never do: the law was disallowed. The reasons were stated by Mr. Huskisson in a long despatch, very liberal of compliments for what had been done—most patient in explanations of what had been left undone,—full of regret at the course which it had been necessary to pursue—and of hope that they would speedily pass another Bill free from

* Parliamentary Papers, 1826 (2), p. 5.   † Ibid. 1828 (1), p. 60.

those insuperable objections. At the same time the Governor was reminded of the instruction which forbade him to sanction any law infringing on religious liberty, unless it had a suspending clause.* But the Assembly were not to be argued into liberality, or complimented into co-operation. They resolved that "the disallowed law contained every real and substantial improvement which could be adopted with safety to the country and benefit to the slave; they could not (for the purpose of gratifying the Parliament and Government of Great Britain) agree to adopt measures incompatible with the best interests of the colonies; and as the Governor was forbidden to sanction any bill on the subject of religion unless it had a suspending clause, and *as they would never make a deliberate surrender of their undoubted and acknowledged rights, by legislating in the manner prescribed*, they would not present any Bill respecting the slave population."† This was in December 1827. Thus the "slow and steady course" had now continued for four years; and the slave law was scarcely better by a single clause than it had been in 1784. A long reply to Mr. Huskisson's objections, and a long rejoinder from him, consumed one season more; and then a change of Government made fresh explanations necessary. Sir George Murray, adopting the policy and the tone of his predecessor, pointed out the various measures to which the Government and Parliament were pledged by the resolutions of 1823; and urged them, for their own sakes, at least to pass some measure which might satisfy people that *something* was about to be done; for the people were impatient, and it would be impossible much longer to avoid some efficient and authoritative interference.‡

A few years before this prospect might have alarmed them, But what did they care for such a threat now, when they had been braving it for the last five years with impunity? The disallowed Bill was brought in again, and passed the House in precisely the same words as before, with the difference only of dates; and the Governor of course refused his assent.§ Still no

---

* Parliamentary Papers, 1828.   † Ibid. 1828, p. 8.
‡ Parliamentary Papers, 1829, pp. 5–9.
§ Sir J. Keane's Despatch. Parliamentary Papers, p. 10.

symptons of coercion. A new Governor was going out, and perhaps he would find a new people. But Lord Belmore himself could not prevent a third Act from passing which contained the same obnoxious clauses, only more rigorous than before; and Sir George Murray had no choice but to disallow it. Still, however, as if each successive Secretary of State felt bound to reject as irrelevant all the experience of his predecessors, he persevered in hoping that on reconsideration the Assembly would abandon their present course;* and, when pressed in the House of Commons to say what he meant to do, he seemed to think this quite enough. "The resolutions of 1823 were, in his opinion, sufficient warrant for him"—to do what? To come down to Parliament for powers to carry them into execution? No—"to continue urging these ameliorating measures as rapidly as they could be urged."† In other words, the "course of temperate but authoritative admonition" had been pursued for seven years without intermission; nothing had been gained by it, except accumulated proofs of its fruitlessness; *therefore*, it might still go on.

At length, however, this wretched hope was cheered with a brief gleam of encouragement—a lightening before death. In February 1831, a law was actually passed (without the inadmissible clauses,) by which the Ministers were at length able to say that, upon the whole, the existing slave code would be improved. It was accepted, as usual, with many compliments and thanks; and the many defects which made it utterly inadequate to its professed purposes, were, as usual, patiently pointed out;—of course with the usual result. The Assembly declined to hazard any further changes in a law so recently passed.‡

There was now no further colour for prolonging the experiment. It was clear that Parliament must either recede from its determination, or prepare to enforce it by some other means; and it was resolved to try whether the co-operation which could not be conceded to reason, to entreaty, or to menaces, might not, after all, be had for money. A new law was framed for the Crown Colonies, embodying all the measures of amelioration

---

* Parliamentary Papers, 1830, p. 35.   † Debate of July 13, 1830.
‡ Parliamentary Papers, 1832, p. 19.

which were then thought requisite, and relief from certain fiscal
burdens was promised to all the legislative colonies which should
adopt them. The strength of the principle so often avowed by
the Assembly of Jamaica, and never for a moment receded from
—not to endure *dictation* in whatever form it might come—was
now to be fairly tested : and it stood the test bravely. The
proposition was met by a direct refusal " to entertain any proposition for the further amelioration of the slave population,
which did not emanate from themselves." This determination was
communicated by the Governor on the 8th of March, 1832, with
an intimation that nothing could be gained by a dissolution.
Thus, in the ninth year of its progress, the " slow and steady
course of temperate but authoritative admonition," which had been
growing slower and steadier every year, at last stood quite still ;
and the hope of ending the difference without a quarrel was
finally extinguished. Surely not too soon ! But all its fruits were
not yet gathered. Had it led to nothing more than a nine years'
postponement of the commencement of a work most urgent and
necessary, that fact would have been enough to condemn it.
But this was not all. The long vexation of these questions had
fretted the Planters into wild and impotent fury. During
1831, Jamaica swarmed with parochial meetings, where language
was used, and resolutions were adopted, which filled the slaves
with such terror and suspicion—such vague surmises of evil
meditated against them by their masters, and of good unjustly
withheld—that the next year they rose up in open insurrection.

We might almost stop here, and leave Sir Robert Peel and his
locus pœnitentiæ to be judged by the very example to which he
had the simplicity, or the effrontery, to appeal. A course of
treatment is tried for the cure of an enormous and admitted
evil : for eight years it produces nothing but barren controversy,
and in the ninth a rebellion—the evil remaining all the while
unmitigated. Is this a course of treatment to be tried again ?
But we must still go on ; for another experiment upon the gentler
sensibilities of this Assembly was still in store ; another result
of experience was to be laid up for our guidance.

For a few years, indeed, it appeared that the last lesson had
not been taught in vain. Conciliation was abandoned. Com-

mittees of both Houses of Parliament were appointed to inquire into the question; and their Report was speedily followed by the Act for the total abolition of slavery throughout the British dominions. The Jamaica Assembly were induced to co-operate in this work by a clause declaring the compensation money payable only on that condition;—effectual co-operation the condition, Government the judge. Among the innumerable inducements which had been held out with the same view for the last forty years, this, it will be seen, was the first which answered its purpose. A prudent statesman would have been the more careful to keep it in reserve till the work was done. But in this there seemed something ungracious, as implying suspicion; and something impolitic, as tending to check the growth of that friendly feeling which can never thrive under the consciousness of distrust. There were many instances on record (especially in works of fiction) in which a generous nature had won the entire confidence of another heart by suddenly bestowing all his own; or escaped a fight by simply throwing away his weapon; or changed an inveterate enemy into an eternal friend by putting himself entirely in his power; and Lord Stanley resolved to try a similar experiment upon the Jamaica Assembly. By paying the money before all the work was done, he could at once give them a clear proof that he did really confide in the fairness of their intentions, and an excellent opportunity for showing that his confidence was not misplaced. This was the last experiment. The particulars we need not detail here, as they may be found in a former number of this Journal;* but we must briefly notice the result. Out of this very display of unnecessary and misplaced confidence, there grew the necessity for three separate acts of super-legislation; three separate violations of the constitution of Jamaica within the space of three years; and finally, the precipitate, if not premature, breaking up of the whole system. To conciliate the Assembly, Lord Stanley had shut his eyes to many serious defects in their first Abolition Act, and trusted to them for the removal of the rest. In gratitude to Lord Stanley, the Assembly consented to adopt many of his suggestions *for one year;* but

* *Edinburgh Review*, No. 134, p. 488. See above, p. 48.

after that they were inexorable. They presented a third Bill more objectionable than the first; and with one or other of those Government was to be contented. The second, the partially amended Act, was re-enacted, in 1836, by a unanimous Parliament. But this was not the end. Out of the many defects which had been allowed to remain in this Act (Lord Stanley having, from delicacy to the Assembly, refrained from insisting on the removal of them), there arose that brood of practical abuses and oppressions of which we have all heard too much;—which, in spite of unwearied exertions on the part of Lord Sligo first, then of Sir Lionel Smith—in spite of the most earnest representations, remonstrances, and lastly admonitions, of the Government—the Assembly would not stir a finger to remedy;—which were allowed to go on month after month, and year after year, unabated, rather aggravated, by the discussion; which finally set all England in an uproar, and raised a storm of opinion that swept everything before it; and ended in another Act of "super-legislation," against which, though most stringent and arbitrary in its provisions, not a single voice was raised in remonstrance. This same clamour it was that drove the Assembly to abandon the Apprenticeship of their own accord; and lastly, out of the sudden announcement of that resolution, arose the necessity of suddenly passing the very Prisons Act, which has brought everything to a standstill.

From all this miserable history of delays, disappointments, and disasters, it must, we think, appear that the quarrel between Parliament and the Jamaica Assembly (whatever may have been the particular occasion of the last outbreak) is not about the terms of a Despatch or the form of a communication; but about the possession of substantial powers for working effects of great practical moment. They think our whole policy with regard to the negroes wrong, and are determined to defeat it if they can; we think it right, and are determined that it shall prevail. For carrying this policy into effect, no means have been left untried; and two only have been successful;—namely, the direct application of authority, and the payment of sterling money. Our money has been already paid away; and the question now is, whether our authority is to be promised away—which, as things at present stand, would be nothing less than an abandonment of our policy. That this is the real condition which the Assembly demand, and that they really mean to be satisfied with nothing less, cannot, we think, be reasonably doubted by any one who, bearing in mind the events which we have already gone through, attends to their words and deeds during the few months which preceded the final rupture.

We have seen how jealous they have always been of interference in all its shapes. Not merely super-legislation by Parliament, not merely authoritative advice proceeding from the Secretary of State, but even the exercise of the Royal Veto, has always been regarded as a grievance. Since the abolition of slavery this power has been called for very often, as occasions for fresh legislation with reference to the negroes (that is, for fresh attempts on their part to defeat the policy of this country) have become more frequent. Towards the end of the Apprenticeship the number of disallowed laws had become so great as to induce a distinct declaration that if their power of legislation was to be thus fettered and controlled it were better they should be deprived of the power at once.* While they were making this complaint, the Abolition Act Amendment Bill (the history of which is sufficiently familiar to our readers) was passing through Parliament without· a dissentient voice. On its arrival in Jamaica it was received with an indignant protest; as a usurpation of their privileges hardly compatible with their continued existence as a legislative body. It might indeed be enforced; "but *there could not be two Legislatures in one State.* If the British Parliament was to make laws for Jamaica, it must exercise that prerogative without a partner; the freeholders of Jamaica would not send representatives to a mock Assembly, nor would representatives be found to accept a service so docked and crippled; the popular branch of the legislature would cease to exist, and, if any taxes were demanded, they must be demanded at the point of the sword."† Such was *their* feeling with regard

* See Report of Committee, dated March 24, 1838: published in the *Jamaica Gazette*, p. 319.

† Protest of Assembly, Parl. Papers, p. 50.

to an Act which was carried with approbation so undivided that even Mr. Burge did not hazard a protest against it, and which Mr. Gladstone has since described as "not involving any assumption or aggression on the part of the British Parliament, but as only a part of the great compact of 1833."* But to do the Assembly justice, they have never been wanting in courage, however wanting in all those other qualities without which courage is apt to become a public nuisance; and they now determined to bring the question between them and Parliament to an immediate issue. They resolved to abolish the remaining term of Apprenticeship at once; and, having thus got rid of the compact, to make a resolute stand against any further super-legislation. In announcing their intention to pass such a Bill, they took occasion to express an "anxious hope that they would then be left in the exercise of their constitutional privileges, *without any further Parliamentary interference.*† Now it so happened that another case of this very interference which they so much deprecated was inevitably brought on by this very announcement. We believe that the consequence was unforeseen, but it was not the less unavoidable. It will be remembered that the worst abuses which had arisen under the Apprenticeship law were owing to the prison regulations, over which the Executive Government had no control.‡ To transfer the management of all places of confinement, so far as Apprentices were concerned (and almost all the inmates were Apprentices), from the parish vestries to the Governor in Council, was one of the main objects of the Abolition Act Amendment Bill. This law was to continue in force so long as the Apprenticeship lasted; and so long, its provisions were stringent enough to prevent any evils that could reasonably be apprehended. But the moment the Apprenticeship expired those provisions expired with it; and under his new name of free labourer, every negro who might be committed to a house of correction by any Justice of the Peace, was in danger of all the collars, chains, cart-whips, and solitary cells, of the familiar application of which under the management of the parish vestries such ample evidence had been produced. It was

---

* Speech on Jamaica Bill, May 7. † 5th June, Parl. Papers, p. 45.
‡ *Edinburgh Review*, No. 134, p. 519. See above, p. 82.

absolutely necessary, therefore, as soon as news came from
Jamaica that the Apprenticeship was to cease on the 1st of
August by Act of Assembly, to pass through Parliament, without
a moment's delay, a fresh Bill to revive those provisions; and
such was the object of all that was obnoxious in the Prisons Act
—an Act hurried through Parliament, not without notice, though
altogether without opposition.

The Assembly saw at once that, now or never, they must
make their intended stand. They no sooner met in November
than they resolved that the Prisons Act was illegal and ought
not to be obeyed; and—seeing "the continued aggressions of
the British Parliament, and the confusion and mischief which
must result from the present anomalous system of government"
—they proceeded to declare, that "they would abstain from the
exercise of any legislative function, except such as might be
necessary to preserve inviolate the faith of the island with the
public creditor, *until they should be left to the free exercise of their
inherent rights as British subjects.*"* Upon this, Sir Lionel
Smith prorogued them for a few days, that they might have
time for reconsideration; and, in calling them together again,
reminded them of the many measures which it was important to
pass, and of the many explanatory communications from the
Secretary of State which he had to lay before them. But it
would not do. They wanted no explanations; they were well
aware of the difficulties in which their conduct would place the
colony; but "their legislative rights had been violated, and *so
long as those rights continued to be invaded,* they must adhere to
their resolutions."† As it was plainly impossible for Sir Lionel
to promise them either satisfaction for the past or security
against future invasions of these privileges, he could only dissolve
them at once. A new Assembly met on the 18th of December;
but their spirit was not changed. They also felt the evils
attending their course; they knew how much laws were wanted;
"but the power was no longer left in their hands to apply the
remedy;" "their legislative rights had been invaded by Parliament;" and "even in their ordinary legislative proceedings they

* Address, 2nd Nov., Parliamentary Papers, p. 154.
† Parliamentary Papers, p. 156.

were fettered by an over-ruling authority" (meaning the Veto of the Crown);—they must, therefore, "adhere to the determination which was come to by the late House of Assembly."*

Now we put it to any unbiassed man, whether the meaning of all this is not as gross and palpable as words and actions can make it. Doubts, we know, have been raised upon this point; and curious interpretations have been devised, which considering the quarter they proceed from, we can only regard with unfeigned wonder, as specimens of the desperate ingenuity of a very clever man, who has placed himself very strangely in the wrong. For ourselves, we must be permitted to believe that the Assembly mean neither more nor less than this—that they will not proceed with their work till some security be given them against further Parliamentary interference. We believe that they not only meant to say this, but mean to stand by it; that nothing short of some assurance of the kind will satisfy them; that no such assurance can be given which would not be construed into a distinct renunciation of the *right* to interfere; and that, had the Government pretended to understand their words in any other sense, they would have been justly chargeable with stooping to a miserable and most unseemly quibble, for fear of frankly accepting a challenge which could not have been more frankly offered.

Such, then, being the condition on which alone they offer to resume their functions, the question is, whether it ought or ought not to be complied with? That it ought to be complied with, no one has ventured directly to maintain; and only one speaker of note seemed disposed to recommend. Lord Stanley, we think, implied as much; though it is not easy to disentangle his *argumentum ad rem* from the *argumenta ad homines* in which it is wrapped up. For although he *praised* Sir Robert Peel's proposal of a *locus pœnitentiæ* backed by a threat, he *recommended* something very different;—namely, a mode of dealing at once "plain, frank, sincere, *and conciliatory;* "—conditions which it is plainly impossible to combine in any course which does not involve a promise of non-interference for the future. As Lord Stanley's personal experience in dealing with the Assembly gives a peculiar

† Parliamentary Papers, p. 160.

weight to his opinion in such a matter, we must explain our own reasons for believing that there never was a time at which such a promise could have been less safely made; or at which a prompt and decided refusal was more urgently called for.

That the interests of all classes in Jamaica demand the enactment of many new laws, adapted to their new relations, will hardly be disputed. The means which have hitherto been available for protecting the mutual interests and regulating the mutual duties of the different classes into which society is distributed, and for guiding the labour of the population into profitable channels, have suddenly ceased to exist. Hitherto seven-eighths of the population have been held under a supervision and control, which provided sufficient securities for the peace of society, the productiveness of capital, the competent supply of labour, the orderly subsistence of the lower classes, the relief of the poor and infirm, and the prevention and punishment of crime. But these ends were attained by sacrificing the freedom of seven-eighths of the population. They must now be secured without that sacrifice. Without interfering with the freedom of locomotion, of speech, of intercourse between families, of assemblage for lawful and inoffensive purposes, of choice of abode, sufficient securities are yet to be taken against crime, riot, vagrancy, squatting, and the like. To the labourer the profits of his labour are to be secured—to the capitalist the produce of his capital. For the improvement of the social , condition of Jamaica much more is required; but thus much, at least, is necessary for the protection of the mere *rights* of each class.

Now, that these ends are not duly provided for by the existing code of Jamaica might be proved by reference to the practical working of all her institutions, from her high courts of justice to her parish vestries; for it must be remarked, as one consequence of the long controversy in which she has been engaged with this country, that, pending that controversy, all public objects have been neglected. But a single illustration will be sufficient. The following case may occur at any time;—may be occurring whilst we write.—It is known that the great mass of labourers are tenants at will of their former masters, and have no homes but such as belong to them. The manager (having previously given to all or any of the labourers dwelling on the estate three months' notice to quit—a precaution which in many cases has been actually taken) calls on them to enter into a contract, involving heavy duties and small pay, and lasting for a long time. If they consent, they bind themselves to a bad bargain; and in case of any kind of failure to fulfil the entire conditions of it *(which need not be expressed in writing)*, they may be deprived of all their wages, or imprisoned with hard labour for three months in a Jamaica prison, at the discretion of any justice of the peace.* If they refuse, they are liable, at the discretion of any two justices, to be summarily ejected from the estate : † being ejected, they may be brought before the nearest justice as vagrants, proved to have been found " wandering abroad," homeless, "not having wherewith to maintain themselves;" and to have "refused to work for the usual and common wages;" and thereupon sentenced to hard labour in the house of correction for six months.‡ If they have wandered far from their native parish before they are taken up, they may besides (be they males or females) receive thirty-nine lashes; and so be sent from parish to parish the nearest way to the place they came from; where the original alternative awaits them. Various other mischances might be pointed out to which they would be exposed in the event of their escaping these. But this is enough to show that the existing law of Jamaica, far from providing adequate protection for the labouring population, may readily be used to deprive almost the whole of that population of their liberty.

Does it, on the other hand, afford sufficient protection for society? Far from it. The police law has expired. The trespass law has expired. There is no law to prevent squatting. The courts of law are so overcrowded with business (350,000 persons having been recently brought within their jurisdiction, in addition to the 50,000 which it formerly embraced), that the Chief Justice complains of the consequent delay as "almost amounting to a denial of justice."§ The prisons are at once

---

* Contract Law.   † Apprenticeship Abolition Act.
‡ Vagrancy Law.   § Parliamentary Papers, I. p. 162.

I

badly regulated and insecure; judges are incompetent; juries
are corrupt; the colony is deeply in debt, and money is ex-
travagantly dear.

Lastly, does the existing law provide sufficient protection
even for the proprietary body, by whom and for whom it was
made? We believe that in this also it will be found to fail.
We believe that the planting interest has grasped at so much
that it is in imminent danger of losing all. The contract law is
so severe that no one dares to enter into a contract. The eject-
ment law, connected with the contract law, may be made such
an instrument of oppression that arrangements have been made
in some places by benevolent individuals to provide independent
locations for all labourers who may be ejected from estates.
The vagrancy law, boldly executed, is indeed stringent enough to
compel the peasantry into contracts of service; but, so executed,
it would be a tyranny too tremendous to be safely enforced
without the aid of soldiers. The local magistracy have so much
of the confidence of the planters that they can enjoy no confidence from the other party.

The effect of all these laws put together is general discontent,
distrust, and alarm. The peasantry feel their liberties insecure.
They begin to be unsettled in their thoughts and habits, and
anxious to be independent. A few months more of this uncertainty, and we shall see them rapidly drawing off the estates,
and establishing themselves in independent freeholds; or, if any
attempt be made to enforce a more rigorous discipline, we may
see them marching off in bodies and taking possession of unoccupied lands, which abound in Jamaica, and where in the present
state of the law it would not be easy to prevent them from establishing themselves, still less easy to dislodge them when once
established, probably impossible to tempt them back to a life of
regular labour.

Such is the state of the law as at present in force in Jamaica;
and such it must remain unless the Assembly choose to alter it,
or unless Parliament interfere. Is there, then, any reason to
hope that the Assembly would consent to make such alterations
in the law as are required by the exigency? And is the reason
strong enough to justify Parliament in encountering the danger

of delay? Surely there is no ground whatever for such a hope. Look back through the last half century. From November 1784 to December 1838, what can you see but bad laws, no laws, nugatory laws, or laws enacted by the Parliament of Great Britain? Has the civilization of the colony during all these years been advanced a single step by its own agency? Yes, one!—one gleam of light to make the darkness visible! Free people of colour have been admitted, first, to give evidence in the courts of justice; and next, to the same political privileges with their whiter neighbours: yet even these measures were only conceded for the purpose of strengthening the white interest against the great body of the black. What, then, has happened now to work the sudden conversion of the Assembly? Circumstances have changed; but the dispositions and interests of the planters (their immediate interests at least) remain unaltered. It has been said that their consent to terminate the Apprenticeship before its time "proved them to possess moderation and firmness." We say, no: it proved only that they felt, in common with the proprietary body and their friends in England, that the violence of public opinion could not at that time be safely or successfully resisted. It has been said that "their interests are now identified with the interests of the whole community." We say, no: it is their interest to oppress the labouring population as much as they can, and as much as they dare; and (only let them have the making of their own laws and the support of the Government in executing them), they will be able to do much in that way, and will perhaps *dare* still more. It has been urged that their dispositions must have changed with their circumstances. Again we say, no: what their dispositions were in the times of Slavery, the same they continued in the times of Apprenticeship; and every manifestation of their feeling during the last year—reports, protests, addresses, resolutions, debates —show that they continue the same still.

Suppose, then, that between the smiles of Lord Stanley and the terrors of Sir Robert Peel, the Assembly should consent to abandon their present position, and resume their functions:— What will be the consequence? First, with regard to the protection of the labouring classes, two courses are open to them

They will (unless their spirit is indeed changed, the probability of which it lies with the asserter to make out) either simply refuse to repeal the existing laws, which have been shown to be utterly insufficient to secure the labourers from a fresh Apprenticeship deprived of the protection which they enjoyed under the old one (and this would be the most favourable case; because a flat refusal would be met at once by suspension or abolition, which need not take more than ten or twelve months to carry); or, secondly, they will have recourse, as in former cases, to evasion and delay. They will pass amendment laws—that is, laws professing to be amended, and really altered. These laws must be sent home, examined, reported on, and disallowed. Then other alterations will be introduced—amendments, perhaps, so far as they go—but still not going far enough to reach the object. The same process must then be gone through again. The existing Vagrancy and Contract Laws might receive successive amendments for ten successive years, and still be unallowable. Yet all this time there might occur no single period in the controversy at which they could be convicted so clearly as now of a deliberate determination not to co-operate with the Government for the protection of the newly emancipated population. At this moment distrust and disapproval of the policy of the mother country are written on every act and every expression; and they have deliberately chosen their own ground to try which is the stronger—which policy is to prevail.

So much for the chance of obtaining adequate laws for the protection of the labouring classes. Now for society. Acting in the same spirit, they will pass a Police Bill speedily enough; but it will contain the same clauses which on the 11th of April, 1838—(in violation of their constitutional privileges—Lord Stanley himself standing by)—were repealed by a unanimous Parliament. Both in the Report of their Committee of the 24th March 1838, to which we have alluded, and in the debates which followed the announcement of the Amendment Act, the repeal of these clauses is spoken of in terms of complaint which leave no doubt that they will be obstinately adhered to. Their Police Act, therefore, must be disallowed. Then they will pass a Trespass Act; but it will contain some clause which may be used to prevent labourers from visiting each other's dwellings without the express permission of the overseer. This Act must likewise be disallowed. A law for the prevention of squatting may easily be made to contain most dangerous and oppressive provisions; and this law must be disallowed like the rest; though it is much wanted even now, and, if the present state of things be suffered to continue, it will soon become indispensable. Again, what will they do for the improvement of the prisons? What do they care about the loathsome condition of these places, or their defective discipline? They can think of nothing but the violation of their constitutional privileges by the Prisons Act. This Act, therefore, will remain inoperative, so far as the improvement of the system goes, for want of funds.* Will they agree to provide a new court of law, and a new judge with an adequate salary? Will they take measures to cleanse the existing courts, and invent some new machinery for dispensing equal justice to all complexions? Will they take the election and control of the militia out of hands that are likely to abuse their power?—for if we are prepared for another beginning of the "slow and steady course" of 1823, we should be prepared also for another termination like that of 1832; and we have not yet forgotten the bloody work in which the Jamaica militia then figured; not in the fight only, but in the courts-martial, regular or at the drum-head, after the fight was over. Will they pass a law declaring the validity of marriages celebrated by dissenters and missionaries? Will they make proper provision for the destitute and aged, without reserving to the planter that quantity of discretion in granting it, which may make the relief an act of indulgence, and the threat of withholding it a means of oppression? Is it not evident that every one of these laws will raise questions for dispute between two authorities which think differently on all the subjects with which they are connected? Yet the worst of the laws which will be proposed (bad as it will probably be) may perhaps produce less practical evil than the non-existence of any law at all.

Such, we believe, would be the practical result of any measure which should imply any kind of promise that the system of

* Parliamentary Papers, I. p. 169.

super-legislation shall hereafter be abandoned. Since the Assembly have declared as distinctly as their gift of speech enables them to do, that they will not be satisfied with anything less than such a promise ; since such a promise would be thus highly inexpedient.; and since Jamaica cannot . be safely left at this juncture without a legislature of some kind or other—it follows, that they must be dealt with as a body which cannot be satisfied, and ought therefore to be superseded.

For these reasons (for in the foregoing pages we have but explained and justified the allegations contained in the preamble of the defeated Bill)—and to meet promptly an occasion which can ill brook delay—the Ministry proposed to transfer to the Governor and Council, for a limited time, the power of making laws for Jamaica. Such a constitution would have differed from the existing constitution of our Crown colonies in two material points only; three salaried commissioners, selected in England for that office, were to be added to the Council ; and all legislative proceedings were to pass more immediately under the supervision of Parliament. It was to last for two years and a half. That such a Government would have been much better, and much more truly representative of the entire people of Jamaica (counting, of course, the 320,000 blacks), and of her several interests, than any Government she has yet had, or can hope to have under the existing law for many years to come, no one, we presume, can seriously doubt.* Once admit that Parliament ought not to abandon its authority (and in such a case to hesitate is to give way), once admit that *some* coercive measure is required, and the objections to the measure proposed—such as the danger of enforcing it, which is nothing ; the fear that it may be *permanently* enforced, which it cannot be without a fresh Act of Parliament ; the difficulty of determining whether to call it a penal measure or a measure of general policy (seeing that it is in fact a measure of general policy brought on by the misconduct of the parties whose privileges it happens to interfere with)— these and the like objections may be safely left to themselves.

---

* The House of Lords has produced, since this was written, an illustrious exception. The Duke of Wellington seriously believes, that under such a government no white man could have remained in Jamaica! The Duke's authority is fairly against us, we admit. But no authority can give weight to such an opinion.

The advantages, direct and collateral, which would have flowed
from such a measure to Jamaica first, and through her to all
our West Indian possessions, would be a more fruitful topic.
But it is idle to dwell upon them now, since the occasion for
securing them has been so miserably thrown away. The mischief is already done, and will hardly be retrieved. The Bill now
before Parliament, if it be allowed to pass, will save something
from the wreck. Three important measures will be gained; but
the rest is to be left to chance. The management of this most
critical time, in which five-sixths of the people of Jamaica are
passing from slaves into citizens—in which "the full light of
liberty is suddenly let in upon the scarcely unsealed eyes;" *—
this most difficult and delicate task of securing to the negroes
the enjoyment of real freedom, and at the same time making it
their real interest, and making them feel and understand that it
is their real interest, to remain in the condition of a labouring
peasantry in the service of their former masters—a task requiring, if ever any did, both strength, and skill, and zeal—is to be
trusted to the present House of Assembly; a body how qualified
at any time for such a task we know too well, and now worse
disposed than ever;—irritated by opposition, insolent from a
victory over the Government, and emboldened by a belief that
Parliament no longer cares, or no longer dares, to interfere.†
Meantime, this very body is standing on the brink of a vast, a
sudden, and (cheerfully as our Conservatives regard it) we must

* Canning in 1823.

† This was a mistake, as the event showed. The vigour of the attempt, and the
narrowness of the escape, did in fact convince them that Parliament both cared and
dared, and in that respect had the same effect as if it had succeeded. This, added
to the timely death of several principal members of the Assembly, which happened
that year, the Admirable judgment of Sir Charles Metcalfe in choosing his position,
and the no less admirable temper of Lord John Russell in supporting him in it,
brought the affair to a very different issue from that which I had anticipated.

[This note was written in the margin of my copy of the Review, in June 1844·
But the history of the next twenty years proved that the anticipated issue, though
postponed, was not escaped. The legislative action of the Assembly during those
years brought the affairs of the colony by degrees into such a condition, that in 1865
they gave up their constitution in despair, their legislative functions were transferred to the Crown by their own desire, and the Government of Jamaica was reduced
for good (in both senses of the word) into the condition in which the bill of 1839
proposed to place it for two years and a half.]

add, a very perilous change. For one or two years more, it will continue to represent the existing constituency of 2000 whites, who were slave-drivers a few months ago; the year after, that constituency may be augmented by an overwhelming and rapidly increasing majority of blacks, who a few months ago were slaves. Who can tell how such a change will work hereafter, or how the temper of the Assembly may be affected by such a prospect now? Thanks to the Conservative party, we have lost the means of watching and guiding the present, and of preparing to meet the future. A competent Legislature on the spot, desiring the real welfare of the whole community, and able not only to make laws but to superintend their operation and remodify them as occasion may suggest—able to feel their way as they proceed —they will not let us have. For what to them is the good of a distant colony, though linked with the prosperity of a mighty cause, when weighed against the inconvenience of a majority for Ministers?

IV.

TALES BY THE AUTHOR OF "HEADLONG HALL."*

THERE was an officer attached to one of the ancient regal establishments whose business was to appear before the king every morning and gravely remind him that he was mortal. How long this office was endured, and what was the fate of the person who first held it, we are not informed. It probably soon sank into a sinecure, its active duties being discharged in deputy by a death's head, till the times of change came when among other bulwarks of that constitution it was swept away altogether. But though names change and salaries cease, wants remain. Courts still stood in need of some such monitor; and in the person of the king's jester the old office was revived in an improved form and with additional duties. The jester was licensed to utter other and newer truths than that one, so long as he did not seem to be uttering them in earnest; and the king could listen patiently to speeches by which his own follies were anatomized, so long as it was understood that the speaker, not himself, was the fool. The profession of the jester was simply to make sport for the great; but his real use was to tell unwelcome truths; his privilege to tell them without offence; and his great art and faculty (supposing him duly qualified for his office) was one in which no lover of truth should omit to exercise himself,—that of detecting secret resemblances between things most distant and in common esti-

1. "Headlong Hall." "Nightmare Abbey." "Maid Marian." "Crotchet Castle." (Standard Novels, No. 57.) 8vo. London: 1837. 2. "Melincourt." London. 3. "The Misfortunes of Elphin." London. (*Edinburgh Review*, January, 1839.)

mation most unlike; and of searching the substance of popular judgments by turning the seamy side outward. It was a sad day for kings when that divine right passed from them of hearing reason only from the lips of fools. It came however in its appointed time. Truths of the most uncourtly kind found their way to courts unbidden and undisguised, and the jester's office became obsolete. But though in courts it is now perhaps but little needed, there are many places in which it might, we think, be revived with great advantage. The immunity which passed from the Crown was divided among the public. Every man's house became his castle. Every man's peculiar set, creed, system, or party became a kind of court, in which he might live surrounded by the echoes of his own thoughts and flattered by a convincing uniformity of sentiment, as secure as kings were once from the intrusion of unwelcome censures. But this is a security which a man who duly distrusts his own skill or courage in self-dissection can hardly wish to enjoy; though if he distrusts likewise his resolution to court annoyances because they are wholesome which he might exclude because they are disagreeable, he will wish it broken as inoffensively as possible, and with as few of those shocks and mortifications from which correction, in whatever form it comes, can never be wholly free. It is for this purpose that, if it were possible to restore dead fashions to life, we would revive the office of jester. It is by the squandering glances of the fool that the wise man's folly is anatomized with least discomfort. From the professed fool he may receive the reproof without feeling the humiliation of it; and the medicine will not work the worse, but the better, for being administered under the disguise of indulgence or recreation. It would be well indeed if every man could keep a licensed jester who, whether in thought or action, has too much his own way. All coteries, literary, political, or fashionable, which enjoy the dangerous privilege of leading the tastes and opinions of the little circle which is their world, ought certainly to keep one as part of their establishment. The House of Commons, being at once the most powerful body on the earth and the most intolerant of criticism, stands especially in need of an officer who may speak out at random without fear of Newgate. Every philosopher who has a system, every theologian who heads a sect, every projector who gathers a company, every interest that can command a party, would do wisely to retain a privileged jester. The difficulty is to find a becoming disguise under which the exercise of such a privilege would be pleasant or even endurable. The motley and the coxcomb are obsolete. They belonged to the "free and holiday-rejoicing" youth of England, and have no mirth in them for us. To the nineteenth century, in which every hour must have its end to attain and its account to render, and every soul must be restlessly bent on providing wares for the market or seeking a market for its wares (which is what we now mean by "doing well"), the foolishness of fools is only folly. A modern Jacques, desirous of a fool's license to speak his mind and of procuring from the infected world a patient reception of his cleansing medicines, must find some other passport into its self-included and self-applauding circles,—some other stalking-horse than professional foolery,—under which to shoot his wit. But in one form or other the heart of man will have its holiday; and whichever of the pursuits of the day has in it most of relaxation and amusement and least of conscious object, whichever is most popular yet least prized—the favourite that has no friend—will supply a suitable mask under which freedom of speech may still be carried on. This in our day is unquestionably the novel. It is over novels in three volumes that the mind of this generation relaxes itself from its severer pursuits into that state of dreamy inadvertency which is the best condition for the alterative treatment which we recommend. It is a maxim that "the mind is brought to anything better, and with more sweetness and happiness, if that whereunto you pretend be not first in the intention, but *tanquam aliud agendo*,"—and certainly the mind of a modern novel reader, forgetting its graver purposes in a pleasureable anxiety for the marriage of the hero and heroine,—purified by terror and pity,—perpetual pity for their crosses, and occasional terror for their fate,—may be brought by the way to imbibe many strange and salutary lessons, which, if formally addressed to it, would have been rejected at once as tedious, mischievous, or unprofitable. The truth of this has in practice been largely recognized. Politics, religion, criticism, metaphysics,

have all used this introduction to the heart of the public; and
the disguise is at least equally well fitted for the purposes of that
philosophy, the function of which is to detect the sore places in
favourite creeds, doctrines, or fashions, by the test of half-earnest
ridicule; to insinuate the vanity of popular judgments which
are too popular to be openly assailed with success; to steal on
men's minds some suspicion of the frauds and corruptions and
inanities and absurdities, which pass current in the world under
the protection of names too sacred to be called in question without impiety.

The author of the works which we are about to review is in
many respects eminently qualified for this office; in which he
has for some years been labouring with great skill and assiduity.
His influence indeed does not seem as yet to have been considerable. The popularity of his works has been just sufficient to
make them scarce; which implies that they are highly esteemed,
but by a limited circle of readers. In fact, an early popularity
was not to be expected for them; and it may be doubted whether
they will ever attain a place in our circulating literature. Their
rare excellence in some qualities carries them too high above the
taste of ordinary readers; while their serious deficiency in some
others will prevent them from obtaining a permanent value in
the estimation of a better class. The refined beauty of the composition, pure as daylight from the glaring colours by which
vulgar tastes are attracted, "as wholesome as sweet and by
very much more handsome than fine," is of itself sufficient to keep
them on the upper shelves of circulating libraries; while certain
shallows and questionable regions in the author's philosophy will
make them uninteresting to many deeper judges.

For our own part however we are not so easily deterred.
Good books are not so plentiful that we can afford to throw them
away because they are not better; and though fully prepared to
be just judges in public, we must take the liberty to be familiar
in private, and keep a copy of these questionable volumes within
reach of our easier chair. In truth we much doubt the wisdom
of living only in the company of such as are perfect. It is to go
out of the world before our time; to deal with the children of the
world as if they were no wiser in their generation than ourselves.

Mental and moral obliquities are to be censured of course wherever we meet them, and if possible amended. Yet it cannot be denied that they help to perform much necessary service which could not be done so well without them. The economy of the world requires characters and talents adapted to various offices, low as well as high; and it is vain to deny that the lower offices will be most readily undertaken and most efficiently discharged by minds which are defective in some of the higher attributes. There is work to be done in the state which a man may be too good to qualify himself for without in some degree contracting the circle of his goodness; and there is work to be done in the province of knowledge and literature to which the deepest and largest and best-balanced intellects cannot address themselves with eager interest or undivided attention. We must have spies as well as soldiers, hangmen and informers as well as magistrates and lawgivers, advocates as well as judges, antiquaries as well as historians, critics as well as poets, pullers down as well as builders up, scoffers to scourge falsehood as well as philosophers to worship truth. There is a place as well as a time for all things, and a hand for every work that is done under the sun.

Whether indeed these works are so necessary as to justify us in *educating* workmen to excel in them, we are happily not concerned to enquire. There is no danger of a scarcity. When we have done all we can to extend education and raise the tone of public feeling, and train all men to the noblest functions of which they are capable, there will still be more than enough of coarse grain and tortuous growth, whose abilities will be well enough adapted to the narrower spheres, whose aspirations will not rise higher, and who will really, in performing these necessary works, be cultivating their talents to the best advantage. Being there, the only question is how they shall be dealt with; whether they shall be acknowledged as good after their kind, or cast out as unworthy of our better company; praised for being faithful over a few things, or condemned because so few have been entrusted to them. For ourselves we have no hesitation in preferring the humaner alternative. It is our favourite belief that there is in every man and in every thing a germ of good, which, if judiciously educed and fostered, may be made gradually to prevail over the surrounding bad, and convert it more and more into its own likeness. But this must be done by favour and encouragement. It is not by whipping the faults, but by expressing a just sympathy with the virtues, that the final predominance of the better nature is to be brought about. And if it is for their interest that this treatment should be adopted, it will be our own fault if we do not turn it to advantage for ourselves. The labours of men who are pursuing anything with an earnest desire to find it can never be positively worthless. They are sure to make out something which is worth knowing; the possession of which can only be injurious when improperly applied or valued at more than its real worth; the pursuit of which can only become mischievous or unprofitable when it involves the sacrifice or interferes with the attainment of something better. Wealth, distinction, power, though not worth living for, are well worth having while we live. A fragment of truth is a good thing so far as it goes. Wit does not lose its value as wit when it mistakes itself for wisdom. The things themselves are of sterling worth; they lose the value which they have only by arrogating a value which they have not; and it is our own fault if we cannot restore them to their proper place, and make that good *for us* by regarding it in its true character, which is bad where we find it only because it affects a higher.

It is not to be denied that this faculty is called into unusual activity by the works before us. The reader must bring with him his own philosophy, moral, religious, and political. The feast is ample and various, but every man must help and digest for himself. Indeed the very aim and idea of them requires that it should be so. That the author should come before us not as a teacher but as a questioner of what others teach, is of the essence of his privilege. For this purpose something of waywardness and levity; some apparent looseness, inconsistency, or absurd liberty; some daring claim to allowance and indulgence too extravagant to be meant or taken in earnest,—is as necessary to him as motley to the jester, or bluntness and oddity of manners to the humorist. It is the pretext and excuse for his raillery; the illusion (more or less discerned, but willingly sub-

mitted to) which disarms resentment and makes censure and
earnest opposition seem ridiculous and out of place; which
enables us, in the words of Jacques,—

> "To weed our better judgments
> Of all opinion that grows rank in them
> That he is wise."

He must not mean all he says, or he could not say all he means.
It is for us to find out for ourselves how much is to be taken in
earnest. He appears not as a judge, but as an advocate;
licensed to espouse either side, and to defend it by bad evidence
as well as good; by sophistry where sound arguments are not
forthcoming; and by improvements on the truth where the
simple truth will not serve his turn. It is for his opponent to
argue the question on the opposite side; and for us the judges to
bear a wary eye and catch the truth which is struck forth from
the collision of the two. The motto which he has prefixed to his
earliest work gives us the key to all—

> "All philosophers who find
> Some favourite system to their mind;
> In every point to make it fit,
> Will force all nature to submit."

He is the disturber-general of favourite systems; the self-re-
tained advocate of nature against all philosophers who affect to
discern her secrets.

Among the various offices, high and low, by which the purposes of society are served and for which a supply of fit candidates is never wanting, we shall not be suspected, after what we
have said, of placing this too high in point of dignity, whatever
we may think of its usefulness. But that which justifies a man
in following any vocation, is not its dignity, but its adaptation to
his own nature; and it would be hard to find another for which
our author is so well fitted by natural constitution and capacity
as for this. A wandering and contemplative turn of mind; a
patient conviction of the vanity of all human conclusions; an
impatient sense of the absurdity of all human pretensions,
quickened by a habitual suspicion of their insincerity; an eye
and a heart open enough to impressions and opinions of all
kinds, so that vanity be the end of all; a perception of the

strangeness and mystery which involves our life, keen enough
to enliven the curiosity, but not to disturb or depress the spirit;
with faith in some possible but unattainable solution just sufficient to make him watch with interest the abortive endeavours
of more sanguine men, but not to engage him in the pursuit
himself; a questioning, not a denying spirit,—but questioning
without waiting for an answer; an understanding very quick
and bright,—not narrow in its range, though wanting in the
depth which only deeper purposes can impart; a fancy of
singular play and delicacy; a light sympathy with the common
hopes and fears, joys and sorrows of mankind, which gives him
an interest in their occupations just enough for the purposes of
observation and intelligent amusement; a poetical faculty, not
of a very high order, but quite capable of harmonizing the
scattered notes of fancy and observation, and reproducing them
in a graceful whole;—such, if we have read him rightly, are the
dispositions and faculties with which he has been turned forth
into this bustling world of speculation, enterprise, imposture,
and credulity, with its multiplying spawn of cant, quackery, and
pretension;—such the original constitution which seems to point
out as his natural and genial vocation the hue and cry after
folly in its grave disguises; the philosophy of irreverence and
incredulity; the light and bloodless warfare, between jest and
earnest, against all new doctrines, accepted or proclaimed for
acceptance,—clamorously hailed by the many, or maintained in
defiant complacency by the self-constituted "fit and few."

The impartiality with which he quits himself in this warfare
is marvellous, and scarcely explicable unless on the supposition
that he has within a deeper and more substantial faith to repose
on than any which he allows to appear. Naked scepticism,—
blank privation of faith and hope,—can never be really impartial;
it is an uncertain succession of fleeting partialities; vain, queru-
lous, discontented, full of quarrel and unquietness, full of spite
and favouritism, full, above all, of itself. Not so with our
author. He stands among the disputing opinions of the time,
a disengaged and disinterested looker-on; among them, but not
of them; showing neither malice nor favour, but a certain
sympathy, companionable rather than brotherly, with all; with

natural glee cheering on the combatants to their discom-
fiture, and as each rides his hobby boldly to the destruction
prepared for him, regarding them all alike with the same smile
of half compassionate amusement.   Of all the philosophies
which are encouraged to expose themselves in these pages, we
have endeavoured in vain to conjecture which enjoys the largest
or which the smallest share of his sympathy.   Could we find
one constantly associated with more agreeable personal qualities,
or with more brilliant conversation, or with sounder argument,
than any other;—were there any which he seemed to handle
with peculiar tenderness, or in the showing up of which he
appeared to take peculiar pleasure; we might suspect that we
had discovered the secret of his preference or aversion.   But no
such clue is offered to us.   The instances of the kind which we
have been able to detect serve only, when rightly understood, to
baffle us more completely.   It might certainly seem that his
respect for the good old times of roast-beef and quarter-staff,
and his contempt for the "march of intellect," have a touch of
earnestness in them;—that of all theories of human life, that
which maintains the superiority in all that concerns man's real
welfare of the twelfth century to the nineteenth, has most of his
secret sympathy; and that that which is advocated in broken
Scotch by certain imaginary members of our own fraternity, and
which may be called the politico-economical theory, is most to
his personal distaste; that of all characters his favourite is the
worldly man who boldly proclaims and acquiesces in his infirmity;
his aversion, the worldly man whose weakness is disguised by
himself under the affectation of something better, or protected
from the censure of society by the sanctity of his profession or his
order.   But, rightly considered, these apparent sympathies and
antipathies are not to be taken as an index to his real feelings.
It is not their greater or less conformity to his own tastes, but
their greater or less acceptance in the world, by which he is
repelled or attracted.   We see in them only the working of a
scepticism truly impartial and insatiable, which, after knocking
down all the opinions which are current in the world, proceeds
to set up an opinion made up of all that is *not* current in the
world, that when that falls too, the desolation may be complete.

K

Hence his tenderness to the twelfth century. The worshippers of the twelfth century are a race extinct. It is a fallen image, to insult which would be to flatter not to oppose the dogmatists of the time. That which has no friends he can treat with tenderness; that which others have thrown aside as false, his vocation requires or his genius moves him to seek some truth in. Our own philosophy, on the contrary, is of a newer fashion. It draws the largest audience; therefore the largest variety of folly, pretension, and credulity, as well as of their opposites. It is the article which best meets the wants of the time, and is therefore most puffed, hawked, and counterfeited. It provides him, we need not care to confess, with a great deal of legitimate work; nor do we desire to exclude him from our precincts. The light shafts which he employs cannot hurt us where we are sound; and where they do touch us, we are not above profiting by the hint. We will not fall into the common error of taking what we see to be good physic in our neighbour's case to be poison in our own. His apparent predilections with regard to personal character are to be explained in the same way. Some predilection for something, it was necessary to feel or feign. Otherwise, his fictions would have wanted warmth and a body. They would have wanted that reference to something positive, without which his world of negations could not have been made palpable; that standard of substance, without which the emptiness of the surrounding shadows could not have been explained. Being obliged to represent some character or other as an object of sympathy, he naturally fixes on that with which no one professes to sympathize. Projects for the diffusion of knowledge, the suppression of vice, the advancement of science, the regeneration of philosophy, or the purification of politics, are entertained as amusing vanities; but a genuine devotion to good eating and drinking, neither disguised nor excused, but studiously indulged and boldly professed as the natural occupation of a sound mind in a sound body, is a quality on which his eye pauses with an enjoyment almost akin to love. Not that he really esteems it (we know nothing of him, but imagine him a temperate man, with a thorough contempt for made dishes), but because it is his calling and his delight thus audaciously to reverse the opinion of the world; and to make all the idols for the worship of which men quarrel appear hollow and ridiculous in the presence of that which they agree in despising. On the same principle it may be observed that the desire of Dinner is in these novels the one touch of nature that makes the whole world kin; the one thing good for man all the days of this vain life which he spendeth as a shadow, on which all philosophers agree, —the one thing which abides with him of his labour. All conflicting theories shake hands at the sound of the dinner-bell. All controversies, however divergent, where the disputants are growing ever hotter and wider asunder as they proceed, strangely converge and meet in the common centre of the dinner-table. The following discussion, much injured by the necessary reductions, may serve as an example :

"*Mr. Crotchet, jun.* Pray, gentlemen, pocket your manuscripts; fill your glasses; and consider what we shall do with our money.

"*Mr. MacQuedy.* Build lecture rooms and schools for all.

"*Mr. Trillo.* Revive the Athenian theatre; regenerate the lyrical drama.

"*Mr. Toogood.* Build a grand co-operative parallelogram, with a steam-engine in the middle for a maid of all work.

"*Mr. Firedamp.* Drain the country, and get rid of malaria, by abolishing duck-ponds.

"*Dr. Morbific.* Found a philanthropic college of anti-contagionists, where all the members shall be inoculated with the virus of all known diseases. Try the experiment on a grand scale.

"*Mr. Chainmail.* Build a great dining-hall; endow it with beef and ale, and hang the hall round with arms to defend the provisions.

"*Mr. Henbane.* Found a toxicological institution for trying all poisons and antidotes. I myself have killed a frog twelve times, and brought him to life eleven; but the twelfth time he died. I have a phial of the drug which killed him in my pocket, and shall not rest till I have discovered its antidote.

"*Rev. Dr. Folliot.* I move that the last speaker be dispossessed of his phial, and that it be forthwith thrown into the Thames.

"*Mr. Henbane.* How, sir? my invaluable, etc.

    *   *   *   *   *   *   *

"*Mr. Crotchet, jun.* Pray, gentlemen, return to the point. How shall we employ our fund?

"*Mr. Philpot.* Surely in no way so beneficially as in exploring rivers. Send a fleet of steamboats down the Niger, and another up the Nile. So shall you civilize Africa, and establish stocking factories in Abyssinia and Bambo.

"*Rev. Dr. Folliot.* With all submission, breeches and petticoats must precede stockings. Send out a crew of tailors. Try if the king of Bambo will invest inexpressibles.

"*Mr. Crotchet, jun.* Gentlemen, it is not for partial, but for general benefit, that this fund is proposed: a grand and universally applicable scheme for the amelioration of the condition of man.

"*Several voices.* That is my scheme. I have not heard a scheme but my own that has a grain of common-sense.

   *   *   *   *   *   *

"*Rev. Dr. Folliot.* Well, of all these schemes, I am for Mr. Trillo's. Regenerate the Athenian theatre. * * * But, sir, I further propose that the Athenian theatre being resuscitated, the admission shall be free to all who can expound the Greek choruses, constructively, mythologically, and metrically, and to none others. So shall all the world learn Greek: Greek, the Alpha and Omega of all knowledge. At him who sits not in the theatre shall be pointed the finger of scorn: he shall be called in the highway of the city, 'a fellow without Greek.'

"*Mr. Trillo.* But the ladies, sir, the ladies.

"*Rev. Dr. Folliot.* Every man may take in a lady: and she who can construe and metricise a chorus, shall, if she so please, pass in by herself.

"*Mr. Trillo.* But, sir, you will shut me out of my own theatre. Let there at least be a double passport, Greek and Italian.

"*Rev. Dr. Folliot.* No, sir; I am inexorable. No Greek, no theatre.

"*Mr. Trillo.* Sir, I cannot consent to be shut out from my own theatre.

"*Rev. Dr. Folliot.* You see how it is, Squire Crotchet the younger: you can scarcely find two to agree on a scheme, and no two of those can agree on the details. Keep your money in your pocket. And so ends the fund for regenerating the world.

"*Mr. MacQuedy.* Nay, by no means. We are all agreed on deliberative dinners.

"*Rev. Dr. Folliot.* Very true; we will dine and discuss. We will sing with Robin Hood, 'If I drink water while this doth last;' and while it lasts we will have no adjournment, if not to the Athenian theatre.

"*Mr. Trillo.* Well, gentlemen, I hope this chorus at least will please you.

> ' If I drink water while this doth last,
> May I never again drink wine:
> For how can a man, in his life of a span,
> Do anything better than dine?
> We'll dine and drink, and say if we think
> That anything better can be;
> And when we have dined, wish all mankind
> May dine as well as we.'

"'The schemes for the world's regeneration evaporated in a tumult of voices." —*Crotchet Castle*, p. 325.

It may seem superfluous to observe that this is not a conclusion in which it is meant that we should rest. It is but a more substantial vanity held up for a while to define and relieve the less palpable, then left to fall of itself; a grosser bubble among bubbles, which, having swallowed up the rest, breaks and leaves a blank, shutting up the story of the vanity like a dream within a dream;—the vanity of vanities, which gone, all is vanity. We close the volume, and from the masque and fantastic mockery of the world, we wake refreshed and not uninstructed into the world itself; there to build up for ourselves our own theory that shall not pass away; or to muse in vain, what, after all, may be the secret faith by which the author lives, in the silent assurance of which he can thus bear to dally with perplexity and dwell among confusions. Doubtless his spirit has a home of its own to go to, or it could not so take its ease in its inn.

We have been unconsciously led into this discussion of the genius and intention of our author, by a wish to justify the pleasure which, whether justifiable or not, we certainly do take in his company. If our theory be good for nothing else, it may serve him to make sport with in his next production. In the meantime the fact remains, that his books are to us very pleasant reading, and fertile enough in grave suggestions to the mind that can take them rightly.

Assuming the legitimacy of his general design, the praise of great skill in the execution will hardly be denied him. He shows a free delight and a prevailing thirst for excellence in his art, which places him in our estimation decidedly among men of *genius*, properly so called; men, that is, whose minds are moved and controlled by an inner spirit, working restlessly towards some end of its own, in the simple attainment of which, independently of any use to be made of it, and in that alone, it finds satisfaction. Hence his rare accomplishment in the use of his weapons, which he wields with a grace, a dexterity, and (excepting a few cases, in which, not content with public conduct and opinions, he undertakes, not very happily, to interpret motives and exhibit personal qualities) with a gay good-humour which takes away all offence from his raillery, and secures for him a free toleration in the exercise of his privilege. The spirit of frolic exaggeration in which the characters are conceived, —each a walking epitome of all that is absurd in himself, —the ludicrous felicity of self-exposure with which they are made to talk and act,—and the tone of decided though refined caricature which runs through the whole, unite to set grave remonstrance fairly at defiance. And while the imagination is thus forced into the current of his humour, the taste is charmed by a refinement of manners, and by a classical purity and reserved grace of style, which carries all sense of coarseness or vulgarity clean away; and the understanding is attracted and exercised by the sterling quality of the wit, the brilliancy, fullness, and solidity of the dialogue, the keenness of observation, the sharpness and intelligence, if not the delicacy or philosophical depth, of satire; and a certain roguish familiarity with the deceitfulness of human nature, from which we may derive many useful hints, to be improved at pleasure. Add to this, that although he dwells more habitually among doubts and negations than we believe to be good for any man, he is not without positive impulses,—generous and earnest, so far as they go,— which impart a uniformly healthy tone to his writings. There are many things both good and bad which he does not recognize; but the good which he does recognize is really good; the bad really bad. Explicit faith of his own he seems to have none; the creeds, systems, and theories of other men he treats alike as toys to play with; his humour, though pure, is shallow: his irony covers little or none of that latent reverence and sympathy, —rarely awakens within that "sweet recoil of love and pity,"— which gives to irony its deepest meaning, and makes it in many minds the purest, if not the only natural language of tender and profound emotion; his general survey of life has something of coldness and hardness, so that much good seed falls in vain and withers on the surface. But his nature bears no weeds, and the natural products of the soil are healthy and hardy. Inhumanity, oppression, cant,* and false pretensions of all kinds are hated

* Except, perhaps, in the case of men whose opinions have been modified by age and experience into better accord with the majority. There are some passages in which he seems to countenance the doctrine that when a man, who in the glow of youth and hope has chiefly signalized himself by an impassioned proclamation of the *rights* of men, turns in his maturer age to warn them of their *duties*,—such change can only be considered as an act of deliberate apostacy from the truth, in consideration of value received. This we call cant; and we would almost stake the justice of the censure upon his own answer to a plain question—Did he, when he spoke of Edmund Burke as "having prostituted his own soul, and betrayed his country and mankind for £1200 a-year," really believe that he was speaking the

with a just hatred; mirth, sunshine, and good fellowship are relished with a hearty relish; simplicity, unassuming goodness, and the pure face of nature never fail to touch him with natural delight. It is most pleasant and encouraging to observe these better qualities gradually prevailing and exercising in each successive production a larger influence. The humour seems to run deeper; the ridicule is informed with a juster appreciation of the meaning of the thing ridiculed; the disputants are more in earnest, and less like scoffers in disguise; there is more of natural warmth and life in the characters; and, altogether, there is a humaner spirit over his later works, and a kindlier sympathy with his subject.

A corresponding improvement may also be observed in the management of his plots—in the skill with which the incidents are interwoven with the conversations, and made to assist in developing the humours of the dialogue. In the two earliest of them indeed, "Headlong Hall" and "Melincourt," the whole story might be stripped off, so as to leave a series of separate dialogues scarcely injured by the change. We should miss only, what indeed we should be very sorry to miss, the picturesque grouping and lively satirical narrative by which they are accompanied and relieved. In "Nightmare Abbey" this could not be so easily done. Without the successive situations which form the story, the humour of *character* (which is more considerable in this than in the two foregoing tales) could hardly be brought out. Scythrop, the gloomy and mystical regenerator, who builds

---

truth? Had it, in fact, ever occurred to him to consider whether the thing he was saying was true or false? He could surely give but one answer. That Burke was wrong—that his feelings being too much ahead of his judgment, all facts came before him through a fiery medium of pity or indignation, or religious love—and that his understanding working on data thus distorted, led him to unreasonable conclusions,—any man with a mind differently constituted from Burke's may easily believe. But that his adoption of those conclusions can only be regarded as an act of deliberate and venal falsehood, is a monstrous proposition, which the man who can truly believe, must have a narrower understanding and a shallower heart than we can believe our author to possess. No—he has in this instance, and in some others (which, lest our censure should preserve the allusions from becoming unintelligible, we pass by silently), allowed himself to adopt a species of cant, familiar and excusable amongst schoolboys, but as much to be hated in a grown man as any of the many cants which are so successfully held up in these volumes to the scorn they deserve.

morbid hopes for the future upon a morbid discontent with the present,—Mr. Glowry, the large-landed misanthropist, to whose table all men are welcome, who can find nothing in the world for a reasonable man to enjoy,—and Mr. Toobad, the Manichean millennarian, who can see nothing there except the devil himself, having great wrath—could hardly have been displayed in full character without the loves, jealousies, and contradictions which it is the business of the narrative to develope. In "Maid Marian" and "Crotchet Castle," the interest lies in a kind of commentary on the action; which would lose its meaning if the scene and story were taken away. In "Crotchet Castle," the incidents are employed to bring out the humours of individual character, and are so well wrought into the texture of the work, that, slight as they are, they could not be separated from it without material injury. It is not that truth to nature is more strictly preserved in the later than in the earlier tales, for the spirit of exaggeration and caricature is still kept up; but that the caricature is deeper and more pervasive, and better harmonized. In the later, the characters *live* upon their hobbies; in the earlier, they only mount them to dispute upon.

But though the management of the plots is in this respect very skilful, the author has wisely abstained (except in one instance, which we shall notice presently) from attempting to give them any independent interest as stories. They are of the simplest construction, and the incidents are taken from everyday life. A hospitable house, a variety of guests, and an occasion which may bring them together on easy terms, are all he wants; no matter whether it be a Christmas party, a wedding party, a party of speculators in philosophy or in the stooks, or a party of rival suitors to an attractive heiress. The course of true love cannot run too smoothly; virtue cannot triumph with too little help from accident or superhuman effort,—need not indeed triumph at all; the true heir cannot be in too little danger of losing his inheritance; the meeting of the guests cannot be too easily brought about, or the parting cause too few tears. The business of the fiction lies in the dialogues, and would only be injured and embarrassed by any independent interest that might be combined with it of an exciting or pathetic nature.

The importance of observing this principle may be best seen in the effect which, in the instance to which we have alluded, is produced by a departure from it. Anthelia Melincourt is an heiress endowed with all virtues of mind and body,—not without an estate of ten thousand a-year to make them manifest to the apprehension and operative upon the happiness of mankind. These combined attractions draw together a sufficient variety of suitors, and supply them with a fair opportunity for exhibiting their peculiarities. Aristocracy, landed propriety, established churchmanship, political economy, match-making maternity, barouche-driving baronetcy, and chivalry in modern attire,—all gather round her as principals or as seconds. They must disperse again as soon as her choice is made. In the meantime there is plenty of mutton to eat, of wine to drink, and of subjects to dispute about. Such circumstances would in the common course of things breed crosses and misunderstandings quite enough for all the author's purposes, without extorting from nature any unnecessary exertions. But instead of contenting himself with these, he has borrowed on this one occasion the common-place-book of a melodramatist, and tried the fortitude of his heroine by a forcible abduction, and the constancy of his hero (and indeed of his reader) by an anxious pursuit. She is carried off by a noble suitor, and shut up in a solitary castle, nobody knows where. Her lover sets off on foot to find her; accompanied by a political economist with whom he may hold dialogues by the way. He wanders about for some days, discussing in a very calm and philosophical spirit a variety of questions suggested by the scenes through which they pass—such as paper-money, surplus population, epitaphs, apparitions, the probable stature of the Patagonians, mountains, and the hopes of the world—but meets with no trace whatever of the heroine; till at length, by the most fortunate accident in the world, he suddenly stumbles upon her, at that precise moment of time when, if he had not,—the author must have found some difficulty in going on. The dialogues and conversations by which the weariness of this journey is beguiled are most of them very elegant and spirited compositions; but they have so little to do with the heroine or the story, that they might be left out without diminishing the interest of the tale, and published as separate papers without losing any of their own. And, indeed, every reader who feels anxious for the fate of Anthelia—which, to confess the truth, we ourselves do not—had better pass at once from the first chapter of the third volume to the last, and read the rest at his leisure as an independent work of a quite different character. He cannot have sympathy in him for both at once.

Nor is this the only demand which is made on the reader in this work for moods of sympathy incompatible with each other. It presents a worse combination than that of moving accidents and melodramatic escapes with miscellaneous dialogue of a philosophical cast;—a combination, to our taste still more inharmonious, of the reality with the masquerade of life; the comedy with the farce; of grave questions for the conscience with the merest buffooneries of wit; of touching appeals to the affections with absurd assaults upon the risibility. And no attempt seems to have been made to reconcile these incompatible moods—to make them blend with each other by the interfusion of some sentiment common to both, or relieve each other by the force of just and harmonious contrast.

It was probably from a consciousness of these defects that the author determined to exclude this tale from the collection before us, though it is evident that no small pains have been bestowed on it; and we suspect that at the time of composition it was a favourite. Its purposes appear to be graver, its pretensions loftier than the others; and although from the defects we have mentioned it must be pronounced a comparative failure, it contains, if we mistake not, indications of a capacity for a better and a higher strain than he has yet attempted.

To make this appear, it will be necessary to go somewhat into detail, and to hazard another speculation as to the history and development of his mind. The pains will be well repaid, if he should be induced to reconsider the capabilities of the work and recast it for some future collection in a more perfect form.

Our theory is, that during the composition of "Melincourt" a struggle was going on in his mind between his better and his

worse genius, and that the contest was neither decided nor com-
promised, but drawn,—each party claiming the victory, and setting up a trophy, after the fashion of the Greek armies in Thucy-
dides, on its own side of the field. We have already adverted to
his tenderness for the former times, and ascribed it to the natural
reaction in a mind like his against the clamorous pretensions of
modern refinement. And we have little doubt that it began in
this ; but had the tale before us been fresher in our memory, we
should not perhaps have asserted so roundly that his mind was
really as free from bias in this direction as in others. He began
in joke, but he seems to have narrowly escaped ending in earnest.
He amused his fancy, or gratified his spleen, by setting forth the
rival pretensions of the barbarous ages, till he fell in love with
the picture he had drawn,—half persuaded himself that civilization was a downward progress, and had more than half a mind
to turn preacher against it in good faith.' But here his habitual
scepticism, aided probably by his sound sense of the ridiculous,
stands in the way. He has not faith enough to turn devotee.
He shrinks from the solemnity of the task in which the consistent pursuit of such a purpose must involve him ; and, after
a brief struggle during which he wavers indecisively between
the graver service of truth and the more exciting persecution
of error, he relapses into the original condition which we
have already endeavoured to describe—betakes himself to the
work of destruction rather than edification—to the pulling down
of other men's systems instead of building up a better of his
own.

It is at least certain that this question concerning the respective pretensions of the dark and of the enlightened ages did at
one time occupy an unusual space in his contemplations ; that
throughout his two earliest works it is distinguished by very
marked attentions,—with this difference, that what was only
flirtation in the first, assumes the aspect of a serious intention in
the second ; and that for some reason or other the serious tone
is afterwards abandoned, and the flirtation renewed, though in a
more sober way. In "Headlong Hall" the argument on the side
of deterioration is conducted by Mr. Escot with great force and
spirit ; but enough of extravagance, inconsistency, and caricature

is mixed up with it, to mark it as a theory to which the author is in no way committed; which reason and nature have nothing to do with; and which leads to no conclusion. If Mr. Escot holds that the manners of this generation are worse than those of the last, he holds also that each succeeding generation has in like manner been worse than its predecessor, ever since men learned the use of fire. If he denounces animal food as noxious, sinful, and unnatural, it is while he is helping himself to a slice of cold beef. If he inveighs against dancing, as foreign to the calm and contemplative habits of the original wild man of the woods, it is only when he is waiting to stand up again with the beautiful Cephalis. Moreover, the argument on the opposite side is maintained with equal spirit, and rather less inconsistency, by Mr. Foster the perfectibilian; and the last word remains clearly with Mr. Jenkinson the *statu-quo-ite*, who, believing that all opposing arguments are held in eternal equipoise, sets up no theory on any subject; but on all questions which present themselves for practical solution, gives the casting vote to his inclination for the time being.* Add to this, that though this question forms the principal topic of discussion, the *action* is unaffected by the decision of it. The deteriorationist and the perfectibilian dine, drink, dance, and are married, just as if neither deterioration nor perfectibility had ever been thought of. The question is dissolved, rather than solved; it disappears, and the action closes over it.

In "Melincourt" the same subject is resumed, but in a graver strain. The motto, the opening, the purpose proposed, are all grave. The heroine is very grave. The title-page informs us that, if the maxims of romance and chivalry have come to be ridiculous in our eyes, it is not because our minds are more enlightened, but because our manners are more corrupt. The first chapter introduces the heroine herself, as a character "really romantic and unworldly," made up of all the cardinal virtues, without a spark of fun. The business is to fit her with a

---

* "In the controversy between animal and vegetable food," said Mr. Jenkinson, "there is much to be said on both sides; and the question being in equipoise, I content myself with a mixed diet, and make a point of eating whatever is placed before me, provided it be good in its kind."—p. 7.

husband—also a grave matter; more especially when coupled with the following formal enouncement of "her ideas on the subject of marriage:"—

"She explicitly made known to all her suitors her ideas on the subject of marriage. She had never perverted the simplicity of her mind by indulging in the usual cant of young ladies that she should prefer a single life; but she assured them that *the spirit of the age of chivalry manifested in the forms of modern life would constitute the only character on which she could fix her affections.*"

Without stopping to discuss this specimen of "simplicity" (which we suspect to be no true growth either of chivalry or of Old England, but a manufacture quite as modern as the affectations with which it is contrasted), it is enough to say that it is certainly meant to be received as the genuine article; that the problem thus enounced is certainly not an absurd one, and is proposed with all apparent gravity for practical solution in the course of the three volumes; that a suitor does at length appear who embodies, in no high Quixotic phrensy, but in a useful, honourable, consistent, and perfectly sane life, the very spirit which she loves; and that after passing through various scenes, in which the sincerity of his principles is attested by his practice, and the wisdom of his practice is justified by its operation, he is duly accepted as the very character which she had believed it possible to find,—a gentleman "in a brown coat in the nineteenth century," yet as true a knight-errant as any that wore golden armour in the days of Charlemagne. "Oh, Forester," said Anthelia, "you have realized my highest wishes. I have found you the friend of the poor, the enthusiast of truth, the disinterested cultivator of the rural virtues, the active promoter of the cause of human liberty. It only remained that you should emancipate a captive damsel, who, however, will but change the mode of her durance and become your captive for life." And then they are married and the story is done.

This, then, is no jest, but a serious thing;—a grave delineation of two lives, shaped according to a peculiar theory, such as anybody in these days might lead (anybody, at least, with sufficient landed property)—yet so pure, prosperous, and prevailing, that, were the example generally followed, there would be neither poverty nor distress in the world. Forester, though in some respects only a reproduction of Escot, is a character far more life-like and earnest; free from contradictions and inconsistencies; an enthusiast indeed, yet one whose enthusiasm is neither wild nor vain, but a noble hope for human nature, an inspired confidence in truth and virtue, and an absolute devotion to their service. Anthelia, "howbeit that we endure her not," is a character of the same mould. There is nothing in either which seems meant to be ridiculous; their theories, though romantic, are not chimerical; the measures by which they hope to realize them are not only sane but successful; nature herself is represented as sanctioning their enterprizes; substantial virtue and happiness spring up beneath their footsteps.

Had the business ended here we should have thought that the author's better genius had prevailed. We might indeed have questioned many of his doctrines, both social and political; and shown cause to doubt whether in the faithful bosom of real nature they would yield so fair a harvest as in the more accommodating soil of fiction. But we should have met him with undivided sympathy, as no idle talker on no trivial theme. This, however, his worse genius interferes to prevent. He has only a half faith in the cause he has espoused, and dares not let go his interest with the other party. It is as if, having in sport or curiosity raised the veil of truth, he had felt rebuked by the severity of her aspect, and turned for relief to more than usual levity and mockery. Hence the perpetual interruption of the serious and affecting, and sometimes even awful, interest which belongs to the main argument of the piece, by scenes of farcical and extravagant caricature, which might be pleasant enough as varieties in that farce of unreason with which he usually entertains us, but which, coming upon the mind in a state of serious emotions, are offensive and disagreeable. The two styles appeal to two opposite and incompatible moods; and it is impossible so to govern the imagination or the sympathies as to be in the humour for both. If you are not disgusted with the lighter, you cannot but be wearied with the graver.

The incongruity is indeed so remarkable, especially in so artist-like a writer, that we have many times paused to consider whether Forester and Anthelia may not after all have been meant to be laughed at too. But if so, the theory by which they live must be in our author's eyes more obviously and intrinsically ridiculous than we can well believe : if not, then it bears an application to the life of every man who reads, too urgent and vital to be a proper subject of buffoonery. Yet in what other light can we view the introduction of Forester's friend, the dumb Baronet? His theory concerning the true and original man might have passed for the dream of an enthusiast. But when coupled with the introduction in person of Sir Oran Haut-ton, Bart.,—that is to say, of a real Oran Outang, caught young in the woods of Angola, brought up in society, and now mixing freely with his degenerate fellow-creatures, and wanting nothing of the civilized man except his vices and his powers of speech,— what is it but buffoonery? and what sort of nondescript does it make of Forester himself? And how are we to regard but as buffoonery, more or less Aristophanic, the election for the borough of One-vote—the description of Cimmerian Lodge, and the symposium at Mainchance Villa? All these are farce ; the two former of the best kind, the two latter of the worst ; but broad farce all : quite inadmissible even between the acts of a piece in which any natural character or quality is allowed to appear, or any train of serious feeling to be awakened.

The author may indeed have persuaded himself that such gross pictures of corruption, quackery, and worldliness, would heighten by contrast the beauty of the opposite qualities as set forth in the life and doctrine of the principal characters. So, he might say, Caliban sets off Miranda. But the cases are not alike. If Caliban, instead of being a real monster, had only been a Christian gentleman endued with the qualities of a monster, he would have been as much out of place in the Tempest as the humours of Mainchance Villa are out of place in Melincourt. As it is, this affected contrast, instead of bringing the virtue of his hero into stronger relief, serves only to make more conspicuous his own want of constancy to his purposes and faith in his principles.

We should not have dwelt so long upon the faults of a work like this, had it been too late to mend them. But the author may yet have occasion to republish it in a future collection. In that case, we would earnestly suggest to him the expediency of separating the better from the worser half of it. Let him turn it into two distinct tales; the election of Sir Oran for the Borough of One-vote being the subject of one, in which (if, after having lived and thought for twenty years longer, he still continues to admire them) he may introduce the humours of Mainchance Villa; the graver question concerning the realization of the spirit of chivalry under the forms of modern society being the argument of the other, with Forester and Anthelia for the central figures. If he would but set about this latter task in a faithful spirit, we do not fear to predict, from the specimen which the tale before us even in its present state exhibits, that he would produce a work of a far higher and more enduring interest than any he has yet attempted. As an indication of his capacity for such a task, we select from many passages in a similar spirit the following fragment of a conversation which, though immediately referring to a question with which England is happily no longer concerned, will not lose its meaning or its force so long as there is a national object left to be attained, or a private duty to be done.

"*Sir Telegraph Paxarett.* Be that as it may, every man will continue to follow his own fancy. The world is bad enough, I dare say, but it is not for you or me to mend it.

"*Mr. Forester.* There is the keystone of the evil—mistrust of the influence of individual example. 'We are bad ourselves, because we despair of the goodness of others.'* Yet the history of the world abounds with sudden and extraordinary revolutions in the opinions of mankind, which have been effected by single enthusiasts.

"*Sir Telegraph Paxarett.* Speculative opinions have been sometimes changed by the efforts of roaring fanatics. Men have been found very easily permutable into *ites* and *onions*, *avians* and *arians*, Wesleyites or Whitfieldites, Huntingtonians or Muggletonians, Moravians, Trinitarians, Unitarians, anythingarians; but the metamorphosis only affects a few obscure notions concerning types, symbols, and mysteries, which have scarcely any effect on moral theory, and, of course, *a fortiori*, none whatever on moral practice: The latter is for the most part governed by the general habits of the society we live in. One man may twang responses with the parish-clerk; another may sit silent in a Quaker's meeting waiting for the illumination of the Spirit; a third may groan and howl in a tabernacle; a fourth may breakfast, dine, and sup, in a Sandemanian chapel; but meet any of the four in the common intercourse of society, you will scarcely

---

* Coleridge's *Friend.*

know one from another. The single adage, *charity begins at home*, will furnish a complete key to the souls of all four; for I have found, as far as my observation has extended, that men carry their religion in other men's heads, and their morality in their own pockets.

" *Mr. Forester.* I think it will be found, that individual example has in many instances produced great moral effects on the practice of society. Even if it were otherwise, is it not better to be Abdiel among the fiends, than to be lost and confounded in the legion of imps grovelling in the train of the evil power?

" *Sir Telegraph Paxarett.* There is something in that.

" *Mr. Forester.* To borrow an allegory from Homer : I would say society is composed of two urns, one of good and one of evil. I will suppose that every individual of the human species receives from his natal genius a little phial containing one drop of a fluid, which shall be evil if poured into the urn of evil, and good if into that of good. If you were proceeding to the station of the urns with ten thousand persons, every one of them predetermined to empty his phial into the urn of evil, which I fear is too true a picture of the practice of society, should you consider their example, if you were hemmed in in the centre of them, a sufficient excuse for not breaking from them and approaching the neglected urn? Would you say, ' the urn will derive little increase from my solitary drop, and one more or less will make very little difference in the urn of ill; I will spare myself trouble, do as the world does, and let the urn of good take its chance from those who can approach it with less difficulty?' No : you would rather say, ' That neglected urn contains the hopes of the human species; little, indeed, is the addition I can make to it, but it will be good so far as it goes;' and if, on approaching the urn, you should find it not so empty as you had anticipated, if the genius appointed to guard it should say to you, ' There is enough in this urn already to allow a reasonable expectation that it will one day be full, and yet it has only accumulated drop by drop through the efforts of individuals who broke through the pale and pressure of the multitude, and did not despair of human virtue;' would you not feel ten thousand times repaid for the difficulties you had overcome, and the scoffs of the fools and knaves you had abandoned, by the single reflection that would then rush upon your mind,—*I am one of these?*

" *Sir Telegraph Paxarett.* Gad, very likely : I never considered the subject in that light."—Vol. i. p. 56–62.

" That strain we heard was of a higher mood ! "

It has been silent since, and we would gladly hear it tried again. Yet though this transient passion—this struggle towards a more earnest life—has yielded to a relapse, its salutary effects have not been wholly obliterated. The hope may have faded, the pursuit may have been abandoned, but the genial glow which it inspired has not departed with it; and its influence may still be traced, mellowing the cruder thoughts, softening the harsher touches, making the heart and head work more harmoniously together. Even in "Nightmare Abbey," which was produced in the following year, we seem to perceive traces of this improvement, especially in a point which we have already noticed,—the better development of the humour of *character* as distinguished from the mere battle of opinions. This is a quality which it is of course difficult to exhibit in an extract; but we may refer as a striking illustration to the difference between the two representations of transcendentalism in this and the preceding work—between Moly Mystic, whose conversation seems to be mere jargon, quite unworthy of the writer,—exposing nothing except his own inability to see any meaning in what he is laughing at; and Ferdinando Flosky, in whose person he deals many sharp and dexterous strokes, which, though passing wide enough of the individual at whom they appear to have been aimed, do much wholesome execution elsewhere. Here is a specimen :—

"*Mr. Flosky.* It is very certain, and much to be rejoiced at, that our literature is hag-ridden. Tea has shattered our nerves; late dinners make us slaves of indigestion; the French Revolution has made us shrink from the name of philosophy, and has destroyed in the more refined part of the community (of which number I am one) all enthusiasm for political liberty. That part of the *reading public* which shuns the solid food of reason for the light diet of fiction, requires a perpetual adhibition of *sauce piquante* to the palate of its depraved imagination. It lived upon ghosts, goblins, and skeletons (I and my friend Mr. Sackbut served up a few of the best), till even the devil himself, though magnified to the size of Mount Athos, became too base, common, and popular for its surfeited appetite. The ghosts have therefore been laid, and the devil has been cast into outer darkness, and now the delight of our spirits is to dwell in all the vices and blackest passions of our nature, tricked out in a masquerade dress of heroism and disappointed benevolence; the whole secret of which lies in forming combinations that contradict all our experience, and affixing the purple thread of some particular virtue to that precise character in which we should be most certain not to find it in the living world; and making this single virtue not only redeem all the real and manifest vices of the character, but making them actually pass for necessary adjuncts, and indispensable accompaniments and characteristics of the said virtue.

"*Mr. Toobad.* That is because the devil has come among us, and finds it for his interest to destroy all our perceptions of the distinctions of right and wrong.

"*Marionette.* I do not precisely enter into your meaning, Mr. Flosky, and should be glad if you would make it a little more clear to me.

"*Mr. Flosky.* One or two examples will do it, Miss O'Carroll. If I were to take all the mean and sordid qualities of a money-dealing Jew, and tack on to them, as with a nail, the quality of extreme benevolence, I should have a very decent hero for a modern novel; and should contribute my quota to the fashion-able method of administering a mass of vice under a thin and unnatural covering of virtue, like a spider wrapt in a bit of gold leaf and administered as a whole-some pill. On the same principle, if a man knocks me down, and takes my purse and watch by main force, I turn him to account, and set him forth in a tragedy as a dashing young fellow, disinherited for his romantic generosity, and full of a most amiable hatred of the world in general, and his own country in particular, and of a most enlightened and chivalrous affection for himself: then, with the addition of a wild girl to fall in love with him, and a series of adventures in which they break all the Ten Commandments in succession (always, you will observe, from some sublime motive, which must be carefully analyzed in its progress), I have as amiable a pair of tragic characters as ever issued from that new region of the belles lettres, which I have called the Morbid Anatomy of Black Bile, and which is greatly to be admired and rejoiced at, as affording a fine scope for the exhibition of mental power."—p. 118.

We must here observe, however, that the persons in this tale are not represented as natural characters, but as masks through which the writer speaks under an ironical assumption of the character, on a principle similar to that laid down by Mr. Sarcastic, in Melincourt:—" I ascertain the practice of those I talk to, and present it to them as from myself in the shape of theory; the consequence of which is, that I am universally stigmatized as a promulgator of rascally doctrines."

Mr. Skionar, transcendentalist of " Crotchet Castle," is yet again an improvement upon Mr. Flosky; the rather perhaps because he says very little. What he does say has so much of the sound and movement of the true transcendentalism, that it requires some knowledge of the matter to detect the counterfeit. And as many of the characters reappear in each succeeding Tale under new names, the progress of the author's mind may be easily traced by comparing them with each other. Compare, for instance, Squire Headlong in the earliest of them with Mr. Hilary in the next, and again with the Baron in Maid Marian; —all belonging to that class of men who take life as it comes, and enjoy it, without caring to understand or to mend it. Observe how crude and thin a creation is Mr. Escot, with his wild man of the woods and his skull of Cadwallader, when compared with Mr. Chainmail and his old baronial hall hung with old armour and banners,—his boar's head and wassail bowl, his old poetry and old manners copied from the twelfth

century. Or observe the various representatives of the Church
established,—the Rev. Dr. Gaster, the more genial Mr. Larynx,
and the most genial Dr. Folliot. It is easy to see that the difference is not accidental, but springs from the deeper and kindlier
impulses under which the later characters were moulded. It is
like the difference between a Bobadil and a Falstaff, which might
be taken as a measure of the humanity of the hearts, not less
than of the pregnancy of the wits in which they were conceived.
But this progressive triumph of the gentler nature is nowhere
displayed so strikingly as in his heroines. The mere misses
and coquettes who fill that place in his earlier works (Anthelia
Melincourt we have already noticed as an exception, though not
a very successful one) seem to have been created solely for the
purpose of making a story to set the dialogues in; yet even
there, the secret delight in beauty shows itself at intervals in
shy touches of delicacy and grace. Gradually the feeling growing
stronger and more impatient insists on a fuller utterance, and is
at length permitted to have its way, and to mould the entire
characters of Maid Marian and the heroine of Crotchet Castle
at its own delighted will, for its own pure satisfaction. The
difficulty of finding quotations to justify our praise is itself a
praise of no common order. Though it would be easy to fill a
considerable volume with very choice " beauties " selected from
these volumes, it would be hard to find one of them which would
not lose half its beauty by separation from its native context.
We cannot introduce Maid Marian in person without dimming
her brightness ; but brother Michael shall set forth her graces
in the following racy description.

　　" ' A mad girl, a mad girl,' said the little friar.
　　" ' How a mad girl ? ' said brother Michael. ' Has she not beauty, grace, wit,
sense, discretion, dexterity, learning, and valour ? '·
　　" ' Learning ! ' exclaimed the little friar; ' what has a woman to do with
learning ? And valour ! who ever heard a woman commended for valour ?
Meekness, and mildness, and softness, and gentleness, and tenderness, and
humility, and obedience to her husband, and faith in her confessor, and domes-
ticity, or, as learned doctors call it, the faculty of stay-at-homeitiveness, and
embroidery, and music, and pickling, and preserving, and the whole complex and
multiplex detail of the noble science of dinner, as well in preparation for the
table, as in arrangement over it, and in distribution around it to knights, and

squires, and ghostly friars,—these are female virtues; but valour—why, who ever heard'——

"'She is the all in all,' said brother Michael, 'gentle as a ring-dove, yet high soaring as a falcon: humble below her deserving, yet deserving beyond the estimate of panegyric: an exact economist in all superfluity, yet a most bountiful dispenser in all liberality: the chief regulator of her household, the fairest pillar of her hall, and the sweetest blossom of her bower: having in all opposite pro-posings, sense to understand, judgment to weigh, discretion to choose, firmness to undertake, diligence to conduct, perseverance to accomplish, and resolution to maintain. For obedience to her husband, that is not to be tried till she has one: for faith in her confessor, she has as much as the law prescribes: for embroidery, an Arachne: for music, a Siren: and, for pickling and preserving, did' not one of her jars of sugared apricots give you your last surfeit at Arlingford Castle?'

*   *   *   *   *   *   *

"'Indeed, reverend father,' said Sir Ralph, 'if the young lady be half what you describe, she must be a paragon: but your commending her for valour does somewhat amaze me.'

"'She can fence,' said the little friar, 'and draw the long bow, and play at single-stick and quarter-staff.'

"'Yet, mark you,' said brother Michael, 'not like a virago or a hoyden, or one that would crack a serving-man's head for spilling gravy on her ruff, but with such womanly grace and temperate self-command, as if those manly exercises belonged to her only, and were become for her sake feminine.'"—*Maid Marian*, p. 180.

The story is the happiest, in our judgment, of all our author's productions. The plan of the tale, requiring that the bright instead of the blank side of the manners he is describing should be turned towards us, keeps him throughout in his most genial mood, and calls forth all the warmth and sunshine of his nature. To exhibit the inconsistency of the popular theory of legitimate government by gravely applying it to the case reversed, is the idea with which he sets out. That "to the principles of free-bootery, diversely developed, belong all the qualities to which song or story concede renown;" that legitimate authority always means the authority of the stronger party; and that the common principle of all governments is to "keep what they have and to catch what they can,"—are his cardinal maxims, assumed in silent gravity. His idea is to be worked out, not by degrading kingcraft to the level of "freebootery," which would have involved him in a course of detractive satire, but by drawing such a picture of freebootery as may raise it to the level of king-craft. The irony and the moral, without being allowed to

cucumber the narrative or obstruct the flow of the humour, are
yet kept sufficiently in sight to conciliate the sympathy of the
reader.   Sherwood Forest is the scene, and Robin Hood is the
hero, in whose person and court the manners, virtues, principles,
and prerogatives of a prince are to be displayed in their fairest
colours.   Never was there a more fortunate congeniality between
the taste and the task. All the irony of his nature finds a happy
vent in disclosing the more latent qualities of legitimacy ; all his
sympathy with beauty, inward or outward, is called forth to
ennoble and embellish them.   A pure delight in the freshness
of uninclosed nature pervades and inspires the whole.   The
scenery is not described, but present as in life: " Wherever the
free range of the hart marks out the bounds of the forest," the
natural greenwood, with its glades and thickets, stretches beyond
us, "rolling its verdant gulfs of every hue."   We seem to hear
the songs of the friar coming before himself through the trees,
and to feel the silent presence of Maid Marian diffusing health
and purity through all.   Nor is the human world out of keeping
with the place and season.   Himself a kind of outlaw—his own
vocation as a writer being to make depredations upon received
opinions, and to redress the inequalities in our popular morality
by raising those who are too poor in the world's esteem at the
expense of those who are too rich,—he has a natural fellow-
feeling with the dynasty of Sherwood.   He paints them as if he
loved them.   In no real commonwealth, and not in every Utopia,
is there to be found a community so happy and well ordered, a
court so pure and loyal, a rule so mild, subjects so obedient,
justice so equally administered.   Whatever may be our graver
conclusions, it is certain that the principles and practice of the
forest, of which the following speech of Friar Tuck supplies a
succinct recapitulation with appropriate commentary, command
our affections for the time.

   " 'I am in fine company,' said the baron.
   " 'In the very best of company,' said the friar, 'in the high court of Nature,
and in the midst of her own nobility. Is it not so ? This goodly grove is our
palace : the oak and the beech are its colonnade and its canopy : the sun, and the
moon, and the stars are its everlasting lamps : the grass, and the daisy, and the
primrose, and the violet, are its many-coloured floor of green, white, yellow, and
blue ; the may-flower, and the woodbine, and the eglantine, and the ivy, are its

decorations, its curtains, and its tapestry : the lark, and the thrush, and the linnet, and the nightingale, are its unhired minstrels and musicians. Robin Hood is king of the forest both by dignity of birth and by virtue of his standing army ; to say nothing of the free choice of his people, which he has indeed, but I pass it by as an illegitimate basis of power. He holds his dominion over the forest, and its horned multitude of citizen-deer, and its swinish multitude or peasantry of wild boars, by right of conquest and force of arms. He levies contributions among them by the free consent of his archers, their virtual representatives. If they should find a voice to complain that we are "tyrants and usurpers to kill and cook them up in their assigned and native dwelling-place," we should most convincingly admonish them, with point of arrow, that they have nothing to do with our laws but to obey them. Is it not written that the fat ribs of the herd shall be fed upon by the mighty in the land? And have not they withal my blessing? my orthodox, canonical, and archiepiscopal blessing? Do I not give thanks for them when they are well roasted and smoking under my nose? What title had William of Normandy to England, that Robin of Locksley has not to merry Sherwood? William fought for his claim. So does Robin. With whom both? With any that would or will dispute it. William raised contributions. So does Robin. From whom both? From all that they could or can make pay them. Why did any pay them to William? Why do any pay them to Robin? For the same reason to both : because they could not or cannot help it. They differ indeed in this, that William took from the poor and gave to the rich ; and Robin takes from the rich and gives to the poor; and therein is Robin illegitimate; though in all else he is true prince. Scarlet and John, are they not peers of the forest? lords temporal of Sherwood? And am not I lord spiritual? Am I not Archbishop? Am I not Pope? Do I not consecrate their banner and absolve their sins? Are not they State, and am not I Church? Are not they State monarchical, and am not I Church militant? Do I not excommunicate our enemies from venison and brawn, and by 'r Lady! when need calls, beat them down under my feet? The State levies tax, and the Church levies tithe. Even so do we. Mass! we take all at once. What then? It is tax by redemption, and tithe by commutation. Your William and Richard can cut and come again, but our Robin deals with slippery subjects that come not twice to his exchequer. What need we then to constitute a court, except a fool and a laureate? For the fool, his only use is to make false knaves merry by art, and we are true men and are merry by nature. For the laureate, his only office is to find virtues in those who have none, and to drink sack for his pains. We have quite virtue enough to need him not, and can drink our sack for ourselves.' "—*Maid Marian*, p. 231.

" Crotchet Castle " recalls us to the less genial atmosphere of the nineteenth century. But the presiding genius of Dr. Folliot, the delineation of whose character must have been a work of sincere enjoyment, and the touching simplicity of the heroine, unite to throw over it a warmth of life, and a glow of romantic beauty, which make it as good perhaps in its kind as

Maid Marian.   It abounds in passages which we should be glad
to extract.   But our limits are full, and with a hearty recommendation to general acceptance as a most witty, shrewd, and
entertaining companion, we take our leave of this disturber of
the peace of coteries.

V.

THE WAKEFIELD THEORY OF COLONIZATION.*

WE have observed with great satisfaction the general and increasing interest which has recently been shown concerning the condition and management of our colonies; and especially the stream of enterprise which is daily setting more and more strongly towards Australia. Not only are emigrants of the lower classes proceeding thither annually by thousands instead of by hundreds; but gentlemen whose fortunes are to seek are beginning to suspect that those countries offer a better field than the overcrowded liberal professions for ripening competency into affluence —large capitalists begin to look thither for the chance of a larger dividend upon their capital—companies are formed for all manner of enterprises, and the shares are at a premium in the market—thousands of pounds are paid down in London for property in lands at the Antipodes, of which nothing is known beyond the latitude and longitude—the surveyor is despatched before to mark out the site of the capital—the governor, the public officers, the people, and the capital itself—houses, churches, and public buildings—follow him within a few months and boldly commence their national existence and their newspaper. It is partly, no doubt, to the natural restlessness of a people who must be doing, and have nothing to

* 1. "Letter from Sydney." 12mo. London: 1829. 2. "Report of the Committee on the Disposal of Lands in the British Colonies." Printed by Order of the House of Commons: 1836. 3. "Instructions to the Colonial Lands and Emigration Commissioners:" 1840. (*Edinburgh Review*, July, 1840.)

do; and partly to the uneasy longing for elbow-room and pros-pect in minds weary of the crowd and the beaten ways of an old and overpeopled country, that we must ascribe this sudden rush of adventure to the opposite corner of the globe: but we believe it must be in a still greater degree attributed to a recent dis-covery in colonization, now familiarly talked of under the name of "the Wakefield Principle;" dignified with capital letters, and notorious to all readers of the *Spectator*, the *Colonial Gazette*, and the *Weekly Chronicle*, as the one thing needful to make mankind rich, virtuous, and happy, for the rest of their time on earth—a specific for all the disorders of the world, so simple and so efficacious that the whole efforts and skill of the Colonial Office can hardly prevent it from taking effect.

But though the name and the pretensions of this principle have become so familiar, we have some doubts whether the prin-ciple itself has been much studied or generally understood. It has not indeed had its fair chance of free examination and dis-cussion; because, while many persons are deeply interested in persuading others to believe in it, nobody has anything to gain by calling it in question. There is no opposition principle bid-ding against it in the market; nor has it become a field for party contention in Parliament. On the other hand, large sums of money have been wagered upon it; and every shareholder is directly interested in raising the public opinion of its virtues, in which opinion resides the value of his share. The greater his own misgivings, the more will he strive to sustain the confidence of his neighbours; and all the tricks of the money market must be expected to be employed in magnifying the evidences of success and concealing all indications the other way. Even those who have taken up the scheme, as the originators did, as a purely political speculation, without any notion of making money by it, must be supposed to have contracted undue prejudices in its favour, and undue suspicions of persons less sanguine than them-selves and less disposed to make all other considerations give way to the pretensions of the favourite theory. It must also be remembered that these persons have happened, or have contrived, in advocating their cause to stand in a position peculiarly favourable for producing an effect upon disengaged bystanders.

Without ever exposing themselves to explanation or contradiction, they have adopted the tone of thwarted and misrepresented men. Fortunate is the disputant who seems to stand on the defensive, because the sense of justice and the hope of a fight secures him sympathy and a hearing ; more fortunate still, if his supposed antagonist be not in a condition to meet and answer him, because then he gets all the credit of a victory without risking the chance of defeat. The advocates of the " Wakefield theory of colonization " have formed a small compact body, with great vigour, ability, and perseverance ;—not restrained by any diffidence, or by many charitable scruples on their own part ; not crossing the path of any opposing interest, and therefore unchecked by hostile criticism from others. For the last eight or nine years they have been attacking without remorse all persons hostile, or supposed to be hostile, to any of their views ; coolly charging them, as if on the authority of personal knowledge (which, by the way, it is hardly credible that they can possess), with the basest motives and the most disingenuous artifices ; and these attacks they have been repeating week after week, without calling forth any one to contradict or question them—not because they are unanswerable, but because the only persons concerned to answer have been either ministers, who cannot enter into controversy with the periodical Press, or subordinate officers responsible only to the chief under whose directions they are presumed to act—who, in their official capacity, and therefore in defence of their official conduct, can say nothing except what he directs them to say. Thus, while there are so many motives abroad, and so much opportunity for preaching up the theory, there is no corresponding inducement to preach it down. Its patrons have had all the talk to themselves, and the other side is still to be heard. Until some equally active party shall be engaged in opposition and set themselves with the zeal of partisans to detect failures and obstructions, it will be difficult for any one to form a fair and comprehensive estimate of the real merits of the theory in question, and of the amount of substantial benefit which may be reasonably expected from its practical operation.

We have thought it the more necessary to suggest these considerations, because we have no intention of undertaking that

task ourselves ; and we wish our own speculations on the matter
to be taken with all due cautions and abatements, and to pass
for no more than we feel them to be really worth. So far as we
can understand the system, and foresee its probable working—
which, considering the novelty of all the circumstances and the
imperfect knowledge under which for the present we must be
content to labour, we cannot pretend to do with any confidence—
we believe it to be sound in principle and heartily wish it success.
The magnificent achievements which are promised in its name
we cannot hope to see completely realized : unforeseen reverses
are, no doubt, lying in wait for it ; the large historical experiences
which are quoted in its behalf we cannot receive in evidence
without further cross-examination ; the expectation that it will
be successful in all quarters of the world alike, without consideration of position, habits, or natural advantages, we may reject
at once as arguing the want of a discriminating judgment ; and
all charges against public men of groundless enmity, jealousy,
or trickery (advanced to account for the lamentable but indubitable fact, that the condition of mankind has not materially
changed nor the prosperity of all classes commenced its career
during the ten years which have now passed since the revelation
was first made), together with all the anecdotes told in illustration, we must be allowed to entertain with simple incredulity.
Knowing by daily experience how transactions of which every
part has passed in public, and been placed on record accessible
to every body, are hourly misrepresented, not only by newspapers,
but by gentlemen with unhidden faces—noble, right-reverend,
learned, and honourable persons, who desire to speak the truth
and expect to be believed—we cannot consent to take any impression whatever from newspaper histories of official transactions, or to believe any assertion whatever on the strength of
private information quoted by an anonymous writer. Such
stories are easily made up ; plausibly enough, perhaps, to impose
on the teller himself. By first framing a theory of the proceeding he wishes to describe, and then fitting into it such discon-
nected points of information as he can pick up, any man with a
bad opinion of his neighbour and a good opinion of himself may
misrepresent the truth to any conceivable extent. . Whenever

Lord John Russell shall undertake in addition to his other duties the task of answering the weekly attacks upon him and his office in the *Spectator* and the *Colonial Gazette,* we shall be in a condition to estimate the real worth of what might be called the Wakefield theory of the Colonial Office. In the meantime, we must be permitted to set it aside, together with all the stories on which it rests, and all the others which rest upon it, as involving moral improbabilities which it would require very strong authority to overcome, while they depend upon authority which is worth nothing. It is much easier to believe that Mr. Wakefield overrates himself and his theory than that all secretaries and under-secretaries of State are in a perpetual conspiracy to defeat his efforts for the good of mankind.

Subject, however, to these explanations and allowances, we believe, as we have said, that the new theory of colonization is a sound one ; and though we cannot repose such absolute faith as some do in its superiority to all accidents, and its universal applicability as a remedy for all disorders, we can truly say that few things would disappoint us more than the failure of the experiment ; few things give us greater pleasure than its entire success.

We shall confine ourselves for the present to an explanation and examination of the principle, as applicable to countries like Australia, which offer the fairest field for its undisturbed operation, and with a view to which it was, in fact, originally suggested ; and we wish to be understood as desiring rather to invite attention to the subject and engage other minds in the study of its many bearings than to establish any peculiar doctrine of our own.

It is a serious defect in the constitution of our executive Government, that it keeps no minds at work to foresee difficulties before they come, and prepare to meet them ; and the practical inconvenience arising from this defect is strikingly illustrated by the history upon which we are about to enter. The gradual encroachment of population upon territory, with its attendant evils of labourers wanting work and capitalists wanting employment for their capital, was no new phenomenon in the history of the world. Sooner or later, and more or less, it must, we conceive,' have been experienced in every country of not unlimited territory which ever prospered. The chief difference was, that in former times the means of relief were at hand, and the evil was no sooner felt than remedied. If the parent hive became too full, there were trees enough in the land; the surplus population had but to swarm, and make for themselves another. The faster the mother city grew, the sooner her boughs touched the earth, and became daughters to renew and cherish instead of burdens to exhaust her. At length however, by the continual pressure of population upon subsistence, the world has been partly peopled; and some of the peopled parts have grown so full that no vacant spaces are left in the neighbourhood into which the superabundance may be drawn off, as it used to be. If Ireland were at this moment uninhabited, those who are now uneasy with the elbowing and competition in England would straightway cross the Channel and set up a more comfortable England for themselves. Malthus might still be studied by a few political economists and denounced by a few priests and sentimentalists. But neither the Government, nor the Parliament, nor the people, would ever trouble themselves about the law of population, or care to anticipate the day when, Ireland being filled as full as England, and her sons nevertheless continuing to increase and multiply, the competition and elbowing should begin again;—when no second Ireland should be at hand, to offer a retreat to the discontented and subsistence to the unemployed;—when, if any man should find his lot at home press hard upon him, he must either make up his mind to endure it, with the prospect of its growing daily worse, or else raise money to cross the Atlantic, and summon courage to face, with wife and family, the unknown conditions of existence which might wait for him on the other side. Yet that such a day must inevitably come, though Ireland were at this hour as empty as New Holland, would not be less certain than that (Ireland being long since brimful) such a day has already arrived. The state of things which became visible in England soon after she settled into peace might have been predicted at least half a century before, as a state which she was rapidly approaching, and must, unless some season of calamity should intervene, soon reach.

A Government duly equipped and duly vigilant should have had some mind on the watch to understand and anticipate that day; to anticipate it at least in imagination; and to consider what might be done with it when it came. There would not have been wanting in the history of the rise and fall of nations indications of the quarter in which the remedy must be looked for, as well as proofs that it would certainly be needed. The means of making distant colonies available for drawing off a surplus population at home should have been for the last half century a familiar study, if not to all statesmen, at least to many capable minds set to work by statesmen for their instruction.

But sufficient unto the Government of the day are the evils of the day; and before any thought had been taken to meet the approaching emergency it was already upon us and around us. A preternatural thirst for speculation, rushing into the void left by the preternatural excitement of the war, hastened the crisis. Banks breaking, discontents rising, masses of people thrown out of employment, the poor starving for want of work, the rich impoverished by maintaining the superfluous hands which could not raise so much produce as they consumed, rents eaten up by rates;—these instant and surrounding disasters awoke our legislators to the necessity of inquiring whence they came and how they were to be dealt with. It was found upon inquiry that the people had indeed been multiplying too fast, and that they were now too many for the land. The theory which accounted for the fact was still indeed open to debate; and some time was lost in disputing whether the increase and multiplication of mankind, which had always been regarded as both a duty and a blessing, could lead to evil; but about the fact itself there could be no doubt; and the majority were content to believe, since the event had certainly come, that it had come according to the laws of nature. It was found likewise (as might also have been anticipated) that the natural and the only discoverable way of re-adjusting the proportion between the claimants for wages and the fund out of which wages were paid was emigration. The recognition of this fact was a great point gained; for it immediately turned the inquiry towards the much more difficult and really novel question—how such emigration might be effected on a scale adequate to the emergency. This question was elaborately investigated by two Committees of the House of Commons in 1826 and 1827. They reported that the British colonies supplied room enough; and that by the assistance of the Government, though at great cost, a sufficient number of the labouring population to relieve the immediate pressure might be enabled to go over and settle on colonial wastes. We need not particularize the measures adopted or contemplated during the next four or five years for carrying this project into effect. It is enough to say that no considerable progress was made. The heavy expense to be borne in the first instance by the public, and the difficulty of obtaining repayment from the parties more immediately benefited, made the operation too costly to be popular. The parishes, though by the removal of so heavy a burden upon their funds they would upon the whole have been the greatest gainers, shrank from the heavy debt in which it must involve them, and preferred to hope that times would mend. From the emigrants themselves, though out of the profits of their labour in Canada they might within a few years have easily repaid the whole cost, it was hardly practicable to enforce the repayment. The Canadian capitalists, though they too must have been benefited by the immigration, did not derive from the settlement of paupers upon the waste lands any advantage equal, or nearly equal, to the cost of the proceeding. Moreover, while the country was thus deterred from offering to the pauper population the means of emigration, rumours of the many evils and accidents to which poor settlers on colonial wastes were exposed discouraged the paupers themselves from taking advantage of the offer. Hence, during these years, though much good was done by the agitation of the measure and the better understanding of the difficulties to be surmounted, the immediate relief secured was not considerable. It may also be observed that the measures proposed, had they been carried out to the full extent, would not have reached the seat of the disorder. The remedy, with all its expenses and difficulties, was after all only a remedy for the day. It aimed only by a violent effort to relieve an extreme pressure, not to provide what was really wanted—a natural and continual source of relief for a pressure which must be continually recurring. It did nothing towards bringing the under-peopled colony within easy reach of the actual and immediate sufferers from the first approaches of over-population in the mother country. For preventing the recurrence of such another crisis, we were to trust to a better internal administration, to hope and chance, and to the ingenuity of those whom it might more directly concern. Enough for us to throw off the disease: to restore and invigorate the constitution would be work for another day.

It was during the pressure of these difficulties that Mr. Edward Gibbon Wakefield was led to take an interest in the condition of the colonies in New South Wales and Van Diemen's Land, and to inquire whether something might not be done to improve them. In those colonies he found all the raw materials of prosperity and civilization lying about, abundant and inexhaustible;—a genial climate ; a fertile soil of unbounded extent; exportable produce, unlimited in quantity, unrivalled in value, and raised with little difficulty and at little cost; ports and harbours ; an enterprising population; and a revenue already flourishing. But civilization itself—the powers, the arts, the virtues, and the enjoyments of social man—did not appear to be advancing with corresponding rapidity. Even their commercial prosperity did not seem to have grown naturally out of all those natural advantages ; but to depend upon an accidental arrangement, itself one of the main obstructions to civilization, and a source of infinite moral pollution—the quantity of penal labour at command. Had there been no convicts, where would have been the wealth of New South Wales? Lying hidden within the bosom of the land, or standing ungathered along the surface of the sheep-walks. Stop the supply of convicts, and what would become of it even now? Yet there were at this time in the colony 50,000 free persons of British origin, who, had they been thrown together in an English county, would have formed a very civilized community. Why should they not do here as they would have done in England, follow the same pursuits, set up the same institutions, and enjoy the same comforts? The answer to this question explained the case. In an English county, so many people living together could not all have been

M

landholders, nor able to purchase land. Some would have looked to live by wages; they would have tilled the soil;—some by trade; they would have kept shops;—some by handicraft; these would have made houses, clothes, furniture, and utensils;— some, again, would have taught, some preached, and some would have lived by managing their neighbours' quarrels. But here, where every man might live upon his own estate, why should he labour on another's? Where all might be masters, why should any be a servant? "Because" (it will be said, and said with truth) "the life of a servant, in a country where servants are plentiful and well paid, is more eligible than the life of a master, where servants are not to be had; and therefore, by voluntarily doing here what they would have been forced to do in a country where land was scarce, they would have promoted not only the general interests of all, but the individual comforts of each." This we believe to be strictly true; and we believe, moreover, that if all these individuals could have been endowed with one mind to understand their interests and control their movements, this is precisely what they would have done. They would have remained together, observing "degree, priority, and place," each consenting to forego his immediate gratification for the sake of the greater share which (all the rest acting on the same principle) would have fallen to him in the end. They would have been as "members one of another." In some particular circumstances indeed, and in some small degree, examples of such conduct have been actually seen; and cases may be readily imagined in which a religious community, for instance, or a Highland clan, or even a sensible family settling in the wilderness, might set such an example, and the happy consequences of it might induce others to follow and so bring it into fashion. In like manner, it is possible to conceive that some particular crowd may, on some remarkable occasion, have been induced to go out of a theatre on fire without trampling each other to death, or choking up the avenues. But in general it must clearly be assumed that many minds will not be governed by one intention, and that where a crowd is left to its own guidance within reach of objects of desire the shares will be settled by scramble, not by distribution. So with the settlers in a new colony. Instead of remaining together like civilized men, and combining their industry to make the territory yield its largest produce, that so the share of each may be the larger, they rush abroad in all directions to obtain land, of which, for want of combination, they can make no use when they have got it. To obtain the fruits of civilization therefore, it is necessary that the population should remain together; and since they are not likely to resist of their own accord the temptation to disperse, they must be prevented. Settling upon land must be made more difficult.

These views Mr. Wakefield put forth in 1829, in a small volume, entitled "A Letter from Sydney," which professed to record the experience of a gentleman, who, having been tempted by the cheapness of land to settle in New South Wales, was speedily convinced, by a series of difficulties, disappointments, and disgusts, that this very cheapness was the main impediment to the civilization of the colony; because, so long as land was cheap, the population would be scattered; and so long as population was scattered, the land would be worthless and the society barbarous. The story is, of course, a fiction, and the facts it records invented, we presume, for the purpose of illustration. The very striking picture, too, which it exhibits of the habits, manners, tastes, and occupations peculiar to a new country, is probably drawn in a great measure from imagination. But the object of the book, light and lively as it reads, is serious and business-like; and the argument is contrived with great skill to lead the reader on by easy but inevitable approaches to the important conclusion—(peculiarly important for its bearing on the question of emigration from Great Britain, to which we shall presently return)—that the root of all evil in a new colony is the superabundance of territory in proportion to the labouring population; that by fixing a sufficient price upon new land and requiring the money to be paid down, it would be at once arrested; and that, by applying the proceeds of all future sales to introduce labouring families, it would be speedily removed.

Hence it appeared that the cure for the diseases of the old country, which was too full, and of the new country, which was not full enough, would be found by creating a channel through which the population of the one should overflow into the other. To make the overflow at once natural and continual, it was only necessary that it should support itself—that is, that it should be accomplished in the ordinary course of commerce, without requiring from any of the parties concerned any unusual sacrifice or exertion. Already it was the immediate interest of the parishes to be relieved from their pauper population; of the pauper population to go; of the Government to facilitate their going; and of the colonists to receive them. It only remained to make it the immediate interest of somebody to pay the expense. Now, so long as waste land might be obtained in the colony for the asking—(and the system of granting titles at once, on conditions to be performed afterwards, did, in fact, come very nearly to this; for the conditions were almost always evaded)—the tendency above noticed, to disperse and settle, made the influx of a labouring population almost useless. No sooner did they touch the colony than they ceased to be a labouring population; labour was almost as scarce as ever, and the demand for it was greater; new territory was appropriated, while the value of that already occupied was hardly increased. But once refuse to grant away another acre without a considerable price paid down, and every shipful of poor immigrants helps to fill the labour-market and enrich the land; and it becomes the interest of every estate in the colony to contribute something towards the cost of their passage. The rapid accumulation of wealth through the labour of convicts—the only labour which can be commanded in New South Wales in sufficient quantities and at reasonable cost—shows what large sums might be profitably laid out on immigration, provided the prices of land were so adjusted as to keep the labour-market at all times sufficiently full. By the same process, while the landlords grew rich, the community would be civilized. The people would be kept together. All the blessings that wait upon plenty, and progress, and human neighbourhood, would gradually develope themselves—churches, schools, hospitals, colleges—light from the intercourse of minds, strength from the combination of hands, activity from the communion of wants; all the conveniences, the luxuries, and the graces of life; all, in short, that man in combination with man can do, create, or enjoy—all that men, scattered and separated, must do without.

Here then is the very channel which we want, costing no more than it will amply repay even in money's worth, and promising advantages which money cannot purchase or measure to all parties concerned;—a channel through which, when a few experiments shall have made it familiar, it seems not unreasonable to hope that a continual stream may flow, of poor men going to be made rich—of the superfluous numbers, that would otherwise be feeding on the life of England, going to infuse new life and strength into her remote dependencies.

Such were the main features of the scheme suggested by Mr. Wakefield in this volume (to which an outline was annexed of the principal regulations which would be requisite to carry it into effect), and such the great ends to which, if faithfully followed out, it might eventually lead. It is now ten years since it was announced; and considering the many prejudices to be overcome, the many minds and interests that must be induced to co-operate, the many unforeseen difficulties and obstructions which must be dealt with one by one, the many lions which are seen by ingenious and thinking men of a certain class in every strange path, the many questions of more immediate interest, and if not larger, at least larger looking, which have occupied the public attention during these years—the Poor-laws, for instance, and the Reform Bill;—above all, considering the long prevalence of an opposite system, and the heavy growths of evil which must die out before the fruits of the new one can be put fairly forth, we see no just reason to be discouraged by the rate of its progress. On some other occasion we may probably resume the consideration of the subject more in detail; but at present we must content ourselves with a rapid sketch of the progress which it has actually made, and the position in which it now stands.

The "Letter from Sydney" soon attracted attention; and in 1830 a society was formed under the name of the National Colonization Society for promoting the scheme. The society was broken up shortly after, by a disagreement among its more prominent members; but its effects remained in the very able pamphlet which had been put forth in explanation of its principles, and a series of controversial letters which followed. Early in the following year, the principle of selling all new lands was adopted by the Government; and the governors, both in Canada and Australia, were forbidden by Lord Ripon (then Secretary of State for the Colonies) to make any more grants of territory belonging to the Crown: in future, all land which was disposed of at all, was without exception to be disposed of by sale to the highest bidder —the upset price being five shillings per acre. About the same time a Commission was appointed by Government to take measures for the encouragement of emigration and the protection of emigrants. Through the exertions of the Commissioners, a great deal of useful information was circulated through the country relative to the condition of the colonies and the attractions they presented to persons of the labouring class; arrangements were made, by which the cost of a passage to New Holland was reduced by almost a half; money was advanced from the English Treasury, and applied by way of loans (which were afterwards converted into gifts) to pay the passage-money of families of working people, and in bounties towards the conveyance of single women. The general effect of these proceedings was to call into existence a disposition on the part of our labouring population to resort to Australia; and so give an effectual commencement to a system of voluntary emigration thither, which has been increasing since. During the four years before the operations of the Commissioners commenced, the total emigration annually to the Australian colonies was on the average only 1469; during the five years succeeding, the number of persons annually assisted to go by the Government, alone exceeded that average; while the entire number of emigrants reached an average of 3124. During the latter portion of this period—the Emigration Commission having been dissolved in 1832, and Mr. Frederick Elliot (who had acted as secretary to that Commission, and on whom the duty of carrying on the system which they had set on foot had practically devolved) being absent in Canada—things appear to have gone wrong. Complaints were made with regard to the selection of the emigrants, and disease and irregularities broke out in some of the vessels. Soon after

Mr. Elliot's return to England, the whole department was again placed under his management, as agent-general for emigration. In the mean time the revenue from the sale of lands in New South Wales (upon which, after several projects for raising an additional emigration fund from other sources, the whole burden seems ultimately to have fallen) was rapidly increasing; and though, in 1831, the annual proceeds of the sales had not been estimated at more than £10,000, Mr. Elliot found, when he entered on his new office, an income from that source of upwards of £182,000 realized during 1836, and of £120,000 estimated for the two following years. The measures which he adopted to make the emigration commensurate with the fund, we shall give in his own words: —

"It is scarcely surprising that so extraordinary a fruit of the rapid development of wealth in this flourishing colony far outstripped the arrangements which had been instituted at home for its beneficial application; neither were the demands for labour quite so urgently pressed then as since. But in entering on my duties, I felt very desirous, in conformity with what I knew also to be your Lordship's wish, to extend the emigration in some proportion to the increased funds, and the increased wants of the colony.

"In the year 1837, therefore, there were despatched to New South Wales and Van Diemen's Land ten ships, hired, fitted, and provisioned by the Government, containing, within a few, 3000 men, women, and children. Of these people 300 sailed for Van Diemen's Land; but no more have been sent there since, in consequence of Sir J. Franklin's despatch to your Lordship, dated the 12th of April, 1837, which seems to show that there is not any longer, in that colony, a demand for the introduction of large bodies of labouring people. The remaining 2700 emigrants were destined to New South Wales.

"In 1838 five ships have gone, up to the present date of the 28th of April, and arrangements are made for seven more to sail before the end of June, all twelve to New South Wales; which, even though the average number in each be estimated so low as 260, will take from hence upwards of 3100 souls in the first six months of this year. Of these ships four have been filled from England, four from Scotland, and the remaining four from Ireland. A more detailed statement of the ships, and of the number and description of the passengers, sent in 1837, will be found in the Appendix.

"The average annual number of emigrants sent to New South Wales, previously to the present system, has been mentioned above to have been 800; more than three times as many, therefore, were sent to the colony last year; and about four times as many are to be sent in the first half of this year, being at the rate of eight times as many per annum. The people may be said to be now going as fast as is required for the complete expenditure of the fund applicable to the object. Further advices may show a fresh augmentation of this remarkable branch of revenue; but by the Report of a Committee of Council which accompanied Sir Richard Bourk's despatch of the 8th of September, 1837, the proceeds of the lands, for two years to come, seem estimated at £120,000 per annum, of which one-third is reserved for the bounties, payable in the colony, on account of emigrants introduced by resident settlers. The remainder is £80,000, which is not a sum that would admit of more than twenty ships being sent in the year. In leaving this part of the subject, it is gratifying to state, that while the number of people sent out in public vessels has been so largely extended, there does not appear to have been any diminution, but on the contrary, an increase of emigration through other channels.

"There was not at first much alacrity to emigrate from England in the public vessels. Dr. Galloway stated that he had to travel over a considerable part of Wiltshire, Dorsetshire, and Hampshire, and also to visit the eastern part of Sussex, in order to provide a sufficient number of passengers for the small ship *Augusta Jessie*, which sailed from Portsmouth in June, 1837; and in July, I found it expedient to take the occasion of a temporary pressure in the weaving districts of Gloucestershire, to send a ship from Bristol with people taken from that part of the country. In the autumn a vessel was allotted to the county of Norfolk; but, although the measure had been settled for some months, and expressly to meet the convenience of the parties, the whole of them changed their minds at the last moment; and, within a fortnight of the time appointed for the ship's sailing, with a certain expenditure of between £4000 and £5000 incurred, we found ourselves with just three families who remained willing to go. This is a specimen of the difficulties to which the service is exposed. I did not hesitate, however, what course to pursue. Late as the time had become, I immediately issued advertisements, and opened a rendezvous at Lieutenant Lean's office in London; and I declined listening to any intimations of a fresh change of disposition in Norfolk; for it seemed to me of paramount importance to the interests of all concerned, that people should be led to understand that the benefits so liberally held out through the funds supplied from the Colony are not to be trifled with. I am happy to say, that the vessel was filled from other quarters by the time appointed; and that, owing to the efforts which were made, I have every reason to hope that the passengers selected for her will prove as useful an acquisition to the Colony as any that have sailed.

"Circumstances are much changed this year. We have found no difficulty in filling four ships already from the county of Kent alone, and have numbers of candidates there besides, whom we have been obliged to reject for want of room. I also look forward to an opportunity of sending from Wiltshire and Hampshire later in the year; in fact, we may be said to have more need of exertion, just at present, in preventing ourselves from being overflowed with applications, than in obtaining all that our resources could possibly satisfy.

"From Scotland and Ireland the supply of emigrants has never been scanty since the first months of 1837."—(*Report, April* 8, 1838.)

Our limits will not allow us to enter into the very interesting account of the reforms which Mr. Elliot then proceeded to introduce in the management and superintendence of his

emigrant ships.   We are glad to find that the new arrangements
have been universally approved and adopted; and that the
results have been even more favourable than could have been
anticipated.   The advance which emigration has made under
his auspices may be seen from the following statement :—Up to
1836, the average number of emigrants proceeding annually
to Australia by the assistance of Government, was 1569 ; the
average emigration of all kinds, only 3124.   In 1837, the
number of emigrants sent by Government was 2991 ; the
number altogether, 5054.   In 1838, the number dispatched by
Government was 6463; the entire number, 14,021.   In 1839,
" in consequence of the accounts of the continued drought, and
the high prices of provisions, accompanied by a falling off in the
land revenue, and a temporary diminution of candidates to
emigrate from home," it was not thought advisable to send out
in the Government ships more than 4096 ; but the total number
of emigrants to the Australian colonies during that year was not
less than 15,786.

Had this been the sole practical result achieved by the new
principle within the first ten years after the announcement of it,
there would have been no cause for discouragement.   In all
such cases, the first grand object is to clear and try the way
and to taste the fruits.   Accidents and oversights will commonly
occur, which, if experienced on a small scale, may be rectified,
and the experience will inspire confidence rather than alarm.
But a single great mistake in the outset, however easily prevented from recurring—a single fatal disaster on the threshold
of the enterprise, however certain the precautions which might
be taken against a second of the kind—would probably stifle the
experiment in its birth.   A heavy return of mortality among
the emigrants to Australia during the first year, either on the
passage or on their first settlement, might have procured an Act
of Parliament to prohibit emigration.   The tentative process
which has been followed, while it has happily been unattended
by any serious calamity, has at the same time suggested such
improvements and precautions as may fairly set at rest all
apprehensions on that score.   The channel is now shaped out,
and the stream may henceforth flow as fast as it will.

But this is not all that has been done.   In New South Wales, so much land had already been granted away under the system which prevailed up to 1831, the settlers were so scattered, and society so little advanced,—whilst the continued importation and assignment of convicts had filled the country with a population so depraved, and so ill-proportioned as to sexes,—that the better system could not for many years be expected to put forth its full fruits.   Its advocates determined, therefore, to seek a fairer field, and try a more decisive experiment.   Persons who had visited the southern coast of Australia had returned with news of good harbourage and anchorage for shipping; of one or two rivers, seen or suspected; of fresh water to be had by digging for it; of a fine and healthy climate; of woody and grassy tracts that appeared to stretch inland; of great scarcity of men, and great plenty of kangaroos, seals, and whales; and all this in a part of the continent sufficiently remote from the penal settlements.   In this region, a square portion containing nearly two hundred millions of acres was marked out upon the map, and granted by the Crown in trust to Commissioners, for purposes and under conditions defined by an Act of Parliament. The land was to be sold at a price of not less than twelve shillings an acre; the whole proceeds to be employed as an emigration fund,—the expenses of settlement and government were to be defrayed by money borrowed on the security of the future revenue; a sum of £20,000 in the funds was to be vested in trustees, as a guarantee against any charges which might be entailed on the public; and nothing was to be done until £35,000 had been realized in this country by the sale of the lands.   The legislative and executive powers were to reside in a governor and council, as in the Crown colonies; the sale of land and the emigration were to be managed by the Commissioners. The Act was passed in August, 1834, and a company was soon after formed with a large capital, to be employed in the improvement of the colony.   In the course of the following year, the preliminary arrangements were completed.   On the 24th of February 1836, the governor was gazetted.   The surveyor with his staff reached the colony in August, and chose the site of the first settlement.   In December, arrived the governor with the first body of settlers, and the province of South Australia was proclaimed. Unhappily, the first thing he did was to quarrel with the surveyor about the site of the capital; and a furious controversy followed between the Government party and the Commissioners' party, which divided against itself the infant and yet unbuilt city; stopped the progress of the surveys; and ended in the indignant resignation of the surveyor-general and his whole staff (though the Commissioners seem to have done what they could to support him), and we believe in the recall of the governor. This quarrel however, though it must have made the settlement uncomfortable, does not seem to have materially retarded its growth or damped the spirit of speculation; for we find that at the close of 1838, the population was supposed to be not less than 7000 (5322 having emigrated from this country); that the land sales had been gradually increasing up to the date of the latest account; and that the sums received on that account amounted altogether to £111,055. What may be the ultimate prospects of this enterprising community, it is of course impossible to say, until we see what it can do for itself in the way of exports and revenue. At present we can only conclude that its prospects are well thought of in the money market, and that if it fail to thrive it is not for want of encouragement. We are glad to avail ourselves—in the following extract of a letter which was called forth from Colonel Torrens by some depreciating statements—of the latest intelligence from an unsuspected quarter that has fallen in our way.

" The colony attained the age of three years, on the 28th of last December, and its third anniversary was celebrated by a public dinner given by the colonists to Colonel Gawler, the governor and resident commissioner. On this occasion, Colonel Gawler thus expressed himself:—' It is in point of numbers and importance an old colony. We have a population of from 10,000 to 11,000, a town as large as the capital of most of the older British colonies, with an interest extending over a distance of 120 miles, and an immense commerce. It has been said that we have tracts of barren country. True, we have some tracts of barren land; but I would ask, what country has not? England has its tracts of barren land, and they are not few in number; America, where I have been, has large tracts of barren land; the continent of Europe has large tracts of barren land; and our neighbours of New South Wales have large tracts of land which is of little use. Here we have some barren land as well as they; it is out of the question to think of having a country containing nothing but fertile valleys. But then look at the good land we have, and we may safely put up with a few hundred acres of barren land at intervals.   There is only one other topic to which I would advert; and this is the amelioration of the condition of those from whom we derive this fine country.   Let us do what we can to civilize and Christianize them.   And now, gentlemen, let British capital continue to flow into this province; let us keep up a high tone of society ; let us bring our sable brothers into a more comfortable state, and there will not be such a colony in the world as our colony.'—In a despatch which is now before me, dated October 5, 1839, and addressed to the colonization commissioners, Colonel Gawler states, that in the province of South Australia, ' private pursuits are so lucrative to really intelligent, honourable, and experienced men, that they will hardly accept even permanent situations under Government.' "—(*Morning Chronicle.*)

No doubt—" Let British capital continue to flow "—and many people will grow rich upon it ; but British capital flows nowhere without expecting something to come back with the ebb. South Australia must cultivate something more exportable than a high tone of society, or British capital will turn to other shores.   We confess a great anxiety to hear of exports ; for the continued flow of capital, though a sufficient proof that much is expected, is no proof that anything is to come.   Many a bubble has found as many capitalists willing to stake their fortunes upon its substantiality.

It is honourable to all parties concerned in this enterprise that the protection of the *Aborigines* has from the first formed a main feature of the scheme—and it may be regarded as a fair experiment, not only to test the practical working of the new theory of colonization—but to try whether the decline and rapid extermination of the native races, either by violence or by disease, be an unavoidable, as it has hitherto been an invariable, consequence of white men settling upon their shores.   Unless it can be shown that these races are already in decay ; that their business on earth has already been accomplished, and that they were destined from the beginning to die out in these times and leave room for a superior people—(a supposition neither incredible nor inconsistent with the great ordinances of Life and Death throughout the world)—we may well doubt whether civilization carries with it any divine commission to undertake so awful a responsibility ; and we could have wished to see the results of this experiment before we proceeded further in the course. On this account we cannot but regret the measures which have forced us into the colonization of New Zealand, before the success of the precautions taken in South Australia has been fairly proved ; neither can we regard without apprehension the example which has been thus set of a few private speculators compelling the authorities of the country to undertake one of two responsibilities—either to assume the control of an enterprise which they disapprove, or, by refusing, to leave the undertakers of it without any control whatever—a course which certainly might, and probably would, lead to disorders and aggressions against which the good intentions of the projectors are no security. In this case however (whatever measures may be taken against a repetition of it) the decision appears to have been inevitable ; and the Colony of New Zealand is already planted; with every prospect, we trust, of advantage to Great Britain—though too probably to the destruction of the finest of the aboriginal races that has yet been discovered.

Thus far, then, has the new theory had all necessary opportunities (and one, as we think, more than necessary) of trying its fortunes in the world. To the promulgation and agitation of it must be ascribed one other consequence, which we regard with unmixed satisfaction ;—the general recognition of the importance of a proper management of the vast colonial territories at the disposal of the Crown, and the constitution of a competent superintending authority. The whole subject was closely investigated by a Committee of the House of Commons in 1836 ; by which the general principles advocated by Mr. Wakefield and already in successful operation in the United States were approved, and recommended for adoption throughout the colonies, under the control of a central Board of Commissioners, to be appointed for that office, and resident in London. In the beginning of this year such a board was constituted by Lord John Russell, under the title of "Colonial Land and Emigration Commission;" and upon that Board the superintendence of this whole department will henceforth devolve ;—the duties hitherto separately discharged by the South Australian Commissioners and the Agent-General for Emigration being united and transferred to it.

Such, then, has been the progress actually made within the last ten years, towards the colonization of New Holland on the improved principle. To this extent the channel has been made, and the stream of emigration has begun to flow;—a progress small, no doubt, when compared with that which remains to be accomplished; and slow, perhaps, if measured by the anticipations of confident and sanguine theorists; but compared with a movement in the opposite direction, vast and full of encouragement. The impulse has been given, and the way made clear: unless the substantial benefits it is to lead to have been much overrated, the natural attraction of mutual advantage may be trusted for the rest. The many important and difficult questions which remain to be discussed and arranged have been referred by Lord John Russell to the consideration of the new Commissioners; who are to make a general report, twice in each year, of the progress and the results of their labours. These reports will, we presume, be laid before Parliament; and will probably afford us an opportunity of resuming the subject, and entering more at large into the doubtful or disputed topics which it presents.

It may be well, however, before we conclude, to point out the main differences—the differences in principle—between the Government and the original patrons of the scheme. We have been both gratified and surprised to find that these are neither many nor material in their practical bearing. The recommendations of Mr. Ward's Committee in 1836, may be taken, we believe, as satisfying the views of the party at whose instance that Committee was appointed; and in all that is most material in those recommendations, whether as respects the general principle or the subordinate regulations, the Government appears to have concurred so cordially, and to have taken such effectual measures for carrying them out, that we find it difficult to account for the spirit of opposition and the tone of scorn with which it has been assailed. Let us first review the points of agreement. That the prosperity of the colonies mainly depends upon the abundance of combinable labour in proportion to occupied territory;—that this abundance is to be secured by introducing labourers from overpeopled countries, and taking measures to keep them for some considerable time in the condition of labourers living by wages;—that the revenue derived from the sale of new land is the fund out of which the cost of introducing them ought to be defrayed;—that the most convenient way of preventing them from rising too rapidly from labourers into employers of labour is to sell the new land at a sufficiently high price;—that the adjustment of that price, and the application of the fund derived from it in promoting the emigration of fit persons, should be entrusted to a Central Board of Commissioners resident in London;—that the emigrants should consist of men and women, as nearly equal in numbers and with as few young children as possible—young married people without children being, if willing to go, the most eligible of all; and that the minimum price of land in any colony being once determined, the rule of selling no land whatever, within the limits of that colony, at a lower price, should be fixed and unalterable :—thus far all parties agree. The points of difference appear to be only these :—*First*, It was recommended by Mr. Ward's Committee that the principle of Lord Ripon's regulations in 1831 should be affirmed by an act of the legislature, and not be allowed to rest only upon a secretary of state's instruction, which another secretary may revoke. This has not yet been done; and though we certainly think it most desirable that such an act should be passed, it seems not less desirable that it should be postponed for the present, until the experience of the Commissioners may be made use of in drawing it up. No harm can happen in the mean time; for on this point the Government is so pledged, that no succeeding government could in practice alter the regulation. A secretary of state's instruction, the revocation of which would attack so many pockets and awaken so much just complaint, is in practice quite as irrevocable as an act of the legislature. *Secondly*, the committee recommended that " the net proceeds of the land-sales, in all colonies the climate of which is not unfavourable to the European frame, should be employed as an emigration fund ; each colony being furnished with emigrant labour in exact proportion to its own land sales." On this resolution the Committee were equally divided, and it was carried by the casting vote of Mr. Ward himself. On the principle which it involves, there appears to be a decided opposition between Mr. Ward's adherents and the Government. The ground and extent of the difference will be best explained by the following passage from Lord John Russell's instruction to the Colonial Land Commissioners. "The funds raised by the sale of lands in the colonies will be applicable to the conveyance of emigrants thither, so far, but only so far, as the use of the fund may be compatible with a due regard for the pressing and necessary demands of the local governments, for which no other resource can be found. While fully admitting and insisting on the principle that the Crown lands in the colonies are held in trust, not merely for the existing colonists, but for the people of the British empire collectively, it is perfectly consistent with that principle to maintain, that in applying the proceeds of the sales to the essential purposes of local good government, which must be otherwise unprovided for, the real interests of the empire at large, not less than that of the colony itself, will be best consulted. I shall, however, be happy to find the colonies providing for such purposes by import-duties and other means, thus leaving the produce from the sale of lands free for the promotion of emigration from the United Kingdom." Practically, therefore, we trust that the refusal of the Government to declare the land-fund absolutely inapplicable to any other purpose than emigration will not make any material difference in the amount actually applied in that way. Theoretically, they appear to us to be clearly in the right. Indeed, setting aside the political considerations involved, we cannot but think that, with a view merely to economy and judicious farming, it would be unwise to insist that no part of the land-fund shall ever be spent otherwise than in the importation of labourers; nor can we see any reasonable ground for restricting the Government in the application of this fund, except the assumed tendency of government to abuse all the liberty it has; from which it follows that the less it has the better. And this we believe to be the feeling which is really at the bottom of the objections in this particular case.

We are aware, however, that Mr. Wakefield has endeavoured to place the question upon more scientific grounds. We have done our best to understand his position and his arguments, and it is only because they seem to us so utterly inconclusive, that we are led to doubt whether we have understood them rightly. As his authority in this matter is not to be lightly set aside, we will explain, as fairly and as clearly as we can, both his views and our own reasons for remaining unconvinced by them. Mr. Wakefield's doctrine appears to us, then, to be this—There is a certain ratio between the supply of labour in the market and the surface of land under cultivation—a ratio varying indeed with the varying circumstances of the case, but in each case discoverable—by which the greatest quantity of produce will be raised. If you miss this ratio either way, you fall into the evils, on the one side of an underpeopled country, in which the land is scratched and the population scattered; in the other, of an overpeopled country, in which the competition of labourers reduces wages to a minimum, and the competition of capitalists reduces profits to a minimum, and the land will not yield enough to feed the people. To keep up always the proper ratio, you must keep the ratio constant between the immigration of hireable labourers and the price of unsold land; and this must be done by first fixing the just price, and then determining to apply the *whole* of that price to the introduction of immigrants. You might indeed fix a higher price in the first instance than would be necessary to bring in the just supply of labour, and in that case you might use the surplus fund for other purposes, without losing the desired proportion between land and labour: but you would introduce an evil of another kind—you would place an *unnecessary* restriction upon the field of cultivation: with a lower price, the same money would have been spent in buying more land, which land would have supported more labourers, which labourers would have raised more produce: and the money you want would be obtained at less cost by taxing the produce raised, than by taking the fund which goes to raise it.

On the same principle, Mr. Wakefield has latterly objected to the sale of lands by auction—a plan which he originally recommended. Find your sufficient price, and let the first man who comes and pays it carry away the title in his pocket. There are many objections to auction,—as delay, favouritism, etc.—and if your fixed price be sufficient there can be no advantage ; the only object of the auction being to raise the price, which by the supposition is itself no good, but an evil. We have not quoted Mr. Wakefield's own words ; the form in which his opinions were delivered makes that hardly practicable ; but we believe that we have faithfully represented his doctrine, as explained before Mr. Ward's committee.

Now this view of the matter has so many advantages, on the ground of simplicity and certainty of operation—saves so much trouble, and promises a growth of prosperity, at once so rapid, so secure, and so unlimited—that we greatly wish we could see it well made out. We are bound, however, after much study of the evidence and repeated endeavours to find some reason for believing that a theory which certainly has other recommendations possesses that of being true, frankly to confess that we can make nothing of it. So far from finding it well made out, we greatly doubt whether it has been well considered. We are at a loss to understand how this " sufficient price," this " due proportion between land and labour," this " golden mean between dispersion and density of population," or by whatever name it may be called, is to be determined ;—by what calculations it is to be discovered; by what signs recognized when we have it. If, indeed, the rate of wages were invariable, a little experience would show how many labourers could be profitably employed upon a given surface of land ; and this might be set down as the due proportion. Or again, if the rate of wages were such as could not be reduced without introducing the evils incident to an overpeopled country, then we might ascertain how many labourers could be imported without reducing wages—and this might be regarded as the mean between dispersion and density : a greater number would be injurious to the general interests of society. But it appears to us that, so long as land is dear, an increase in the number of candidates for employment would cause a reduction of wages, and thereby enable the landholder either to employ a greater number of hands and so increase his produce, or the same number at a less cost and so increase his profits ;—and, on the other hand, that so long as wages are high enough to enable an industrious man to save his £20 a-year, the effect of a reduction

would be to keep him longer in the condition of a labourer, but
not to contract the comforts attached to that condition.   If this
be true, where is your measure of the due proportion?   How
will you know when you have got your sufficient price?   Tell us
what proportion of labourers can cultivate the land well, and we
will tell you of a proportion which will cultivate it better.   Name
any price which will secure a large produce, and we will name
one which will secure a larger.   So long as a larger amount of
human skill and industry can be had for the same cost, and can
be applied to quicken the productive powers of nature, it seems
vain to suppose that you have obtained the maximum of produce;
and so long as the produce can be increased without increasing
in proportion the non-productive consumers of produce, you have
not reached the highest point of prosperity which the land will
bear.

To make our meaning clearer, we will suppose a case : It is
reckoned by Colonel Torrens, that in South Australia four agricultural labourers would suffice for 100 acres ; meaning, we presume, not that the labour of six could produce no more out of
100 acres than the labour of four, but that the new hands would
absorb as much as they could produce ; therefore, that (wages
remaining the same) the additional produce would not pay for
the additional cost of production ;—in short, that if the farmer
had the offer of two more hands he would not employ them.
Now, let us suppose the price of land raised, and the importation
of labourers increased in proportion, so that there should be (say)
six men in search of employment where only four are wanted.
What would be the consequence?   Surely they would underbid
each other, and so bring down wages to such a rate as the farmer
could afford to pay ; then, whatever work he might put the new-
comers to—whether to the more effectual tillage of the soil, the
tending of stock, the making of roads, the draining of marshes,
or the cutting of water-courses, (for it is not to be supposed that
four men can do all that can be done for the improvement of 100
acres in South Australia)—it would be just so much gain : his
estate and the colony would be just so much the better for it.   It
would appear, therefore, that the more people you can introduce
into a new colony, who cannot subsist without labour, and can

subsist comfortably with it, the more rapidly will the colony thrive; that the only "due proportion of labourers to land" is that proportion which you can induce to remain contented on these conditions;—the only "sufficient" price of land is the highest which anybody thinks it worth while to give. And if this—the highest degree of *production*—be really the object at which, in regulating the price of land, it is necessary to aim, we know not how it is to be pursued with any chance of success, unless by selling the land to the highest bidder, and applying the proceeds to the introduction, not of "a certain amount of combinable labour," but of as much combinable labour as the landowners can afford to employ, at such wages as will keep the labouring class in comfort and contentment. The *minimum* price need only be so high as to interrupt any fatal tendency to dispersion by which the source of combinable labour would be drained away; and the quantity of land offered to public competition at that upset price should not be otherwise limited. By this rule, the field of production would not be unnecessarily restricted; the amount of productive labour would be the greatest possible; yet, for all that, there might be a portion of the land-fund remaining which could not be profitably applied in bringing in more labourers, and might be profitably applied in other ways. If we were asked how we should know when the supply of labour began to exceed the just measure, we should answer that there would be many sufficient indications observable, long before any of the evils of an overpeopled country began to appear. The competition of rival settlements, and the facility of settling on unoccupied lands, would immediately correct any mistake on that side; while the prices offered for lands sold by auction would supply a test of their actual value, which might be useful in adjusting the upset price.

Let us not be misunderstood. We are not aware of the many objections and inconveniences attending the auction plan; nor do we mean to maintain that they are overbalanced by the advantages. The system of a uniform price, and an immediate unconditional sale of all lands without exception, has the advantage in almost all other respects; and the experience of the South Australian Commissioners tells strongly for it. But whatever may be the superiority of that plan, we must think that it has not been argued upon the proper grounds; and that Mr. Wakefield especially rests his decision in favour of it upon an assumption which he certainly has not succeeded in justifying—which we can hardly believe he has taken any pains to examine,—and which, in our judgment, will not bear examination. That assumption—(namely, that there is some definite ascertainable ratio between land and labour—therefore, some definite ascertainable price of land—which "should be both the maximum and the minimum;" which "would tend to make the produce of industry as great as possible;" which "would tend to the greatest possible profits to be divided between capitalists and labourers")—appears to us to run through the whole of his reasoning upon this part of the subject. Grant it; and nobody, we think, can dispute his conclusion, that every impediment to the obtaining of land beyond the exaction of this price, every difficulty or delay interposed, must be an evil. But before we grant it, we must ask how it is to be ascertained. We do not ask what it is; for he would very reasonably say that that depends upon the circumstances of each particular case; but we are entitled to ask on what principle, in any given case, he would go about to discover it. On this point, he was closely cross-examined in the Committee. The question was put to him in various forms, and it is remarkable that he seems to have been totally unprepared for it. Not only was he betrayed into several inconsiderate and inconsistent answers, hardly to be expected from so bold and so ready a disputant; but we really believe—though we have not come to the conclusion without wonder and hesitation—that he had no answer to give. The inconsistencies we pass over, because they may have arisen from hurry or accident; what we want to arrive at is the sum. We believe it is to be found in the following sentences—we have searched curiously, and this is all we can find:—1st, "The sufficient price is such a price as will keep the wages of labour and the profits of capital at the maximum—as high as possible." (868.) 2nd, "I look to no other proof of the sufficiency of the price." (870.) "By having attained the maximum of profits and wages I ascertain that I have reached the proper price." (873.) 3rd, "How do you ascertain when you have reached the maximum of profits and wages? The answer to that question requires a good deal of reflection, and a full answer would require a good deal of explanation. *But I should be quite satisfied that I had attained the maximum, if I had attained a higher rate of profits and wages than had ever existed before in any other colony;* OR EVEN IF THE RATE OF PROFITS AND WAGES WERE HIGHER IN THAT COLONY THAN THEY HAD EVER BEEN BEFORE." Mr. Wakefield was not asked whether he was satisfied that the maximum has been attained at Swan River, which was at that time recovering itself from a state of no profits and no wages. We are sorry the question was not put, for we should have been curious to see his answer. But the meaning of all this is just what we should have expected. The "maximum of production" and the "sufficient price" are, after all, merely arbitrary terms: —a *reasonable* amount of production would do just as well, and a *fair* price—such a price, in short, as Mr. Wakefield would not think either too high or too low; and such an amount of production as Mr. Wakefield would be satisfied with. Neither are we prepared to say that this is an unreasonable way of settling the matter. It is Mr. Wakefield who insists upon precision—not we. We can well believe that a uniform price, judiciously guessed at, and not far wrong, would be much better, though you sacrificed some revenue and permitted too much dispersion in consequence, than the highest price you could get by the auction system; and we are glad to see that Lord John Russell has referred this question specially to the consideration of the Colonial Land Commissioners.*

---

* In a book published in 1849 (" A View of the Art of Colonization "), Mr. Wakefield noticed this passage; and after observing that his motive for declining to "name a price and attempt to justify the decision by reasons," was that, if he had, he would have "got into a mess," proceeded to explain at great length how "the sufficient price" was to be practically determined. If I collect his meaning rightly (of which I am not sure, for it is defined with less precision than is usual with him), the practical process would be this. The legislature in Downing Street must ascertain what price would be *sufficient* in each case " to prevent labourers from turning into landowners *too soon.*" The evidence upon which it must form its judgment " would be *all the facts which shew whether labour is scarce or superabundant, or neither the one nor the other.*" " If the lawgiver *saw* that labour was scarce, and the price too low, he would raise the price; if he saw that labour was superabundant, and the price too high, he would lower the price; if he saw that labour was neither scarce nor superabundant,

To return for a moment to the other favourite doctrine of Mr. Wakefield, which we have already adverted to as the point on which Mr. Ward's Committee and the Government are most decidedly at variance—the maxim that, in order to secure the most rapid progress of the best sort of colonization, *the whole proceeds of the land-fund, without exception, should be employed as an immigration fund*. This maxim also will be found to rest entirely upon that assumption, the grounds of which we have just examined. It seems to be a doctrine which requires some special justification; for it is not by any means the most natural view of the matter. The most natural idea would have been, that supposing such a price fixed on land and such a portion of it spent on immigration as should secure a *competency* of combinable labour (meaning by competency, not the greatest quantity which could be turned to advantage, but enough to enable the colony to advance and prosper)—we should have thought it would then become a question for consideration, which would hasten that advance the more rapidly—a still greater amount of such labour, or a judicious application of the existing amount upon works of general benefit? And here again we will put a case—a case, we should think, very likely to occur. Sup-

he would not alter the price, because he would *see* that it was neither too high nor too low, but sufficient." For the knowledge of all the facts which would enable him to see all this, he must rely upon the legislature of the colony; for "a Downing Street legislature judging for the distant colonies . . . . would be apt to make terrible mistakes;" but the colonial legislature, "possessing an intimate knowledge of the colony," and being "deeply interested in coming to a just judgment," would have no difficulty: the facts by which to determine the question "whether labour was too plentiful or too scarce" would be plain to the dullest eye. An answer which he need not (so far as I can see) have withheld from the committee of 1836; but upon which the natural comment would have been, "Then you mean that the price which is found upon trial to prevent labourers from becoming landholders *sooner than the colonial legislature thinks desirable, is* the sufficient price."

With regard to the private history of this article which is given in p. 352, Mr. Wakefield must have been misinformed as to my part in it. The first I heard of the matter was in a letter from the editor of the *Edinburgh Review* to myself, requesting an article on the subject of colonization—a subject which I had never thought of taking up. Having ascertained that there would be no objection to my dealing with it in my own way, I undertook it. I never wrote anything under less restraint, or with less direction either to help or hinder. No one except the editor saw what I wrote before it was published; and all that he did was to strike out a few expressions in which I had spoken of the theory more hopefully than he thought prudent, and which I have now restored.

pose two fertile valleys separated from each other by a barren tract. On the uniform price system, the fertile would be bought up and cultivated, the barren left waste and unappropriated. An easy communication between these fertile tracts would no doubt increase the value of both; but whose interest would it be to make it? Import as much combinable labour as you will, two hands will not be combined for this object. As fast as you can pour it in, it will be bought up by the purchasers of the good land, so long as any good land remains to be purchased. Yet it is not the less certain, that by employing a portion of the labour actually in the colony, to make a good road between the two, you might increase the value of both in a much greater degree than the temporary subtraction of that labour from cultivation would diminish it. Not to mention the political and social advantages that would come from thus correcting the evils of dispersion, every individual proprietor of that fertile land would gain more in the actual value of the produce of that land, than he would have gained by his share of the additional combinable labour which the same sum spent on immigration would have placed at his command. How can it be said that in such a case, by the application of a portion of the land-fund to such an object, the progress of the best sort of colonization would be retarded? Yet to the reservation of any such discretionary power, Mr. Wakefield decidedly objects. Why? Because, either by disturbing the ratio between land and labour, (which was assumed to be the exact ratio that would make profits and wages as high as possible), or by altering the price of land (which was assumed to be the exact price that would keep up that ratio), it would diminish the produce of the colony; and would therefore, however desirable the object, be an expensive method of obtaining it. It is clear to us that, unless this ratio and this price can be determined with the precision which Mr. Wakefield's assumption implies, the whole of this reasoning falls to the ground; and until we can find some more promising clew to the discovery of them than Mr. Wakefield's evidence supplies, we must continue to believe that there are occasions when some portion of the land-fund may be appropriated to other uses than the introduction of immigrants, not only without injury, but with the greatest benefit to those who paid it; and therefore that the Government was quite right (if it were for this consideration alone) in refusing to divest the Crown of such discretionary power. We agree with Mr. Wakefield that the land-fund ought to be wholly spent in promoting the best interests of the colony: we agree with him that the introduction of immigrants is one of the most effectual ways to advance those interests; we differ from him only in supposing that it is not the only way.

These, as far as we can make out, are the only points of difference with regard to the principles and main objects of Australian colonization between Mr. Wakefield and the Government: compared with the points of agreement we cannot but think them of very small moment. Other differences no doubt there are, and will always be, concerning matters of detail—concerning the manner of carrying those principles into practice—and concerning the complex questions which will arise when collateral objects are to be taken into the account. Such differences have arisen with regard to New Zealand, to Port Natal, to the West Indies, to Canada, to the convict establishment in New South Wales; they must be expected to arise in many other quarters; and where all the authority, the responsibility, the duty of taking into consideration contending and collateral principles and purposes, and we may add, where all the authentic information is on one side—whilst all the facilities of writing and talking, and, if not all the zeal, at least all the partiality for a favourite theory, is on the other—we must expect to find such differences made the most of, and imputed to the corrupt will of office. But into such questions it is useless to enter at all, without being prepared to go fairly through them. At present we will only suggest by way of caution, that in these times a writer in a newspaper, a private gentleman, an orator at a public meeting, or even an independent Member of Parliament, has much less to fear from making an unjust charge against a responsible minister, than that minister has to fear from exposing himself to a just one.

For our own part, after what we have said concerning the nature and objects of the new theory, we can hardly be suspected of entertaining any hostility to it. If we have succeeded in showing that the resistance of the Government to some of the doctrines of its propagators and more zealous advocates, may be accounted for in other ways than by supposing them secretly hostile to it or incapable of carrying it out ; still more, if we have succeeded in turning the attention of those advocates to a reconsideration of their doctrines ; and above all, if we have interested in the progress and prospects of the system minds not hitherto engaged in the consideration of it ; this paper, imperfect as it is, will not be without its use.

VI

SOUTH AUSTRALIA IN 1841.*

———◦◦◦———

In the discussion of the "Wakefield Theory of Colonization,"
which appeared in a former number of this Journal, we briefly
noticed the settlement of South Australia as an experiment,
devised by the especial patrons of that theory, for the purpose of
bringing its merits to a practical proof—an experiment of which
the issue was still to be seen. We explained the circumstances
out of which the scheme arose, the general principles by which
it was distinguished from previous enterprises of the same kind,
and its progress up to the date of the latest accounts then accessible to the public; and without presuming to treat it as a
failure, merely because the boasted evidences of success appeared
to us to be fallacious, we confessed a growing anxiety to receive
some indications of stable and permanent prosperity more substantial than the value of Bonds in the market, or the number
of capitalists who might be willing to stake large sums of money
upon the chances of the speculation turning out well. For at
that time, though we had heard much of the increasing value of
land, as indicated by the enormous prices paid for lots in favourable situations—much of the unexampled "attractiveness" of
the new colony, its streets, squares, wharfs, public buildings,
and club-houses—much of the rapid influx of settlers and of
British capital, and something of a growing revenue derived

* Second Report from the Select Committee on South Australia. Ordered by
the House of Commons to be printed, 10th June, 1841. *Edinburgh Review*, April
1842.

from customs' duties upon goods imported ; we had as yet heard nothing of exports or of internal production—nothing of new sources of wealth opened in the colony itself—nothing, in short, of the creation of that promised fund from which was to be derived the interest upon all the capital permanently invested there, as well as the means of repaying all the borrowed money which had been laid out in making the colony "attractive." Of the creation and growth of this fund we were anxious to hear ; because, unless the bosom of the new land should prove capable of producing supplies of new wealth sufficient to remunerate the capitalist for his advances, it was plain that—how long soever the game of speculation might be carried on, how long soever the money might be shifted from hand to hand, how many fortunes soever might be made and lost before the cheat was finally detected, and upon whomsoever the loss might ultimately fall—it must end at last in failure and disaster.

Not many weeks after our remarks were written, serious apprehensions began to prevail that all was not so well in South Australia as it had been represented, and South Australian revenue Bonds were no longer negotiable ; and these apprehensions were shortly confirmed by the refusal of the Commissioners to honour bills drawn upon them by their own officer resident in the colony—a virtual declaration of insolvency ; and a reference of the whole matter to Government, on the ground that they could no longer carry out the provisions of the act without further powers than those with which it entrusted them. The result of this reference, as our readers are aware, was the appointment of a select Committee of the House of Commons, by whom the whole case was minutely investigated, and on whose recommendation a temporary advance of £155,000 was made by Parliament to enable the Commissioners to meet the immediate emergency. Their second Report, containing a series of recommendations as to the future government of the colony, lies before us (with evidence and appendix) in one of those huge folios in which our legislators think it expedient to seclude from idle curiosity the fruits of their graver deliberations, and will, according to an intimation given by Lord Stanley in the House of Commons, speedily occupy the attention of Parliament. Had the getters up of this and similar experiments used a similar vehicle for the conveyance of their communications to the public, we might have been content to leave this history of the progress and issue of it to make its own impression. But advertisements, prospectuses, leading articles in newspapers, and even pamphlets, find their way into heads where no folio can follow them; and we hope, therefore, that in reducing to a circulable shape the more material results of this important investigation and committing them to the wings of our lighter octavo, we shall be performing no unacceptible service to the idler public, whom it much concerns to be truly informed of the fate of such projects; inasmuch as it is to the idler public that all new projects, requiring borrowed money to set them on foot, especially address themselves. The broad fact, indeed, that up to this period the experiment has proved a failure, is sufficiently notorious. The creation within so short a time of so great a financial embarrassment—the demand upon the public for £155,000 before four years were out, to save from absolute ruin a colony in behalf of which it had been constantly promised that it would at least cost nothing to the mother country—speaks for itself in language which everybody can understand and nobody can dispute. Which of the parties concerned has been most to blame may admit of controversy; but the result which they have brought out among them will not be popularly recognised under any better name than failure. Admitting, then, that the experiment has failed, the question is, what and how much we are to infer from the failure; what light does it really throw upon that theory of colonization which it was *meant* to bring to the test; and whether, giving up as vicious the principles of the South Australian colonization act, we must give up the "Wakefield principle" along with them. Our own opinion is, that the question as to the soundness and practical efficacy of that principle, as expounded by us on a former occasion, remains exactly where it was, and is not at all affected by the issue of this experiment; the miscarriage of which is sufficiently accounted for by other parts of the scheme quite apart and separable from it, though unfortunately placed in the same boat. The principles of navigation are not answerable for the wreck of a vessel entrusted to an ignorant pilot or sent out without proper equipments; nor must Mr. Wakefield's theory of colonization be too hastily condemned because it has not been able to overcome the threefold disadvantage under which he was content that it should be tried —of a territory unexplored and unfavourable, a Board of managers inexperienced and irresponsible, and a supply of money drawn from a source at once expensive and uncertain. We formerly intimated our opinion that, in expecting it to triumph over all natural disadvantages, its patrons expected too much from it. Our belief that it was sound, and our hope that results of great practical importance might be expected from its operation, we as yet see no reason to abandon. But to make our conclusions more intelligible, it will be convenient to begin with some account of the negotiations and the abortive schemes that preceded the introduction of the measure which was finally adopted.

That Mr. Wakefield, once satisfied as to the value of his theory, should be in a hurry to see it at work, was natural and laudable; that he should be duly cautious and ·deliberate in maturing his plans and surveying his ground, was hardly to be expected. How soon after the promulgation of his doctrine South Australia was fixed on as a fit field of operation, we are not informed: but the choice seems to have cost very little trouble. Of the huge cantle which was to be cut out of the globe for this purpose, scarcely anything was then known— except the latitude and longitude, the general temperature of the climate, and the aspect of the land as seen from the coast. How far the fertility extended inwards, whether the appearances of fertility on the coasts were not themselves superficial, what supply there was of water, what the soil was capable of growing, whether the selected territory consisted chiefly of grass or jungle, sand or rock, mountain, plain, or swamp—all this was left to the imagination. But where nothing is known, more may be hoped—and, whatever might be the qualities of the land, at all events it was waste, and remote from other settlements. The very beauty of the theory was, that by securing the just proportion between the surface of the land and the labouring population, it would make all lands alike fertile. If the soil proved less rich than was expected, it was only to bestow more labour upon it—if more labour were wanted, it was only to pour in emigrants more rapidly—if more means of emigration were required, it was only to raise the price of land. Certainly an only child does not suffer more from the blindness of parental affection than an only theory. The territory "lying between the 132nd and 141st degrees of east longitude, and between the 20th parallel of south latitude on the north, and the Southern Pacific Ocean on the South," was voted "eminently fit for the reception of emigrants or settlers"—and negotiations commenced accordingly with the Colonial Office in the beginning of 1831.

Lord Howick, then Under Secretary for the Colonies, thought favourably of the principle, and was disposed, under proper cautions, to make the trial; and Lord Ripon had no objection, provided it could be done without an additional item in the estimates, and without involving the Government, should the scheme prove unsuccessful, in the discredit of the failure. To provide against this, it was proposed that the Government should have nothing to do with it; but that it should be undertaken by a Company with a paid-up capital, upon whom, along with the management, would devolve all the risk and all the responsibility. A company, with a capital of £500,000, was to undertake the charge of founding, peopling, and governing the new settlement; of managing the land sales according to certain principles to be defined in their charter; of applying the proceeds to emigration; and of advancing money to defray the preliminary outlay; and if, on trial, the plan did not succeed—*i.e.* if the population did not reach a certain amount within a certain period—it was to be given up; *i.e.* the peculiar principles on which the Colony was to be established were no longer to be insisted on: South Australia was to be as New South Wales, or as Van Diemen's Land. This sounded fairly. But if the Company were thus to undertake all the responsibilities of Government, they must, of course, be trusted with the authority of Government likewise; and the authority which they required amounted to little less than a delegation of all the substantial powers of sovereignty. This Lord Ripon was not prepared to sanction; and without this the project could not proceed. Accordingly, after a year and a half spent in fruitless endeavours to adjust the difficulty, the proposition was abandoned. And in truth it might as well have been given up at first; for the condition required by Lord Ripon was obviously impracticable. Unless it could have been contrived that in case of failure not only the pecuniary losses, but the social and political consequences also, should fall upon the projectors alone, it was plainly impossible for Government to escape responsibility for the issue of an experiment which could not be tried without its express sanction. By deputing others to conduct it, Lord Ripon might indeed throw upon them a subordinate responsibility; but so far from absolving the Ministers of the Crown by that means of the responsibility in chief, he would rather involve them in a double responsibility—making them answerable, not only for the propriety of the experiment, but also for the fitness of the instruments.

Up to this point, it might be thought the obstacle to this undertaking lay solely with Lord Ripon, who demanded a condition from the undertakers which he refused them the means of fulfilling. But from the correspondence which took place on the revival of the project during Lord Stanley's administration of the Colonial department, it appears that this condition of the scheme—namely, that the Government should have no concern in the practical management—was one which the undertakers themselves were prepared to insist on quite as obstinately as Lord Ripon; for Lord Stanley interposed no such stipulation, but, having made up his mind to sanction the experiment, was quite ready to take his share in the charge of it. The idea of a *Sovereign* Company being now abandoned, the following plan was next proposed:—The limits of the Colony being marked out, a guarantee was to be given by Government that no land should ever be sold within those limits below a certain price—that the whole of the sum derived from the sale of land should be employed in conveying to the Colony young pauper labourers of both sexes in equal proportions—and that the maximum price of Government land, though it was to be advanced from time to time, should never be reduced. The Governor and all the

officers were to be appointed by the Crown: and upon the
Governor was to devolve the whole power and responsibility of
the government, " until the Colony should be thought sufficiently
advanced to receive the grant of a Legislative Assembly." But
since the entire revenue derived from land sales was to be spent
in emigration, a fund would still be wanting for the purposes of
the civil government. Provision was to be made for this by a
Joint Stock Company, who were to make themselves "responsible
to the Government for a paid annual income" during a certain
period—the money so advanced constituting a colonial debt: in
consideration of which they were to have the pre-emption of
100,000 acres, to be selected within a given time, at the *first
minimum* price; and the privilege, so long as those advances
should be continued, of selecting the emigrants.

This scheme was at least intelligible and feasible. South
Australia was to be a Crown colony, governed in the usual way;
only that the expenses of Government, instead of being provided
by a Parliamentary grant, were to be advanced on speculation
by a Joint Stock Company trading in land, and looking to the
profits of that trade to pay the interest and cover the risk. To
a project framed on these principles, Lord Stanley was ready to
accede, subject to certain stipulations; of which the chief was,
that the security for the fixed income applicable to the civil
government should be good. This was in August, 1833. But
though the proposal originated with the South Australian Association, it appears to have been premature. If the conditions satisfied
Lord Stanley, they certainly did not satisfy the Association.
Whether it was that capitalists hung back, and would not subscribe on such conditions; or that the distrust of the colonial
office had been revived by the intervening discussions; or that
the practical management had got into other hands; or that the
plans had been originally proposed in the hope that Lord Stanley
would object, as Lord Ripon had done before, to risk his credit
by taking any direct part in carrying it out, and that so the
demand for larger powers might seem to be forced upon the
Association against their own desire; whatever may have been
the cause, certain it is, that when the plan came to be drawn out
in detail, it had assumed an aspect so different that it can hardly

be recognized as the same. By the draft Charter, which was submitted to Lord Stanley in February, 1834, it was proposed to transfer to the proposed Company not merely all the requisite powers for managing the emigration and trading in the land, but the entire authority of government, checked by a veto on the part of the crown. They were to have power to make, or delegate the power of making, all laws, institutions, ordinances, &c.; to constitute all courts; to appoint all governors, judges, and magistrates; and to levy all rates, taxes, and duties. To the Crown was reserved the power of disallowing any of their acts and appointments in the first instance, and of removing their officers in case of misconduct; but it was to originate nothing; nor could it otherwise interfere. When Lord Stanley objected to this delegation of authority, and refused to entertain the project further unless it were agreed that "the government of the colony should be left in the hands of the Crown and its constitutional advisers until it should be able to govern itself," he was informed by Mr. Grote, writing in behalf of the Association, that his objection was "fatal to the project of a chartered colony; for, of course, no body of persons would consent to take the trouble and responsibility of such an undertaking, without at the same time obtaining sufficient authority for carrying their objects into effect;" and as he declared, at the same time, that to be a joint stock company for the purchase of land never was the object of the Association, and that "for such a company to purchase land at a lower price than that which should afterwards be paid by others," would be directly contrary to one of their first principles,* it was plain that that project was at an end.

---

* These assertions contrast so strangely, not only with the actual provisions, but with the professed object of the original scheme, that one would almost think an entire chapter, in the course of which the views of both parties had completely changed, had dropped out of the correspondence. On the 6th July, 1833, Mr. Whitmore forwards to Lord Stanley "a project for founding a new colony on the southern coast of Australia, by the means of the purchase of waste lands from Government, by a joint stock company and by individuals;" and the views of this proposed company he thus explains:—"The inducement to the company to found this colony is this right of pre-emption at the first minimum price. Having the first choice of land, they will be able to select that upon which the seat of government will be placed, &c. The profit of the company will arise from the additional value which the increase of population, and the growth of capital, always confer

It appears, however, that the difficulty was not in finding persons who would take the "trouble and responsibility," but who would purchase shares, "without having sufficient authority to carry their objects into effect;" for it was next proposed to try whether the project of a colony founded on Wakefield principles would not have credit enough in the money market to enable them to raise the requisite fund by way of loan, on the security of its future revenues. The fundamental principle of selling the land at the *minimum* price, and spending the entire proceeds upon immigration, was to be established by act of Parliament; the management of the land sale and the immigration to be entrusted to a Board of Commissioners, who were to be further charged with the duty of raising the loans; the powers of government to be vested in the Crown. To this proposition Lord Stanley was also ready to accede, provided he could be satisfied that the territory selected was fit for the purposes of colonization —that at least £35,000 would be invested in the purchase of land—that there were persons ready to embark for the colony with a capital of not less than £50,000; and that an annual income, applicable to "the support of such parts of the establishment of the colony as might seem to her Majesty's Government

upon land, and from the increase in the minimum price at which the Government land will be sold; while the price paid by the company for their land will be uniform at whatever period it may be taken up." On the 21st March, 1834, Mr. Grote replying, in the absence of Mr. Whitmore, to Lord Stanley's remarks on the draft charter, says:—"It is true that at the interview to which you refer, Mr. Stanley suggested that the Association should be a joint stock company for the purchase and sale of land; *but this never was the object of the present Association;* and I may add, that the proposal at the conclusion of your letter, for bestowing land on such a company at a lower price than hat which should afterwards be paid by others, is directly contrary to one of the chief objects of the Association; viz. that in the intended colony land should be uniformly sold upon equal terms to all applicants." It would appear that there must have been somebody behind the curtain who understood the objects of the Association much better than its more prominent members; for we observe that in the draft charter, though it was provided that the company, instead of any right of pre-emption, should have the whole territory conveyed to them in trust,—therefore, that in their corporate capacity they could not trade in land,—yet, by the 34th clause, they were to have the power of incorporating as many land-trading companies as they pleased, on such conditions as they pleased —a privilege much more extensive, and one which might be made much more profitable. For it does not seem that they were precluded from incorporating themselves, or any number of themselves, for these purposes.

absolutely essential," of £5000 for the first three years, £8000 for the next three, and £10,000 for the four following, could be effectually guaranteed. The Committee of the Association undertook to satisfy him upon all these points; but before the negotiations were concluded Lord Stanley resigned his office, and the final decision upon the proposition devolved upon his successor. In urging the new Secretary not to delay that decision, the Committee represented the plan as one which had been already approved—every condition required by his predecessor having been complied with; and which only waited for an official announcement of the official sanction which it had already received. How far this representation was just, we cannot tell —Lord Stanley's latest views having been explained at an interview of which there is no record in these papers. All we can say is, that if he was really prepared to sanction the measure in the shape which it ultimately assumed, he must either have misapprehended the effect of some of its provisions, or altered his mind on two important points which, once at least, he had been prepared to insist on. The question as to the fitness of the territory for colonization was expressly waived as one on which those who proposed to emigrate must judge for themselves; and the clauses relating to the revenue fund, instead of securing *to the Crown* a fixed income for carrying on the government of the colony, left to the Commissioners (apparently, however, through some oversight) not merely the duty of raising, but the right of appropriating, the loan at their own discretion, without any check whatever; except one which made the arrangements with regard to salaries contingent upon the approbation of the Treasury. By this arrangement, whether attributable to oversight or to foresight, the clauses which reserved to the Crown all the ordinary powers of government became practically useless. The blood and sinews of the Government being under the control of the Commissioners, the Crown with all its powers had no effectual authority. The Commissioners could do many things without the consent of the Crown; but the Crown could scarcely carry a single point against the Commissioners. Even the power of appointing and removing at pleasure the members of the Commission was one of which practically but little use could be made. The sole chance of getting the project started under such conditions, rested in the confidence reposed by a section of the public in the new principle; and it was notorious that the faith of that section in the Wakefield theory of colonization was not more deeply rooted than their faith in what we have called the Wakefield theory of the Colonial office;—their settled distrust of the capacity, the intentions, and the integrity of all ministers of that department. To intrust the duty of the Commissioners to any person enjoying the confidence of the Government, but not enjoying the confidence of what now began to be called "the South Australian public," would have been the same thing as to crush the scheme. None but the immediate disciples and known supporters of Mr. Wakefield would have had either the zeal or the influence necessary for overcoming the preliminary difficulties. Accordingly, it was left to the chairman of the Association to suggest the names of the Commissioners; and of the eight gentlemen recommended by him no objection was taken to any; and the two others who were added as representatives of the Government, do not appear to have taken any active part in the proceedings. Under these auspices, the great experiment was at length afloat, with every prospect of success—if success were to be ensured by giving the projectors their own way; but with many chances of failure should they prove unequal to the management of it.

It was necessary to go through these details, in order to show clearly in what relation the several parties concerned in this project really stood towards each other—a relation which the mere terms of the act, and the power of the Commission, without reference to the preceding correspondence, from which are to be gathered the feelings and purposes, the understood expectations on one side, and the understood admissions on the other, and all the indirect and unexpressed obligations of the parties, would very imperfectly represent. At this point it will be convenient to examine the project more carefully, and to consider how far it can be regarded as a fair trial of the Wakefield principle, and how far we are bound to abide by the issue.

Now, in the first place, it is to be observed that this project involved not a simple but a complex experiment—not one but three principles of colonization, hitherto untried, were to be tried all at once in the case of South Australia. It was to be a " self-supporting " colony—that was one principle. It was to be a colony governed by a few private gentlemen, without any previous experience in such a task, without any effective check upon their proceedings, without responsibility to any other department of the State, and without any direct interest in the success of their experiment—that was a second principle. And thirdly, it was to be a colony founded on the system of selling the land, and spending the proceeds on immigration. So far as this last is concerned, we will not go so far as to say with Mr. Wakefield that the experiment has been " eminently successful " —but we will say that there has been no indication of failure. The rapid influx of capital and of population during the first three years did not prove that the system was a sound one, but only that many persons believed it to be sound. The sudden check and financial embarrassment in the fourth, did not prove it to be unsound ; but only that speculation had been carried too far, and that the finances had been mismanaged. The tree was in blossom, and has suffered a blight. We must wait for another season before we can know, by proof, what kind of fruit it will bear. Leaving, therefore, the Wakefield theory of colonization as still subject to the remarks with which we quitted it a year and a half ago, we turn to the two collateral novelties involved in the project, concerning which the issue proves much. To the " self-supporting " system, and to the usurpation by private gentlemen of the proper functions of Government, may be distinctly traced the difficulties which have arisen ; and we believe it to be far from unfortunate that these popular parts of the scheme have been so soon and so fairly brought to the test, and illustrated by so conspicuous an example.

By the " self-supporting system of colonization " (the notion of which Mr. Wakefield seems to us to treat with more ridicule than it deserves), we understand that system, on the credit— that is to say, on the *supposed* merits—of which you can borrow the means of founding, settling, and peopling a colony—support-ing it on the *promise* of the future revenue, until such revenue shall be actually forthcoming. Every moneyless inventor who

brings his invention into the market by means of capital
borrowed on the faith of its future value proceeds on the self-
supporting system. The man who persuades his friend that he
has discovered a secret in farming by which he can make his
fortune, and so obtains a loan of money to buy land for the purpose of trying it, is a self-supporting farmer. So the South
Australian Association proclaim a new mode of colonization, by
which a large revenue may be raised within a short time; and,
having no money of their own, persuade people to lend them
money at ten per cent. to carry this scheme into execution. If
they are right—if the new system prospers and creates a revenue
equal to the payment of the debt and the interest—then all is
well. The colony, most strictly speaking, has supported itself.
There it is; and it has cost nothing to anybody.

But though we see nothing absurd in the notion of a self-
supporting colony, nor feel justified in calling the name, as Mr.
Wakefield does, "a kind of puff,"—(though no doubt it has
been much used for puffing purposes)—yet to the manner in
which South Australia has been required to support itself we
see very serious objections; nor can we perceive any corresponding advantage. By refusing to advance any public money, and
throwing the colony upon the money market for supplies, it was
intended to hold the public safe, and throw the whole risk upon
private speculators. And if the failure of the speculation had
involved nothing more than the ruin of those private speculators, the precaution would have been effectual, and not unreasonable. But the fact is, that the insolvency of a colony, established under the sanction of Government, with thousands of
people in it, is a calamity which Government can never throw
aside as the result of a private speculation with which it had
nothing to do. If not bound to uphold its credit (a point which
it would not be easy to maintain) it is at least bound to save
the inhabitants from destruction. If the speculation be a good
one—that is, if the money be lent on good interest and good
security—it is much better that the mother country should make
the advance, which it can do on much better terms to both
parties than private capitalists: if not, then it ought not to be
sanctioned at all. For, if unsafe with public money lent at four

per cent., it must be many times more unsafe with private money
lent at ten; and if it fail, the failure must be a public, and not
a private matter. The mother country must pay for the losses,
whoever may have the benefit of the gains. But there is a more
serious objection to this mode of raising supplies than either its
extravagance, or its futility as a security against expense to the
mother country, or the almost irresistible temptation which
it offers to a system of puffing—namely, its precariousness.
During its earlier years, not only the prosperity of the colony,
but the very lives of the inhabitants, depend upon the regularity
of the supplies; and that regularity depends upon the facility of
borrowing money from private capitalists; who, being only concerned for the security of their own speculations, will refuse to
lend the moment they apprehend any difficulty about the repayment. Twenty accidents, against which no foresight can provide, may discredit the speculation in their eyes. There need
not even be any just ground for alarm. A false rumour will stop
the supplies for the time as effectually as a true one. The
colony may be ruined by a leading article as suddenly as it was
created. A puff may *break* it, as a puff has made. In the short
history of South Australia, something of this has been actually
experienced, and more is suggested. We trust that the lesson
has not been read in vain, and that no second experiment resembling it in this feature will be attempted.

Nor is this short history less valuable for the considerations
it suggests with regard to the other novel feature which we have
noticed—the delegation to private projectors of the duties which
belong properly to the recognized and responsible authorities of
the country. There is scarcely any popular prejudice more unreasonable, but there is scarcely any more prevalent, than that
which leads men to place more confidence in those of whom they
know nothing, than those of whom they know much. Hoping
always for more than we can have, and knowing that we cannot
get what we want from the one, we turn to the other, of whom,
knowing nothing, we do not know even that. Thus it is in the
disputes between Government and projectors. Government has
existed for centuries, and has wrought no miracle; whilst every
year sends forth some sanguine or interested projector, burning

with anxiety to show how some miracle may be wrought. The
objections which he is met with fail to convince him ; the discouragement makes him fierce. The refusal to adopt his views
he attributes to secret hostility. The public take part with the
untried promiser against the tried non-performer. The matter
is brought before Parliament. The ignorant lookers-on (who
form a considerable majority in both Houses) are easily persuaded that the thing is an experiment and ought to be tried;
and that since the responsible officers of the Crown say they
cannot undertake to bring it to a successful issue, the trial must
be made by the projector himself, who says he can. The necessary powers are accordingly conveyed to him by Act of Parliament, and the Government is only too happy to get rid of the
responsibility, the trouble, the importunity, and the abuse, all at
the same time.

Nor is this arrangement without its plausibilities. The pre-
sumptions against Government in respect both to zeal and ability
for making the best of a new thing, are not altogether unfair.
To plod on in the old ruts, to be jealous of all nostrums and
novel theories, will always be the tendency of the executive,
constitute it as you may ; because the credit of success in such
cases bears no proportion to the discredit of failure. They are
the trustees of the nation ; and, like all trustees, are more concerned to keep things from growing worse than to make them
better. Therefore, under the best-constituted executive, many
good things will be left for private projectors to suggest; and
these projectors will have many plausible, and probably some just
grounds of complaint. In the case of our own Government, this
aversion from all that is unprecedented is unduly strong, and
amounts to a serious defect. It is not to be denied that the inventive department, owing to the total want of any agency working in that direction, is weak and languid, and the distrust of
other men's inventions proportionally active. Nor is it less true
that, from want of a better supply of effective servants, and of
stimulants to zeal and activity, many of its duties are neglected
and mismanaged. The popular error is not in apprehending
that the Government will do the work ill, but in assuming that
the projector will do it better ; as if the censure of blunders in

others offered any security that the censurer will commit no blunders himself. The delusion is a gross one, which the least reflection must dissipate; but it is wonderful how few of us are not, more or less, under its power. Let the securities for zeal and ability and integrity in the discharge of their office by the ministers of the Crown be as defective as the most discontented projector can assert; yet it is obvious that they are better than you have anywhere else. However defective the instruments they have to work with, they have at least a more extensive command than any other body of the best instruments that are to be had. However inadequate the responsibility under which they act, they at least act under a more definite and effective responsibility than can be thrown upon any private person or Board of persons. However prone to avail themselves of the privilege of office for the purpose of shielding from inquiry what will not bear inspection, they are at least well known themselves —are liable to be called to a severe account in case of ultimate failure or palpable misconduct; and, conscious of living in the public eye, are deeply sensitive to public censure. Whatever objections may be urged against their methods of transacting business, their methods are at least the gradual growth of many years of trial; they include all the improvements prompted by long experience—all the securities against irregularity, all the precautions, checks, and helps of which time has suggested the expediency. That each man, indeed, should believe of *himself* that he could arrange everything much better (especially having never tried) is not surprising; but why we, his neighbours, should believe it of *him*, is a matter of much wonder, though as old as the world. To anyone who thinks, it must appear undeniable that though the securities for the good management of a new experiment in the hands of Government are bad enough, compared with what they ought to be, yet compared with the security we have when the management of it is transferred to a Board of private gentlemen labouring under a superfluity of public spirit, they are ample, and worthy of all confidence. The case before us supplies as apt an illustration as we could wish. Nearly seven years ago the charge of colonizing South Australia, with all powers and privileges appertaining, was com-

mitted to eight gentlemen unconnected with the Colonial Office ;
because the Colonial Office, not having due faith in the principle, could not be trusted for carrying it out. They had every
facility for conducting their own scheme in their own way. They
were allowed to select their own officers ; and we doubt whether
they could quote a single measure which they were prevented
from taking, or a single important point in which they were
thwarted, from the day of their appointment to that of their
dismissal. It is now notorious that in the hands of these eight
gentlemen (for it is to be observed that the embarrassments had
risen under their instructions, and before the news of the revocation of their commission had reached the colony, though the
duty of dealing with them was inherited by their successors)
this great charge has miscarried; that the result of their five
years' administration has been an advance of £155,000 by the
mother country, as the only means of avoiding immediate and
extensive disasters in South Australia. How many of our
readers can repeat the names of these eight gentlemen ? Mr.
Wakefield was not among them. He abjures all responsibility,
and now declares that he always apprehended some evil results
from the arrangement. Had the responsibility been laid upon
any of the regular departments of state, the issue would have
remained as a personal blot upon the reputation of the minister
at the head of it. As it is, it rests upon who knows whom ?

That it was only an *experiment,* cannot be admitted as an
excuse for thus confiding the conduct of it to inexperienced
hands. There is a mischievous fallacy lurking under that word
experiment. "If you will not try my experiment yourselves,
stand aside and let me try it," is the cry of the projector to a
distrusting Government, and all the people think it reasonable.
Go into the fever ward of an hospital, announce an improved
mode of treatment, and call on the surgeon either to try it himself or to let you try it—he will answer that he has no right
to do either the one or the other—either to make experiments, or
to allow them to be made upon the patients under his charge—
the failure of the experiment may be the death of the patient.
But let the inventor of an improved method of colonization
demand of the State, that if his method be not adopted

generally, he shall at least have a colony made over to him to try it on, and nobody doubts the reasonableness of the demand. It is forgotten that the trial cannot be made at the sole risk of the inventor, and that the State is fully as answerable for evils that may arise from permitting hazardous experiments to be tried by others, as for refusing to adopt wise and safe ones itself. The duty of the Government in such cases is plain—to entertain all projects for the good of the community; to take up and give effect to those of the wisdom of which it is satisfied; and resolutely to refuse its sanction to all such as it is not prepared to adopt.

We have dwelt thus long on this part of the subject, because we regard the establishment and the clear convincing illustration of these positions (obvious as they seem) as by far the most important result of this South Australian embarrassment. It is of little consequence comparatively to trace the chain of events which led to it, or to settle who has been most in fault; provided the result itself be set up as a conspicuous and standing example to warn all Statesmen and Parliaments against giving way to these popular delusions, or indulging themselves in this indolent legislation. The remedy for the many defects of our administrative government is to be sought in the improvement, and, if necessary, the reconstitution of the establishment itself—a work which will find all reformers enough to do—not in transferring its duties to other and untried hands.

With regard to the eight South Australian Commissioners themselves, we cannot fairly charge them either with any great negligence, or any great incapacity in the discharge of their trust. They appear to have been active and painstaking—the immigration department seems to have been prosperously conducted—there has been no lack of exact and careful instructions; and, considering the novelty of the circumstances and their own inexperience, we do not know that it could have been reasonably expected of them that they should do the work better. The thing they had to do had never been attempted before—the means by which it was to be done had never been employed before—they themselves had neither precedent to guide them nor previous experience in the kind of duties which had devolved upon them. "The act," (says the Report of the Committee) "required that provision should be made for the reception, in a vast unexplored wilderness, and for the protection and good government of a population flowing in at a rate of unprecedented rapidity. The making of all necessary arrangements for that purpose was confided to a board of private gentlemen, not placed by their commission under any adequate control in the exercise of their duties; and acting at a distance of 16,000 miles from the scene on which the experiment was to be tried. The only provision placed at their disposal for defraying the costs of the undertaking, was a power to borrow money from private capitalists on the security of the future revenues of that unexplored wilderness; a precarious provision therefore, and subject to interruption from a variety of accidents which they could neither foresee nor control.* We do not quarrel with them for failing in the execution of such a charge; their great error was in consenting to undertake it.

To transfer to an unwatered wilderness, root, branch, and blossom, the conceptions which flourished so fairly in Adelphi Terrace, and make them prosper there, was no easy task. Their policy, their plans, and their precautions, read smoothly enough on paper, and everything seems provided for. The design is clearly and carefully drawn. But when we turn to the impression which was actually printed off on the rugged and uneven ground of South Australia, a most distorted, blotted, and imperfect figure presents itself. The internal history of the colony exhibits a series of miscarriages, one treading upon the heels of another. First, the Governor quarrels with the Surveyor-General about the site of the capital; and the colonists split into factions before they have set up their houses. Then the Surveyor-General quarrels with his instructions, and throws up his office in disgust. Then the surveys stand still, to the great inconvenience of the purchasers of land, who have been promised immediate possession. Then, in the urgent necessity of carrying the surveys forward at any cost, vast unforeseen expenses are incurred. Then the Governor quarrels with the resident Commissioner, and must be recalled. Then the resident Commis-

* Report, p. 9.

sioner with whom he quarrelled is convicted of gross irregularities in his capacity of Colonial Treasurer, and is dismissed under
serious suspicion of peculation.   Then this Colonial Treasurer is
replaced by another, "who appears to have been most irregular,"
and who was shortly obliged to be placed in the hands of the
Attorney-General for not rendering his accounts.   Then the
Colonial Storekeeper is found to have been guilty of great irregularity, proceeding "partly from the confusion of the Colony,"
but principally from his "utter unacquaintance with the principles of public duty;" a deficiency for which "several other
heads of departments had to be dismissed," and which "had
been, and still was, a great cause of the difficulties of the colony."
Then the new Governor, in his zeal to correct all these irregularities, is obliged to treble the charges of the civil establishment;
and under the inevitable necessity of providing for the stream of
immigration which was poured in upon him, together with
his great anxiety to prevent what he calls "stagnation," is involved in an expenditure not only beyond his authority, but
beyond his power of calculation, and beyond the utmost means
of the Commissioners to meet;—an expenditure of which he was
unable to form the roughest estimate, but which was increasing
quarter by quarter from a rate of £12,000 per annum to a rate
of £140,000; and all this without even the advantage of a
knowledge on the part of the Commissioners of the demands
which were coming upon them.   Upon a comparison of Colonel
Gawler's despatches, announcing the progress of his expenditure
(which will be found at pp. 220-266 of the appendix to the
report), with the dates of the bills drawn by him upon the Board
in England (which will be found at p. 172 of the same), it may
be distinctly shown that before June, 1840, the Commissioners
had no reason to suppose that the annual demands upon them
would exceed £42,000 per annum; that the bills presented for
payment *during that month* indicated a demand of £140,000;
and that the next month brought them, along with the first
complete financial statement which they had received, a warning
that for some time to come they must expect no less.   This it
was which brought the matter to a crisis; for it was now plain
that the powers of borrowing with which they were entrusted

by the act, even if used to their fullest extent, would not enable them to satisfy all their liabilities. Accordingly, in August, they suspended all further payments, and then threw themselves upon the Government. Colonel Gawler was recalled, and Captain Grey was sent out to declare a bankruptcy and commence a system of rigorous retrenchments ; and all other questions connected with the subject were to stand over until a committee of the House of Commons should have reported upon them.

The recommendations of the Committee are embodied in a series of resolutions, which are introduced by an explanatory report, containing a statement of the grounds of them, a rapid but fair account of the origin and nature of the embarrassment, and a judgment upon the conduct of the several parties implicated. Of the measures recommended by the Committee with a view to the better administration of the affairs of the colony in future, the most important are—

1. The dissolution of the Board of Commissioners ; and the placing of South Australia, as to its general government, on the same footing with other colonies belonging to the British Crown.

2. The making of provision by Parliament for such advances of money as may be necessary for maintaining its existence ; the advances, with interest at not more than four per cent., to be charged to the colony as public debt.

3. The relaxation of the existing rule as to the disposal of land, so far as to allow *one-half* of the proceeds to form part of the general revenue, the other half being still devoted to immigration ; to admit of the reservation by the Crown of any lands required for public purposes, or for the benefit of the aborigines ; and to throw the cost of survey upon the purchaser, by an acreable charge in addition to the purchase money, instead of charging it as heretofore to the general revenue.

4. The establishment, instead of the uniform price system which has hitherto been adopted, of that of public auction at a minimum upset price: with some modifications, however, tending to combine the advantages of both ;—namely, first, a provision that the sales by auction shall take place *periodically ;* second, that between these periods any land which has been put up and

not sold shall be purchasable by the first applicant at the minimum upset price; third, that blocks of land, containing not less than 20,000 acres each, may be sold by private contract, only not below the minimum price; and lastly, that the minimum price itself may be raised above its present amount of £1 per acre, " with a view to the principle of maintaining such an amount as may tend to remedy the evils arising out of too great a facility of obtaining landed property, and a consequently disproportionate supply of labour, *and exorbitant rate of wages.*"

It will be seen, therefore, that if the recommendations of the Committee be adopted, the Wakefield principle will at length have a fair trial in South Australia; as soon, at least, as the arrears due to past mismanagement shall be paid off; for it will no longer be in the same boat with the two companion principles which we have spoken of above. The colony will have a source of supply not liable to fail in a case of extremity, *because* it is a case of extremity; and it will have the best security for good government during its infancy which the nation has been able to devise. At the same time the "Wakefield principle of coloni- zation," properly so called, is retained entire; excepting only those parts of it (relating to the "sufficient" price and the application of the *entire* proceeds to immigration, and to the *uniform* price as distinguished from the auction system), against which we argued at length on a former occasion; and one of which at least Mr. Wakefield himself has now given up.

The only part of these recommendations to which we are disposed to demur, is that which relates to the raising of the minimum price. Not that we have any positive reason for thinking that the price of land in South Australia will not bear to be raised higher, but we do not see our way through the process by which it is proposed to determine it. It appears to us that there lie at the bottom of the reasoning on this matter, two assumptions which will not be found to bear the test of experience. The first is, that the *value* of the land may be increased to any extent by increasing the *price*. The second is, that by regulating the minimum price and the quantity of immigration, it is possible in a new country to reduce the price of labour; that is, to place the labourer so far at the mercy of his employer as to force him to be content with less than he wants. "In a colony," says the *Report*, "where the extent of available land may, when compared with the population, be practically considered as unlimited, ordinary land, if all were allowed to appropriate what they pleased, would have no value whatever, and it only acquires a value from the policy of not allowing it to be appropriated, except by those who purchase it on certain terms." All this we admit ; but we are not so clear as to the inference which is drawn from it in the next sentence. "As the value acquired by land under such circumstances is artificial, so it may be made *higher* or lower *at the discretion of the authority by which it is created.*" Now, surely there are other limits to the *value* of land besides the *price* demanded for it. By raising the price as high as you please, you may make it as difficult as you please to get; but not therefore as much worth having. You may make a thing so dear that it is not worth buying at the price. You may make a penny roll as dear as a quartern loaf, if you have the command of the wheat market, but you cannot make it feed as many people. Make bread so dear that people cannot buy enough to live on, and they will feed on potatoes. So with land. So long as the produce of the soil will pay a reasonable interest on the price demanded, you can raise the value by creating an artificial scarcity ; but as soon as the price rises above that point, the artificial scarcity will operate only as a prohibition upon the sale. The question is, how high you can price waste land in South Australia without making the purchase of it a bad investment of capital, or a worse than can be had elsewhere.

If indeed by applying the additional price to the introduction of labour, you could be sure to cheapen labour in proportion, this artificial value might be increased indefinitely, until the productive powers of the land, as well as the value of its produce, reached their maximum. But this brings us to the other question : Is it practicable by *any* regulations to make a labouring population in a new colony so dependent upon the employer of labour, that the rate of wages shall sink in anything like that proportion —or indeed that it shall sink at all ? Certainly no tendency of the kind has appeared in South Australia. And we strongly

P

suspect, that if the principle recommended by the Committee be adopted, of " progressively increasing the price of land until the object of establishing a due proportion between the supply and demand for labour, and between the population and the extent of territory occupied by it, shall have been accomplished "—or as it is expressed in another page, until such a price be imposed " as shall prevent a greater quantity of land from being bought than the number of inhabitants is sufficient to make use of to advantage "—one of two things must happen; either such a price must be demanded as no capitalist can afford to give; or such stringent regulations with regard to the labouring population must be adopted, as no Government will be able to enforce. Labour may be made more plentiful, we doubt not; but we doubt whether within any assignable period it will become more cheap. The value of the land will in that case be determined by the nett profits of the produce which it can be made to yield; and the price must follow the value.

There is one other point on which the Report is not quite satisfactory to us. In their judgment upon the conduct of the several parties who have been implicated in the affairs which have led to this embarrassment, they appear to us to have extended their indulgence to Colonel Gawler too far. No doubt, a man who has not had an opportunity of making his defence is entitled to large allowances; and although it is difficult to believe that he has not done things on too grand a scale, and been far more liberal in his expenditure for the benefit of the colony than its pecuniary circumstances justified, we are not masters of the circumstances sufficiently to say positively that, had he not determined to incur that expenditure, a worse result might not have happened. But the charge against him is not merely that he involved his employers in a debt so far beyond his authority, and beyond even their means to pay—circumstances may be imagined in which an officer is justified in assuming such a responsibility—but that he did it without giving them any adequate warning of the extent to which he was prepared to go. He not only drew bills upon them for thousands upon thousands beyond his authority, without specifying the particular services for which they were drawn—this, in the

confused state of affairs, it may have been impossible to do with
exactness—but he did not furnish them with the means of con-
jecturing within any reasonable limits of approximation what
amount they were to be prepared for.   It is true that he kept
warning them in general terms that he was forced to incur
" enormous " expenses, the responsibility for which " filled him
with anxiety ; " but what did an " enormous " expenditure mean,
when the authorized expenditure was £12,000 a year?   Was it
twice as much, or three times, or four times as much ?   The
only account (previous to that upon the receipt of which the
Commissioners threw up their charge) on which any definite
conjecture could be built as to the total amount for which they
must in future be prepared, was that which accompanied the
half-year's report dated 26th November 1839, and must have
been received by them in February 1840.   In this despatch he
recounts the causes which have made his actual expenditure so
much exceed the regulated estimate; gives a list of the things
he has had to do ; and adds, all this *has been done* (not " has yet
to be done ") " *in a very expensive period.*"   This account therefore did not indicate an increased, but rather a diminished
expenditure thereafter.   Now, the bills drawn by Colonel Gawler,
in excess of the regulated estimate, for the services of this year,
amounted to £42,000 ;—an excess quite large enough to answer
the general terms in which he had spoken, and to justify his
anxiety.   But while this account was on its way home, at what
rate was Colonel Gawler actually drawing upon them ?   At a
rate of £50,000 per annum, or £60,000, or £100,000 ?   No, but
of £140,000 !   Now, we contend that Colonel Gawler—however
impossible it may have been for him to form an exact estimate,
or even an estimate nearly approaching to accuracy, of the
expenditure for the half year before him—ought to have been
able to make a guess within a hundred thousand pounds.   He
should have been able to give his employers some idea whether,
when he talked of enormous excesses above the regulated estimate, he meant twice as much, or twelve times as much.   And
this was the rather required of him, because the very ground on
which he justifies his assumption of such responsibility is the
total incapacity of the Commissioners to form any judgment for

themselves; and because he knew that their resources were not unlimited, and that his drafts must be trespassing very closely on the limits of them.

The Committee say that they " are not prepared to affirm the insufficiency of the grounds on which he has alleged his inability to furnish information as to the specific services for which he was about to draw, or to supply *any* estimates of the total amount he should be compelled to draw in the course of the year." It appears to us that the Committee *ought to have been prepared* to allege the insufficiency of these grounds; and that from the principle involved in their hesitation to do so inferences may be drawn, of which very inconvenient and dangerous applications may be made by all officers serving the Government in distant places. If the excuse is good for the expenditure of unauthorized hundreds of thousands, it is as good or better for the expenditure of unauthorized millions; inasmuch as the inability to " furnish information as to the specific services, and to supply estimates of the total amount;" would be ten times as great. We regret this piece of false candour and indulgence on the part of the Committee; because it may be construed into an intimation that there were not sufficient grounds for recalling Colonel Gawler—a measure than which none was ever more imperatively called for. In other respects the Report appears to us to contain a fair judgment upon the conduct of all parties.

The evidence contains a good deal of interesting and conflicting testimony as to the natural productive capacities of South Australia; of which Mr. Angus has a high opinion. But there is so little solid experience as yet to build on, that such opinions can be entertained only as conjectures; and, as we said before, we must wait to see what fruit the tree will bear, and what it will sell for, before we can form any grounded conclusions. What is certain is, that a very large proportion of this selected territory turns out to be unavailable from natural sterility—so barren that it will be worth nothing to a purchaser, however much you may make him pay for it—and so much of it, that it was at one time thought advisable to alter the boundaries of the colony, for the purpose of taking in a more fertile tract between it and Port

Philip. Some considerable tracts of very good land have however been discovered since; and we hope that the barren parts will only operate as an anti-dispersive, and that no practical evil will result from the unfortunate selection of the field of operations. With regard to this part of the question however, pending the arrival of some more decisive indications, we must be content with quoting, in their own words, the result of the inquiries of the Committee as to the present position and prospects of the province :—

"The public debt charged on the future revenues of South Australia, including the sums raised by the Commissioners, the advance recently made by Parliament, and the proposed further advance to the Emigration Fund, will amount to £296,000. The annual interest payable upon it will be about £15,000. The number of inhabitants is supposed to be about 15,000. The ordinary revenue, which has been progressively increasing, may now be estimated at about £30,000 per annum. The ordinary expenditure, which has been increasing still more rapidly, is now proceeding at a rate amounting, together with the interest of the loan, to about £70,000 a year; and although it may be hoped that some reduction may be effected by the present Governor, your Committee are unable, from want of detailed evidence in this country, to speak with any confidence on the subject.

"With regard to the natural resources of the colony, the value of the produce and the amount of revenue which it may hereafter yield, your Committee have not been able to obtain sufficient data to justify them in pronouncing a decided opinion; they would, however, refer to the evidence given by Mr. Angus, as showing the recent progress of agriculture, and the aptness of the soil for raising grain, and for pasturage; to that of Mr. Elliot in explanation of the quantity of available land still unsold; to a statistical report transmitted by Colonel Gawler, and to the general tenor of his despatches, as encouraging the hope that, after making allowance for very large tracts of wholly unavailable land, the natural capacities of the colony are considerable; and that as its tillage extends, and its stock multiplies, it may in due time yield an ample revenue, and become a valuable appendage to the British Crown. For the present, however, it does not appear to your Committee that there are any certain grounds for expecting either such an increase of revenue or such a reduction of expenditure as would obviate the necessity of making provision out of some fund, over and above the ordinary revenue, for an annual deficit of a large amount."—(*Report*, p. x.)

VII.

EXPEDITION TO THE NIGER IN 1841. CIVILIZATION OF AFRICA.*

———◆◇◆———

SIR T. BUXTON's estimate of the extent of the African Slave Trade, the probable efficacy of the measures which he proposes for the extinction of it, and the general character of his work, were discussed in our last number. To this part of the subject we do not here propose to return. For the present we shall confine ourselves to the consideration of the preliminary measure in furtherance of Sir Thomas Buxton's views which the Government has consented to adopt—a measure which has been much praised and much censured, but of which the true scope and grounds have not, as it appears to us, been duly considered. That three iron steam-vessels have been built by Government, and are on the point of proceeding, under the command of three captains of the royal navy, up the Niger—that the object of the expedition is to prepare the way for the extinction of the Slave Trade by means of the civilization of Africa—and that it is to cost £61,000—are facts sufficiently well known, and upon which

* 1. Correspondence relative to the Niger Expedition. Printed by order of the House of Commons. February, 1840. 2. Appeal to the People and Government of Great Britain against the Niger Expedition: a Letter addressed to the Right Honourable Lord John Russell. By ROBERT JAMIESON, Esq. London: 1840. 3. Letters to the Right Honourable Lord John Russell, on the Plans of the Society for the Civilization of Africa. By Sir GEORGE STEPHEN. London: 1840. 4. Address of Joseph R. Ingersoll at the Annual Meeting of the Pennsylvania Colonization Society. 1838. 5.' Address on African Colonization. By R. R. GURLEY. 1839. 6. Seventh Annual Report of the Colonization Society of the City of New York. (*Edinburgh Review*, January, 1841.)

much debate has arisen. One party sees in the enterprise only
the final overthrow of the hated slave trade; another regards it
as nothing better than the opening of a new unhappy chapter in
the history of African colonization—another costly and miserable
failure, fraught with great waste of British life and treasure,
and bringing no good to Africa. The great meeting in Exeter
Hall is still fresh in remembrance, at which the most eminent
persons of all parties laid their differences aside to sanction and
promote the Niger expedition, and claim a share in the glory
and responsibility of the work; whilst Mr. Jamieson's appeal in
behalf of the mercantile community against the intermeddling of
Government in matters which would prosper better without its
aid, and the wilder denunciations of the *Times* newspaper, have
drawn attention, though rather late in the day, to the doubts
and difficulties by which the project is certainly not unattended.
But what the expedition is *to do*—what are the immediate purposes, and what the probable issues of it—upon what grounds
of knowledge and reasonable expectation the attempt is justified
—what will be the extent of evil if it fail, and of good if it
succeed—these are points which seem to be lost sight of in the
controversy. The indignation of the *Times* flies much too high
to touch them, and the statements on which Mr. Jamieson rests
his appeal might, as it seems to us, be quoted with more propriety on the other side. The expedition, as we understand it,
has one object—namely, to explore and survey the ground, with
a view to ascertain the practicability of further measures and
the most effectual way of conducting them : and there is one
question to be previously determined—namely, whether the
reasons for expecting some considerable benefit to issue from
such a survey are strong enough to justify the risk and outlay
which must attend it. Our present object is simply and briefly
to set forth our grounds for deciding this question in the affirma-
tive. To us it appears that within the last few years a new hope
has been opened for Africa—a new opportunity, distinct in some
essential features from any that has hitherto presented itself, of
bringing into cultivation some portions, at least, of this vast
neglected estate, to the great benefit of the world ; that it lies
with England to improve this opportunity; and that the first

and indispensable condition of any successful movement in that direction, is to send out an expedition duly equipped and appointed to examine and explore the path ;—the information which we now possess being sufficient, as we think, to prove that *much* may be done; but neither full enough nor certain enough to teach us either how much, or what, or in what way. If it be reasonable to believe that we can carry into Africa the seeds of a civilization which shall take root and spread, then we hold the expedition to be justified; if otherwise, not.

The position, the extent, the inexhaustible fertility, and the many natural advantages of the central region of this continent, as well as the worse than neglected state in which its vast capabilities are still left, and the scanty measure in which man has done his duty by them, are matters on which, as notorious and undisputed, we need not dwell. But inasmuch as there lies a *primâ facie* presumption against the intrinsic capacity for improvement of what has so long resisted the efforts of man and the improving influences of time, it is necessary in the first place to look somewhat more narrowly into the nature of the experiments which have been already made and the opportunities which have presented themselves. Now the great civilizer of mankind is intercourse between nation and nation; and from this the middle regions of Africa have been almost entirely shut out. There have been but four channels through which the arts, manners, and experiences of people farther advanced in civilization have had any chance of making their way thither; first, the transatlantic slave trade; secondly, the European settlements planted along the western coast; thirdly, the palm-oil trade; and fourthly, the trade with the northern parts of the continent carried on by Arab and Moorish merchants across the Great Desert.

Of the first of these it is scarcely necessary to say that it has done much more to obstruct than to advance civilization. Some specimens of European manufacture—guns, powder and ball, rum, Manchester cottons, Portuguese cloths, pots and pans, buttons, &c.—it may have brought the natives on the coast acquainted with; but it has not had the effect of carrying even these far inwards. In the mean time, the manners and habits which have been imported along with them are of the worst kind—more fitted to corrupt than to improve. And while the advantages this trade brings are thus trifling in themselves and confined in their operation, it is not so with the evils. Of the European productions derived through this channel all traces are quickly lost; but the European demand for slaves carries its message into the heart of the continent, and offers such a premium upon internal rapine and disorder that industry and ingenuity have neither peace nor leisure to try their fortune there. So long as the export trade of Africa consists chiefly of slaves, it is vain to hope that any systematic and effectual attention will be paid to the cultivation of cotton, coffee, or ginger.

The effects of the English and American settlements on the western coast have given rise to disputes, into the merits of which we cannot at present stay to enter. But the truth seems to be that although if we measure them either by the expense of life and treasure which they have involved, or by the aims and hopes of their founders, or by the ends which remain to be accomplished, they may be pronounced failures; yet their operation has been, with reference to those parts of Africa, decidedly, and in no trifling degree, beneficial.* The countries in the immediate neighbourhood of these settlements are in a better condition than they were; property is more secure; the culture of the soil is more attended to; the advantages of commerce are beginning to be felt; Christianity has made some small advances; the people have shown some anxiety to have their children educated; and the slave trade has entirely (or almost entirely)

* In the Reports of the *American Colonization Society*, and the addresses of Mr. Gurley and Mr. Ingersoll, the titles of which appear at the head of this article, much information will be found concerning the proceedings and views of that society. To these interesting, and in this country little known tracts, we must be content to refer our readers. The number of coloured persons who may be disposed to emigrate to Africa rises into a question of unusual importance, now that an opening is made for colonization on a larger scale, which can hardly be effected without a lamentable destruction of life by Europeans; and the encouragement of this spirit is one of the great objects of the society. The official reports of the progress of *Liberia* (the name of the American colony)—though conveyed in a style so glowing and rhetorical as to suggest some doubt whether they can be relied on as the results of dispassionate inquiry—strike us as most encouraging, and as indicating a regular advance in the right direction, not inconsiderable even now, and which may be expected to proceed every year with increasing rapidity.

forsaken those shores. But why have they done no more? for
if this is to be all, it becomes a serious question whether it be
worth the sacrifice; whether the same lives, energies, and sums
of money might not be better employed elsewhere. A glance at
the map answers the question. These settlements are all on
the outside, as it were, of the continent, and in a place where
they have no means of getting in. Indeed, considering the
broad belt of *malaria* which nature has drawn along the tropical
coasts of Africa, and the savage manners and habits with which
the slave trade has lined them, we may almost say that the
largest of the navigable rivers in those parts does not penetrate
beyond the husk and rind of the continent, and cannot, therefore,
bring us into contact with the sensible and vital parts. The
utmost efforts to civilize Africa through Gambia, Sierra Leone,
Cape Coast Castle, or Liberia, can be but as a flesh-brush
applied to an elephant; they can never affect the *circulation*.
Or, to take a less remote analogy, suppose England were still as
Cæsar found her; suppose a settlement were planted at the
mouth of some brook on the Welsh coast, and an attempt made
from that as from a centre to diffuse laws, arts, and manners
through the country; and suppose, at the same time, that slave-
trading merchants in great numbers frequented the mouth of
the Thames,—what wonder if the slavers carried the day, and
the influence of the civilizers were felt only through a county
or two on the coast, while theirs circulated all through the land?

The palm-oil trade is young, and labours under some heavy
disadvantages. For though the locality commands a wide range,
it is a locality already occupied by the slave trade, against the
immediate competition of which the new comer is involved in an
unequal struggle; and besides, the command of the inner country
is in some degree thrown away upon a trade which is essentially
a *coast* trade, inasmuch as the produce in which it deals does not
grow far inland. Moreover, the climate and the difficulty of
navigation throws the Liverpool trader too much into the power
of the chiefs inhabiting the delta of the Niger, whose interest it
is to keep the trade as much as possible to themselves, and to
prevent communication with the interior. We cannot, therefore,
expect from this trade such an extensive circulation of commer-

cial intercourse as may reach the heart of Africa and materially affect its condition : neither the Liverpool traders themselves, nor the agents in their employment and in direct communication with them, have been induced to traverse the interior, nor even until lately to pass up the river. Yet in this case also the results are encouraging so far as they go. The trade has done considerable good within the limited range of its operation, and might probably in no long time grow strong enough, if not to expel the slave trade from the river, at least to compete successfully with it in the immediate neighbourhood.

The desert trade with Northern Africa has penetrated further than any of these, and produced more effect, and would by this time have laid secure foundations for a better order of things, but that it also labours under some heavy and peculiar disadvantages. The greatest is, that the Arab merchants come chiefly for *slaves :* and hence the trade they drive does nearly as much to obstruct the civilization of Africa by stimulating wars and slave-hunts as to advance it by the introduction of knowledge and the intercourse it opens between the Africans and a superior race. Next, the Arabs are not good civilizers; ignorant, unsettled, lawless, rapacious, cruel, and deceitful, they are bad instructors to impart knowledge and to teach the value of security, mutual confidence, settled habits, and the like. Moreover, the religion which they bring, though superior to the Paganism which they find, is not a *civilizing* religion : it is very good for conquering, but very bad for improving the conquered. Further, the length, difficulty, danger, and cost of the passage across the desert drags so heavily upon this trade that it cannot thrive properly, and interposes such a gulf between the merchants who venture and the countries from which they come, that it cannot be subjected to proper authority and regulations. Their own government, if it had the will, has not the hands to reach them at such a distance. Nevertheless, when we follow Captain Clapperton along the route of the caravans from Bornou to Soccatoo, and read the accounts which are given of Timbuctoo and Jenne, and observe the superiority in respect of government, organization, industry, and manners of the kingdoms lying between these points along the borders of the desert, we cannot doubt that in spite of all its drawbacks this trade has actually effected something considerable towards the improvement of the country.

Now, with regard to this traffic, let us suppose four things changed. Suppose, first, that in the parts of Africa whence these traders come *there were no market for slaves*; suppose, secondly, that there were a market of unlimited extent for raw cotton, or some other natural production of Central Africa not requiring much skill or capital to raise it; suppose, thirdly, that between the two there were no Desert, but a canal, a navigable river, a railroad, or any other easy and safe approach for merchants with heavy goods; suppose, lastly, that these merchants were not Arabs, professing the religion of Mahomet, and subject to Morocco, Tunis, or Tripoli, but of a nation eminent for order, honesty, and humanity—professing a religion which teaches the equality of all men in the eye of God, inculcates at once self-respect and humility, and insists in an especial manner upon the duty of justice and mercy from every man to every other man—subject to a government vigilant enough to superintend, strong enough to control, scrupulously respectful of the rights of others, and inexorable in enforcing fair dealing wherever its authority extends. Suppose all this—who can doubt that the whole face of Africa would speedily be changed?

Upon this consideration it is that we rest our hopes of much better and larger results from the enterprise now in contemplation, and refuse to admit the failure of previous experiments or the non-improvement of previous opportunities in evidence against it. Now, for the first time, these four things meet. Between the richest regions of Central Africa and the most insatiable market in the world for the produce of those regions, a communication, safe, expeditious, and available for the cheap carriage of heavy goods, is now for the first time opened. The traders who supply this market are Englishmen and Christians; and while they will buy as much raw cotton as the industry of man will ever raise in Africa, they will *not* buy a single man, woman, or child. If there were in Africa any authority capable of understanding the full benefit of opening this communication, and with power to enforce the necessary conditions and regulations, there can be no doubt, we think, that a flourishing trade would immediately commence, and that the spirit of civilization would begin to spread. How fast and how far it would spread would depend mainly upon the judgment and energy of missionary and commercial and agricultural societies, and all the rest, for whose labours a fair field would be opened. But in the mean time the doubtful question is, whether in the present circumstances of Africa—looking at the disorganized condition of society, the universal prevalence of the slave trade, and the fatal qualities of the climate which may perhaps make it impossible for English merchants to transact their own business there—it be practicable to set the trade well on foot; to make such a commencement that the benefits shall be felt at once, and felt widely enough to secure for it the necessary protection from those who have influence enough to afford it.

For the climate, it must be admitted that appearances are against it; yet it *may* turn out that, in the interior at least, it is not more fatal to European constitutions than other tropical climates. Of the many travellers who have died there, we cannot hear of one who has been in a condition to take proper care of himself. A gentleman is attacked with fever or with dysentery; takes a sharp dose of calomel; is obliged, though hardly able to sit on his horse, to spend all the day in travelling; gets wet above the middle in crossing a river; lets his clothes dry on his back; and when at length he stretches himself on his mat for a night's rest, is stung to distraction by mosquitoes and black ants. That anybody has survived such attacks is a greater wonder than that so many have died under them, and can only be ascribed to that excitement of novelty and exertion which bears the frame up under hardships, half of which would kill most of us who are living at ease in England. It must also be remembered that medical science has yet to be brought to bear upon this question. It is not impossible that a few precautions and a better method of treatment may make the climate innoxious. Should it however prove invincible, it will still be practicable to employ negroes or men of colour to transact business in the interior; of whom we do not doubt that there will be found many equal to that work.

As for the slave trade, though it will retard the growth of a legitimate commerce, it will not, we think, universal as it is, have power to strangle it. There is room for a commencement; and when once both are fairly in the field together, the more profitable will carry the day.

The disorganized condition of the country does indeed present some serious difficulties. It limits the power of the chiefs, causes kingdoms to change hands rapidly, raises hostile neighbours and unruly subjects, compels authority to be violent and arbitrary, unsettles the minds and habits of the people, and induces that carelessness of human life which naturally follows where its tenure is so precarious. Here you find a chief eager to embrace your offers, enforce your regulations, and protect your people; but his neighbour prefers wars and slave-hunts; or his more distant subjects are hard to manage, and he cannot afford any effectual protection beyond his own immediate territory. This year you find an honest man and a friend; next year a knave and an enemy has taken his place. Your traders, who are courted and protected this month, may perhaps be robbed and murdered the next. Nay, the same man may be your friend to-day and your enemy to-morrow; the same childish delight in novelties which made him embrace you at first, making him suspect you soon after.

These are serious difficulties, which in such a case as this it would be worse than weak to overlook or neglect. The question is whether, looking them fairly in the face, they appear insurmountable. Are the elements of society so disordered and uncertain that no lasting impression can be made upon them, and that every attempt to organize them must simply fail? Shifting and chaotic as they are, is there not after all among these African nations coherence, order, and intelligence enough to retain something at least, however little, of whatever civilizing influences we may pour in; so that, while much is wasted and rejected, *some* may go to convert and alter the system?

It appears to us that there is reason to think so; and in order to prove it, we would point out the various *centres* of trade already existing in the country, and the circumference of the trade which centres there; from which it will be seen that, in spite of all the drawbacks and disadvantages under which commerce labours, there does actually exist both the spirit of traffic to a very great extent, and security to a considerable extent; and that in all the articles for which there is any demand, an active trade is continually going on from one end of the country to the other. The facts we have to state are familiar to all readers of African travels; but their bearing upon this question may probably have escaped those who have not put them together for the purpose. The most convenient way of approaching the subject will be to follow the course of the expedition.

Passing as quickly as possible through the delta of the Niger, where the malaria is most fatal and the inhabitants most wretched and demoralized, we come to *Eboe*, a town with a population of 50,000 or 60,000, "the most enterprising and industrious traders (says Mr. Laird) on the Niger;" governed by King Obie, who boasts himself to be the greatest of the palm-oil kings, has the command of the river, and insists that all traders shall buy and sell with him before they go further up. From his dominions (passing however through the hands of the chiefs on the coasts, who no doubt deduct their full share of the profits,) the Liverpool traders at the mouth of the river Nun—who have for many years past been carrying on, though at a miserable expense of life and health, a regular and rapidly increasing trade in palm-oil—receive their largest supplies of that article. In exchange for their palm-oil, the people of Eboe receive various articles of English manufacture—guns, powder and ball, showy Manchester cottons, looking-glasses, knives, rum, &c.—the exchange being commonly effected through the medium of shells or cowries, which are their money, and pass current far into the interior of Africa.

Above this town the trade is carried on still more busily. The banks of the river are thickly studded with towns and villages, between which there is a great deal of intercourse; the population of a superior character; life and property more secure; men, women, and children all engaged in their several ways in traffic; of which (according to Dr. Briggs, who accompanied Mr. Laird) there appeared to be twice as much as on the upper part of the Rhine. The great centre of all this traffic lies more than a hundred miles above Eboe, and is well known through all that part of the country under the name of *Bocqua* or *Iccory*. It is situated not very far below the confluence of the Shadda with the Niger; and is celebrated for a market, or rather fair, which lasts for three days at a time, and is held every ten days; when it is attended by traders from all the towns on the Niger, both above and below, within a range of more than a hundred miles, and by great numbers from the interior. Some notion of the importance of this place may be drawn from the fact stated by Mr. Laird, that while his vessel lay aground in the neighbourhood for some months he used to observe as many as twenty-five canoes, each containing from forty to sixty people, passing every ten days on their way to attend the market; and such is the throng which it brings together, the bustle, the animation, the variety, not only in the wares brought for sale, but in the dress, features, and complexion of the sellers, that even Mr. Oldfield rises into liveliness as he describes it. To this market the Eboe traders bring for sale the European goods they have received from the coast— red cloth, velvet, mock coral beads, knives, snuff-boxes, looking-glasses, etc.—while the traders from the upper and inner countries bring (besides slaves, which here as elsewhere are the chief article of commerce) cloths of native manufacture, ivory, horses, saddles and bridles, tobes, straw hats, country-made mats, and various kinds of food; the traffic being carried on as at Eboe, not by barter, but by money in the form of cowries.

The range and attraction of this market extends, as we have intimated, to a considerable distance both upwards and inwards. About three days' journey to the east lies *Fundah*, once a kind of entrepôt where the Arabs and Fellatahs from the north exchanged European goods for slaves, and a place of considerable trade. The trade is now interrupted by the disorders of the country beyond; but the fact that it did flourish does not the less indicate an aptitude by natural position for commerce, which will revive when the disorders subside. Here native cotton is raised, " of a very fine staple," out of which they manufacture " durable and heavy cloths; " there are also considerable dye-works; and plenty of iron and copper, which are wrought into various articles. About thirty miles further to the east, and within fifty of the.

navigable Shadda, lies *Toto*, a town not yet visited by any of our travellers, but said to be the largest in that part of the country; having a king who is anxious to trade, and a population at once warlike and industrious, and skilful in the working of copper and iron. Goods purchased at Bocqua are occasionally carried thither for sale; and ivory, Arabian horses, bullocks, sheep, camels, &c., may be had there in exchange.

Further than this, in this direction, we know nothing. The Shadda was ascended for more than a hundred miles; but the natives being then in continual dread of incursions by the copper-coloured Fellatahs (a complexion which there passes for white) would enter into no communications with the white strangers. Returning, therefore, to Bocqua, and turning northwards up the Niger for forty or fifty miles, we come to *Kattam Karafi;* another well-known market place for the usual inland produce, both raw and manufactured, which is brought down the river in canoes. A few miles further on we pass *Kakunda*, the capital of an independent kingdom lying to the west; the people peaceable and industrious, and though apparently not very adventurous, in the habit of trading down the river as far as Bocqua. Advancing still farther in the same direction, we reach a more important place, *Egga*; a populous town and much frequented—having a large market filled with sharp bargainers, whose custom it is "as in every other part of *Africa*" (so says Mr. Oldfield,) "to get the most for every article;" and with the usual variety of wares, which make the shops of the large traders look like English toyshops. Here too they raise indigo of a superior quality, and a little very fine cotton; dyeing yards are also to be seen of considerable extent; spinning walks and weaving machines resembling our shuttle; and cocoa-nuts (imported from some neighbouring country) are sold in the streets in great quantities. It was here that Lander, in his first descent of the river, first met with Benin and Portuguese clothes in common wear. "The people" (he says) "are very speculative and enterprising, and numbers of them employ all their time solely in trading up and down the Niger. They live entirely in canoes, over which they have a shed that answers every purpose; so that in their constant peregrinations they have no need of any other dwelling

Q

or shelter than what their canoes afford them." It seems also that the desire of wealth in the abstract, independently of any tempting objects to be purchased with it, is not unknown here. Mr. Oldfield found here an old Mallam who had two or three houses (African of course) filled with cowries; he purchased goods to a considerable amount, and would be glad (he said) to purchase ten or twelve ship-loads if they would stay.

At this point we come among a new people; and it is satisfactory to find that as we advance farther into the heart of the country the population improves. The reputation of the people of *Nyffé* for skill and industry reached Captain Clapperton in 1824 at Kano and Soccatoo; it met Lander in descending the Niger from Boussa; and Mr. Oldfield found it in full force as he ascended from Bocqua. They are more especially celebrated for the manufacture of cloths, plain or dyed, which are the best in Africa. Along the borders of this kingdom the river continues to be navigable by an iron steamer, and brings us (some hundred miles further up) to the capital of it, *Rabbah;* where at length the trade—which we have accompanied in its course from the mouth of the Nun upwards—meets and mixes, not indeed with the main tide, but with a kind of overflow or eddy of that main tide of commerce, which, being drawn across the Desert from the shores of the Mediterranean, flows along the northern borders of Central Africa and passes out by the Desert again. The country round about, though disturbed by predatory and civil war, is populous, and abounds with the usual agricultural produce; besides which, they have for the export trade, ivory, indigo, ostriches, camels, leopards' skins, bees' wax, (of which latter it is supposed that any quantity might be obtained, if there was a regular demand for it,) not to mention mats and sandals; in the manufacture of which they are said to be unrivalled. Rabbah has a large market, well regulated, and distributed into separate departments for separate articles—to which the Arabs (for whom, and for all strangers, an enclosure of dwellings in the suburbs of the town is set apart) bring for sale horses, asses, raw silk, red caps from Tripoli, armlets, anklets, and trona or natron, which comes from Bornou, and is used by the natives as a substitute for salt, and given as a medicine to cattle. When Mr. Oldfield was at Rabbah, there were several caravans of merchants staying there from the Haussa country, from Soccatoo, from Kano, and from Tripoli. Some were taking their departure eastward to Bornou, others northward to Timbuctoo. Nor is this all. In the middle of the river, and within sight of Rabbah, lies the flourishing island of *Zagozhie;* mentioned by Lander as one of the most extensive and thickly inhabited towns, as well as one of the most extensive trading places, in the whole kingdom of Nyffé;" and described by Mr. Oldfield, with unusual force, as the "Manchester" of Africa. " The cloths which they manufacture, (says Lander,) and the tobes and trousers which they make, are most excellent, and would not disgrace an European manufactory; they are worn and valued by kings, chiefs, and great men, and are the admiration of the neighbouring countries, which vainly attempt to imitate them. We have also seen a variety of caps, which are worn solely by females, and made of cotton interwoven with silk, of the most exquisite workmanship. The people here are uncommonly industrious, both males and females, who are always busy either in culinary or in other domestic occupations. In our walks we see groups of people employed in spinning cotton and silk; others in making wooden bowls and dishes, mats of various patterns, shoes, sandals, cotton dresses, and caps and the like; others busily employed in fashioning brass and iron stirrups, bits for bridles, hoes, chains, fetters, etc., and others again in making saddles and various horse accoutrements. These various articles, which are intended for the Rabbah market, evince considerable taste and ingenuity." Personally, the inhabitants of this island are represented as superior to other Africans. " They have liberty stamped upon their features: and lightness and activity, so rarely to be seen in this country of sluggards, are observable in all their actions. The generality of the people are well behaved; they are hospitable and obliging to strangers, they dwell in amity with their neighbours, they live in unity, peace, and social intercourse with themselves. They are made bold by freedom, affluent by industry and frugality, healthy by exercise and labour, and happy by a combination of all these blessings." Such were the impressions—heightened

a little, it may be, by the pleasure of turning a good sentence,
but faithful no doubt in the main—which ten days' residence in
the island produced upon the two Landers. We have the rather
given them at length, because the secret of all this prosperity is
peculiarly worth enquiring for, with reference to our present
subject. Whence so many points of difference between these
islanders and their neighbours? They are of the same race—
negroes, as black as coal; the island is not large, only fifteen
miles long, and three broad; the land, though rich, is so low
and moist as to form one continued bog, the greater part overflowed in the rainy season; the houses standing in the water,
and many of them carried away when the river rises very high;
no missionary has been among them; no European trader, not
even an Arab chief or merchant, has taken up his abode there;
with persons of superior race or education they have had still
less communication than their neighbours. What then have
they, which their neighbours want, that they should so far
surpass them? The answer is given in a word—they have
security. The chief of Zagozhie, "king of the dark water," has
a fleet of six hundred canoes, and fears no invasion; his people
are bred to the water, they live secure in person and property
within their wooden walls, they are the only ferrymen, and all
the trade by the river is in their hands.

But to pass on:—cross the river, and within two or three
days' journey, besides the two rising Fellatah towns of Raka and
Alorie, concerning which we have no detailed information, we
find *Katunga;* a city with seven daily markets, the residence of
the King of Yarribah, whose power *de jure* extends westward as
far as the coast of Guinea, and must *de facto* be considerable, if
we may judge from the security, both of person and property,
with which all strangers coming to visit him are conveyed from
place to place. The country round contains many other considerable towns, with well supplied and much frequented
markets; and is traversed in more than one direction by parties
of merchants—branches of the great stream which we have
spoken of—who carry the produce of central Negroland
(elephants' teeth, natron, rock salt, and Nyffé cloths) as far as
Ashantee and the country round Cape Coast Castle.

Thus far, then, we have found a regular chain of commercial intercourse and exchange—rude, indeed, and scanty, but un-interrupted—by which each impulse given to commerce at the mouth of the Nun, makes itself felt, however feebly, for several hundred miles up the Niger, and over considerable spaces on either side. We have seen that European goods, purchased with palm-oil or with slaves, are carried from Eboe to Bocqua; and thence dispersed through the adjoining countries, or carried up to Egga and Rabbah, where they are exchanged for the ivory and the manufactures of the Upper Niger, which are thus carried down to Eboe; and again, that the goods which thus make their way to Rabbah, are carried (or would be, if duly selected to hit the wants or fancies of the people) on one side into the heart of Negroland, and the regular caravan route from Bornou to Tim-buctoo; and on the other side through Yarribah to the Atlantic; —that the channel therefore is formed, and the stream does already flow in some quantity; and that, be it as meagre and as much obstructed as it may, there can be no doubt that if more were drawn into it more would flow. It would not be lost as in a swamp nor absorbed as in a desert, but would enter into the veins and enrich the natural circulation.

Here then, if necessary, we might be content to stop. Open at Rabbah an extensive market for European goods and an ex-tensive demand for the productions of the interior, and it would not be long before some considerable portion of the main stream would be drawn thither; the tendency of which must plainly be to raise the value of man's labour, and to diminish the (ex-changeable) value of man himself; and so give birth to a rival trade, which, if it prosper, must ultimately swallow up the slave trade. How fast the transmutation may proceed, it is hardly possible to form any well-grounded conjecture. It must depend upon many facts of which we are not informed and many accidents which we can neither foresee nor control. But that a slip thus planted would take root and grow—that there would be life in it—we do not see on what principle any one can doubt.

But we have stopped short of our full case. Some damage done to the machinery of Mr. Oldfield's vessel, made it unsafe to put on power enough to ascend the current further; and how

far above Rabbah the river continues navigable for a vessel of
that size we cannot tell.   It appears however that Lander, who
had the best means of judging, was not without hope of advancing some hundred miles further ; as far as the ferry at
Comie.   They would then have been no longer on the borders
and outskirts, but at once in the very highway of that portion of
the inland traffic which branches off from the main route of the
caravans ;—the way by which all the merchants who trade to
the countries west of the Niger pass out of the central region.
From this ferry, along this much-frequented road, it is but three
days' journey to one of the great centres of the inland traffic,
the town of *Coolfu* ; in which all the larger streams meet, and
from which all the smaller radiate.   Of the nature of the traffic
at this place, we have a full account from Captain Clapperton,
who, on his second journey, was detained there a good while ;
and his account is well worth the attention of all who wish to
know, not only the natural capabilities of Africa for sustaining
a large commerce with England, but the extent and depth of the
channels which are already there, waiting to receive and diffuse
it.   Presuming then that an iron steamer, laden with goods
from Manchester and Liverpool, may be brought without loss,
damage, or danger (the danger from the climate excepted),
within easy reach of Coolfu ; and remembering that the countries
round have never (we believe) enjoyed a settled peace, but have
always been exposed to disturbance by conquests, insurrections,
or petty predatory warfare ;—that at the very time when the
account was written, a civil war had been "desolating the
country for the last seven years," during which the inhabitants
had been twice burned out of the town ;—that there does not
appear to exist at Coolfu, more than in any other part of the
country, any settled constitution or form of government :—therefore, that all the *accidents* by which commerce is promoted or
depressed were at that time against, not for, it ;—bearing these
things in mind, let us see what is the actual state of it—what
progress, with opportunities so limited and against such heavy
disadvantages, commerce has actually made.

   At Coolfu then, besides the daily market attended by the
inhabitants, there are two markets held weekly which are re-

sorted to by strangers. The extent of their attraction may be
thus explained. From Bornou, far to the east; from Cubbi,
Yaoori, Zamfra, and the borders of the desert, on the north;
from Yarribah and the Gold Coast, westward; and from Benin,
Jaboo, and the furthest part of Nyffé, to the south; there resort
to this market parties of regular merchants, bringing the produce
of their several countries for sale : as, for instance, salt from the
north; red wood, peppers, and European cloths from the south;
kolla and goora nuts, gold, woollen cloths and printed cottons,
brass and pewter dishes, earthenware, and muskets, from the
western coast; horses, natron, unwrought silk, undyed tobes,
from Bornou; besides a variety of articles which find their way
across the desert—Venetian beads, Maltese swords, Italian
looking-glasses, gums and scented woods of the east; silks,
turbans, and tunics of checked silk and linen from Egypt; and
many more ; all of which are to be had at Coolfu, and meet with
a ready sale. Some of these merchants erect tents for themselves outside the walls, where they sell their wares; others send
them by their slaves to the market, and round to the different
houses; others entrust them to brokers, of whom there are many
in the town, both male and female; others live in the houses
of their friends. And besides these regular merchants, there is
a great number of petty traders, chiefly women, who come from
the towns lying to the west of the Niger in Yarribah and Borgoo,
many days' journey distant; carrying their goods on their heads,
and trading at the several markets as they pass. These lodge
in the town, and, while they attend the markets daily, support
themselves by spinning cotton during their spare time. As soon
as they have sold what they have, and bought what they want,
they return to their homes again. The inhabitants likewise (not
excepting the artizans and manufacturers, of whom there are
many), are mostly engaged in buying and selling.[*]

From these facts some notion may be drawn of the dispositions and habits of people in this part of Africa with regard to
trading. The demand must be considerable which draws together such a variety of goods from such distant places; the
enterprise must be considerable which carries people such long

* Clapperton, p. 135, et seq.

journeys to buy or sell them; the security considerable which
makes it practicable to accomplish these journeys with safety.
At present, no doubt, their wants are simple and few, and it may
be asked whether there is any reason to expect that they will
expand; the supply, it may be thought, has hitherto followed
the demand, such as it is; but the demand being now satisfied,
and the vessel full, any further supply would only be wasted.
And certainly, knowing so little as we do of the history and
growth of their wants; not knowing whether they have preceded, or kept pace with, or lagged behind their opportunities;
hardly knowing for certain whether they are at this moment increasing or declining—we must admit this question to be a fair
matter of doubt and speculation. It appears however to us
that the manners and customs of these people indicate anything rather than an indifference to superfluous luxuries or a
disposition to rest contented with a bare supply of the more im-
portunate wants of nature. "Allow not nature more than
needs, man's life is cheap as beast's"; which is by no means
the case in Negroland. Their life is full of toys and superfluities
and social vanities; and their appetite for these appears to be
as insatiable as a child's. The following sketch of the daily life
of the inhabitants of Coolfu is worth attention, as showing how
far they have advanced in artificial habits—a better measure of
the nature and strength of their wants than that eagerness for
new ornaments and playthings of which accounts reach us in
every page; because the existence of such habits proves not
only their taste for superfluities, but the systematic and diligent
cultivation of it :—

"At daylight the whole household arise; the women begin to clean the
house, the men to wash from head to foot; the women and children are then
washed in water, in which the leaf of a bush has been boiled, called Bambarnia;
when this is done, breakfast of cocoa is served out, every one having their separate dish, the women and children eating together. After breakfast the women
and children rub themselves over with the pounded red wood and a little grease,
which lightens the darkness of the black skin. A score or patch of the red
powder is put on some place where it will show to the best advantage. The eyes
are blacked with khol. The mistress and better-looking females stain their
teeth and the inside of their lips of a yellow colour with gora, the flower of the
tobacco plant, and the bark of a root; the outer part of the lips, hair, and eye-
brows, are stained with shani or prepared indigo. Then the women who attend

the market prepare their wares, and when ready, go. The elderly women prepare, clean, and spin cotton at home, and cook the victuals ; the younger females are generally sent round the town selling the small rice balls, fried beans, &c. The master of the house generally takes a walk to the market, or sits in the shade at the door of his house, hearing the news or speaking of the price of natron or other goods. The weavers are daily employed at their trade ; some are sent to cut wood and bring it to the market ; others to bring grass for the horses that may belong to the house, or to take to the market to sell; numbers, at the beginning of the rainy season, are employed in clearing the ground for sowing the maize or millet ; some are sent on distant journeys to buy or sell for their master and mistress, and very rarely betray their trust. About noon they return home, when all have a mess of the pudding called waki, or boiled beans ; and about two or three in the afternoon they return to their different employments, in which they remain till near sunset, when they count their gains to their master or mistress, who receives it and puts it away carefully in the strong room. They then have a meal of pudding or a little fat stew. The mistress of the house, when she goes to rest, has her feet put into a cold poultice of the pounded henna leaves. The young then go to dance and play if it is moonlight, and the old to lounge and converse in the open square of the house, or in the outer coozie, where they remain till the cool of the night." *

Whether a population which has reached this stage shall stand still or go on, will depend in a great measure upon accidental facilities, opportunities, and temptations. The demands of the body being satisfied, and objects of ambition being presented to the mind, simple indeed, but sufficient to exercise the faculties and engage them in pursuit, they may remain content with what they have, so long as nothing is presented to them which they like better. The King of Eyeo or Kiama glories in gilt brass buttons ; and will not cease to glory in them, until he finds that they tarnish, while golden buttons retain their brightness. But as soon as he knows this, his desire changes ; he despises brass, and sends a score of his more elderly wives, laden with the work of their hands, to bring him gold buttons from the furthest parts of Ashantee. The spinning women at Kano and Soccatoo are all equipped with pocket mirrors, which they carry in their cotton baskets ; appealing to them every five minutes to reflect the pleasure of the vanity. Though these mirrors are no flatterers, and can embrace only a feature or two at a time, their owners are nevertheless well pleased, and will continue to smile upon them until some brighter rival shall

* Clapperton, p. 140.

appear—larger, and showing a fairer image; from which moment every spinning woman in Kano and Soccatoo will be more or less unhappy until her basket shall be equipped with a better looking-glass. All will turn on the opportunity and encouragement which shall be afforded. Throw in their path better things than they now have, and if they can be made to understand the superiority, no doubt they will wish to have them; ask in exchange for these such articles as they can best afford to supply, and they will soon learn to apply themselves to the production of those articles. Hitherto they have never been asked for raw cotton, hardly for ivory. Only spread before them the glittering treasures of Birmingham and Manchester, asking for these in return, and they will soon begin to raise cotton for export, and to circumvent the elephants which infest their forests.

Following the caravan route eastward (for be it remembered that we are still within three days' journey of our own vessel), and passing several populous towns with considerable markets, we arrive in about thirty days at *Kano*, the next great centre of trade, lying halfway between the capitals of the two most powerful nations of central Africa, the Bornouese and the Fellatahs. Here again we find a population by no means unprepared to profit by new opportunities and examples of civilization; a people ingenious and industrious, and full of the spirit of traffic; some curious manufactures; a well-frequented and well-supplied market; an organized and regulated trade, and all the operations of buying and selling in full activity. Here is Captain Clapperton's account of the regulations of the market, taken from the narrative of his first journey in 1824:—

"The soug or market is well supplied with every necessary and luxury in request among the people of the interior. . . . There is no market in Africa so well regulated. The sheikh of the soug lets the stalls at so much a month, and the rent forms a part of the revenues of the Governor. The sheikh of the soug also fixes the prices of all wares, for which he is entitled to a small commission, at the rate of fifty whydah or cowries on every sale amounting to four dollars, or 8000 cowries, according to the standard exchange between silver money and this shell currency. There is another custom, regulated with equal certainty, and in universal practice; the seller returns to the buyer a stated part of the price, by way of blessing, as they term it, or of luck-penny according to our less devout phraseology. This is a discount of 2 per cent. on the purchase money; but if the bargain is made in a hired house, it is the landlord who receives the luck-penny. I may here notice the great convenience of the cowrie, which no forgery can imitate; and which, by the dexterity of the natives in reckoning the largest sums, forms a ready medium of exchange in all transactions, from the lowest to the highest. Particular quarters are assigned to distinct articles; the smaller wares being set in booths in the middle, and cattle and bulky commodities being exposed to sale in the outskirts of the market place; wood, dyed grass, bean straw for provender, beans, Guinea corn, Indian corn, wheat, etc., are in one quarter: goats, sheep, asses, bullocks, horses, and camels, in another: earthenware and indigo in a third: vegetables and fruit of all descriptions, such as yams, sweet potatoes, water and musk melons, papau fruit, limes, casheu nuts, plums, mangoes, sha'ldocks, dates, etc., in a fourth, and so on. . . . The interior of the market is filled with stalls of bamboo, laid out in regular streets, where the most costly wares are sold, and articles of dress, and other little matters of use or ornament made and repaired. Bands of musicians parade up and down, to attract purchasers to particular booths. Here are displayed, coarse writing-paper of French manufacture, brought from Barbary; scissors and knives of native workmanship; crude antimony and tin, both the produce of the country; unwrought silk of a red colour, which they make into belts or slings, or weave into the finest cotton tobes; armlets or bracelets of brass; beads of glass, coral, and amber; finger-rings of pewter, and a few silver trinkets, but none of gold; tobes, turkadees, and turban shawls; coarse woollen cloths of all colours; coarse calico; Moorish dresses; the cast-off gaudy garbs of the Mamelukes of Barbary: pieces of Egyptian linen checked or striped with gold; sword-blades from Malta, etc. The market is crowded from sunrise to sunset every day, not excepting their Sabbath, which is kept on Friday. The merchants understand the benefits of monopoly as well as any people in the world; they take good care never to overstock the market, and, if anything falls in price, it is immediately withdrawn for a few days. The market is regulated with the greatest fairness, and the regulations are strictly and impartially enforced. If a tobe or turkadee, purchased here, is carried to Bornou, or any distant place, without being opened, and is there discovered to be of inferior quality, it is immediately sent back as a matter of course; the name of the *dylala* or broker being written inside every parcel. In this case the *dylala* must find out the seller, who, by the laws of Kano, is forthwith obliged to refund the purchase money." *

It was here that Captain Clapperton was surprised to find *English green cotton umbrellas* not uncommon.† They were brought from the shores of the Mediterranean, by the way of Ghadames; how much less convenient a road than the Niger!

Since the people of Nyffé (among whom, it will be remembered, our steamer must remain) will be the chief receivers and transmitters of our goods, it is satisfactory to know that they bore as high a reputation at Kano in 1824, as we have seen that

* Vol. iv. p. 31.   † Vol. iv. p. 38.

they now do all along the Niger. "Of all the various people who frequent Kano, the Nyfféans are most celebrated for their industry ; as soon as they arise, they go to market and buy cotton for their women to spin, who, if not employed in this way, make *billam* for sale, which is a kind of flummery made of flour and tamarinds. The very slaves of this people are in great request, being invariably excellent tradesmen ; and, when once obtained, are never sold again out of the country." *

Captain Clapperton then proceeds to describe with some minuteness the several processes of spinning, weaving, preparing indigo, dyeing, tanning, and manufacturing leathern jars ; in all of which the people of Kano show considerable skill.

Eastward of Kano, some thirty days' journey, lies *Kouka*, the capital of Bornou ; where, according to Major Denham, writing in 1824, the Sheikh El Kanemy—by whose vigour and wisdom the kingdom had within a very few years been delivered from subjection to the Fellatahs, and subjected to law and government of its own—was extremely anxious to promote commerce ; where all the merchants who have ventured thither are encouraged and treated with liberality—and some are known to have returned, after a residence of less than nine years, with fortunes of 15,000 or 20,000 dollars ; where Englishmen especially are sure of a kind reception : and where "the roads are probably as safe as in England." Beyond this lies the Desert on one side, and on the other barbarous nations of which we know nothing.

Westward of Kano, some twenty days' journey, we come to *Soccatoo*, the capital of the Fellatah empire—the most populous town which Captain Clapperton had seen in Africa—where we again find the usual appearances of order and social life, with its established customs, and formal vanities, and round of daily occupation. It seems to be less of a trading place than Kano, though it lies in the route of the caravans ; but we find the usual species of traffic going on, and the ordinary works both in agriculture and manufacture ; grain in abundance ; indigo and cotton plantations ; dyeing-houses, weaving machines, tan-yards, etc. ; and Captain Clapperton is said to have declared that in

* Vol. iii. p. 196.

this town he could have negotiated a bill on the Treasury of London.

Of the countries lying between this city and the famous Timbuctoo, towards which the caravan route now takes its way, our information is less detailed and not so much to be relied upon; though if it be true that between Mushgrelia and Haussa there are more boats employed on the river than between Rosetta and Cairo, and that the fields are enclosed and irrigated by canals and water-wheels,* it seems to indicate a state of advancement and a capacity for improvement not inferior to that which we have been describing.

But we have already proceeded far enough to make out a *primâ facie* case for trying the experiment of a trade up the Niger. To this conclusion we wish for the present to limit ourselves. The establishment of factories, the acquisition of territory, and the organization of companies, involve questions of great moment and difficulty, upon which we cannot now enter. The course and final destinies of the work it would be idle to speculate upon: but it is important, in this more than in almost any other enterprise, that we should proceed with eyes open and feelings uninflamed—as there is none in which a false step, or a fall across the threshold, is likely to involve more important consequences. We are not among those who regard no public undertaking as justifiable which is likely to cost good lives and limbs in the prosecution of it. No great thing is accomplished without great sacrifices on the part of those who lead the way. Not in wars only, but in religion, in politics, in civilization, in commerce, even in science and literature—each in its several kind—the world has always marched on to take possession of its conquests over the dead bodies of the forlorn hope:—a melancholy thing to reflect upon, did not reflection likewise teach us, that between the few who die to win the conquest and the many who live to enjoy it, the real difference amounts after all but to this—the first die, having done something, to-day; the others die, having done nothing, to-morrow. And certainly, when we consider the infinite nature of the benefit which will be secured if this vast continent should ever be reclaimed to Christianity

* Buxton, p. 475.

and the use of man, we cannot but think that human life may be worse wasted than in taking whatever measures may be in the first instance necessary for setting the work on foot.

The opportunity is now before us; it lies with England to take the first step. If England does nothing, nothing will be done. If the Government does nothing, nothing will be done as it should be. Private adventurers, pursuing their own ends in their own ways, cannot act largely or systematically enough; cannot make the sacrifices which will occasionally be required by consistent dealing on a great scale. They will sometimes be reduced to straits which will tempt them to acts of violence or of subterfuge, ruinous to the moral effect of example, and destructive of the confidence upon which all prosperous intercourse must be built. What then is the step which the Government is called on to take? We recur to our original position: it is the business of Government to lead and feel the way; neither keeping aloof, as Mr. Jamieson recommends, and leaving the work wholly to private adventure; nor plunging, as others would have it, headlong and irrevocably into the middle; but sending out proper persons to explore the ground; to open communications with the several chiefs; to make them understand the advantages of a commercial intercourse with England; to persuade them to agree to certain conditions of protection and immunity; to establish a regular system of duties and customs; to devise, if possible, some unobnoxious method of enforcing the observance of such conditions and regulations by either party; to provide our traders (which will probably prove the most difficult, as it is one of the most important, points to accomplish) with some better way of obtaining redress, when they are cheated, than those to which the Liverpool expedition was reduced—namely, the pointing of great guns, the firing of villages, and the seizure of innocent persons for hostages; to make, or to report upon the practicability of making treaties for the suppression of the slave trade; to examine the probable advantages or disadvantages of erecting a fort on the Niger, to be commanded by an officer who may act as arbiter in disputes, protector of British subjects, and representative of the British Government; and, above all, to supply more accurate and more complete information than we now possess concerning the condition of the country, the systems of law and government (if such they can be called), and the proper way of infusing into them a better life, and establishing permanent and prosperous relations. If these things can be done, the trade which has already commenced will immediately be placed upon a much better footing, and we shall be able to proceed to the adoption of further measures with some knowledge of what we are about. Such we take to be the objects of the forthgoing expedition, and on such grounds we hold it to be good.

NOTE.

THE expedition sailed at the time appointed. But though every precaution had been taken which science could suggest for the prevention or mitigation of the coast fever, the mortality proved so great that nothing could be done, and the outcry at home so vehement that no second attempt of the kind under the authority of the Government could ever be thought of. And though private vessels have since made their way up and down the Niger on private business without exposing their owners to public reprobation, no important advance appears to have been made (as indeed little was to be expected) in the way of opening a civilizing intercourse with Negroland by that road. That the Government should have been compelled to abandon all further attempts of the kind is the more to be regretted, because the exceptional mortality in this expedition appears to have been due to an oversight which could be easily avoided. When I was at Washington in 1842, I met a gentleman who had just returned from Liberia. He was a medical man, and had served for some years as the chief medical officer of the Government there. The news of the fate of our Niger expedition had reached me 'not long before, and I asked him whether he thought that in an expedition up the Niger with a European crew the risk of such a number of deaths was unavoidable. He thought not: "But then," he said, "you must have *acclimatised constitutions* for your crew." Now I believe that in our enterprise, that was the one precaution which was *not* taken. The selection of the crew was, of course, the last of the preparations. The others had taken so much time that there was danger of the season passing by. What remained was done in a hurry, and the crew consisted chiefly, I believe, of healthy young Englishmen or Scotchmen,—the favourite victims of the African coast fever. Let us hope that the measures now in progress for carrying commerce and civilization into the interior of Africa from the eastern side will prove more fortunate.

VIII

DICKENS'S AMERICAN NOTES.*

———•◦•———

TRAVELLERS should be well-instructed and conscientious men, for the reputation of nations is in their hands. Lawyers, physicians, and clergymen, must pass their examinations, and receive their credentials, before they can give opinions which the public are authorized to confide in; but for a man who has been where no man else has been, it is enough if he can write—spelling, punctuation, and syntax, will be furnished by his publisher; and there is no continent so large but he can pronounce upon the character of its laws, government, and manners, with an authority which few professors enjoy. If there be any Englishman living who has smuggled himself through the interior of China, ascertained the colour of the Emperor's eyes and beard, eluded the officers of justice, and escaped from bowstring and bastinado down the river Yang-tse-Kiang, now is his time for a book on China and the Chinese. For three months to come, he will be an absolute authority on all the internal affairs of a third of the human race. Everybody will read his book, and everybody will believe all he says. But he must not lose his tide; if he let anybody get the start of him, his authority will go for little more than it is worth —unless he be able, not only to write, but to write the more readable book; for it may be generally observed, that where we have conflicting accounts of a foreign country, the opinion which carries the day is not that of the person who has taken most

* "American Notes for General Circulation." By CHARLES DICKENS. 2 vols. 8vo. London: 1842. *Edinburgh Review*, January, 1843.

pains, or had the best opportunities, or is best qualified by education and natural ability, for forming a judgment, but that of the most agreeable writer.

We say this only of the " reading public " in general. Very many, no doubt, there are amongst us of whom it is not true. Very many there are, who are more particular about the formation of their opinions on such matters—who hold it to be not foolish only, but wrong, to let false impressions settle in the mind ; and who, remembering that a few weeks' residence among strangers will not qualify a man to judge of the character of nations and governments, whose opinion nobody would ask on the working of the Poor Law or the Corporation Act in his own parish, require some better assurance of the worth of a traveller's judgment before they will take the character of a continent from his representation. With such fastidious readers, in entering upon a book of travels, to learn something of the character and capacity of the writer is a primary object. Unfortunately, printed books having no physiognomy, but being all alike plausible, it is an object scarcely attainable, except where the writer has the rare art of impressing his character upon his composition, or where he has already written on matters which others understand. It is on this account that we have looked forward with considerable interest to a work on America by Mr. Dickens ; —not as a man whose views on such a subject were likely to have any conclusive value, but as one with whom the public is personally acquainted through his former works. We all know " Boz," though we may not have seen his face. We know what he thinks about affairs at home, with which we are all conversant —about poor-laws and rich-laws, elections, schools, courts of justice, magistrates, policemen, cab-drivers, and housebreakers— matters which lie round about us, and which we flatter ourselves we understand as well as he. We know, therefore, what to infer from his pictures of society abroad ; what weight to attribute to his representations ; with what caution and allowance to entertain them. If his book abound in broad pictures of social absurdities and vulgarities, we know that he commenced his literary career as an illustrator of Seymour's cockney caricatures, and that his tendency in that direction is so strong, that, though possessing sources of far finer and deeper humour, he can hardly refrain from indulging it to excess. If he draw bitter pictures of harsh jailers and languishing prisoners, we know that his sympathy for human suffering sometimes betrays him into an unjust antipathy to those whose duty it is to carry into effect the severities of justice. If he grow learned on questions of government and politics, we know that his opinions on such matters are not much enquired after at home. We know, in short, where we may trust his judgment, where we must take it with caution, and where we may neglect it.

Mr. Dickens has many qualities which make his testimony, as a passing observer in a strange country, unusually valuable. A truly genial nature; an unweariable spirit of observation, quickened by continual exercise; an intimate acquaintance with the many varieties of life and character which are to be met with in large cities; a clear eye to see through the surface and false disguises of things; a desire to see things truly; a respect for the human soul, and the genuine face and voice of nature, under whatever disadvantages of person, situation, or repute in the world; a mind which, if it be too much to call it original in the highest sense of the word, yet uses always its own eyes, and applies itself to see the object before it takes the impression—to understand the case before it passes judgment; a wide range of sympathy, moreover—with sweetness, and a certain steady self-respect, which keeps the spirit clear from perturbations, and free to receive an untroubled image;—a mind, in short, which moves with freedom and pleasure in a wider world than has been thrown open to the generality of men. This happy combination of rare qualities, which Mr. Dickens's previous works show that he possesses, would seem to qualify him, in some respects, beyond any English traveller that has yet written about the United States,—if not to discuss the political prospects of that country, or to draw comparisons between monarchical and republican institutions,—yet to receive and reproduce for the information of the British public a just image of its existing social condition. To balance these, however, it must be confessed that he labours under some considerable disadvantages. His education must have been desultory, and not of a kind likely to train him to habits of grave and solid speculation. A young man, a satirist both by profession and by humour, whose studies have lain almost exclusively among the odd characters in the odd corners of London, who does not appear to have attempted the systematic cultivation of his powers, or indeed to have been aware of them, until they were revealed to him by a sudden blaze of popularity which would have turned a weaker head—who has since been constantly occupied in his own peculiar field of fiction and humour—how can he have acquired the knowledge and the speculative powers necessary for estimating the character of a great people, placed in circumstances not only strange to him, but new in the history of mankind; or the working of institutions which are yet in their infancy, their hour of trial not yet come—in their present state resembling nothing by the analogy of which their tendency and final scope may be guessed at? Should he wander into prophecies or philosophic speculations, it is clear that such a guide must be followed with considerable distrust. Nor, indeed, can his opinions be taken without abatement and allowance, even in that which belongs more especially to his own province—the aspect and character of society as it exists. As a comic satirist, with a strong tendency to caricature, it has been his business to observe society in its irregularities and incongruities, not in the sum and total result of its operation; a habit which, even in scenes with which we are most familiar, can hardly be indulged without disturbing the judgment; and which, among strange men and manners, may easily mislead the fancy beyond the power of the most vigilant understanding to set it right. It is the nature of an Englishman to think everything ridiculous which contrasts with what he has been used to; and it costs some effort of his reflective and imaginative powers to make him feel that the absurdity is in himself, and not in the thing he sees. In a strange country, where the conventional manners and regulations of society are not the same as in England, every room and every street must teem with provocations to this kind of amusement, which will keep a good-humoured English traveller, of average reflective powers, in continual laughter. And though Mr. Dickens *knows* better, it is too much to expect of him that he should have always acted upon his better knowledge; especially when we consider that he had his character as an amusing writer to keep up. The obligation which he undoubtedly lies under to keep his readers well entertained, (failing which, any book by "Boz" would be universally denounced as a catchpenny,) must have involved him in many temptations quite foreign to his business as an impartial observer; for any man who would resolutely abstain from seeing things in false lights, must make up his mind to forego half his triumphs as a wit, and *vice versâ.* Even his habits as a writer of fiction must have been against him; for such a man will always be tempted to study society, with a view to gather suggestions and materials for his creative faculty to work upon, rather than simply to consider and understand it. The author of "Pickwick" will study the present as our historical novelists study the past—to find not what it is, but what he can make of it.

It is further to be borne in mind, in estimating Mr. Dickens's claims to attention, that the study of America does not appear to have been his primary object in going, nor his main business while there. He is understood to have gone out as a kind of missionary in the cause of international copyright;* with the design of persuading the American public (for it was the public to which he seems to have addressed himself) to abandon their present privilege of enjoying the produce of all the literary industry of Great Britain without paying for it;—an excellent recommendation, the adoption of which would, no doubt, in the end prove a vast national benefit. In the mean time, however, as it cannot be carried into effect except by taxing the very many who read for the benefit of the very few who write and the present for the benefit of the future—to attempt to get it adopted by a legislature over which the will of the many has any paramount influence, would seem to be a very arduous, if not an altogether hopeless enterprise. In this arduous, if not hopeless enterprise, Mr. Dickens, having once engaged himself, must be presumed, during the short period of his visit, to have chiefly occupied his thoughts; therefore the gathering of materials for a

---

* With regard to this sentence, which gave great offence to Mr. Dickens, see the note at the end of the paper.

book about America must be regarded as a subordinate and incidental task—the produce of such hours as he could spare from his main employment. Nor must it be forgotten that in this, the primary object of his visit, he decidedly failed; a circumstance (not unimportant when we are considering his position and opportunities as an observer of manners in a strange country) to which we draw attention, the rather because Mr. Dickens makes no allusion to it himself. A man may read the volumes through without knowing that the question of international copyright has ever been raised on either side of the Atlantic.

Our catalogue of cautions and drawbacks grows long; but there is yet another point to which, as it does not appear on the face of the book itself, we must advert. Though Mr. Dickens does not tell us of it, it is a notorious fact, that throughout his stay in the United States he was besieged by the whole host of lion-hunters, whose name in that land of liberty and equality is legion. In England, we *preserve* our lions : to be admitted to the sight of one, except on public occasions, is a privilege granted only to the select. Persons of a certain distinction in the fashionable world are alone licensed to exhibit him; and the exhibition is open to those only whom such distinguished persons may choose to honour by admission. In America (always excepting a skin of the right colour), the pursuit of this kind of game requires no qualification whatever; for though society seems to form itself there, just as it does with us, into a series of circles, self-distinguished and excluded one from the other, yet there does not appear to be any generally acknowledged scale of social dignity. Each circle may assert its own pretensions, and act upon them; but they are not binding upon the rest. One citizen may not choose to dine with another, just as one party may refuse to act with another in politics; but they are not the less equal in the eye of the law. In the eye of the law and of the universe, a citizen is a citizen, and, as such, has a right to do the honours of his country to a stranger; and though there are doubtless many circles in which the stranger is pitied for having to receive such promiscuous attentions, there is none which seems to consider itself excluded from the privilege of offering them. Of the evils which necessarily beset a man whom everybody is agog to see, this is a very serious aggravation. In London his condition is bad enough; for the attentions which are prompted not by respect but by this prurient curiosity must always be troublesome and thankless. But in America the whole population turns out, and the hunted animal has no escape. The popularity of Mr. Dickens's works is said to be even greater there than it is at home. Copies are circulated through all corners of the land at a tenth of the native cost; readers therefore are ten times as numerous. The curiosity to see him, hear him, and touch him, was accordingly universal; and (if we may trust current report) his time must have been passed in one continual levee. It was not merely the profusion of hospitable offers—the crowd of callers that besieged his lodgings,—the criticisms upon his person,—and the regular announcement of his movements in the newspapers:—But if he walked in the street, he was followed; if he went to the play, he had to pass through a lane formed by rows of uncovered citizens; if he took his seat in the railway car a few minutes before the time of starting, the idlers in the neighbourhood came about him, and fell to discussing his personal appearance; if he sat in his room, boys from the street came in to look at him, and from the window beckoned their companions to follow (vol. i. p. 277); if he took the wings of the evening, and fled to the farthest limits of geography, even there his notoriety pursued him. As he lay reading in a steam-boat, between Sandusky and Buffalo, he was startled by a whisper in his ear (which came, however, from the adjoining cabin, and was not addressed to him), "Boz is on board still, my dear." Again, after a pause (complainingly) "Boz keeps himself very close." And once more, after a long interval of silence, "I suppose that Boz will be writing a book by-and-by, and putting all our names in it." This is the very misery of kings, who can enjoy no privacy, nor ever see the natural face of the world they live in, but see only their own importance reflected in the faces of the gaping crowd that surrounds them. We set down the circumstance among Mr. Dickens's most serious disadvantages—not because we suppose his judgment to have been biassed by it, for he has too much sense to be gratified by this kind of homage, and too much

good nature to take it unkindly; but because it must have prevented him from seeing society in its natural condition : it must
have presented the New World to his eyes under circumstances
of disturbance, which brought an undue proportion of the sedi-
ment to the surface, and thereby made his position as an observer
very unfavourable. In the New World as in the Old, and in all
classes, from the highest to the lowest, the curiosity which besets
the paths of every much-talked-of man is essentially vulgar;
and, in such a case as this, can hardly fail to leave upon the
mind of the sufferer an undue impression of disgust.

Such being our opinion of Mr. Dickens's faculties and opportunities for observation, we expected from him a book, not without
large defects both positive and negative, but containing some
substantial and valuable addition to our stock of information
with regard to this most interesting country—interesting not
only for the indissoluble connexion of its interests with our
own, but likewise as the quarter from which we must look for
light on the great question of these times,—What is to become
of *Democracy*, and how is it to be dealt with ? We cannot say
that our expectations are justified by the result. Though the
book is said to have given great offence on the other side of the
Atlantic, we cannot see any sufficient reason for it. To us it
appears that Mr. Dickens deserves great praise for the care with
which he has avoided all offensive topics, and abstained from
amusing his readers at the expense of his entertainers; and if
we had an account of the temptations in this kind which he has
resisted, we do not doubt that the reserve and self-control which
he has exercised would appear scarcely less than heroical. But,
on the other hand, we cannot say that his book throws any new
light on his subject. He has done little more than confide to
the public what should have been a series of letters for the
entertainment of his private friends. Very agreeable and
amusing letters they would have been; and as such, had they
been posthumously published, would have been read with interest and pleasure. As it is, in the middle of our amusement
at the graphic sketches of life and manners, the ludicrous incidents, the wayside conversations about nothing, so happily told,
and the lively remarks, with which these " Notes " abound—in

the middle of our respect for the tone of good sense and good
humour which runs through them—and in spite of a high appreciation of the gentlemanly feeling which has induced him to
refrain from all personal allusions and criticisms, and for the
modesty which has kept him silent on so many subjects, concerning which most persons in the same situation (not being
reminded of the worthlessness of their opinions by the general
inattention of mankind to what they say) are betrayed into the
delivery of oracles—in the middle of all this we cannot help
feeling that we should have respected Mr. Dickens more if he
had kept his book to himself; if he had been so far dissatisfied
with these "American Notes" as to shrink from the "general
circulation" of them; if he had felt unwilling to stand by and
see his nothings trumpeted to all corners of the earth, quoted
and criticised in every newspaper, passing through edition after
edition in England, and settling in clouds of sixpenny copies all
over the United States.   That he had nothing better to say is
no reproach to him.   He had much to say about international
copyright, and that, we doubt not, was well worth hearing; we
only wish it had been heard with more favour.   But, having
nothing better to say, why say anything?   Or why, at least,
sound a trumpet before him to call men away from their business
to listen?   To us it seems to imply a want of respect either for
himself or for his subject, that he should be thus prompt to
gratify the prurient public appetite for novelty, by bringing the
fruits of his mind into the market unripe.   This, however, is a
matter of taste.   In reputation, so easy and abundant a writer
will suffer little from an occasional mistake.   Though this book
should only live till New Year's Day, it will have lived long
enough for his fame; for on that day we observe that he is himself to come forth again in a series of monthly numbers, so that
none but himself will be his extinguisher.   In the mean time,
as a candidate for "general circulation," it stands before us for
judgment, and must be dealt with according to its deserts.

Concerning America in her graver aspects, we have already
said that it does not add much to our existing stock of information.   In comprehensiveness, completeness, and solidity, the
fruits of a judicial temper, patient and persevering observation,

and a mind accustomed to questions of politics and government, it is not to be compared to the work entitled "Men and Manners in America," by the author of "Cyril Thornton." Any one who is curious about the state of things in that country, and wishes to form some idea of its real condition, should look there for it, and not here. There he will find the matter discussed and illustrated; here he will find little more than a loose record of the travelling impressions of Mr. Dickens. Still, even this is not without its value. To know the impression made by the first aspect of a country upon a mind like his, is to know something of the country itself. The good things he has been able to say, and the good stories he has met with in his travels, are things of less real interest, though a good deal more entertaining. Good stories grow wild in all societies; no man who can tell one when found had ever any difficulty in finding one to tell. Sketches of odd characters, specimens of the slang of coachmen and porters, ludicrous incidents, picturesque groups, whimsical phrases, or such as sound whimsical to strange ears—these things (though it is of such that the better part of these volumes consists) tell us nothing about a country. We want to know the total aspect, complexion, and constitution of society; these are only its flying humours. Leaving these, therefore, to the newspapers (which have rarely come in for such a windfall during the recess) we shall apply ourselves to discover from such hints as these volumes supply, what kind of people these transatlantic brethren of ours really are, and what kind of life they live. We shall not, indeed, inquire at what hour they dine; whether they wear their hair long or short; how they pronounce certain words; how they take their tobacco; and whether, when they wish to soften the absoluteness of their positives or negatives, they say, "I guess," or "I suppose," "I *expect*," or "I *suspect*." In these and the like matters, the nations have our good leave to please themselves. We want to know how they act and feel in the substantial relations and emergencies of life; in their marryings and givings in marriage; in their parental, conjugal, filial duties; in the neighbourly charities; in the offices of friendship. The fireside, the market-place, the sick-room, the place of worship and the court of justice, the school, the library—it is in the arrangement of these that the life and being of a people must be looked for, not in their dress, or dialect, or rules of etiquette.

We must confess, indeed, that to gather any sound knowledge, and form any just opinions on these points, is a matter of extreme difficulty; and when we say that Mr. Dickens has not given us much information about them, we are far from meaning it as a reproach. "He that hath knowledge spareth his words"—and the stranger who thinks to understand a people in a fortnight, is not wise. In all his observations on a strange society, a man must have a reference, more or less direct, to that with which he is familiar at home. Without reference to some such standard he cannot explain his feeling to himself—much less to another. Yet to compare a familiar world with a strange one,—what is it but comparing the ore as it comes out of the smelting-house, with the ore as it comes out of the mine? In remembering his own country, a man takes no account of the dross; in observing another, he values the gross lump—dross and gold together. At home he has made himself comfortable—that is, he has gradually settled into the ways he likes, gathered about him the people he likes: of the things he did *not* like, he has got rid of what he could, reconciled himself to what he must, and forgotten all about the rest. Out of a hundred persons whose acquaintance he might have cultivated, he has cultivated ten. Out of a dozen places of resort that are open to him, he resorts to one. He has tried three or four servants, and at last found one that suits him. They gave him damp sheets and a bad breakfast at the Crown Inn: instead of making a note of the fact for general circulation, he went to the Bell, where they serve him better, and forgot it. And thus, out of the jarring elements of the world into which he was born, he has shaped out a small peculiar world expressly for himself, which fits him; and this private world it is that he boasts of to others, grumbles at to himself, and carries about in his thoughts as a standard to measure foreign pretensions by. In the foreign world, meanwhile, he can make neither selections nor distinctions; he looks at everything alike, and everything he looks at he sets down as alike characteristic. Some delusion from so unequal a comparison it is impossible to avoid. But it may be partly corrected—some estimate at least may be formed of the extent of correction required—by taking any given surface of ground at home, the inhabitants of which have been drawn together, not by any common interest or pursuit, but each by his several occasion; supposing yourself suddenly set down among them without any previous knowledge of their characters; and endeavouring to imagine the impression you would take of the place and people during the first exchange of visits; how they would figure in your journal in that period of probation, before you had learned to treat them according to their qualities —to cultivate the estimable, to avoid the disagreeable, to be inattentive to the tiresome, and to think nothing about the greater number.

Fully aware, no doubt, of all this—desiring to be just and liberal in his observations—intending to write a book, but remembering withal that "in the multitude of words there wanteth not sin," and firmly resolved to violate neither the confidence of social intercourse by revealing private conversations, nor the decency of manners by publishing criticisms upon the character and appearance of the ladies and gentlemen at whose houses he might be received—(a modern practice which, considering the activity of the press, the rapidity and regularity of communication between the two countries, and the scandalous appetite for personal sketches which afflicts both, is little better than to talk of people before their faces; and can be compared to nothing so aptly as to the conduct of the street boys in Baltimore, who came to inspect "Boz" as he sat in the railway car *)—Mr. D. landed at Boston on the 22nd of January 1842. Having remained there about a fortnight, he proceeded towards New York, where he arrived on the 13th of February. How long he stayed we

---

* " Being rather early, those men and boys who happened to have nothing particular to do, *and were curious in foreigners*, came (according to custom) round the carriage in which I sat; let down all the windows; thrust in their heads and shoulders; hooked themselves on conveniently by their elbows; *and fell to comparing notes on the subject of my personal appearance, with as much indifference as if I were a stuffed figure I never gained so much uncompromising information with reference to my own nose and eyes, the various impressions wrought by my mouth and chin on different minds, and how my head looks from behind, as on these occasions.*" —(Vol. i. p. 277.) The street boys we can excuse; but our literary ladies and gentlemen should know better.

cannot learn ; but in the middle of March we find him at Richmond in Virginia, having already seen all he meant to see of Philadelphia, Washington, and Baltimore, and now turning his face towards the great West. The next six or seven weeks must have been spent almost entirely in coaches and steam-boats ; for we find him passing from Richmond back to Baltimore ; thence up the valley of the Susquehanna to Harrisburg ; across the Alleghany mountains to Pittsburg ; down the whole length of the Ohio river to its junction with the Mississippi ; up the Mississippi to St. Louis ; back again as far as Cincinnati ; thence across the State of Ohio, two or three hundred miles northward, as far as Sandusky ; from Sandusky traversing the whole length of Lake Erie ; and so proceeding by way of Buffalo to the Falls of Niagara, which he reached about the end of April, and remained there for ten days, in a confusion of sublime emotions, upon which he has enlarged in a passage which is meant to be itself sublime ; though we think it would tell better as burlesque. The next three weeks were devoted to Canada ; after which he had only time for a rapid journey to New York by way of Lake Champlain, and one spare day, which he devoted to the "Shakers" at Lebanon.

If to these dates (which we have gathered with some difficulty) we could add an account of the distances between place and place, (distances of which we, who are confined within our four seas, can form no practical conception), it would be sufficiently apparent that, during the last half of Mr. Dickens's sojourn in the United States, he did not stay long enough in any one place to become even tolerably well acquainted with its society ; and that his impressions of social character throughout the vast regions lying to the west of Washington, must have been drawn entirely from the company he travelled with—a class of persons whose manners must, in all countries, be far below the average. Any general judgments he may hazard must therefore be taken with the requisite allowance. A fortnight well spent in Boston, and a month between New York, Philadelphia, and Washington, may enable a wise man to say something about the people. The rest of Mr. Dickens's experience qualified him admirably well to tell us what to expect in coaches, canal boats, railway carriages, and hotels; and in these matters, if allowance be made for his habitual exaggeration—(a fault, by the way, and a vulgarity which, we fear, increases upon him)—we dare say his authority is as good as any man's. But, as we should be sorry to have the character of England inferred from the manners of the road; or indeed to have any conclusions drawn as to our own personal proficiency in the courtesies of life, from our demeanour in the traveller's room; we shall leave his westward observations un-noticed, and endeavour to make out what kind of people he found in the drawing-rooms at Boston, Philadelphia, and Wash-ington.

Every country—especially a new one—has a right to be judged by the best of its natural growths; for the best is that towards which the rest aspire. Of the manners and character of the best class in America, Mr. Dickens (in common, we believe, with every gentleman who has had an opportunity of judging) gives a very favourable impression. On quitting New York, after not more than a fortnight's stay there, he says:—" I never thought that going back to England, returning to all who are dear to me, and to pursuits that have insensibly grown to be a part of my nature, I could have felt so much sorrow as I endured, when I parted at last on board this ship with the friends that accompanied me from this city. I never thought the name of any place so far away, and so lately known, could ever associate itself in my mind with the crowd of affectionate remembrances that now cluster about it." And then follows one of Mr. Dickens's fine passages, which we wish to be understood as quoting, not because we admire it, but because it shows that the last sentence was not strong enough to satisfy his feelings :—
" There are those in this city who would brighten, to me, the darkest winter day that ever glimmered and went out in Lapland; and before whose presence even home grew dim, when they and I exchanged that painful word which mingles with our every thought and deed; which haunts our cradle-heads in infancy, and closes up the vista of our lives in age."—(Vol. i. p. 230.) And in his concluding remarks, he deliberately repeats the same sentiment as applicable, not to New York only, but to the nation generally :—" They are by nature frank, brave, cordial, hospitable,

and affectionate. Cultivation and refinement seem but to en-
hance their warmth of heart and ardent enthusiasm: and it is
the possession of these latter qualities in a most remarkable
degree, which renders an educated American one of the most
endearing and most generous of friends. I never was so won
upon as by this class; never yielded up my full confidence and
esteem so readily and pleasantly as to them; never can make
again, in half a year, so many friends for whom I seem to
entertain the regard of half a life."—(Vol. ii. p. 288.) Acknow-
ledgments, scarcely less strong than these, of the merits of the
best class of American gentry, are scattered through Captain
Hamilton's book; and even Captain Basil Hall, in spite of his
prejudices and conventional feelings—his horror at words wrong
pronounced, and meats ungracefully swallowed, and his com-
placent persuasion that whatever is the fashion in England is
right in the eye of the universal reason—tells us, in his gossiping,
good-humoured way, the very same thing. Of the manners and
distinguishing qualities of the class to which the individuals
belong, who called forth the above expressions of admiration, we
regret that little or nothing more can be collected from these
volumes. The tone of society in Boston is only described as
being " one of perfect politeness, courtesy, and good breeding."
The ladies, we learn, are beautiful; and " their education much
as with us." Their parties take place at more rational hours,
and the conversation " may possibly be a little louder and more
cheerful" than with us. In other respects, a party in Boston
appeared to Mr. Dickens just like a party in London. In New
York, we are only told that " the tone of the best society is like
that of Boston: here and there, it may be, with a greater in-
fusion of the mercantile spirit, but generally polished and refined,
and always most hospitable. The houses and tables are elegant;
the hours later, and more rakish; and there is perhaps a greater
spirit of contention in reference to appearances, and the display
of wealth and costly living: " the ladies are again described as
" singularly beautiful." Of the society in Philadelphia, we only
learn that " what he saw of it he greatly liked "—but that it was
more " provincial " than at Boston or New York; and apparently
rather too blue for his taste. But his stay was very short. At

Washington he confines himself to legislators; and of them he speaks only as he finds them in the arena where they exhibit. His remarks on them we shall pass over—for, being in quest of the best manners in the country, we must of course avoid all places consecrated to public debate. To learn the true character and manners of the English bar, you must look at lawyers anywhere but in court; and before we pronounce upon the breeding of a member of Congress, we must see him in a private drawing-room. The only persons whom he speaks of as having personally known, are those whom he specially excepts from his general censures. Of these—" the foremost among those politicians who are known in Europe "—he says—" to the most favourable accounts that have been written of them, I more than fully and most heartily subscribe : and personal intercourse and free communication have bred within me, not the result predicted in the very doubtful proverb, but increased admiration and respect. They are striking men to look at, hard to deceive, prompt to act, lions in energy, Crichtons in varied accomplishment, Indians in fire of eye and gesture, Americans in strong and generous impulse ; and they as well represent the honour and wisdom of their country at home, as the distinguished gentleman who is now its minister at the British court sustains its highest character abroad." (Vol. i. p. 292.) This is another of those ambitious sentences, from which we can gather no distinct idea except that these gentlemen have inspired Mr. Dickens with a strong desire to pay them a splendid compliment. We cannot doubt that his admiration of them is sincere; and we may take his known character and ability as a guarantee that it is well founded.

We do not suppose that his conversation has lain much among professors, or that his thoughts on Universities are entitled to much authority; but we must not omit to mention, in this place, his notice of the University of Cambridge, and its influence upon the society around. " The resident professors at that University are gentlemen of learning and varied attainments ; and are, without one exception that I can call to mind, men who would shed a grace upon, and do honour to, any society in the civilized world. Many of the resident gentry, in Boston and in its neighbourhood, and I think I am not mistaken in adding, a large majority of those who are attached to the liberal professions there, have been educated at this same school. . . . It was a source of inexpressible pleasure to me to observe the almost imperceptible, but not less certain, effect wrought by this institution among the small community at Boston; and to note, at every turn, the humanizing tastes and desires it has engendered—the affectionate friendships to which it has given rise—the amount of vanity and prejudice it has dispelled."

As we are not writing an essay upon the social condition of America, but trying to collect Mr. Dickens's impressions of it, we must be content with these somewhat meagre notices of the manners and character of its best society. For further evidence as to its qualities, we must look to its fruits. And the fruits of the social character, as distinguished from the political regulations, of a country, are to be looked for in those matters in which (the baser appetites and worse dispositions of men having no temptation to interfere), sense, character, knowledge, and virtue have their natural influence. Not, therefore, in the Legislature; for the composition of that depends upon the law of election and the amount of qualification; nor in the Press, for the character of that depends upon the cost of printing and paper, and the amount of taxes, direct and indirect, upon what by courtesy is called knowledge. The Press and the Legislature react upon the social character, but are not to be taken as representing it. The composition of the House of Representatives is not so much an index to the feelings and opinions of the American gentry, as to the number of Irish labourers who have votes. And the character of the daily and weekly Press is a measure rather of the number of uneducated persons who can read, than of the taste of the educated. But there are some departments in the social establishment, which the worse half of society silently leaves to the care and taste of the better. Among these, the most conspicuous are charities of all kinds, public and private; arrangements for the education of the people; asylums for persons labouring under natural defects; provisions for the relief of sick persons and young children; for the treatment of prisoners, and the like. Institutions of this kind are probably the fairest expression that can be had of the feeling and character of a people, properly considered; reckoning, that is, not by numbers but by weight—counting every man as two whose opinion carries another along with it. Now, in these matters, Mr. Dickens's testimony is not only very favourable and very strongly expressed, but really of great value. Prisons and madhouses have always had strong attractions for him; he went out with the advantage of a very extensive acquaintance with establishments of this kind in England; and, wherever he heard of one in America, he appears to have stayed and seen it. His report leads irresistibly to the conclusion, that in this department New England has, as a people, taken the lead of the civilized world; and that Old England, though beginning to follow, is still a good way behind. And the superiority lies not merely in the practical recognition of the principle that the care of these things belongs properly to the state, and should not be left, as with us, to the charity and judgment of individuals, however securely that charity may be relied on; but in the excellence of the institutions themselves in respect of arrangement and management. Our limits will not allow us to follow him through his observations and remarks on this subject; which are, however, upon the whole, the most valuable and interesting part of the book. He carefully inspected not less (we think) than ten institutions of this class; and of these he has given minute descriptions. Those at Boston, he believes to be "as perfect as the most considerate wisdom, benevolence, and humanity can make them." . . . . . "In all of them, the unfortunate or degenerate citizens of the State are carefully instructed in their duties both to God and man; are surrounded by all reasonable means of comfort and happiness that their condition will well admit of; are appealed to as members of the great human family, however afflicted, indigent, or fallen; are ruled by the strong heart, and not by the strong (though immeasurably weaker) hand." And the rest, (with the exception of a lunatic asylum in Long Island, and a prison nicknamed "The Tombs" at New York), appear to deserve, so far at least as the design and the management go, the same praise. Upon one doubtful and difficult question, which has of late excited a good deal of controversy in England, Mr. Dickens's observations will

be read with great interest—we allude to the effects of the
solitary as contrasted with the *silent* system.   Against the
solitary system Mr. Dickens gives his most emphatic testimony;
which will, no doubt, have due weight with the department on
which the consideration of this question, with reference to our
own prison system, devolves.   For our own part, we must
confess that, highly as we esteem his opinion in such a matter,
and free as we are from any prejudice in favour of the system
which he condemns, we are not altogether satisfied.   His manner
of handling the question does not assure us that he is master
of it.   His facts, as stated by himself, do not appear to us to fit
his theory.   If not inconsistent with it, they are certainly not
conclusive in favour of it.   We sometimes cannot help doubting
whether his *judging* faculty is strongly developed, and whether
he does not sometimes mistake pictures in his mind for facts in
nature.   He is evidently proud of his powers of intuition—of his
faculty of inferring a whole history from a passing expression.
Show him any man's face, and he will immediately tell you his
life and adventures.   A very pretty and probable story he will
make of it; and, provided we do not forget that it is all *fiction*,
a very instructive one.   But, in discussing disputed points in
nature or policy, we cannot admit these works of his imagination
as legitimate evidence.   The case before us supplies a striking
illustration of Mr. Dickens's power in this way; and likewise,
we suspect, of his tendency to be misled by it.   We shall take
the opportunity of quoting a long passage, which will serve the
threefold purpose of exhibiting a favourable specimen of Mr.
Dickens's style, of justifying the doubts we have expressed as to
his judging faculty, and of presenting one side of the question
concerning the solitary system in a strong light.

He commences his remarks on the subject by declaring his
belief " that very few men are capable of estimating the immense
amount of torture and agony which this dreadful punishment,
prolonged for years, inflicts upon the sufferers," and that, " in
guessing at it himself, and in reasoning from *what he has seen
written upon their faces, and what to his certain knowledge they
feel within,* he is only the more convinced that there is a depth
of terrible endurance in it, which none but the sufferers them-

selves can fathom, and which no man has a right to inflict upon
his fellow-creature."—(Vol. i. p. 239.) He then proceeds to
describe the regulations of the prison, and the condition and
appearance of several of the prisoners. The sight, and the feelings of awe and pity which the sight awakens, set his "shaping
spirit of imagination" at work, and he thus goes on:—

"As I walked among these solitary cells, and looked at the faces of the men
within them, I tried to picture to myself the thoughts and feelings natural to
their condition; I imagined the hood just taken off, and the scene of their
captivity disclosed to them in all its dismal monotony.

"At first, the man is stunned. His confinement is a hideous vision; and
his old life a reality. He throws himself upon his bed, and lies there abandoned
to despair. By degrees the insupportable solitude and barrenness of the place
rouses him from this stupor, and when the trap in his grated door is opened,
he humbly begs and prays for work. 'Give me some work to do, or I shall go
raving mad!'

"He has it; and by fits and starts applies himself to labour; but every now
and then there comes upon him a burning sense of the years that must be
wasted in that stone coffin, and an agony so piercing in the recollection of those
who are hidden from his view and knowledge, that he starts from his seat, and
striding up and down the narrow room, with both hands clasped on his uplifted
head, hears spirits tempting him to beat his brains out on the wall.

"Again he falls upon his bed, and lies there, moaning. Suddenly he starts
up, wondering whether any other man is near; whether there is another cell like
that on either side of him; and listens keenly.

"There is no sound: but other prisoners may be near for all that. He
remembers to have heard once—when he little thought of coming there himself—
that the cells were so constructed that the prisoners could not hear each other,
though the officers could hear them. Where is the nearest man—upon the right
or on the left? or is there one in both directions? Where is he sitting now—
with his face to the light? or is he walking to and fro? How is he dressed?
Has he been there long? Is he much worn away? Is he very white and
spectre-like? Does he think of his neighbour too?

"Scarcely venturing to breathe, and listening while he thinks, he conjures
up a figure with its back towards him, and imagines it moving about in this
next cell. He has no idea of the face; but he is certain of the dark form of a
stooping man. In the cell upon the other side, he puts another figure, whose
face is hidden from him also. Day after day, and often when he wakes up in
the middle of the night, he thinks of these two men until he is almost distracted.
He never changes them. There they are always as he first imagined them—an
old man on the right; a younger man on the left—whose hidden features
torture him to death, and have a mystery that makes him tremble.

"The weary days pass on with solemn pace, like mourners at a funeral; and
slowly he begins to feel that the white walls of his cell have something dreadful
in them: that their colour is horrible: that their smooth surface chills his

blood: that there is one hateful corner which torments him. Every morning when he wakes, he hides his head beneath the coverlet, and shudders to see the ghastly ceiling looking down upon him. The blessed light of day itself peeps in—an ugly phantom face—through the unchangeable crevice which is his prison window.

" By slow but sure degrees, the terrors of that hateful corner swell until they beset him at all times; invade his rest, make his dreams hideous, and his nights dreadful. At first, he took a strange dislike to it; feeling as though it gave birth in his brain to something of corresponding shape, which ought not to be there, and racked his head with pains. Then he began to fear it, then to dream of it; and of men whispering its name and pointing to it. Then he could not bear to look at it, nor yet to turn his back upon it. Now,. it is every night the lurking place of a ghost—a shadow—a silent something, horrible to see; but whether bird or beast, or muffled human shape, he cannot tell.

" When he is in his cell by day, he fears the little yard without. When he is in the yard, he dreads to re-enter the cell. When night comes, there stands the phantom in the corner. If he have the courage to stand in its place and drive it out, (he had once, being desperate,) it broods upon his bed. In the twilight, and always at the same hour, a voice calls to him by name; as the darkness thickens, his loom begins to live; and even that, his comfort, is a hideous figure, watching him till daybreak.

" Again, by slow degrees, these horrible fancies depart from him one by one; returning sometimes unexpectedly, but at longer intervals, and in less alarming shapes. He has talked upon religious matters with the gentleman who visits him; and has read his Bible, and has written a prayer upon his slate, and has hung it up as a kind of protection, and an assurance of heavenly companionship. He dreams now sometimes of his children or his wife, but is sure that they are dead or have deserted him. He is easily moved to tears; is gentle, submissive, and broken-spirited. Occasionally the old agony comes back; a very little thing will revive it; even a familiar sound, or the scent of summer flowers in the air; but it does not last long now; for the world without has come to be the vision and this solitary life the sad reality.

" If his term of imprisonment be short—I mean comparatively, for short it cannot be—the last half-year is almost worse than all; for then he thinks the prison will take fire and he be burned in the ruins, or that he is doomed to die within the walls, or that he will be detained on some false charge and sentenced for another term: or that something, no matter what, must happen to prevent his going at large. And this is natural, and impossible to be reasoned against; because, after his long separation from human life, and his great suffering, any event will appear to him more probable in the contemplation than the being restored to liberty and his fellow-creatures.

" If his period of confinement have been very long, the prospect of release bewilders and confuses him. His broken heart may flutter for a moment when he thinks of the world outside, and what it might have been to him in all those lonely years; but that is all. The cell door has been closed too long on all his hopes and cares. Better to have hanged him in the beginning than bring him to this pass, and send him forth among his kind, who are his kind no more."

Now this is a most powerful sketch of a *possible* case. Had it occurred in a professed work of fiction, as a description of the actual condition of one of the characters, we should have thought it remarkable not only for force but for truth. It is terrible, but not monstrous ; we can imagine a man feeling and doing all that is described. But when we are enquiring into the actual and ordinary effects of solitary confinement upon the mind of a prisoner, we are constrained to ask Mr. Dickens what authority he has for his many facts ? How does he know that prisoners are affected in this manner ? And, above all, how does he know that it is the general case ? He will say that he saw it in their faces ; they had all the same expression ; and that expression told him the whole story. But he should at least show that his interpretation of the countenance was corroborated by other indications of less doubtful character. Let us refer to the individual sufferers whom he saw and conversed with in several stages of punishment, and see whether their demeanour (as he himself describes it) accords with his supposition. There are but nine cases of which he gives any detailed report : we will take them all, placing them however in our own order. First, a German who had been brought in the day before—he was imploring for work. Second, an English thief, who had been in only a few days ; still savage. These two cases may be set aside : the effects of the system not having had time to show themselves. Third, a man convicted as a receiver of stolen goods ; but who denied his guilt. He had been in for six years, and was to remain three more. " He stopped his work when we went in, took off his spectacles, and answered freely to everything that was said to him. . . . He wore a paper hat of his own making, and was pleased to have it noticed and commended. He had very ingeniously manufactured a sort of Dutch clock from some disregarded odds and ends ; and his vinegar bottle served for the pendulum. Seeing me interested in this contrivance, he looked up at it with a great deal of pride, and said that he had been thinking of improving it, and that he hoped the hammer and a little piece of broken glass beside it would play music before long. He had extracted some colours from the yarn with which he worked, and painted a few poor figures on the wall." Surely

this is not the demeanour, nor these the ways, of a man whose
spirit is crushed and faculties destroyed—who suffers day and
night from horrible fancies. Fourth, a German imprisoned for
larceny; has been in for two years, and has three to come.
"With colours prepared in the same manner, |he had painted
every inch of the walls and ceiling quite beautifully. He had
laid out the few feet of ground behind with exquisite neatness,
and had made a little bed in the centre, which looked, by the by,
like a grave. The taste and ingenuity he had displayed in every
thing were most extraordinary." Here again. is very strange
evidence of the destructive effects of solitude upon the faculties.
Mr. Dickens goes on, it is true, to assure us that "he never saw
such a picture of forlorn affliction and distress of mind;" that
"his heart bled for him," etc. And very unhappy he may well
have been; people are not sent to prison to be made happy; but
the question is, whether he was the worse or the better for it.
Fifth, a negro burglar, notorious for his boldness and hardihood,
and for the number of previous convictions—*his time nearly out.*
He was at work making screws. "He entertained us with a
long account of his achievements, which he narrated with such
infinite relish that he actually seemed to lick his lips as he told
us racy anecdotes of stolen plate," etc. Here, at any rate, we
have a man who has not been made too miserable. Sixth, a
man, of whom we are told no more than that he was allowed to
keep rabbits as an indulgence; that he came out of his cell with
one in his breast, and that Mr. Dickens thought it hard to say
which was the nobler animal of the two. Seventh, "a poet,
who, *after doing two days' work in every four-and-twenty hours,*
one for himself and one for the prison, *wrote verses* about ships,
(he was by trade a mariner,) and 'the maddening wine-cup,' and
his friends at home." Here again! Mr. Dickens must have
selected his examples very oddly—or one would think that
solitary confinement called out a man's resources instead of
paralyzing them. Eighth; at last we come to a case (probably
the case) in point: a sailor who had been confined for *eleven
years,* and would be free in a few months. Mr. Dickens does
indeed here draw the picture of a man stupefied by suffering;
and we can well believe that the picture is just. But the most

strenuous advocates of the solitary system will hardly maintain that there may not be too much of it. Try a man who has been in *two* years, and is going to be released next day, and see whether *his* case is hopeless. And here we have him; number nine. "I have the face of this man before me now. It is almost more memorable in its happiness than the other faces in their misery. How easy and how natural was it for him to say that the system was a good one; and that the time went 'pretty quick considering;' and that, when a man once felt he had offended the law and must satisfy it, 'he got along somehow;' and so forth!" Upon women Mr. Dickens acknowledges that the effect of this punishment is different. He thinks it quite as wrong and cruel in their case; but admits that their faces are humanized and refined by it, and thinks it may be "because of their *better nature*, which is *elicited in solitude*."

Upon the question at issue, we offer no opinion; but with these discrepancies between Mr. Dickens's facts and fancies, we can hardly be rash in saying that his authority, great as it is, should not be taken as decisive. Commending the matter, therefore, to the further consideration of the inspectors of prisons, we shall return to our own proper subject; which is the character of the American people as expressed in their civil institutions. In the case of this Philadelphia prison, Mr. Dickens's objections are confined to the principle. To the intentions, motives, and characters of those who are concerned in the management of it, as well as to the efficacy of the arrangements, he gives unqualified praise.

Another thing on which the true character of a people in its substantial qualities must be expected to impress itself, is the administration of justice; and we wish that Mr. Dickens had frequented the courts a little more. Except on extraordinary occasions, politics and party find no business there; and where that is the case, the ablest man will naturally have the best place yielded to him, and the true interests (as distinguished from the fleeting inclinations) of the public will be consulted in all forms and proceedings; and in this, after all, consists the true health of the body politic. Let person and property be secured from violence, and let affairs be equitably adjusted

between man and man, and what reasonable person would grudge
his legislators their long speeches, their personal altercations,
or even their spittoons ?   From the scanty notices on this head
scattered through these volumes, we should infer that America
has no reason to shrink from this test.   The high character of
the Supreme Court is notorious through Europe.   And Mr.
Dickens tells us that in every place he visited. the judges were
men of high character and attainments ; which is saying much,
considering that in some of the States they are, we believe,
annually elected by the people.   Of their modes of proceeding
he tells us nothing beyond the general picturesque effect; and
we are left to infer from his silence, that the want of wigs and
gowns, and of raised platforms for witnesses and prisoners, does
not obstruct the course of justice.

The condition of the Church in America is another thing
which should throw great light on the character of the people ;
for in this also politics do not interfere : each party can do as it
pleases, and therefore no two need quarrel.   Unfortunately there
is a great want of sound information on this subject in England ;
the popular notion of the style of religious worship in America
being built, we believe, upon Mrs. Trollope's account of a *Revival*.
Mr. Dickens does not tell us much : but from what he does say
we should imagine that the prevailing character of the Church in
New England, has more of old Puritanism in it than of modern
Methodism ; and we have heard it maintained by gentlemen
who have resided in America for months together, and visited
different places of worship, that they have rarely met with any
symptoms of fanaticism or sycophancy in the preacher, or of
enthusiasm in the congregation ; but that the service, whatever
the persuasion, was generally characterized by decency and
dulness.

Of the system of education in the United States and the
provision for it (which should stand, perhaps, next in order as
an illustration of the social character), Mr. Dickens says but
little.   We hear occasionally of a college or a school, and we
gather generally that sufficient provision is made by each State
to enable every citizen to receive some degree of education.   The
proportion of adults who cannot read and write is consequently

extremely small; and among these we believe there are scarcely
any native Americans. Beyond this fact, which is of great importance, we can learn nothing that is much to our purpose. We
could have wished to know, first, the amount of knowledge and
the kind of intellectual cultivation which a man must have, in
order to take rank in general opinion as a well-educated man;
and, next, the style and amount of accomplishments which are
requisite to *distinguish* him in that rank. This would show in
what direction the great body of the intellect of the country is
working. It would also be very interesting to know something
about the composition of American libraries, especially private
ones. What kind of books do you find *permanently* established
on the shelves in a gentleman's study, and of these which appear
to have been most used? We say permanently, because it is of
much less consequence to know which among the publications
of the day are the most popular. These are read, as newspapers
are, not because they are congenial to the taste, but because
reading is fashionable, and they are of the newest fashion. Their
universal popularity indicates little in the national character
beyond a general appetite for light stimulants, and produces
little alteration in it, except perhaps some general debilitation
from swallowing such a deluge of slops. But for the most
part, we believe this kind of literature passes through the mind
with as little effect upon it for good or for evil as the conversation
of a morning caller. It is the favourite, not the fashionable
book that betrays the character of the man; and it is the book
which works itself into public favour *against* the fashion that
indicates the character of the people. That the miscellaneous
writings of Mr. Carlyle had been collected and printed in
America before his name was generally known in England is a
fact which tells much more about the intellectual and spiritual
capacities of the people, than we can infer from knowing that
the whole brood of New Burlington Street are circulated as fast
as they come out for an annual subscription of a few dollars.
The character of the native periodical literature of the costlier
class, and therefore of more limited circulation, would throw
further light on the matter; for it would show not only what the
more select class of readers will pay for, but what the better

class of writers can produce. The North American Review, and the New York, for instance, will give a juster, as well as a higher idea of the tendencies and prospects of American literature, than the most ambitious and elaborate pamphlets, speeches, and state papers—all of which are addressed to a wider, but a lower circle.

Whether Mr. Dickens has much considered the subject of American literature in its true bearings, we are not informed. From these volumes, we can only gather that he is deeply read in their newspapers, the character of which he denounces in his bitterest, and by no means his best, style. Of the justice of his censures, not having ourselves gone through the nauseous course of reading, by which he has qualified himself to speak, we can form no opinion. We shall only say, that, looking at the condition of our own Daily Press, and imagining what it would be were it turned loose in a land of cheap printing and no stamp duties—where everybody could read, and everybody took a part in politics ; and without any capital city in which public opinion might gather to a head and express itself with authority—we can readily believe it to be true in the full extent. Thanks to London, which concentrates and represents the feelings of the British people, the leading London journals (and from them the provincial Press throughout the country takes its tone) are held under some restraint. Gross violations of manners are not countenanced, and wanton slander of private persons would not be tolerated. Moreover, the enormous amount of information which is demanded of an English newspaper, cannot be supplied at first hand without a costly establishment and machinery ; and this, requiring large capital to start with, excludes the worst class of adventurers from competition, and insures in the proprietor that kind and amount of respectability which in England always accompanies substance. A man with something to lose will not offend the feelings of the mass of his customers ; a man with nothing cannot get up a paper which has any chance of general circulation. We fear, however, that it is impossible to answer for more than this. Private houses, we trust, are (from the stamped Press at least) secure. But what conspicuous public man can be insured against the most malignant slander from one party, and the grossest adulation from the other—both equally unprincipled? What measure of what party was ever discussed by the Daily Press, on either side, upon its real merits, or with a desire to represent it truly? What misrepresentation is too gross for our most respectable newspapers to take up? What rumour too injurious and too ill-founded for them to spread? What sophism so palpable, that if it can be used with effect to damage the character of a political opponent, they will not employ it? And the worst is, that in the guilt of this, the Respectability of England is directly implicated. It cannot be said that the disease is incident to liberty, and must be borne with; for, strange to say, this kind of licentious writing (known as it is, and thoroughly understood to be licentious), is what the great mass of news *readers* like. The writer has no interest in his malice; he may be a very good-humoured man, with no wish to injure anybody. But the readers must have what they call *vigour*. Their party spirit must be at once roused and gratified by powerful attacks and powerful vindications. A leading article, written in a spirit of candour and justice (unless it be known to proceed from some responsible quarter, in which case it has a separate and superior interest), is felt to be insipid. It is true that the influence of these compositions is not so great as might appear at first, because they impose on nobody; everybody knows that they are full of falsehoods. Convict a newspaper of the grossest intentional misrepresentation, and which of its "constant readers" will be shocked? Their influence is, however, considerable, and, so far as it goes, most pernicious. We cannot but regard the condition of our own Daily Press as a morning and evening witness against the moral character of the people; for if this kind of scurrility were as distasteful to the public as the grosser kinds of licentiousness are, it would at once disappear. That its condition is still worse in America, we can, for the reasons above indicated, easily believe; but we doubt whether it be fair to draw the same inference from the fact as to the moral tastes and feelings of the people; for the Respectability of America, not having the same means of expressing its will that the Respectability of England has, cannot be held in the same degree answerable. In the mean time, we hope that

Mr. Dickens is mistaken as to the degree in which the Press in the United States expresses and influences the general feeling. We cannot but think that, if his description of it be just, the strength of the poison must act as an antidote. Does any well-educated man in America read these papers *with respect?*

Among other circumstances from which something as to the social characteristics of the people may be safely inferred, certain definite and generally established regulations of society may be mentioned; such, for instance, as the courtesy which everybody is expected, as a matter of course, to pay to women and to strangers. And we should be inclined to draw very favourable inferences from the fact, that in all public places, including public conveyances, a woman is entitled to the best place, *occupied or unoccupied;* for possession on the part of the man goes for nothing; and also from the courtesies of the Custom House, which, we believe, all foreigners will bear witness to. Captain Hamilton, indeed, was so possessed with the notion that this business could not be transacted without intolerable annoyance, that he kept away. But Captain Basil Hall gives a pleasant anecdote, to show in how gentlemanly a manner the thing may be done. And Mr. Dickens commends to our special consideration and imitation the " attention, politeness, and good-humour, with which the Custom House officers at Boston discharged their duty."

We have now nearly exhausted these volumes of the information which they supply, available for the purpose with which we set out. Of the manners of the mass of the people, Mr. Dickens gives many amusing illustrations; most of which have been already quoted in various publications, and have made us all very merry. It is but justice to him, however, to say, that he saw all these things in their true light; and that, while indulging his sense of the ludicrous by a hearty English laugh, he was not betrayed by them into any foolish conclusions, or illiberal (we wish we could add un-English) contempt. The following sensible remarks are worth extracting, not because they tell us anything which is not obvious to any man who thinks; but because so few people trouble themselves with thinking about the matter. The scene is Sandusky, at the south-western extremity of Lake Erie.

" We put up at a comfortable little hotel. . . . . . Our host, who was very attentive, and anxious to make us comfortable, was a handsome, middle-aged man, who had come to this town from New England, in which part of the country he was 'raised.' When I say that he constantly walked in and out of the room with his hat on, and stopped to converse in the same free-and-easy state, and lay down on our sofa, and pulled his newspaper out of his pocket and read it at his ease—I merely mention these traits as characteristic of the country ; not at all as being matter of complaint, or as having been disagreeable to me. I should undoubtedly be offended by such proceedings at home, because there they are not the custom, and where they are not, they would be imperti-nences. But in America the only desire of a good-natured fellow of this kind is to treat his guests hospitably and well : and I had no more right, and I can truly say no more disposition, to measure his conduct by our English rule and standard, than I had to quarrel with him for not being of the exact stature which would qualify him for admission into the Queen's Grenadier Guards. As little inclina-tion had I to find fault with a funny old lady, who was an upper domestic in this establishment, and who, when she came to wait upon us at any meal, sat her-self down comfortably in the most convenient chair, and, producing a large pin to pick her teeth with, remained performing that ceremony, and steadfastly re-garding us meanwhile with much gravity and composure (now and then pressing us to eat a little more), until it was time to clear away. It was enough for us, that whatever we wished done was done with great civility and readiness, and a desire to oblige, not only here but everywhere else; and that all our wants were in general zealously anticipated."—Vol. ii. p. 170.

Further on in the volume, a good story about an American bootmaker, which has been quoted everywhere, is introduced by the following general remark, which has not yet, we believe, been anywhere quoted.

" The republican institutions of America undoubtedly leave the people to assert their self-respect and their equality ; but a traveller is bound to bear those institutions in his mind, and not hastily to resent the near approach of a class of strangers, who at home would keep aloof. This characteristic, when it is tinctured by no foolish pride, and stops short of no honest service, never offended me ; and I very seldom, if ever, experienced its rude or unbecoming display."— Vol. ii. p. 300.

The political condition of the United States has been dis-cussed, on various occasions, in this Journal. Mr. Dickens's *Notes* do not throw any new light upon it ; and, as no peculiar interest attaches to his opinions on such subjects, we do not feel called upon to criticise them. We have treated the work gravely, out of deference to the gravity of the subject; and partly because the superior attractiveness and quotability of the lighter parts are likely, we fear, to give a false impression of the tone and

spirit of the whole.   In thus endeavouring to collect the substance of his more serious observations, we have no doubt, in a
great measure, lost sight of the prevailing character and spirit
of his book.   But of this it is enough to say, that it leaves our
opinion of Mr. Dickens's powers unaltered.

NOTE.

THERE being a passage in this article which brought upon the editor of the
Edinburgh Review a warm remonstrance, and the necessity (as he fancied) of
publicly expressing regret for having admitted into it an unwarranted and
injurious statement; and the fact that such a charge was so made and so
acknowledged being now to be found without further explanation in more than
one book that is likely to hold its place in literature; I cannot let the article go
forth as mine without a counter-statement on my own part, which I have not yet
had any opportunity to make.

It was undertaken at short notice by the editor's express desire; who considered it important that a review of the book should appear in his next number;
his motive for applying to me being partly that I had lately returned from
Washington, where I had spent four months shortly after Mr. Dickens passed
through, and partly that I thought the book had merits which entitled it to
graver and more respectful treatment than it had generally met with.   When
he saw what I had done, he was, for his own part, very well pleased with it.
One or two short passages, which he " thought would be reckoned rather severe,"
he struck out; and (though " some would think it too favourable,") he did not
expect it to " quite please the author;" but he accepted it as " done in the
proper spirit, and with judgment and discrimination," and as " altogether an
instructive and agreeable article "—and this after reading it through in the proof
and making such alterations as he thought expedient.

That my criticism of his book should " quite please the author," was not to
be expected.   Though both in praising what was good and in passing by what
was not so good I had gone quite as far as I felt justified in going, to *him* it
would naturally seem short measure; and I should not have been surprised to
find him treating it with contempt.   But I was not prepared for a charge of
malicious misrepresentation : least of all in the point which he selected as the
ground for such a charge;—which was the allusion to his labours in the cause of
international copyright,—labours which I had all the while been thinking of
with the most respectful sympathy.   Where the offence was, I am still unable
to perceive : but the immediate effect was a letter to the *Times*, written to
clear himself of what by some strange misconception he took for an implied
imputation of something discreditable.   Quoting the words of the article,—" He
went out, if we are rightly informed, as a kind of missionary in the cause of
international copyright "—" I deny it wholly," he wrote.   " He [the writer of

the article] is wrongly informed, and reports without enquiry a piece of information which I could only characterise by using one of the shortest and strongest words in the language."—(Forster's Life of Dickens, ii. 29).

Whatever the offence, the offender was myself only; and I lost no time in writing to the editor: with what result the following extracts will show. I quote in my own part from the rough drafts, which are all I have; but if the fair copies differed from them, the difference was only verbal.

To the Editor.

16 January.

"That Mr. Dickens should be so angry, (see his letter in to-day's *Times*), I certainly did not expect, and I only wish to say that if you can set your relations with him right by mentioning my name as responsible for the article, I have not the least objection. I certainly never inquired of himself or any of his friends what he went to America for; but I think I may answer for it that, in America at least, there was a very general impression that he came chiefly to agitate for international copyright; insomuch that I distinctly remember seeing the word "mission" somewhere applied to his visit. And the tone of a letter which he wrote to a Washington paper before he left America, and still more of one which he addressed to the *Morning Chronicle* when he returned to England, was so much in accordance with the general impression that I never thought of doubting it."

From the Editor.

19 January.

"Whatever may be thought of the tone and taste of Dickens's letter, there can be no doubt that, as the statement was *rather* disparaging, and at any rate made without any *direct* authority, he had good reason to complain. He would not expect any false view of the object of his American visit *from me*, and I confess I am heartily sorry that a statement so uncalled for, and unwarranted, was made and published under my hand. I have written him at some length, and I have also given him, for *publication* if he thinks it worth while, a *retractation* of the offensive statement; expressing, however, that the writer had no intention whatever of injuring or disparaging him. I have not given your name, but I have, as the defence of the writer of the article, quoted what you urge to me as the grounds of your belief. Having retracted the allegation, and laid before him the grounds of belief, I thought I did enough without giving your name."

To the Editor.

21 January.

"In case you propose to insert a note in your next number retracting the aspersion (if aspersion it must be called), I think it would be desirable to add (what is strictly true) that it never crossed the mind of the writer that the word 'missionary' could be understood as implying any reproach or disparagement. Where the offence should be I must confess myself still unable to guess; unless a 'missionary' be supposed to mean a man acting under orders, or for hire,—which I do not think it does. To me the word suggests no ideas but those of self-sacrifice and devotion,—labour voluntarily undertaken for the benefit of others. Neither should it be over-looked that the statement is qualified with an 'if.' I confess that 'if we are rightly *informed*' does look as if the statement had been made on the strength of some definite information, and not merely of general notoriety. But did it stand so in my manuscript? Surely I wrote, '*He is understood* to have gone out, etc.,' or something to that effect. It is so written in my draft, and I cannot conceive why I should have altered it."

This ended the matter, as far as I had any part in it. As I was not to appear and answer in my own person, I could interfere no further. The retractation, with which I had nothing to do (and which was harmless enough; for though very apologetic in tone, it *admitted* nothing more than an erroneous impression as to the *motive* of Dickens's visit to America, which nobody but himself could know) appeared in the next number of the Edinburgh Review, and I heard no more.

I now find however that on the same day on which I offered these suggestions as to the form of retractation, Mr. Dickens was expressing his own feelings as to the matter to be retracted. How the editor had put it to him I do not know; but the effect of the communication will be seen in the following letter, which appears among the selections from the editor's correspondence, recently published.

January 21st, 1843.

MY DEAR SIR,

Let me hasten to say in the fullest and most explicit manner that you have acted a most honourable, open, fair, and manly part in the matter of my complaint, for which I beg you to accept my best thanks, and the assurance of my friendship and regard. I would on no account publish the letter you have sent me for that purpose; as I conceive that by doing so I should not reciprocate the spirit in which you have written to me privately. But if you should upon consideration, think it not inexpedient to set the Review right with regard to this point of fact, by a note in the next number, I should be glad to see it there.

In reference to the article itself, it did by repeating this statement, hurt my feelings excessively; and is, in this respect, I still conceive, most unworthy of its author. I am at a loss to divine who its author is. I *know* he read in some cut-throat American paper this and other monstrous statements, which I could at any time have converted into sickening praise by the payment of some fifty dollars. I know that he is perfectly aware that his statement in the Review, in corroboration of these lies, will be disseminated through the whole of the United States; and that my contradiction will never be heard of. And though I care very little for the opinion of any person who will set the statement of an American editor (almost invariably an atrocious scoundrel) against my character and conduct, such as they may be; still my sense of justice does revolt from this most cavalier and careless exhibition of me to a whole people as a traveller under false pretences and a disappointed intriguer. The better the acquaintance with America, the more defenceless and inexcusable such conduct is. For I solemnly declare (and appeal to any man but the writer of this paper, who has travelled in that country, for confirmation of my statement) that the source from which he drew the "information" so recklessly put forth again in England, is infinitely more obscene, disgusting, and brutal, than the very worst Sunday newspaper that has ever been printed in Great Britain. Conceive the Edinburgh Review quoting *The Satirist* or *The Man about Town*, as an authority against a man with one grain of honour, or feather-weight of reputation.

With regard to yourself, let me say again that I thank you with all sincerity and heartiness; and fully acquit you of anything but kind and generous intentions towards me. In proof of which, I do assure you that I am even more desirous than before to write for the Review, and to find some topic which would at once please me and you.

Always faithfully yours,

CHARLES DICKENS.

I do not know whether the editor was content to accept "acquittal" on these terms. His letter to me was written before he received this; and the only notice taken of it, so far as I am aware, was the apologetic note in the next number of the Review, which implied nothing more than a regret that "Mr. Dickens's visit to America" had been, through misinformation, "ascribed to an erroneous cause." My name not having been mentioned, I was not held to be a party concerned, and remained in happy ignorance of Mr. Dickens's opinion of "the article itself" and of all he "knew" about the writer of it.

But the case is now changed. Appearing in the character of the person against whom these remarks were directed,—as I now do,—I feel that some explanation may be expected from me. The explanation is simple, and (as far as my proceedings are concerned) complete; though it leaves the cause of offence in him more inexplicable than ever.

"The source from which I drew my information" was neither an editor nor a newspaper, but the general conversation of Washington in the spring and summer of 1842; when Congress was sitting, and when therefore it contained samples of American society from all points of the compass. When I arrived there, in April, Dickens and the international copyright were among the commonest topics of conversation; and as he had made no secret of the part he took everybody knew and talked of it. That he entered into the cause of international copyright with what I should call the spirit of a missionary—meaning a man who goes into far countries to preach the gospel—I knew, as I know that Mr. Gladstone took a leading part in the agitation for autonomy in Bulgaria. That he went to America *for the purpose* of helping in that work, I *inferred* from the coincidence of time and place; just as when I hear that Mr. Gladstone has made a speech at St. James's Hall, I infer that he went thither for the purpose of speaking. And since it was obviously impossible for me to *know* what Mr. Dickens's private intentions were, except by putting the question to himself —which he would have thought odd from a stranger—it seemed impossible that anybody could take it for anything more or other than an inference. Nor was the question itself a matter of importance. The material fact was that when he arrived in America a movement was on foot for an International Copyright Act; that he went into it immediately with all his heart, and that it was the business in which he appeared to take the greatest interest, and did play the most conspicuous part, during the first half of his visit. So much the people who formed the society of Washington during the session of 1842 could know and did know; and no one who was living among them could doubt it. To this fact I alluded merely as a thing to be remembered in comparing his advantages and disadvantages as an observer in a foreign country. A cause which interested him so deeply must have interfered, I thought, with his study of the place and the people generally. But I especially mentioned it as a good cause—too good indeed to have much chance of prevailing under the conditions; and so far was I from seeing anything unworthy of him in going from England to America to promote it, that I did in fact look upon his zeal in this business as the feature of his visit in which he showed to most advantage.

What he secretly believed my "statement" to be or to imply, and what he was himself to be understood as "denying" when he denied what he called

T

" *it*," I should have liked to know ; but I had no opportunity of asking. And as both his own letters leave both points entirely unexplained, it seems hopeless now to inquire what offended him, or what the " point of fact " was in which he wished " the Review to be set right." All that is material, however, in the statement itself still admits of easy and ample justification by evidence even more unquestionable than that upon which it was originally made. If anyone wishes to know what I mean by a man who " went out as a kind of missionary in the cause of international copyright," and made the promotion of it " his main employment " during the short period of his visit, let him read the following extracts from Dickens's own Life and Letters. He landed at Boston, it will be remembered, on the 22nd of January 1842.

1.

" His second letter," says his biographer, " was dated from the Carleton Hotel, New York, on the 14th of February ; but its only allusion of any public interest was to the beginning of his agitation of the question of international copyright. He went to America with no express intention of starting this question in any way, and certainly with no belief that such remarks upon it as a person in his situation could alone be expected to make would be resented strongly by any section of the American people. But he was not long left with doubt on this head. He had spoken upon it twice publicly, ' to the great indignation of some of the editors here, who are attacking me for so doing right and left.' On the other hand, all the best men had assured him that, if only at once followed up in England, the blow struck might bring about a change in the law ; and yielding to the pleasant hope that the best men could be a match for the worst, he urged me to enlist on his side what force I could ; and in particular, as he had made Scott's claim his war-cry, to bring Lockhart into the field." Vol. i. 291.

2.

" I spoke, as you know, of international copyright at Boston. I spoke of it again at Hartford. My friends were paralyzed with wonder at such audacious daring. . . . It is nothing that of all men living I am the greatest loser by it " [*i.e.*, by the " atrocious state of the law"]. " It is nothing that I have a claim to speak and be heard. . . . I wish you could have seen the faces that I saw down both sides of the table at Hartford, when I began to talk about Scott. I wish you could have heard how I gave it out. My blood so boiled as I thought of the monstrous injustice that I felt as if I were twelve feet high when I thrust it down their throats.

" I had no sooner made that second speech than such an outcry began (for the purpose of deterring me from doing the like in this city) as an Englishman can have no notion of. Anonymous letters, verbal dissuasions, newspaper attacks. . . . came pouring in upon me every day. The dinner committee were so dismayed that they besought me not to pursue the subject, *although they everyone agreed with me.* I answered that I would, that nothing should deter me. . . . Accordingly when the night came I asserted my right, with all the means I could command to give it dignity in face, manner, and words ; and I believe that if you could have seen and heard me," etc. Ibid. p. 294.

3.

"The effect of all this agitation at least has been to awaken a great sensation on both sides of the subject; the respectable newspapers and reviews taking up the cudgels as strongly in my favour as the others have done against me." Ibid. p. 303.

4.

"I should like to have a short letter addressed to me by the principal English authors who signed the international copyright petition, expressive of their sense that I have done my duty to the cause. I am sure I deserve it, but I don't wish it on that ground. It is because its publication in the best journals here would unquestionably do great good. As the gauntlet is down, let us go on. Clay has already sent a gentleman to me express from Washington (where I shall be on the 6th or 7th of next month) to declare his strong interest in the matter, his cordial approval of the "manly" course I have held in reference to it, and his desire to stir in it, if possible. I have lighted up such a blaze that a meeting of the foremost people on the other side (very respectfully and properly conducted in reference to me personally, I am bound to say) was held in this town 'tother night. And it would be a thousand pities if we did not strike as hard as we can, now that the iron is so hot." Ibid. p. 301.

5.

"I have in my portmanteau a petition for an international copyright, signed by all the best American writers, with Washington Irving at their head. They have requested me to hand it to Clay for presentation, and to back it with any remarks which I may think fit to offer. So 'hoo-roar for the principle, as the money-lender said ven he vooldn't renoo the bill.'" Ibid. p. 310.

6.

"You will see by my other letter. . . . . how there is war to the knife about the international copyright, and how I will speak about it, and decline to be put down." Ibid. p. 312.

7.

A letter from Mr. Carlyle to Dickens, 26th March 1842, begins :—"We learn by the newspapers that you everywhere in America stir up the question of international copyright, and thereby awake huge dissonance, where all else were triumphant unison for you." Ibid. p. 313.

8.

"He" [Mr. Preston, a senator] "so solemnly assures me that the international copyright shall and will be passed, that I almost begin to hope; and I shall be entitled to say, if it be, that I have brought it about. You have no idea how universal the discussion of its merits and demerits has become ; or how eager for a change I have made a portion of the people." Ibid. p. 330.

That to represent the cause of international copyright as Mr. Dickens's primary object and main employment during his visit was " to exhibit him to a whole people as a traveller under false pretences and a disappointed intriguer," is an assertion in which I can see no meaning. For the story, as I understood it, left no room (unless he could have been suspected of secretly wishing the cause to be defeated) for so much as a suspicion either of intrigue or false pretences. But his fancy was working in a wrong direction, and it may be that something had passed between him and one of the editors which made my words seem to mean more than they expressed. *What* else they can have seemed to mean, I cannot guess. But before I should have felt justified in retracting anything at all material which they either expressed or implied, or could have suggested to any-body but himself, I must have had his own express and personal authority for stating that he did *not* take a leading part in the agitation for an International Copyright Act during the first two months of his visit.

IX.

TENNYSON'S POEMS.

————◦✦◦————

[The following article was written in pursuance of an engagement, made when Mr. Tennyson's two first volumes were out of print, that if he would publish a new edition I would try to get leave to review it in the *Edinburgh*. Upon my assurance that, though an intimate friend and an advanced believer, I would not commit the Review to any praises or prophecies that would endanger its reputation, the editor consented. But though I kept carefully within bounds, I found by an alteration in the last paragraph, slight in itself, but considerable in effect and significance, that I had after all gone a little further than he thought prudent. The credit of the Review not being now at stake, I have taken the reputation of the imprudence upon myself and restored the original reading.]

ONE of the severest tests by which a poet can try the true worth of his book, is to let it continue for two or three years out of print. The first flush of popularity cannot be trusted. Admiration is contagious, and means often little more than sympathy with the general feeling—the pleasure of being in the fashion. A book which is praised in all the Reviews, thousands will not only buy but be delighted with; and thus a judicious publisher may contrive, by keeping it cleverly in people's way, to preserve for years a popularity which is merely accidental and ephemeral. But if this be all, the interest in it will cease as soon as it becomes difficult to procure. Let a man ask for it two or three times without getting it, he will take to something else; and his curiosity, unless founded on something more substantial than a wish to see what others are looking at, and a disposition to be

* "Poems," by Alfred Tennyson. 2 vols. 12mo. London, 1842. *Edinburgh Review*, April, 1843.

pleased with what others praise, will die away. If, on the other hand, a new edition be perseveringly demanded, and when it comes be eagerly bought, we may safely conclude that the work has something in it of abiding interest and permanent value; for then we know that many people have been so pleased or so edified by the reading that they cannot be content without the possession. To this severe test the author of the unpretending volumes before us has submitted an infant, and what seemed to many a baseless and precarious, reputation; and so well has it stood the test—for we understand that preparations are already making for another edition—as to give him an undeniable claim to the respectful attention of all critics.

The book must not be treated as one collection of poems, but as three separate ones, belonging to three different periods in the development of his mind, and to be judged accordingly. Mr. Tennyson's first book was published in 1830, when he was at college. His second followed in 1832. Their reception, though far from triumphant, was not inauspicious; for while they gained him many warm admirers, they were treated, even by those critics whose admiration, like their charity, begins and ends at home, as sufficiently notable to be worth some not unelaborate ridicule. The admiration and the ridicule served alike to bring them into notice, and they have both been for some years out of print. As many of these productions as Mr. Tennyson has cared to preserve are contained in the first volume of the present edition. The second consists entirely of poems not hitherto published; which, though composed probably at various intervals during the ten intervening years, have all, we presume, had the benefit of his latest correcting hand. In subject, style, and the kinds of excellence which they severally attain or aim at, they are at once so various and so peculiar, that we cannot affect to convey any adequate idea of the general character of the collection; unless we should go through the table of contents, giving as we go a description and a sample of each poem. Neither shall we trouble ourselves to assign to the author his exact rank among the poets of the day. We trust we have room enough in our hearts for as many true poets, each moving in his just and entire orbit, as the land can produce; we are not, therefore, concerned to inquire how far one differs from another in glory :

Πάντα δέ τ' εἴδεται ἄστρα· γέγηθε δέ τε φρένα ποιμήν.

We shall content ourselves with endeavouring to form a true estimate of the man himself, and his claims upon the public attention, both for what he has done and for what is to be expected of him hereafter ;—which, if we are not much mistaken, (and supposing, what as yet however we have no absolute assurance of, that he possesses the one great faculty of holding all his other faculties in full and sustained exertion,) is something that will make all he has yet produced appear only like preliminary essays and experiments. For the indications of improving taste and increasing power exhibited not only in the results of his later labours, but in the omission of some and the alteration of others among his earlier, lead us to infer that his faculties have not yet reached their highest development; and, even as they are now, he has not yet ventured upon a subject large enough to bring them all into play together.

His earliest published volume—though it contains one or two poems, as "Mariana" for instance, which must always rank among his very best—is to be referred to rather as a point from which to measure his subsequent progress, than for specimens of what he is. The very vigour and abundance of a poet's powers will commonly be in his way at first, and produce faults. But such faults are by no means unpromising. Indeed it is better that the genius should be allowed to run rather wild and wanton during its nonage ; for a poet will hardly have the free command of his faculties when full grown, unless he allow them free play during growth. Too severe a repression of their young activities will stunt and cripple them, so that their aid will not be forthcoming when it is wanted ; while, on the other hand, a free indulgence of them will bring in the end a double advantage— they will be not only more fully developed by exercise, but (having sown their wild oats) more readily brought into discipline when business begins.

Regarded as a crop of wild oats, Mr. Tennyson's first collection of poems, as originally published, cannot but be accounted a production of unusual promise. The natural faults of youth—

exuberance, prodigality, lightness of heart and head, ingenuity wasted upon nothing, the want of sustained effort and a determined course, together with some vanities and fopperies—it may well afford to be charged with. The untried genius needed to be assured of its powers by putting them forth—to feel itself alive through all its capacities by living acts of creation. Hence his early efforts are, many of them, rather exercises than works—gymnastic exercises for the fancy, the intellect, the imagination, the power of language, and even for the feelings—valuable, as the games and tasks of schoolboys are valuable, not for the thing done, but for the practice, strength, and dexterity acquired in doing it. Here we have a succession of vague melodies, in which the power of musical expression tries how far it can go ; there a group of abstract ideas, turned, for the satisfaction of the creative genius, into shapes ready for the sculptor :—here a conceit, in which the fancy admires its own ingenuity ; there a thought, of no great worth or novelty perhaps, but expressed with curious felicity :—presently we find ourselves surrounded by a bevy of first-loves—Adelines, Madelines, and Lilians, more than we can remember—phantoms of female grace in every style, but all belonging to the land of shadows : then again come delineations of every state of mind, from that of the mystic who has nearly reached the highest circle, to the " second-rate sensitive mind not at unity with itself ; " and of every variety of untried being, on earth or in water, or on the earth under the water, from the grasshopper with his " short youth, sunny and free," to the kraken sleeping for ages in the central depths, among millennial sponges and giant-finned polypi : whilst at intervals we recognize a genuine touch of common humanity—a " Character," (p. 44)—a " Circumstance," (p. 67)—or a sketch truly drawn from homeliest nature, which needs, however, no fancy dress to make it beautiful, but will remain for ever fresh when all that " airy stream of lively portraiture " has faded before the increasing daylight :—

> " No matter what the sketch might be ;
> Whether the high field on the bushless Pike,
> Or even a sand-built ridge
> Of heaped hills that mound the sea,

> Overblown with murmurs harsh,
> Or even a lowly cottage whence we see
> Stretch'd wide and wild the waste enormous marsh,
> Where from the frequent bridge,
> Like emblems of infinity,
> The trenched waters run from sky to sky."
> * * * * * *
> " Come from the woods that belt the gray hill-side,
> The seven elms, the poplars four,
> That stand beside my father's door;
> And chiefly from the brook that loves
> To purl o'er matted cress and ribbed sand,
> Or dimple in the dark of rushy coves,
> Drawing into his narrow earthen urn,
>   In every elbow and turn,
> The filter'd tribute of the rough woodland.
>   O! hither lead thy feet!
> Pour round mine ears the livelong bleat
> Of the thick-fleeced sheep from wattled folds,
>   Upon the ridged wolds,
> When the first matin-song hath waken'd loud,
> Over the dark dewy earth forlorn,
> What time the amber morn
> Forth gushes from beneath a low-hung cloud."

Ode to Memory, vol. i. p. 34.

In the course of these exercises, though Mr. Tennyson may not have produced much that he now sets any high value on, yet he made himself master of a great variety of instruments; and his next appearance, only two years after, showed manifest symptoms of the benefit derived both from what he had acquired and from what he had thrown off. The superiority of his second collection of poems lay not so much in the superior workman-ship, (it contained perhaps fewer that were equally perfect in their kind,) as in the general aim and character. If some of the blossom was gone, it was amply repaid by the more certain promise of fruit. Not only was the aim generally larger, the subjects and interest more substantial, and the endeavour more sustained, but the original and distinctive character of the man appeared more plainly. His genius was manifestly shaping a peculiar course for itself, and finding out its proper business; the moral soul was beginning more and more to assume its due predominance—not in the way of formal preaching, (the proper

vehicle of which is prose,)—but in the shape and colour which
his creations unconsciously took, and the feelings which they
were made insensibly to suggest. Considerable faults, however,
still remained; a tendency, for example, arising from the fulness
of a mind which had not yet learned to master its resources
freely, to overcrowd his composition with imagery; a habit also
(caused by that dissatisfaction with himself, which, so long as it
does not depress the spirits too much, a poet ought to cultivate
rather than to repress) of adding, altering, and retouching, till
in trying to improve the form he lost the spirit and freshness of
his work, and blurred the impression;—to which may be added
an over-indulgence in the luxuries of the senses—a profusion of
splendours, harmonies, perfumes, gorgeous apparel, luscious
meats and drinks, and such "creature comforts," which rather
pall upon the sense, and make the glories of the outward world a
little to obscure and overshadow the world within.

In all these respects, the decade during which Mr. Tennyson
has remained silent has wrought a great improvement. The
handling in his later pieces is much lighter and freer; the
interest deeper and purer;—there is more humanity with less
imagery and drapery; a closer adherence to truth; a greater
reliance for effect upon the simplicity of nature. Moral and
spiritual traits of character are more dwelt upon, in place of
external scenery and circumstance. He addresses himself more
to the heart, and less to the ear and eye. This change, which is
felt in its results throughout the second volume, may in the
latter half of the first be traced in its process. The poems
originally published in 1832, are many of them largely altered;
generally with great judgment, and always with a view to strip
off redundances—to make the expression simpler and clearer, to
substitute thought for imagery, and substance for shadow. "The
Lady of Shalott," for instance, (p. 77) is stripped of all her
finery; her pearl garland, her velvet bed, her royal apparel, and
her "blinding diamond bright," are all gone; and certainly, in
the simple white robe which she now wears, her native beauty
shows to much greater advantage. The "Miller's Daughter,"
again, is greatly enriched by the introduction of the mother of
the lover; and the following beautiful stanzas (which many

people, however, will be ill satisfied to miss) are displaced, to make room for beauty of a much higher order :—

> "Remember you the clear moonlight
> That whiten'd all the eastern ridge,
> When o'er the water, dancing white,
> I stepp'd upon the old mill-bridge?
> I heard you whisper from above,
> A lute-toned whisper, 'I am here!'
> I murmur'd, 'Speak again, my love,
> The stream is loud: I cannot hear!'

> "I heard, as I have seem'd to hear
> When all the under-air was still,
> The low voice of the glad new year
> Call to the freshly-flowered hill.
> I heard, as I have often heard
> The nightingale in leafy woods
> Call to its mate, when nothing stirr'd
> To left or right but falling floods."

These, we observe, are away; and the following graceful and tender picture, full of the spirit of English rural life, appears in their place. (The late squire's son, we should premise, is bent on marrying the daughter of the wealthy miller :—)

> "And slowly was my mother brought
> To yield consent to my desire:
> She wished me happy, but she thought
> I might have look'd a little higher;
> And I was young—too young to wed:
> 'Yet must I love her for your sake;
> Go fetch your Alice here,' she said;
> Her eyelid quiver'd as she spake.

> "And down I went to fetch my bride:
> But, Alice, you were ill at ease;
> This dress and that by turns you tried,
> Too fearful that you should not please.
> I loved you better for your fears,
> I knew you could not look but well;
> And dews that would have fall'n in tears,
> I kiss'd away before they fell.

> "I watch'd the little flutterings,
> The doubt my mother would not see;
> She spoke at large of many things,
> And at the last she spoke of me;

And turning look'd upon your face,
  As near this door you sat apart,
And rose, and, with a silent grace
  Approaching, press'd you heart to heart.'
                    Vol. i. p. 109.

In the song of the "Lotos-Eaters"—which, as an expression
of the loathing of exertion supposed to be produced by that plant,
and as a picturesque and melodious assemblage of all images in
nature that can suggest or persuade repose, hardly admitted of
improvement—Mr. Tennyson has added some touches of deeper
significance, indicating the first effects of the physical disease
upon the moral and intellectual nature :—

  "Dear is the memory of our wedded lives,
  And dear the last embraces of our wives
  And their warm tears : but all hath suffer'd change ;
  For surely now our household hearths are cold :
  Our sons inherit us : our looks are strange :
  And we should come like ghosts to trouble joy.
  Or else the island princes over-bold
  Have eat our substance, and the minstrel sings
  Before them of the ten-years' war in Troy,
  And our great deeds, as half-forgotten things.
  Is there confusion in the little isle ?
  Let what is broken so remain,
  The Gods are hard to reconcile :
  'Tis hard to settle order once again.
  There *is* confusion worse than death,
  Trouble on trouble, pain on pain,
  Long labour unto aged breath,
  Sore task to hearts worn out with many wars,
  And eyes grown dim with gazing on the pilot-stars."
                    Vol. i. p. 182.

At the end of the same poem there will be found an alteration of similar tendency, but of still more awful import ; where
for the flow of triumphant enjoyment, in the contemplation of
merely sensual ease and luxurious repose, with which it originally closed, a higher strain is substituted, which is meant
apparently to show the effect of lotos-eating upon the religious
feelings.   The gods of the Lotos-eaters, it is worth knowing, are
altogether Lucretian.

Another instance, more convenient for quotation, of Mr.
Tennyson's growing tendency to seek deeper for sources of

interest is the third and concluding part (which is entirely new) of the " May Queen." Many of our readers are probably familiar with the first two parts of this poem; in the latter of which the natural pathos of the situation—a beautiful girl dying in her prime, before life has lost its freshness, before decay and sorrow have made her familiar with the thought of death—is wrought up with so much truth and tenderness, that there seemed to be little room for more. It is a picture of resignation to a fate felt to be a hard one—the reluctant abandonment of pleasures which she is content to resign since she needs must, but would fain be permitted to keep; the case of thousands, the rudest delineation of which must always be affecting. With Mr. Tennyson's treatment of it no fault can be found. The homely pleasures, the sports, the cares, the vanities of her little life—the familiar places she must leave, the familiar process of the seasons, hitherto bringing to the delighted spirit only a succession of delights, now sad and sacred because watched for the last time —all her shining world, as it was when she moved the centre of it, as it will be when she is no longer there—pass over her mind like shadows, and are touched with exquisite sweetness and simplicity. But he saw in the situation materials for a deeper and loftier strain. Hitherto so full of life, what should she know of death ? A blank negation it seemed; the non-existence to her of all that existed; no positive image. But as she grows familiar with the thought of total separation from all she knows, new interests disclose themselves, and death appears but as the passage to a new life. That life she has long known of, indeed, and looked forward to; but idly, as a thing far off, which did not yet practically concern her; a proposition assented to, but not comprehended; a book possessed and known to contain precious things, but not yet read—or at most read with a truant attention,

> " Like words
> That leave upon the still susceptive sense
> A message undeliver'd, till the mind
> Awakes to apprehensiveness, and takes it."

But now the formless void takes shape and substance as she gazes into it, and draws her whole spirit that way, until already

in imagination death is swallowed up in victory. The theme is
as trite as can be, and the treatment as simple; but it is not the
less original. There are probably not less than a thousand
persons now living who could have made elegant and touching
verses upon it—one set, perhaps, not greatly differing from
another. But of all the thousand poems we will venture to say
that not one would have resembled this:—

> " I thought to pass away before, and yet alive I am;
> And in the fields all round I hear the bleating of the lamb.
> How sadly, I remember, rose the morning of the year!
> To die before the snowdrop came, and now the violet's here.

> " O sweet is the new violet, that comes beneath the skies,
> And sweeter is the young lamb's voice to me that cannot rise,
> And sweet is all the land about, and all the flowers that blow,
> And sweeter far is death than life to me that long to go.

> " It seem'd so hard at first, mother, to leave the blessed sun,
> And now it seems as hard to stay, and yet His will be done!
> But still it can't be long, mother, before I find release;
> And that good man, the clergyman, he preaches words of peace.
>
>   *   *   *   *   *   *   *

> " He show'd me all the mercy, for he taught me all the sin.
> Now, though my lamp was lighted late, there's One will let me in:
> Nor would I now be well, mother, again, if that could be,
> For my desire is but to pass to Him that died for me.

> " I did not hear the dog howl, mother, or the death-watch beat,
> There came a sweeter token when the night and morning meet:
> But sit beside my bed, mother, and put your hand in mine,
> And Effie on the other side, and I will tell the sign.

> " All in the wild March-morning I heard the angels call;
> It was when the moon was setting, and the dark was over all;
> The trees began to whisper, and the wind began to roll,
> And in the wild March-morning I heard them call my soul.

> " For lying broad awake I thought of you and Effie dear;
> I saw you sitting in the house, and I no longer here;
> With all my strength I pray'd for both, and so I felt resign'd,
> And up the valley came a swell of music on the wind.

> " I thought that it was fancy, and I listen'd in my bed,
> And then did something speak to me—I know not what was said;
> For great delight and shuddering took hold of all my mind,
> And up the valley came again the music on the wind.

"But you were sleeping; and I said, 'It's not for them : it's mine.'
And if it comes three times, I thought, I take it for a sign.
And once again it came, and close beside the window bars,
Then seem'd to go right up to heaven and die among the stars.

*   *   *   *   *   *   *

"O look! the sun begins to rise, the heavens are in a glow;
He shines upon a hundred fields, and all of them I know.
And there I move no longer now and there his light may shine—
Wild flowers in the valley for other hands than mine.

"O sweet and strange it seems to me, that ere this day is done
The voice that now is speaking, may be beyond the sun—
For ever and for ever with those just souls and true—
And what is life, that we should moan ? why make we such ado ?

"For ever and for ever, all in a blessed home—
And there to wait a little while till you and Effie come—
To lie within the light of God, as I lie upon your breast—
And the wicked cease from troubling, and the weary are at rest."

These specimens may serve to show that the full blossom
which distinguished the "Poems chiefly Lyrical," contained no
deceitful promise. But it is a small thing that the genius possesses the command of all its instruments, if it be not itself in
tune with nature. All that is of true and lasting worth in poetry,
must have its root in a sound view of human life and the condition of man in the world; a just feeling with regard to the things
in which we are all concerned. Where this is not, the most con-
summate art can produce nothing which men will long care for—
where it is, the rudest will never want audience; for then nothing
is trivial—the most ordinary incidents of daily life are invested
with an interest as deep as the springs of emotion in the heart—
as deep as pity, and love, and fear, and awe. In this requisite
Mr. Tennyson will not be found wanting. The human soul, in
its infinite variety of moods and trials, is his favourite haunt;
nor can he dwell long upon any subject, however remote apparently from the scenes and objects of modern sympathy, without
touching some string which brings it within the range of our
common life. His moral views, whether directly or indirectly
conveyed, are healthy, manly, and simple; and the truth and
delicacy of his sentiments is attested by the depth of the pathos
which he can evoke from the commonest incidents, told in the

simplest manner, yet deriving all their interest from the manner of telling. See, for instance, the story of "Dora," (vol. ii. p. 33,) and "The Lord of Burleigh," (p. 201). What is there in these that should so move us? Quarrels and reconciliations among kindred happen daily. Hopeless affection, secretly, without complaint, cherished to the end, is a grief commoner than we know of. Many a woman marries above her natural rank, and afterwards dies of a decline. How is it that we do not pass these stories by as *commonplace*—so like what we see every day that we want no more of them? It is because they are disclosed to us, not as *we* are in the habit of seeing such things, through the face they present to the outward world—but as they stand recorded in the silent heart, to whose tragic theatre none but itself (and the poet) may be admitted as a spectator. And many a lighted drawing-room is doubtless the scene of tragedies as deep as Hamlet, which pass into the long night unwept, only for want of some *vates sacer* to make them visible. As a specimen of the same kind of power in quite another style, take the following stanzas, entitled "A Farewell," the pathos of which, if it be difficult to account for, it is not the less impossible to resist :—

> " Flow down, cold rivulet, to the sea,
> Thy tribute wave deliver :
> No more by thee my steps shall be,
> For ever and for ever.

> " Flow, softly flow, by lawn and lea,
> A rivulet, then a river :
> No where by thee my steps shall be,
> For ever and for ever.

> " But here will sigh thine alder-tree,
> And here thine aspen shiver ;
> And here by thee will hum the bee,
> For ever and for ever.

> " A hundred suns will stream on thee,
> A thousand moons will quiver ;
> But not by thee my steps shall be,
> For ever and for ever."

A simple touch this—a mere ejaculation of tender emotion, which seems as if it might have escaped from anybody ; yet it shows, as well as a more elaborate performance could have done, how truly the poet's feeling vibrates in sympathy with nature; otherwise how should so simple a tone out of his heart awaken such an echo in our own?

But there are four poems in which Mr. Tennyson has expressly treated of certain morbid states of the mind; and from these we may gather, not indeed his creed, but some hints concerning his moral theory of life and its issues, and of that which constitutes a sound condition of the soul. These are the "Palace of Art," the "St. Simeon Stylites," the "Two Voices," and the "Vision of Sin." The "Palace of Art" represents allegorically the condition of a mind which, in the love of beauty and the triumphant consciousness of knowledge and intellectual supremacy, in the intense enjoyment of its own power and glory, has lost sight of its relation to man and to God.

> "I built my soul a lordly pleasure-house,
> Wherein at ease for aye to dwell.
> I said, 'O soul, make merry and carouse,
> Dear soul, for all is well!'
> *   *   *   *
>
> "To which my soul made answer readily:
> 'Trust me, in bliss I shall abide
> In this great mansion, that is built for me,
> So royal-rich, and wide.'"

There she gathers round her whatever is beautiful in nature, perfect in art, noble and moving in history—all objects, from all climates and ages, that can inspire the imagination, flatter the senses, or charm the heart; in the midst of which she "lives alone unto herself," till she feels beyond the reach of change or chance.

> "Then of the moral instinct would she prate,
> And of the rising from the dead,
> As hers by right of full accomplished Fate;
> And at the last she said:
>
> "'I take possession of men's minds and deeds.
> I live in all things great and small.
> I sit apart, holding no forms of creeds,
> But contemplating all.'"

The very remembrance of human misery and weakness—"the riddle of the painful earth"—though it crosses her thoughts, does

not disturb her triumph. But such immunity from the common
yoke of mortality is not given to mortal; for a man (as our
author expresses it elsewhere)

> "is not as God;
> But then most Godlike, being most a man."

The sin of self-absolution from human cares and duties, finds its
appropriate retribution in the despair which the sense of being
cut off from human sympathy, when it once forces itself on the
mind, inevitably brings;—a truth which Shakespeare has indicated in the case of Richard III.; when he "that had no brother,
that was like no brother,"—"he that had neither pity, love, nor
fear,"—was shaken by his conscience in sleep.

> "There is no creature loves me;
> And if I die no soul shall pity me:—
> I shall despair."

We have not room for the whole passage in which Mr. Tennyson
describes the despair of this soul, when, in the midst of her
solitary delights, "deep dread and loathing of her solitude" fell
upon her. But the concluding stanzas (as conveying the moral,
and especially as showing that it is not the enjoyment, but the
selfish enjoyment, of her intellectual supremacy—not the gifts,
but the gifts as divorced from charity—which he holds to be
sinful) must find a place.

> "Back on herself her serpent pride had curl'd.
> 'No voice,' she shriek'd in that lone hall,
> 'No voice breaks thro' the stillness of this world:
> One deep, deep silence all!'

> "She, mouldering with the dull earth's mouldering sod,
> Inwrapt tenfold in slothful shame,
> Lay there exiled from eternal God,
> Lost to her place and name;

> "And death and life she hated equally,
> And nothing saw, for her despair,
> But dreadful time, dreadful eternity,
> No comfort anywhere;

> "Remaining utterly confused with fears,
> And ever worse with growing time,
> And ever unrelieved by dismal tears,
> And all alone in crime:

" Shut up as in a crumbling tomb, girt round
    With blackness as a solid wall,
Far off she seem'd to hear the dully sound
    Of human footsteps fall.

" As in strange lands a traveller walking slow,
    In doubt and great perplexity,
A little before moonrise hears the low
    Moan of an unknown sea.

" And knows not if it be thunder or a sound
    Of stones thrown down, or one deep cry
Of great wild beasts; then thinketh, ' I have found
    A new land, but I die. '

" She howl'd aloud, ' I am on fire within,
    There comes no murmur of reply.
What is that will take away my sin,
    And save me lest I die ?'

" So when four years were wholly finished,
    She threw her royal robes away.
' Make me a cottage in the vale,' she said,
    ' Where I may mourn and pray.

" ' Yet pull not down my palace towers, that are
    So lightly, beautifully built:
Perchance I may return with others there,
    When I have purged my guilt.'"

As the " Palace of Art " represents the pride of voluptuous enjoyment in its noblest form, the " St. Simeon Stylites " represents the pride of asceticism in its basest. To shadow forth dramatically the faith, the feelings, and the hopes, which support the man who, being taught that the rewards of another life will be proportioned to the misery voluntarily undergone in this, is bent on qualifying himself for the best place—appears to be the design, or the running idea, of the poem. It is done with great force and effect; and, as far as we can guess, with great fidelity to nature. Of this, however, we must confess that we are not competent judges. Holding, as we do, that all self-torment inflicted for its own sake—all mortification beyond what is necessary to keep the powers of self-command and self-restraint in exercise, and the lower parts of our nature in due subjection to the higher—is a thing unblest; and that the man who thinks to propitiate God by degrading his image and making his temple loathsome, must have his whole heart out of tune, and be in the right way to the wrong place—we must confess that we cannot so expand our human sympathy as to reach the case of St. Simeon. We notice the poem for the light it throws on Mr. Tennyson's feeling with regard to this disease of the mind ; which, if we collect it rightly—(for, as the saint has all the talk to himself, it cannot of course be conveyed directly)—is, that selfishness, sensuality, and carnal pride, are really at the bottom of it ; and this, however paradoxical it may appear, we believe to be quite true.

In the " Two Voices " we have a history of the agitations, the suggestions, and counter suggestions, of a mind sunk in hopeless despondency, and meditating self-destruction ; together with the manner of its recovery to a more healthy condition. Though not one of the most perfect, it is one of the most remarkable of Mr. Tennyson's productions. An analysis of the arguments urged on either side, would present nothing very new or striking; and in point of poetical management—though rising occasionally into passages of great power and beauty, and though indicating throughout a subtle and comprehensive intellect, well fitted for handling such questions—it appears to us to be too long drawn out, and too full of a certain tender and passionate eloquence, hardly compatible with that dreary and barren misery in which the mind is supposed to be languishing. The dry and severe style with which the poem begins, should have been kept up, we think, through the greater portion of the dialogue, especially on the part of the " dull and bitter " voice, which sustains the character of a tempting Mephistopheles. These, however, are points of minute criticism, into which we have not room to enter. What we are at present concerned with, is the moral bearing of the poem. The disease is familiar; but where are we to look for the remedy ? Many persons would have thought it enough to administer a little religious consolation to the diseased mind ; but unfortunately despondency is no more like ignorance than atrophy is like hunger ; and as the most nutritious food will not nourish the latter, so the most comfortable doctrine will not refresh the former. Not the want of consoling topics, but the incapacity to receive consolation, constitutes the disease. Others would have been content to give the bad voice the worst of the argument; but, unhappily, all moral reasoning must ultimately rest on the internal evidence of the moral sense; and where this is disordered, the most unquestionable logic can conclude nothing, because it is the first principles which are at issue; the *major* is not admitted. Mr. Tennyson's treatment of the case is more scientific. We quote it, not indeed as new or original,—(it has been anticipated, and may perhaps have been suggested, by Mr. Wordsworth, in the memorable passage at the close of the fourth book of the "Excursion,")—but for the soundness of the philosophy, and the poetic beauty of the handling. The dialogue ends (as such a dialogue, if truly reported, must always do), leaving everything unsettled, and nothing concluded. Then the speaker, having answered the tempter's arguments, but gathered no practical assurance from his own, opens the window and looks forth into the early Sabbath morning:—

" And I arose, and I released
The casement, and the light increased
With freshness in the dawning east.

" Like soften'd airs that blowing steal,
When meres begin to uncongeal,
The sweet church-bells began to peal.

On to God's house the people prest,
Passing the place where each must rest,
Each enter'd like a welcome guest.

" One walk'd between his wife and child,
With measured footfall firm and mild,
And now and then he gravely smiled.

" The prudent partner of his blood
Lean'd on him, faithful, gentle, good,
Wearing the rose of womanhood.

" And, in their double love secure,
The little maiden walk'd demure,
Pacing with downward eyelids pure.

" These three made unity so sweet,
My frozen heart began to beat,
Remembering its ancient heat.

" I blest them, and they wander'd on :
I spoke, but answer came there none :
The dull and bitter voice was gone.

" A second voice was at mine ear,
A little whisper, silver-clear,
A murmur, ' Be of better cheer.'

" As from some blissful neighbourhood,
A notice faintly understood,
' I see the end, and know the good.'

" A little hint to solace woe,
A hint, a whisper breathing low,
' I may not speak of what I know.'

" Like an Æolian harp, that wakes
No certain air, but overtakes
Far thought with music that it makes.

" Such seem'd the whisper at my side :
' What is it thou knowest, sweet voice ? ' I cried.
' A hidden hope,' the voice replied :

" So heavenly-toned, that in that hour
From out my sullen heart a power
Broke, like the rainbow from the shower.

" To feel, although no tongue can prove,
That every cloud that spreads above
And veileth love, itself is love.

" And forth into the fields I went,
And Nature's living motion lent
The pulse of hope to discontent. .

" I wonder'd at the bounteous hours,
The slow result of winter showers :
You scarce could see the grass for flowers.

" I wonder'd, while I paced along.
The woods were fill'd so full with song,
There seem'd no room for sense of wrong.

" So variously seem'd all things wrought,
I marvell'd how the mind was brought
To anchor by one gloomy thought ;

> "And wherefore rather I made choice
>   To commune with that barren voice
>   Than him that said, 'Rejoice! rejoice!'"

The "Vision of Sin" touches upon a more awful subject than any of these;—the end, here and hereafter, of the merely sensual man :—

> "I had a vision when the night was late :
>   A youth came riding toward a palace-gate.
>   He rode a horse with wings, that would have flown,
>   But that his heavy rider kept him down.
>   And from the palace came a child of sin,
>   And took him by the curls and led him in."

Then follows a passage of great lyrical power, representing, under the figure of Music, the gradual yielding up of the soul to sensual excitement, in its successive stages of languor, luxury, agitation, madness, and triumph :—

> "Till, kill'd with some luxurious agony,
>   The nerve-dissolving melody
>   Flutter'd headlong from the sky."

This is the sensual life to which the youth is supposed to be given up. Meantime, the inevitable, irrevocable judgment comes slowly on,—not without due token and warning, but without regard :—

> "And then I look'd up toward a mountain-tract,
>   That girt the region with high cliff and lawn :
>   I saw that every morning, far withdrawn
>   Beyond the darkness and the cataract,
>   God made Himself an awful rose of dawn,
>   Unheeded : and detaching, fold by fold,
>   From those still heights, and, slowly drawing near,
>   A vapour heavy, hueless, formless, cold,
>   Came floating on for many a month and year,
>   Unheeded ; and I thought I would have spoken,
>   And warn'd that madman ere it grew too late :
>   But, as in dreams, I could not. Mine was broken,
>   When that cold vapour touch'd the palace-gate,
>   And link'd again. I saw within my head
>   A grey and gap-tooth'd man as lean as death,
>   Who slowly rode across a wither'd heath,
>   And lighted at a ruin'd inn——"

This is the youth, the winged steed, and the palace—the warm blood, the mounting spirit, and the lustful body—now chilled, jaded, and ruined : the cup of pleasure drained to the dregs ; the senses exhausted of their power to enjoy, the spirit of its wish to aspire : nothing left but "loathing, craving, and rottenness."* His mental and moral state is developed in a song, or rather a lyric speech, too long to quote ; and of which, without quoting, we cannot attempt to convey an idea ;—a ghastly picture (lightened only by a seasoning of wild inhuman humour) of misery and mockery, impotent malice and impenitent regret ; "languid enjoyment of evil with utter incapacity to good."† Such is his end on earth. But the end of all ?

> "The voice grew faint : there came a further change ;
> Again arose the mystic mountain-range :
> Below were men and horses pierced with worms,
> And slowly quickening into lower forms ;
> By shards and scurf of salt, and scum of dross,
> Old plash of rains and refuse patch'd with moss.
> Then some one said, ' Behold ! it was a crime
> Of sense avenged by sense that wore with time.'
> Another said, ' The crime of sense became
> The crime of malice, and is equal blame.'
> And one : ' He had not wholly quench'd his power ;
> A little grain of conscience made him sour.'
> At last I heard a voice upon the slope
> Cry to the summit—' Is there any hope ! '
> To which an answer peal'd from that high land,
> But in a tongue no man could understand ;
> And on the glimmering limit, far-withdrawn,
> God made Himself an awful rose of dawn."

Into the final mysteries of judgment and of mercy let no man presume to inquire further. Enough for us to know what for us is evil. Be the rest left to Him with whom nothing is impossible !

We have dwelt longer on these four poems than either their prominence or their relative poetic merit would have led us to do ; because, though they may not show the author's art in its most perfect or most attractive form, they show the depth from

---

* Berkeley.   † Lamb.

which it springs; they show that it is no trick of these versify-
ing times—born of a superficial sensibility to beauty and a turn
for setting to music the current doctrines and fashionable feelings of the day; but a genuine growth of nature, having its root
deep in the pensive heart—a heart accustomed to meditate
earnestly, and feel truly, upon the prime duties and interests
of man.

Having ascertained the depth and quality, we should next
inquire into the compass, of his power, and the manner in which
it has hitherto been most completely and characteristically
developed. But we have already transgressed our limits, and
must leave the book to speak for itself on these points. Such
poems as the "Morte d'Arthur," the "Pictures," the "Talking
Oak," the "Day Dream," and many others, could derive no
additional interest from any comment of ours; and if there be
persons to whom a few of the lighter pieces—such as "Audley
Court," "Walking to the Mail," "Will Waterproof," or
"Amphion"—appear idle and foolish, we see no help for it;
nor, in the meantime, any harm. Those whose humours (to
borrow Falstaff's phrase) they happen to "jump with," will
relish them: the rest may pass on.

We cannot, however, conclude without reminding Mr. Tennyson, that, highly as we value the Poems which he has produced,
we cannot accept them as a satisfactory account of the gifts
which they show that he possesses; any more than we could
take a painter's collection of *studies* for a picture, in place of the
picture itself. Powers are displayed in these volumes, adequate
to the production of a very great work; at least we should find
it difficult to say which of the requisite powers is wanting. But
they are displayed in fragments and snatches, having no connexion, and therefore deriving no light or fresh interest the one
from the other. By this their effective value is incalculably
diminished. Take the very best scenes in Shakespeare—detach
them from the context—and suppose all the rest to have
perished, or never to have been written—where would be the
evidence of the power which created Lear and Hamlet? Yet
perhaps not one of those scenes could have been produced by
a man who was not capable of producing the whole. If

Mr. Tennyson can find a subject large enough to take the entire impress of his mind, and energy persevering enough to work it faithfully out as one whole, we are convinced that he may produce a work, which, though occupying no larger space than the contents of these volumes, shall as much exceed them in value, as a series of quantities multiplied into each other exceeds in value the same series simply added together.

X.

HARTLEY COLERIDGE.*

It is a common weakness in persons who are not so handsome as they would be, or have been, to abhor a faithful portrait-painter; and a still commoner weakness in their friends to prefer what they call an "idealised" likeness of them, by which they mean, not one in which the true and permanent character prevails over the accidental peculiarities of the face, but one which, being sufficiently like to be recognised, approaches otherwise as nearly as may be to the academical standard of beauty. A similar weakness prevails with regard to men's lives and characters, and a biographer who so portrays his subject that those who did not know the man may know what he was like, must not expect to escape popular censure. Yet we all long to have some definite image both of the features and the character of any man in whom we are interested, whether the interest be excited by his writings or his actions; and it is only when a faithful record of the face or the life destroys some cherished ideal that the minutest personal details are unwelcome. *Then,* indeed, when the real man falls short of the ideal formed of him from his writings, people are apt to exclaim, "Why undeceive us? Why publish what might have been kept private? That part of his life and character which his works reveal is all that the world has interest in; why not leave it to speak for itself?" To this appeal the obvious and sufficient answer is, that if the

---

* Poems by Hartley Coleridge; with a Memoir of his Life, by his Brother. In two volumes. Lond. 1851. *Gentleman's Magazine*, June, 1851.

works bespeak a life and character which does not correspond
with the fact, they speak falsely, and those who so interpret
them are living in a false belief, which to hold unconsciously is
an evil, to cherish deliberately is a sin. Some provinces of the
intellect there are, indeed, which may be said to be independent
of the moral character. We may inherit the full fruits of a life
devoted to science, for instance, without caring to imagine or to
ask what sort of man he was who bequeathed them to us. In
such cases, if the life be otherwise unworthy of remembrance, let
it by all means be forgotten. But it is not so with the poet. All
poetry which is worth anything is a voice out of a human heart,
and every human heart beats in some individual man. We must
sympathize, and we cannot sympathize with an abstraction. If
we do not know what he was like, we imagine him—we make a
picture of him in our mind—and if we imagine him other than
he was, we deceive ourselves, and, so far, the truth is not in us.

To us, therefore, when a poet dies whose works are worthy or
likely to live, a candid account of his personal history shall
always be welcome, and, provided it reveals the truth, it shall
not be the less welcome though the truth be painful. Indeed we
are persuaded that, even where the truth is most painful, it is for
the interest of the poet's own memory that it should be frankly
told. To estimate the strength of a man's virtue we must know
the constitutional weaknesses against which it had to struggle.
In them we shall find at once the explanation and the excuse of
his shortcomings; and far better it is that they should be fairly
expounded by a friend who understands the whole case, than
that scattered evidences of them should be picked up one by one
and exhibited as curiosities and fragments of "truth brought to
light by time,"—such fragments being often only scandals and
errors which truth had in their own day disowned and dismissed
to oblivion.

All this we believe to be eminently true with regard to
Hartley Coleridge, and in the copious and candid memoir prefixed to these volumes we think the editor has not only rendered
a service to literary history, by contributing to it the portrait of
a man in all ways interesting and in many ways remarkable, but
has also performed an office of piety to the memory of his

brother. We should have preferred, indeed, a tone less elaborately apologetic, a more sparing introduction of censures and
regrets, and generally a style of narrative more concise, and
simple, and straight-onward. But when we remember the
relation in which the editor stands to his brother and his family
on one side, and to a jealous and not very reasonable public on
the other, we feel that it would be rash to pronounce judgment
on the execution of a task so very delicate and difficult. Enough
that the story which he has recorded is full of interest and instruction, and as we have good reason to believe that no material
part of the case has been suppressed or misrepresented, those
who are dissatisfied with his treatment of it may treat it better
for themselves.

Hartley Coleridge was born at Clevedon on the 19th of
September, 1796, the eldest son of Samuel Taylor Coleridge, and
therefore with a hereditary title both to gifts of the intellect and
infirmities of the will. About the end of his fourth year his
home was transferred from the banks of the Severn to the lakes
of Cumberland and Westmoreland, and fixed in the house which
will long be remembered as the residence of Southey. He
appears to have been distinguished from other children at a very
early age by a certain oddity of manner and absence of mind,
and by a constitutional inaptitude for all games requiring attention and manual dexterity. This, rather than any premature
devotion to books or aversion from the society of playmates, prevented him from mixing in childish sports, and caused him to
spend the greater part of his time in an imaginary world of his
own, strangely peopled with shadows abstracted from the real
world in which he lived, and of the concerns of which he was at
the same time no inattentive observer. How far he was distinguished from others of the same age by any extraordinary powers
of mind it is not easy to gather. There is hardly any child
whose mind, when subjected to the inspection of poets and meta-
physicians, is not full of wonders; and we may more confidently
infer that Hartley was an extraordinary child from the fact that
he certainly grew up to be no ordinary man, than from the impressions he made on Wordsworth at six years old, or from his
father's report of the metaphysical mysteries with which his

childish understanding perplexed itself.*   Though a clever boy,
and not idle, it seems that he made no remarkable progress in
his school-studies, and it is rather singular that the faculties by
which he was most decidedly distinguished from other boys were
not those which he much cultivated or much excelled in afterwards.   That he lived a great deal in a phantom-world we
should not mention as anything singular—all children do so.
Chairs are turned into carriages and horses, passages into turn-
pike roads, sofas into market-towns, faster than by the slap of
Harlequin's sword.   But in ordinary cases these brain-creations
are abstracted from the simple events of everyday life, and pass
like the day-dreams of maturer age in swift succession, having
no coherency, and leaving no trace.   The instances must be very
rare in which this imaginative faculty is equal to the foundation,
peopling, and government of an empire; rarer still in which it
can maintain the illusion for years together, and carry on the
history of the ideal people through all the vicissitudes of peace
and war and social progress.   Yet it seems that Hartley Coleridge not only imagined such a kingdom at a very early age, and
made a map of it, and peopled it with "many nations, conti-
nental and insular, each with its separate history, civil, ecclesias-
tical, and literary, its forms of religion and government, and
specific national character," but actually continued to *govern* it,
as seriously as an ordinary child rides his stick, for years
together, till he was on the verge of manhood.   This fact rests
upon no vague or doubtful tradition, but upon the distinct
testimony of the editor, who was his brother's companion and
confidant all the time, and to whom the substance of all "letters
and papers from Ejuxria" was regularly imparted as they were
supposed to arrive.   Probably this process of imparting the news

---

* "Hartley, when about five years old, was asked a question about himself
being called Hartley. 'Which Hartley?' asked the boy. 'Why, is there more
than one Hartley?' 'Yes,' he replied, 'there's a deal of Hartleys.' 'How so?'
'There's Picture-Hartley (Hazlitt had painted a portrait of him) and Shadow-
Hartley, and there's Echo-Hartley, and there's Catch-me-Fast-Hartley,' at the same
time seizing his own arm with the other hand very eagerly, an action which shews
that his mind must have been drawn to reflect on what Kant calls the great and
inexplicable mystery, viz. that man should be both his own subject and object, and
that these two should be one."—p. 27.   I venture to guess that he was only
thinking of the difference between the substance and the shadow.

to a listener who seems to have been almost as much in earnest as himself, helped to feed and stimulate the fancy and preserve the outward form of the fiction from its natural dissolution; and the brother of twelve years old may have fancied the brother of sixteen more in earnest than he really was. But, when all allowances have been made, there still remains a very singular and interesting story, well worth recording for the consideration of psychologists. It will be found at pp. 36—42 of the memoir. From this, and other similar amusements of his childhood, it might have been supposed that the creative imagination was unusually strong in Hartley; and yet the productions of his afterlife show scarcely any traces of such a gift.

His tenth year must have contributed largely to the history of Ejuxria. In the days of the terror of Napoleon and the glory of Grimaldi (not to mention the abolition of the slave trade, and the noises of a change of ministry, a dissolution of Parliament, and a general election,) he passed the spring of 1807 at Sir George Beaumont's in Leicestershire, where Wordsworth and Wilkie were; the summer in London with Mr. and Mrs. Montagu; the autumn at Bristol with his mother's family. He "read every word about the battle of Eylau, and was enraged if a doubt were hinted of the Russian victory." He saw the Wood Demon and Jack Bannister at Drury Lane, Mother Goose and Grimaldi at Covent Garden; went over the Tower in company with Wordsworth and Walter Scott; and was introduced to the wonders of chemistry by Sir Humphry Davy: a year of impressions never to be forgotten.

In the summer of 1808 he was sent with his brother to a small school at Ambleside, kept by a gentleman of manly character and vigorous understanding, but no great scholar; fortunate, it seems, in the character of his schoolfellows, and in an ample allowance of leisure and mountain-liberty; eminently fortunate in the neighbourhood of some of his father's most distinguished friends; not very fortunate in his initiation into the nicer mysteries of Greek and Latin. Here he remained for seven or eight years, composing themes and verses, not in any remarkable degree superior to those of his schoolfellows, and with visible effort; wandering at large among the hills with one intimate companion, or gathering desultory knowledge from the libraries and conversation of Wordsworth, Wilson, De Quincey, and Charles Lloyd; helping his school-mates to construe their lessons, or entertaining them with tales; say rather with one continuous tale, having for its moral the injustice of society, which he spun on night after night (we are told) for years together; admired and loved, yet suffering the penalty of his small stature and odd ways in being plagued and teased; joining in no school-games, and forming no intimacies; but "reading, walking, dreaming to himself, or talking his dreams to others."

The immediate result was such as might have been anticipated. He went to Oxford in his nineteenth year with no very accurate knowledge of Greek and Latin, therefore no match for Eton-trained scholars in competition for distinctions awarded according to Etonian standards, but with a mind full of original thoughts and general knowledge, and a rare gift of lively and eloquent discourse. "He would hold forth by the hour (for no one wished to interrupt him) on whatever subject might have been started, either of literature, politics, or religion, with an originality of thought, a force of illustration, and a facility and beauty of expression, which I question (says Mr. Dyce, writing in the year 1849) whether any man then living, except his father, could have surpassed." Whether the popularity at wine-parties which was the inevitable consequence of such a gift, interfered much with his reading during the first year or two of his residence, we are not informed. But in the summer of 1818, as we learn from Mr. C. H. Townshend (who then first met him, and has recorded his impressions in a long and interesting letter) he was certainly reading hard. At Michaelmas following he took a second class *in literis humanioribus;* his deficiencies in what is exclusively, and somewhat arbitrarily, called "scholarship," sinking him below the place to which his "talent and general knowledge" would have raised him. Soon after, he obtained an Oriel fellowship with great distinction; and it seemed as if he were now honourably provided for, and as if the kindness of the friends by whose help he had been sent to college had received its best reward.

Had it turned out so, it is probable that the brief outline

which we have given of his school and college life might have
been thought to contain all that need be remembered of it. It
might not have been suspected that any material feature of his
character remained unnoticed. But a fellow-elect of Oriel has to
pass one year of probation, at the end of which, in case of misconduct, his election may be cancelled. At the close of this probationary year, Hartley Coleridge was judged to have forfeited
his fellowship, "on the ground mainly of intemperance." Great
efforts were made in vain at the time to get the decision reversed;
and severe comments have been made upon it since. We have
ourselves heard it confidently asserted by a very high and grave
authority,—a man by no means given to think indulgently of
intemperance, or suspiciously of dignities, and one whom the
question must have deeply interested at the time,—that the
charge of intemperance was in fact a pretext only, and that the
real offence was of quite another kind, less venial perhaps in the
eyes of college authorities, though not so easily reached by their
statutes, and, in the eyes of the world, no offence at all,—namely,
an indiscreet freedom of speech with regard to University
reforms. Upon this point we can only say that the narrative
before us gives us no means of forming an opinion. We have no
account either of the specific charges, or of the evidence, or of
the answers. Judging, however, from the tenor of Hartley's
subsequent life, we can hardly assume that he had been guilty of
no irregularities which formed a fair pretext for rejecting him,
and (remembering how just his views were, and how pungent his
remarks, upon established institutions in general,) we can have
little doubt that he had *said* many things extremely offensive to
the ears of authority, though perhaps not on that account the less
wholesome, had they been weighed and considered.

But what, it will be asked, *were* these irregularities? And
how did they come upon him? For hitherto we have heard of
no evil tendencies of any kind. To this question neither his
brother's recollections nor the evidence which he has collected
from others, enable us to give a satisfactory answer. We cannot
attach much weight to early manifestations of "intense sensibility" not under proper control; of "impatience of constraint;"
of a disposition to "shrink from mental pain;" of occasional

X

"paroxysms of rage, during which he bit his arm or finger violently;" of a proneness "to yield unconsciously to slight temptations, as if swayed by a mechanical impulse apart from his volition;" for not only are such infirmities incident more or less to the youth of all large and sensitive natures, but it does not appear that they overcame him in the struggle. Where he was left to himself, they led him into no evil that we can hear of. Where, as in the duties of school, he had work to do or constraint to endure, it seems that he did the work and submitted to the constraint. Where the sensibility was most cruelly tried by the thoughtless persecutions of bigger boys—persecutions the remembrance of which became the ever-recurring torment of his dreams in later life—he must have borne them with great patience and sweetness; for we are told that he retained the admiration and love of his school-fellows, though he did not share their amusements. In what respect then was it that "a certain infirmity of the will, the specific evil of his life, had already manifested itself?" It is possible that a school or college companion of his own age, or a little older, could have explained this to us. His brother was too much the younger to "look into him with inquiring eyes;" and we have no report from any other observer who was intimate with him during those years. Nevertheless it is undoubtedly true that "a certain infirmity of the will" did constitute the specific evil of his later life, and it was in all probability connected in some mysterious way with that specific peculiarity of his boyhood, to which we have already alluded. "He never played. He was indeed incapable of the adroitness and presence of mind required in the most ordinary sports. *His uncle used to tell him that he had two left hands.*" Could science anatomize the material organization through which the mind acts upon the body—through which

> —— the brain
> Says to the foot, now move, now rest again,—

it would perhaps be found that in such cases the *will* also has two left hands. That such a constitutional infirmity should prevail more against the grown man than the growing boy, is not surprising. The full flow of hope and youth counteracted but did not extinguish it. Youth and hope ebbing, left the man without energy enough to continue the struggle.

However this may be, Hartley Coleridge—whose spirits were subject to those vicissitudes which so often afflict the *genus irritabile vatum*, especially where the nature is exquisitely tender and affectionate, and a strong thirst for sympathy is irritated by a depressing consciousness of personal disadvantages—had occasionally found a temporary relief from painful sensations in wine. His popularity as a guest exposed him to the temptation; and his constitution was such that a small quantity excited him. Hence a fair pretext, if not a just ground, for taking away his fellowship; and he left Oxford (with £300 given him by the college by way of mitigation) for London, meaning to support himself by his pen. This he could easily have done; for there were few departments of popular literature in which he was not eminently qualified to shine. But infirmities which are not eradicated in youth commonly increase with age. The very habit of introspection, though it be with the purpose of understanding and ejecting them, makes a man familiar with their company, and aggravates the evil. The direction which Hartley's infirmity took was not one of the worst either for body or mind,—certainly not so bad as opium-eating,—but it had a worse name. And though his health was little if at all injured, and his mind not at all corrupted by it, his self-respect (with which self-command is closely allied) was shaken. Then came (to use his own significant words) "that helpless consciousness of faults which conduces to anything rather than amendment." A habit of procrastination followed—part of the same disease. After two years' trial, during which he resided chiefly with Mr. and Mrs. Montagu, it appeared plainly that London was not the best place for him. He returned to Westmoreland; and (yielding against his own better judgment to the urgency of friends) endeavoured to establish himself as a schoolmaster at Ambleside. But, after four or five years' trial, he was obliged to abandon the scheme as a failure.

This was his last attempt to achieve a position in the world. After this he submitted to his destiny, as "a waif of nature:" and, though perhaps no man ever felt a stronger yearning for

the blessings from which his "fault or fate" excluded him, it
was probably the best condition which his very peculiar case
admitted. Here he lived (with one or two short intervals which
we need not stay to describe) the life of a solitary student by the
banks of Grasmere and Rydal ; dependent indeed upon the help
of his relations for what small provision he needed, but requiring
no more than they could cheerfully supply ; condemned indeed
to hopeless poverty and (which to him was a sadder thought) to
hopeless celibacy—but everywhere a welcome guest to the high
and the low, the learned and the ignorant ;· producing little
indeed which brought him money, but much which will be found
to be of more real worth than the most marketable produce which
he could have raised. For it was part of his singular case that
the conditions which steady the character and stimulate the
powers of other men had the contrary effect upon him. By
some strange misdirection of the moral sensibility, which seems
indeed to have been hereditary, a formal engagement to do a
thing frightened him from his purpose, and paralysed his power
of performance. It is Cowper, we think, who somewhere says
that he could sit in his room all day without desiring to go out,
until the door were locked upon him ; but the moment he felt
that he could not let himself out when he pleased, it became a
misery to him to stay in. So Hartley Coleridge could read and
write assiduously and copiously, so long as he did not feel
himself under an obligation to go on ; but a promise to finish
took away his power to proceed.

    The lot therefore upon which he had at last fallen, with all
its privations and disadvantages, gave probably the freest scope
to his peculiar faculties of which they were capable. Here his
defects could do least injury to himself or others ; here his genius
could bear its best fruit. His wanderings were but transient
eclipses. The shadow past, he came forth as pure and bright as
before. Never, perhaps, was a man who was so unlike other men
more justly appreciated by those among whom he lived. We
doubt whether they could have understood him half so well at
Oriel. The breeze which is so healthful and so refreshing in its
native mountains would spread consternation through the Combination Room ; and Hartley's mind flowed where it listed, obedient

to the inner impulses, with little respect for persons or places. What the tutors might have thought of it we do not know; but the "untutored dales" were charmed with the various stream of his talk, so singular yet so unaffected, so familiar yet so unvulgar, so full of drollery and yet by fits so pensive, so unstudied yet so full of wisdom, so keen and pungent and yet so truly genial, liberal, and humane. Those who never heard him talk will get the best notion of his manner from the letters of Mr. Thomas Blackburn (pp. 115—132), who has the art of picturesque narration, and from whom we should be glad to have a fuller reminiscence and a more complete delineation. But no report of what he said can convey the effect, or even the true meaning of his words, unless a notion could at the same time be given of the rapid transitions of his eye and voice from boisterous mirth to thoughtfulness, tenderness, or sadness, as one idea called up another. Therefore the peculiar charm of his conversation will probably live only in tradition. It was not in his conversation however, only or chiefly, that the real spell lay. It was his affectionate and large-hearted sympathy with man, woman, and child, of whatever degree—his true delicacy and generosity of nature—that endeared him to all hearts. Several years ago, when some of his friends thought of asking him to visit them in the south of England, the project being mentioned to Wordsworth, he strongly disapproved of it: "It is far better for him," said he (we heard the words ourselves), "to remain where he is, —where *everybody knows him, and everybody loves and takes care of him*." What can be added to such testimony from such a witness?

The literary produce of these later years, when all is gathered together, will amount to something very considerable, both in quantity and quality. The excitement of conversation did not exhaust, but rather stimulated him, and he would often on returning from a party fall to his desk and continue writing far into the night.

"The quantity, (says his brother, p. 144) the variety, and I venture to add the quality, of the thought which passed through his mind during these latter years, judging only from his note-books and miscellaneous papers, and taking no account of that which perished with him, would surely have ranked him among the most copious and most instructive, as well as the most delightful, writers of his age, had he exerted the resolution or possessed the faculty of combining his materials on any considerable scale or on any given plan. The hope and intention of turning his literary talent to account in this way he never ceased to cherish, and he was not wanting in exertion. He mastered several modern languages, French, Italian, and German, which it had not fallen in his way to acquire in youth. He had commenced the study of Hebrew, expressly with a view to theological investigation, and had begun to apply his knowledge, rudimental as it was, to good purposes. He read and wrote incessantly; he made copious collections; the margins of his books are filled with carefully-written annotations, evidently intended for future use, to which in some few cases they had been actually applied; but by far the largest portion is unpublished. His note-books, which are very numerous, and bear quaint names, are full of original matter, little cycles of speculation, sometimes profound, often acute and sagacious, almost always original and characteristic, but thrown together without an attempt at method. These are always written in the first person, somewhat after the manner of Montaigne. Even extracts from books, lexicography, facts in natural history, etc. are interveined with something of his own, and not unfrequently of himself."

From these note-books, etc. it is intended to publish a selection. We hope it will be a copious one; for we expect to find in such dispersed observations some of the very best fruits of his mind. We do not anticipate the less from them, because they are desultory and without method. Thick books are imposing things, and treatises which comprehend and exhaust the subject they treat of have a value of their own; but in most cases the reader has to pay for the completeness of the whole in an inferior treatment of many parts. The thought which rises to the surface without pressing, generally contains all the cream. And, after all, what worse name do such scattered contemplations deserve than that of essays? Essays they are, according to the true meaning of the word and truest use of the thing: not prize essays, in which the writer labours to say all that can be said, but natural essays, in which, without binding himself to any formal method, he sets down whatever occurs to him as worth saying. From these promised selections, therefore, we hope to derive new and important evidence as to the scope and character of Hartley Coleridge's mind, and it would be premature to attempt an estimate of it until they appear.*

* Since this was written, the "Essays and Marginalia" have appeared, in two volumes; the first consisting of papers formerly contributed to magazines and annuals, with a few others found among the author's MSS.; the second, chiefly of

We have expressed a hope that the selection will be copious. Let us hope also that it will not be timid. He was a devout Christian, but a great foe to sectarianism within the Church as well as without, and if he has spoken his mind freely on the religious questions of the day, he must have said much that neither Oriel nor Exeter Hall will willingly sanction. We trust the editor will remember that he is *not* responsible for his brother's opinions, but that he *is* responsible for giving a faithful representation of them. The views of a devout layman, who has bound himself by no Articles, are very valuable just now; and the editor should consider what his views were, not what will be thought of them.

As a poet, his character must be judged by the volumes before us, which contain all he left which has been thought worth publishing. The poems in the first volume have been familiar to us for the last sixteen years; and, as we find that our interest in them has not abated, we cannot doubt that their worth is genuine and their charm will last. We have left ourselves but little room to speak of them; but they stand in no need of a lecturer to show them off. If we should attempt indeed to fix their exact place in the scale of poetical merit we should have to begin a long discussion. But why trouble ourselves to fix their place? They advance no pretensions; they demand of no man to admire them beyond their worth; but they have a beauty of their own, which those who have a sense for it will feel at once, without being told why or how. Only we will say, by way of warning, that Hartley Coleridge's excellence lies, not in the creative, but in the reflective department of the imagination. He reveals no new worlds; but he can set the profounder emotions suggested by his own experience to a delicate and peculiar music; and when a *thought* strikes him— an intellectual perception, which if dryly told in prose would be

notes written in margins of books; but some extracts from the Note-books are interspersed. These quicken our appetite for a second selection, which is to follow " if the reception of the present volumes justify the undertaking." Of this we trust there can be no doubt. The Essays, though printed before, have lost none of their interest, and to nine readers in ten are new. The Marginalia are all well worth preserving. And the Note-books promise to be better still; for Hartley Coleridge, naturally concise and pithy, writes best when he has most room.

accepted as a fine and striking observation—he can deck it out with a profusion of illustrative imagery, so apt, so fanciful, and so graceful, that it becomes doubtful where the charm most lies —in the sense, the sentiment, or the setting forth.   We must content ourselves with two or three specimens, taken almost at random, for the variety of choice perplexes us.

First, however, let us hear his own estimate of his pretensions as a poet—an estimate which we have reason to believe contains his real and deliberate judgment—before we form an opinion of our own :—

POIETES APOIETES.

" No hope have I to live a deathless name,
 A power immortal in the world of mind,
 A sun to light with intellectual flame
  The universal soul of human kind.

" Not mine the skill in memorable phrase
 The hidden truths of passion to reveal,
 To bring to light the intermingling ways
  By which unconscious motives darkling steal.

" To show how forms the sentient heart affect,
 How thoughts and feelings mutually combine,
 How oft the pure impassive intellect
  Shares the mischances of its mortal shrine.

" Nor can I summon from the dark abyss
 Of time the spirit of forgotten things,
 Bestow unfading life on transient bliss—
  Bid memory live ' with healing on its wings.'

" Or give a substance to the haunting shades
 Whose visitation shames our vulgar earth,
 Before whose light the ray of morning fades,
  And hollow yearning chills the soul of mirth.

" I have no charm to renovate the youth
 Of old authentic dictates of the heart—
 To wash the wrinkles from the face of truth,
  And out of nature form creative art.

" Divinest poesy ! 'tis thine to make
 Age young—youth old—to baffle tyrant time;
 From antique strains the hoary dust to shake,
  And with familiar grace to crown new rhyme.

"Long have I loved thee—long have loved in vain,
    Yet large the debt my spirit owes to thee.
Thou wreath'dst my first hours in a rosy chain,
    Rocking the cradle of my infancy.

"The lovely images of earth and sky
    From thee I learnt within my soul to treasure,
And the strong magic of thy minstrelsy
    Charms the world's tempest to a sweet sad measure,

"Not fortune's spite," etc.

Vol. i. p. 130.

Take next a Sonnet, as an example of his moral vein :—

"Pains have I known that cannot be again,
    And pleasures too that never can be more.
    For loss of pleasure I was never sore,
But worse, far worse it is, to feel no pain.
The throes and agonies of a heart explain
    Its very depth of want at inmost core;
    Prove that it does believe, and would adore,
And doth with ill for ever strive and strain.

"I not lament for happy childish years,
    For loves departed that have had their day,
    Or hopes that faded when my head was grey;
For death hath left me last of my compeers;
    But for the pain I felt, the gushing tears
    I used to shed, when I had gone astray."

Vol. ii. p. 7.

As an example of thought playing with fancy perhaps we cannot choose a better than the lines on " Fairy Land :"—

"My fairy land was never upon earth,
    Nor in the Heaven to which I hoped to go;
For it was always by the glimmering hearth,
    When the last faggot gave its reddest glow,
    And voice of eld waxed tremulous and low,
    And the slow taper's intermittent light
    Like a slow-tolling bell declared good-night.
Then could I think of Peri and of Fay,
As if their deeds were things of yesterday.
I felt the wee maid in her scarlet hood,
Real as the babes that wandered in the wood.
And could as well believe a wolf could talk,
As that a man beside the babes could walk
With gloomy thoughts of murder in his brain;
And then I thought how long the lovely twain

Threaded the paths that wound among the trees,
And how at last they sank upon their knees,
And said their little prayers, as prettily
As e'er they said them at their mother's knee,
And went to sleep. I deemed them still asleep,
Clasped in each others' arms, beside a heap
Of fragrant leaves; so little then knew I
Of bare-bone famine's ghastly misery.
Yet I could weep and cry and sob amain
Because they never were to wake again.
But if 'twas said "they'll wake at the last day,"
Then all the vision melted quite away;
As from the steel the passing stain of breath,
So quickly parts the fancy from the faith.
And I thought the dear babes in the wood no more true
Than Red Ridinghood—aye, or the grim loup-garou
That the poor little maid for her granny mistook.
I knew they were both only tales in a book."

Vol. ii. p. 173.

We cannot attempt to give samples of each variety of excel-lence which the book exhibits, but we must make room for one specimen of the playful-pathetic, which might be mistaken for Cowper :—

TO A CAT.

" Nelly, methinks, 'twixt thee and me
There is a kind of sympathy;
And could we interchange our nature—
If I were cat, thou human creature—
I should, like thee, be no great mouser,
And thou, like me, no great composer;
For, like thy plaintive mews, my muse
With villainous whine doth fate abuse,
Because it hath not made me sleek
As golden down on Cupid's cheek;
And yet thou canst upon the rug lie,
Stretched out like snail, or curled up snugly,
As if thou wert not lean or ugly;
And I, who in poetic flights
Sometimes complain of sleepless nights,
Regardless of the sun in Heaven,
Am apt to doze till past eleven.
The world would just the same go round,
If I were hanged and thou wert drowned;
There is one difference, 'tis true,—
Thou dost not know it, and I do."

Vol. ii. p. 252.

Beautiful and touching as these poems are, we are by no means sure that the editor is right in supposing that it is as a poet that his brother will be best remembered. He was a clear, earnest, and original thinker; and he delivered his thoughts in a manner so perspicuous and lively, with the peculiar humour of his own character so shining through, that his essays, which would be worth studying for the sense they contain, though the style were dull, are among the pleasantest things to read in the language. When all are gathered together they will fill, we suppose, several moderate-sized volumes. If so, and if we are not greatly mistaken as to the quality of the volumes which are to come, we may surely (without raising vain questions as to what he might have done if he had not been what he was) say that the last half of his life, though spent in cloud and shadow, has not been spent in vain.

He died on the 6th of January, 1849, after a short illness, the consequence of an attack of bronchitis. Wordsworth marked out a space for his grave, next to the spot destined for his own, and they now lie side by side in the quiet churchyard of Grasmere,—all that was mortal of them. But

> " The sage, the poet, lives for all mankind,
>   So long as truth is true and beauty fair;
> The soul that ever sought its God to find,
>   Has found him now—no matter how or where."
>
> Vol. ii. p. 58.

XI

ENGLISH HEXAMETERS.*

———◆◇◆———

" THE object of these Lectures " (says *Notes on Books*), " is to
determine the most essential characteristics of Homer's poetry ;
to point out how, from failing to preserve faithfully one or other
of them, every English translation of the *Iliad* up to the present
time has been a false rendering of Homer ; and to give advice to
the future translator as to the best means for retaining these
characteristics in his own version."

Upon the two first branches of the inquiry I have little to
say, except to express my admiration of Mr. Arnold's criticism.
But in his practical advice there is one point which seems to
me to require reconsideration. I agree that a translation of the
Iliad should be " rapid in movement, plain in words and style,
simple in ideas, and noble in manner ; " but I cannot think that
it should be in English hexameter ; and since the recommendation comes from a scholar and a poet, as the result of an inquiry
showing a very remarkable combination of scholar-like taste
with poetic sensibility, it deserves a fuller and graver answer
than I should otherwise have thought necessary. If indeed the
practical question at issue were one in which scholars only are
interested, I would leave them to settle it among themselves.
But if another attempt is to be made to produce a translation of
the *Iliad* for the benefit of those who cannot read the original,
the feelings of the patient should be taken into consideration ;

* " On Translating Homer." Three Lectures given at Oxford by Matthew
Arnold, M.A.   London : Longman and Co.   1861.

and one whose Greek has long been at grass is in some respects
better qualified to understand the case of the "English reader"
than those who have kept it in daily exercise.

According to Mr. Arnold, indeed, the appeal in this case lies
to scholars, and scholars only : for "they alone can say whether
the translation produces, more or less, the same effect upon
them as the original." But this is not exactly the question,
though it comes very near it. The true question, in my opinion,
is this—Does the translation produce upon one who cannot read
the original the same effect, more or less, which the original
produces upon one who can ? Now, the innumerable associations
of which the practised scholar cannot divest himself make it
very hard for him to judge what the effect will be upon those
whose associations are quite different. To him the original
shows through the translation, and gives it new colours and
qualities. In reading the English he feels the Greek within
it; and the illusion thereby produced is seen in no more conspicuous example than that of a scholar reading a page of
English hexameters, and fancying that the "movement" of
them is like that of the Greek or Latin. "Applied to Homer,"
says Mr. Arnold, "this metre affords to the translator the
immense support of *keeping him more nearly than any other metre
to Homer's movement;* and since a poet's movement makes so
large a part of his general effect, and to reproduce this general
effect is at once the translator's indispensable business, and so
difficult for him, it is a great thing *to have this part of your
model's general effect already given you in your metre,* instead of
having to get it entirely for yourself."

Now, to my ear the *movement* of the best English hexameters
which I have seen is so very unlike the movement of any Greek
or Latin hexameters that I remember, since the days when I
had to *scan* the verse in order to understand the measure, counting the feet with my voice by throwing a strong accent upon
the first syllable of each; and the movement produced by the
scanning process was so very unlike that with which even then
I *read* them when I was called up to construe; that unless Mr.
Arnold either reads Homer very oddly, or means by English
hexameter a measure constructed upon a principle totally and

essentially different from any that I have seen attempted, his ear is surely under some strange delusion.

I do not suppose he reads Homer differently from other people. For though in the note on p. 95 he seems to imply that we *ought* to read Greek according to the Greek accentuation—ἀιόλος ἵππος as if it were ἀιολλος ἵππος, Διὸς αἰγιόχοιο as if it were Διόσσ' αἰγιόκχοιο—he seems at the same time to admit that we do not in fact read it so. And since the effect of the Greek upon the ear of a modern scholar is by himself proposed as the only standard of reference, I infer that when he speaks of the movement of Homer he means the movement which the ear of a modern scholar recognises. If not, the whole dispute is at an end. For though there *may* be some way of training the ear to understand the measure so read, it is a training which has to be begun from the beginning with every one of us; nay, further back than that; for before we can begin we must get rid of all our existing prepossessions.

Assuming, then, that Mr. Arnold means the Greek hexameter to be read in the usual way, does he propose any new way of writing the English hexameter? I find no hint to that effect. He says, indeed, that he is not quite satisfied with any attempt that has yet been made in it on any considerable scale. He recommends a freer introduction of spondees (meaning by spondee a foot of two syllables, the first of which takes the accent); a little (and only a little) more attention to quantity; and a good deal of care to make the accents which are suggested by the sense coincide with those which are required by the rhythm. But he suggests no change in the fundamental law of the metre; and it is plain that the measure which he recommends as possessing so much rapidity, so much natural dignity, and a movement so like Homer's, is nothing but the common English hexameter with which we are all painfully familiar, and of which the earliest specimen I ever heard (combining, as by anticipation it does, all the suggested improvements) may serve for a typical example:

> Here we go up, up, up; and here we go down, down, downy;
> Here we go backwards and forwards, and hey for—

But the poet unfortunately had not sufficient faith in his rhythm;

and by introducing here the alien element of rhyme altered its
character. A very slight alteration will remove this blemish,
and then the two verses may stand together as fair representatives of the family—the first exhibiting the spondaic effect, the
second the dactylic ; both being rapid in movement, plain in
words and style, and simple in ideas ; quantity being neither
outrageously violated nor pedantically affected, and the accents
falling of themselves into the right places.

> Here we go up, up, up; and here we go down, down downy ;
> Here we go backwards and forwards ; and hey for the city of London.

What effects the metre of which I seriously assert that these
two lines are a favourable example, may or may not be capable
of in the hands of an artist, I do not undertake to say. But
taking it as I find it, and as managed by the best artists who
have yet made the experiment, I will venture to affirm that it
is the metre which a translator of Homer should of all others
avoid; the resemblance which its movement bears to Homer's
movement being the resemblance not of mimicry but of mockery :
a mere exaggeration of the characteristic peculiarity, without
any of the other features by which it is balanced, softened,
varied, or harmonized ; and the conditions being such, that the
better you make your English hexameter, the more it will
resemble the worst form of the measure which the Greek allows.
And that this must be so, unless an entirely new element be introduced into the English, I think I can show, provided we first
come to a proper understanding as to the difference between
quantity and *accent*.

In all our English metres quantity is held of so little account
—the essential metrical conditions are so independent of quantity—that many people seem to doubt whether our tongues and
ears are capable of distinguishing between long and short. The
Greeks and Romans, it is thought, had some art of pronunciation by which an accented syllable might sound short and an unaccented syllable long ; but an Englishman has no way of mark-
ing length or shortness except by accent or no accent. This I take
to be a mere delusion. The quantity—the length of any syllable
measured in time—is distinguishable in English through all its
degrees, by any ear that will attend to it. *Slumbers* is a word

of two long syllables, with the accent on the first. *Supper* is a word of two short syllables, also with the accent on the first. *Bittern* has its first syllable short but accented, its second long but not accented. *Quantity* is a dactyl; *quiddity* a tribrach: the first syllable in both being accented, but in one long, in the other short. *Honestly* is a word to which we find no parallel in Latin; the first short but accented, the second long but unaccented, the third short. And so on to the end of the dictionary. The degrees of length being infinite in number, there are of course many syllables which are doubtful or common; either you cannot tell whether to class them with the long or the short, or you may make them which you please by your pronunciation. But, in general, you can tell the quantity of every syllable at once, if you only listen for it, and may soon learn to be as much shocked by a false quantity in English, as if you knew it to be against a written rule.

> Sweetly cometh slumber, closing th' o'erwearied eyelid,

is a correct Virgilian hexameter, like

> Ipsa tibi blandos fundent cunabula flores.

> Sweetly falleth slumber, closing the wearied eyelid,

contains two shocking false quantities.

The truth is, that we spoil our ears for this work, not only by want of attention to quantity in English, but by forcing ourselves to overlook a number of false quantities which we habitually make in Latin and Greek. For as no Englishman sounds the double consonant in such words as *annus, tellus, terra, vacca, gemma*, and the like, and the vowel in all such words is short, he has no means of lengthening the syllable. Therefore to distinguish *ănus*, (for instance) from *annus*, he lengthens the short *a*; and generally learns his lesson so well that he fancies he hears a short syllable in *ănus* (pronounced exactly like *cănus*) and a long one in *annus*; whereas he does really hear exactly the reverse. And even the Carthusians, who know better than that, fancy that they hear a long syllable in one of the words, though they pronounce both exactly alike and as short as possible. A long list of similar deceptions of the ear might easily be drawn out. But if any one doubts whether English syllables differ in length as well as in accent, I can assure him that if he will make a little experiment which I have just been making, and of which I will presently exhibit the result, he will become painfully conscious of the fact.

This distinction between accent and quantity being clearly understood, a simple comparison of the rules by which the classical and the English hexameter are respectively governed, is enough to show how unlike they must be in movement. Let us avoid all questions of dimeter and trimeter, all talk of dactyls, spondees, and catalexis, and all phrases which are encumbered with disturbing associations; and merely describe the two in such English as any lady will understand.

First, what is an English hexameter?

A regular English hexameter is a line containing six *distinctly accented* syllables; of which (the first syllable in the line being always one) the first, second, third, and fourth are each followed either by one or by two *unaccented* syllables; the fifth by two; the sixth by one. Any series of words in which the accents can be so placed without violence, is within the law of the metre. *Quantity*—that is, length measured in time—may be entirely disregarded. Any of the seventeen syllables which the line admits may be either long or short, by nature, by position, or by both. The rhythmical effect depends, of course, upon quantity, pause, division, alliteration, and many other conditions; but it is the peculiar arrangement of the accents which makes the metre. With the accents placed according to the rule which I have given, a line may be good or bad, smooth or rough, quick or slow, but it is certain to be an English hexameter. With the accents placed otherwise, it may easily be a much better thing, but it will not be recognized as a hexameter by any English-trained ear.

What, on the other hand, is a classical hexameter?

A regular Virgilian hexameter is a line containing six *long* syllables, of which (the first syllable in the line being always one) the first, second, third, and fourth are each followed either by two *short* syllables or by one long; the fifth by two short, the sixth by one which may be either long or short. This is the complete and invariable rule with regard to quantity. But

Y

quantity, though the fundamental and indispensable, is not the only condition of the metre.   Of these groups of long and short syllables (which we commonly call feet) either the second or the third must be divided between two words—must be part in one word and part in another; this is the rule for what they call the *cæsura*.*   The accent also must be distributed according to certain laws.   Of the six long syllables the two last *must* be accented.   Of the remaining four, any one, two, or three *may* be accented.   All four must *not*.†   Subject to these conditions, the accent may be placed anywhere, and the rhythmical effect depends mainly upon the management of it; but any series of Greek or Latin words in which these conditions are fulfilled will be found to be a correct and regular hexameter.

Thus it appears that the only points in which the laws of the two metres concur, are the number of the syllables and the place of the two last accents.   In all other respects they are different, and in one contradictory.   The English takes account of accent only, and pays no regard to quantity or *cæsura*.   The Latin is inexorable as to quantity and *cæsura*, requires the time of each syllable to be distinctly felt and measured, and allows no choice but between one long and two short; while with regard to accent it gives much liberty.   The English insists that the first four accents shall all be placed where the first four long syllables are placed in the Latin; the Latin insists that all four shall never be so placed.

I take the laws of the classical hexameter from Virgil, because his is the most perfectly developed form of the metre under conditions which enable us to judge of it.   For whatever mistakes we make in sounding his vowels and consonants (and I have no doubt we make many), yet, as far as accentuation goes, we do pronounce Latin as Virgil did.   The rule of pronunciation, as explained by Quintilian (*Inst. Orat.* i. 5, 30), amounts in effect to this:—Every word takes one accent, and only one.   In a word of more than two syllables, it is always placed on the last

---

* The Lucretian line "Et membratim vitalem deperdere sensum" breaks this rule. But to my ear it is not a hexameter.

† There are, however, several lines in Virgil in which the accents do coincide with the long syllables. See Munro's paper on the Inscription at Cirta, p. 16.

but two, except where the last but one is long ; in that case, and
in disyllables, always on the last but one. And this is an exact
description of our English practice. Of the Greek pronunciation,
all we know is that the rule of accentuation was in Quintilian's
time different from the Latin. What it was in Homer's time,
Quintilian himself probably did not know. Our mode of reading Homer, therefore, may be right or may be wrong. But in
the meantime we do read Greek, in respect of accent, exactly as
we read Latin; and we find that the Homeric hexameter, so
read, is in its fundamental conditions the same as the Virgilian.
In regard to quantity, it is quite as regular and inexorable ; the
greater licence which it admits being in the pronunciation, not
in the measure. In Homer we have sometimes to dwell on a
syllable naturally short so as to *make* it long, in a way which we
are rarely or never called on to do in Virgil, as in

ἢ δεῦρο μὲν ἕποντο νέεσσ' ἐνὶ ποντοπόροισιν·

But we are just as much obliged to *feel* the length of it ; and if
the ear once misapprehends the *quantity*, we have to correct it
and begin the line again, in order to make the measure intelligible ; whereas in English we have to do this only when we
happen to misplace the *accent:* a mistake in quantity may make
the measure clumsy, but never makes it unintelligible. With
regard, again, to the placing of the accents, the Homeric hexameter, though less strict than the Virgilian, follows ordinarily
the same rule. In Homer we do find now and then a line which
reads like an English hexameter—viz., a line in which all the
six long syllables are accented, as

αὖτις, ἔπειτα πέδονδε κυλίνδετο λᾶας ἀναιδής ·*

or (to take a less exceptional example, and one which, owing to
some peculiar effect of the cæsura, reads well in Greek, although
a similarly constructed line would read well in English) :—

ὡς δ' ὅτ' ἐν οὐρανῷ ἄστρα φαεινὴν ἀμφὶ σελήνην.

Such lines are rare, even in Homer, as any one may satisfy
himself if he will read a few pages of the *Iliad* as if he were

---

* I doubt whether even this would have been allowed without the long pause
after αὖτις, which is connected with the preceding line. Even in a case of imitative
sound, I suspect that ἀυτὰρ ἔπειτα πέδονδε, etc., would not have been endured.

scanning the verses, and count the number of lines which read naturally so. Still they do occur here and there ; and so far the Homeric hexameter does, no doubt, come nearer to the English. But to balance this, it admits freely and frequently another irregularity, which we never, or hardly ever, meet with in Virgil. It does *not* insist absolutely that the two last accents shall coincide with the two last long syllables ; and thus allows lines of which the measure would be quite unintelligible in English. What, for instance, could be made of a line like

τὸν δ' αὖτε προσέειπε βοὴν ἀγαθὸς Διομήδης.

Try an Englishman with

> Then straightway said in answer honest General Garibaldi,

(which, in accent and quantity both, is really a correct Homeric verse),—he will not know how to read it into metre at all.

These general considerations sufficiently explain the difference of the effect which the two metres have always had upon my ear ; and they ought, I think, to suggest to those who have not yet perceived it, that a difference there is and must be as long as their respective laws are so widely and radically at variance. But general considerations are dry, and an example or two will make the case clearer.

First, therefore, to show how very widely the respective systems of accentuation differ, let us take a few lines of Virgil, and observe how often the accent coincides with any of the four first long syllables. I distinguish the long syllable by the usual mark, and the accented syllable by italics.

> Mē verō prīmūm dulcēs ante ōmnia Mūsæ,
> Quārum sācra fero, īngentī percūlsus amōre,
> Accípiānt : cœlīque viās et sīdera mōnstrent :
> Dēfectūs solis variōs, lunǣque labōres ;
> Ūnde tremŏr terrīs ; qua vī maria ālta tumēscant
> Ōbjícibūs ruptīs, rursūsque in se ípsa resīdant :
> Quīd tantum ōceanō properēnt se tīngere sōles
> Hībernī, vel quǣ tardīs mora nōctibus ōbstet.

Here we see that the accent coincides with one of the first four long syllables, in the 1st, 3rd, 6th, 7th, and 8th lines only once ; in the 2nd and 5th only twice ; in the 4th not at all ; while the places in which it falls are scarcely twice alike.

Now let us try a few of Mr. Arnold's. We may as well take the first that come, p. 93.

> *So* shone *forth* in *front* of *Troy*, by the *bed* of *Xanthus*
> *Between that* and the *ships*, the *Trojans'* numerous *fires.*
> *In* the *plain* there were *kindled* a *thous*and *fires:* by *each* one
> *There* sate *fifty men*, in the *light* of the *ruddy fire.*
> *By* their *chariots stood* the *steeds*, and *champed* the white *barley,*
> *While* their *masters sate* by the *fire*, and *waited* for *morning.*

Here we find the six accents punctually falling every time in exactly the same places; varied a little in effect, indeed, by the different degrees of violence which are required to force them in, but bound to occupy those places and no other, upon peril of confounding the metre. All relations of quantity are so disordered or disregarded, that I presume Mr. Arnold seeks in that mode of irregularity some relief from the monotony which, in a succession of three or four smooth lines, becomes intolerable. If it were not the special object of his work to recommend hexameter, I could even think that he meant to extend the irregularity to the accents also, allowing the reader to drop the first altogether, and so begin the line with two unaccented syllables—a liberty which in five lines out of the six would be a great relief. But that would transform it at once into another metre, which could have no pretence to the name of hexameter. And yet, from his obvious dislike to begin the line with a word which will *naturally* bear the accent, I almost think that this is what he privately does himself, and that that other metre is what he hears in his own head. Does he really read "*Between* that and the ships," "*In* the plain," "*There* sate fifty men," "*By* their chariots," "*While* their masters?" Would any of these lines *read itself* so? Read any of them naturally, and what happens? It becomes immediately a line with only *five* accented syllables—an ordinary blank verse, in fact, varied and made dactylic by the introduction of a few redundant unaccented syllables (after the manner of that variety of the ordinary octosyllabic couplet with which Scott and Byron have made us familiar.

> But it is not to list to the waterfall
> That Parisina leaves her hall;
> And it is not to gaze on the heavenly light
> That the lady walks in the shadow of night, etc.)

A metre of which very good use might probably be made, and which may possibly prove after all the best English representative of the classic hexameter, but certainly not itself a hexameter, and certainly not that which Mr. Arnold meant to write and means to recommend. I may say more of it presently; but I want first to dispose of the first question, which relates to the respective *movement* of the Greek and English hexameter properly so called.

In Mr. Arnold's lines I have distinguished by italics the syllables on which I presume that he intends the accent to fall. Compare with them the original Greek, accented according to our pronunciation.

> Τόσσα μεσήγυ νέων ἠδὲ Ξανθοῖο ῥοάων
> Τρώων καιόντων πύρα φαίνετο Ἰλιόθι προ.
> Χίλι' ἀρ ἐν πεδίῳ πύρα καίετο· πὰρ δε ἑκάστῳ
> Εἴατο πεντηκόντα, σέλᾳ πύρος αἰθομενοῖο.
> Ἵπποι δε, κρὶ λεύκον ἐρεπτόμενοι καὶ ὀλύρας,
> Ἑστάοτες παρ' ὀχέσφιν, εὔθρονον ἠῶ μίμνον.

Here we see that the accent coincides in each line with only two of the first four long syllables; and in what respect the movement of the English resembles that of the Greek, I profess myself unable to perceive.

But the most effective mode of exhibiting the contrast would be by producing, if it were possible, specimens of both in the same language. If one could but construct with Latin words a hexameter on the English model, or with English words one on the Latin model, I think no ear could help perceiving that the movement is essentially and irreconcilably different. It is not easy to do this in either case, so many words in each language are by the conditions excluded; but if sense be not too strictly insisted upon, the sound may be obtained.

> Incipe parve puer risu cognoscere matrem :
> Matri longa decem tulerunt fastidia menses,
> Incipe parve puer : cui non risere parentes,
> Nec Deus hunc mensa, etc.

Can anybody produce me an English hexameter resembling, in the succession of sounds, any one of these three lines? I think not. But if I shift the accents a little, and write,

Incipe parve puercule, risu noscere matrem.
Matri longa tulērunt sex fastidia menses :
Incipe parve puercule, fac ridere parentes,—

do we not all recognize at once the movement of our new friend ?

Why dost thou prophesy so my death to me, Xanthus? It needs not, etc.

Two or three lines in Latin made of words exactly corresponding in length, divisions, pause, accent, and all other metrical conditions (except quantity, which is of course out of the question), with the component words of two or three approved English hexameters, would be a fairer and more satisfactory test; but I doubt whether they can be made. I find, however, that true Virgilian hexameters—accent, cæsura, quantity, and all—may be constructed in English words, and in that way the true movement of the classical measure may be fairly contrasted with that of its modern representative.

In the following hexametrical dialogue, A speaks in Virgilian measure, B in that of Longfellow.

A.

Verses so modulate, so tuned, so varied in accent,
Rich with unexpected changés, smooth, stately, sonorous,
Rolling ever forward, tidelike, with thunder, in endless
Procession, complex melodies—pause, quantity, accent,
After Virgilian precedent and practice, in order ɩ
Distributed—could these gratify th' Etonian ear-drum?

B.

How should Etonian ears that are trained in Virgil and Homer
Follow a measure like that? Where, where are your dactyls? I counted
Two in each line at most. Hexameter always in my time
Stept on his dactyls along, like a toe-tripping queen of the ballet.
Yours on accents false goes hobbling. Vain your endeavour
Long to distinguish from short: long or short is all one to us English.

A.

Virgil *my* model is: accent, cæsura, division,
His practice regulates; his laws my quantity obeyeth.

B.

Longfellow most pleases me; no trouble his quantity gives me,
Each verse bounding along like a ship that bounds through the waters.

*   *   *   *   *   *   *

How different the movement of these two measures is will probably be made manifest by a practical test; for I fully expect that Etonian ears will at first be quite puzzled by A.'s verses, and that ears *not* trained in Virgil and Homer will not be able to make out the metre at all, while B's will be understood at once by everybody.

To me, I confess, the effect of the metre constructed upon A's system is not bad. But unless the same effect can be obtained by some other process than that of composing it with words resembling Latin or Greek words in their metrical conditions, it is useless for any practical purpose; because it excludes more than half the words, and I suppose nine-tenths of the combinations of words, in the language. I can conceive it possible indeed that a new English metre may be invented, resting upon six regularly recurring accents as the ground, and made musical by some variation played upon it with quantity; just as the Latin takes quantity for its ground, and obtains its variations through the management of the accent. But it will take some time to invent, and more to make it familiar. And in the meantime, what need is there to seek for a new metre at all?

Mr. Arnold is curiously coy on this point. He carefully avoids all mention of the word hexameter, until he has passed in review what we are to consider as *all* the remaining alternatives, and successively rejected them. When he has led us to the brink of despair, he at last tells us that there is still one metre remaining which has not been condemned; and we seem to be driven to the dilemma of accepting this or making up our minds to go without any translation of the *Iliad*. If this were so, I should have no objection to an attempt being made in English hexameter, provided I am not myself bound to read it. But Mr. Arnold's enumeration of the possibilities appears to me to be very arbitrary and very incomplete. When he is reminded that hexameters have not been used in English on any considerable scale with success, he is content to reply (p. 76), *Solvitur ambulando :* the objection may be removed by *producing* good English hexameters. Yet the ten-syllable couplet is rejected because rhyme, *as Pope uses it,* "tends to pair lines which in the original are independent, and thus the movement of the poem is changed;" and because *Chaucer's* narrative manner, "though a very good and sound manner, is neither grand nor Homeric."

Ten-syllable stanzas with interwoven rhymes are rejected, because, if the simpler system of correspondences changes the movement of Homer, the more intricate system of correspondences must change it more profoundly. All varieties of ballad-metre are rejected, because *Dr. Maginn* has turned a passage of the *Odyssey* into a jig; and *Walter Scott*, not being "one of the five or six supreme poets of the world," has failed to attain "the grand manner." Blank-verse is condemned because Milton's movement, though grand, is unlike Homer's; because Cowper imitates Milton; because Tennyson has written three lines in which the thought belongs to another order of ideas than Homer's, and the rhythm to another order of movement; while the blank-verse in which the most rapid passages of Shakespeare's plays are written forms a mould into which Homer could not be poured without being first entirely broken up, melted down, and composed afresh. And this, as far as I can make out, is all. Surely one may reply in Mr. Arnold's own words, *Solvitur ambulando:* the objections may be met by *producing* a form of the rhymed couplet, of the ten-syllable stanza, of the ballad-stanza, or of blank-verse, of which the movement is *not* at variance with the movement of Homer. The paces to which Pope trained the heroic couplet, Milton the blank-verse, Scott the octo-syllabic rhyme, are surely not the only paces of which those several metres are capable. If Chaucer failed to rise to the true epic dignity, it was not because his *measure* kept him down. The rhymed couplet, as he manages it, follows freely wherever the imagination leads; and if he had had an *Iliad* in him would have served him for a vehicle of expression perfectly well. The measure which is best for a ballad is not likely to be good for an epic; and therefore I should not look among Percy's relics for the best metre to imitate Homer in; but the common ballad-metre admits of many variations of movement; and we do not know what might be done with it if a man of genius took it in hand. For large and long-sustained effects, however, I suppose the line of five accents, in one form or another, will always be the favourite in English. The Alexandrine, which has six, is too slow, and indeed intolerable, except as recurring at measured and rather distant intervals; or by way of an occa-

sional change, as at the close of a Drydenian triplet. The
octo-syllabic, which has four, is too light in its rapidity: it
wants stateliness. But among the various arrangements of the
ten-syllable line in stanza with rhyme, there are some which
lend themselves with great facility to almost any movement
which is wanted. The *Don Juan* stanza, for instance, has a
remarkable power of rising and sinking, of passing from grandeur
to familiarity, from the pathetic to the playful, and *vice versâ*,
without effort or abruptness: and this is one of the requisites
which a translator of Homer cannot dispense with. He must be
able to pass at once from the famous nod of Jupiter (*Il.* i. 528)
to his altercation with Juno (of the nobleness in manner of
which, by the way—an invariable Homeric attribute, according
to Mr. Arnold, p. 36—we should be better judges if we could
compare it with the prose Billingsgate of Homer's day); then to
the relenting smile of the white-armed goddess, when Vulcan
intercedes and offers her the cup; and the inexhaustible merriment of the Olympian party as he hands it round; and to do
this easily and naturally.

> Therewith to all the gods in order due
>   He poured sweet wine, and played the cupbearer;
> And the gods laughed with all their hearts to view
>   Lame Vulcan like a young page serving there:
> And so they feasted all the long day through,
>   Till the sun set, and feasted well they were.
> To grace the feast his harp Apollo strung,
> And all in parts the sweet-voiced Muses sung.

The necessity, however, of having two sets of triple rhymes
in every stanza limits the resources of the translator incon-
veniently, and forms a serious objection to this measure, as well
as to Chaucer's seven-line stanza; either of which might otherwise be used with very good effect. But where is the objection
to our own natural blank-verse?—a measure into which English
speech rises of itself the moment it aspires to speak in measure
at all—a measure in which we know from Shakespeare that every
condition of feeling, every action of intellect, every mood of
imagination, can find fit utterance—a measure with the normal
structure of which all our ears are so familiar, that any variety
of modulation may be introduced without danger of confusion—a

measure in which if Tennyson has written three lines of which
the movement is too slow for Homer, he has written hundreds in
which all the characteristic qualities which Mr. Arnold finds in
Homer—rapidity of movement, plainness of words and style,
simplicity and directness of ideas, and above all, nobleness of
manner, are as conspicuous as in Homer himself—a measure of
which the very difficulty lies in the abundance of its liberty and
resources, which are dangerous to those who do not know how
to use them, but an unmixed advantage and facility to those who
do. Where is its defect? I cannot think that the difference in
length, as compared with the hexameter, forms any objection;
for the different constitution of the languages makes it impossible
to present the thoughts in the same order and within the same
spaces, clause for clause, and cadence for cadence; as we may
learn at once from Mr. Arnold's prose version of one of the
passages selected for illustration :—

> τόσσα, μεσηγὺ νεῶν ἠδὲ Ξάνθοιο ῥοάων,
> Τρώων καιόντων πυρὰ φαίνετο.

Presented in this order, the Greek words are as simple, natural,
and straightforward as possible. Present the best English
equivalents in the same order, and the construction is involved,
unnatural, and hardly intelligible. To make it read like sense,
Mr. Arnold has been obliged to alter the order of the clauses.
By that necessary alteration he has quite changed the cadence
and emphasis; and after all, he has not succeeded in giving
even the meaning correctly. " So many in number, between the
ships and the streams of Xanthus, shone forth in front of Troy
the fires kindled by the Trojans." " So many in number shone
the fires," is not the same as τόσσα πυρὰ φαίνετο—" so many
fires shone;" and the closing of the sentence with Τρώων
καιόντων, instead of πυρὰ φαίνετο, alters the effect far more than
a much more extensive change of construction need have done.
This Mr. Arnold has himself felt, and in his metrical version has
put the clauses together in a different way, though without
attempting to keep the order of the original. In fact, if Homer
is to be translated into English at all, whether in prose or verse,
the translator must be prepared to break him up and reproduce
him; and even if he had a metre exactly the same, it does not

follow that he could make it fit. What he wants is not a line of
the same length, but a measure which is easy, flowing, familiar,
stately, unshackled, and capable of variety. Any such measure,
however different it be in structure, will supply means of representing the metrical effect of the Homeric hexameter, just as the
English language supplies means of representing the sense; but
it must do it in its own way.

Mr. Arnold will perhaps ask for an example; for of his own
attempts he speaks very modestly, and he may fairly claim to
have his translation judged by comparison, not with the original,
but with another translation. Well, the question is as to the
metrical effect involved in rival metres; for otherwise I have no
exception to take to the principles which he lays down. Now
we have seen his translation into hexameter of the passage last
mentioned. Here is one in blank verse:—

> Not fewer shone before the walls of Troy,
> Between the rolling Xanthus and the ships,
> The camping Trojans' watch-fires. In the plain
> A thousand fires were burning, and by each,
> Grouped round the ruddy light, sate fifty men;
> While the steeds mouthed their corn aloof, and stood
> Beside the chariots, waiting for the dawn.

Take a man or a woman who cannot read Greek; would the
hexameters convey to him or her a truer idea of Homer's manner,
an impression more like that which the original conveys to Mr.
Arnold himself, than the blank verse? I suspect not.

But Mr. Arnold may perhaps insist on appearing by his
champion, and refer me to Dr. Hawtrey.

"The most successful attempt (says he) hitherto made at rendering Homer
into English, the attempt in which Homer's general effect has been best retained,
is an attempt made in the hexameter measure. . . . . . The passage is
short; and Dr. Hawtrey's version of it is suffused with a pensive grace, which is
perhaps rather more Virgilian than Homeric; still *it is the one version of any
of the 'Iliad' which in some degree reproduces for me the original effect of
Homer:* it is the best, and it is in hexameters."—(p. 77.)

I have already said that the proper issue is not how far the
translation *reproduces for Mr. Arnold* the effect which is produced
on him by the original; but how far it *produces* that effect upon
one to whom the original is unknown. Upon this issue the
challenge is fair, and I accept it.

As readers of *Fraser* do not all carry a *Homer* in their pockets, it may be convenient to begin with the original :—

Νῦν δ' ἄλλους μὲν πάντας ὁρῶ ἑλίκωπας Ἀχαιούς,
Οὕς κεν ἐὺ γνοίην, καὶ τοὔνομα μυθησαίμην·
Δοιὼ δ' οὐ δύναμαι ἰδέειν κοσμήτορε λαῶν,
Κάστορα θ' ἱππόδαμον καὶ πὺξ ἀγαθὸν Πολυδεύκεα,
Αὐτοκασιγνήτω, τώ μοι μία γείνατο μήτηρ.
Ἢ οὐχ ἑσπέσθην Λακεδαίμονος ἐξ ἐρατεινῆς ;
Ἢ δεῦρο μὲν ἕποντο νέεσσ' ἐνὶ ποντοπόροισι,
Νῦν δ' αὖτ' οὐκ ἐθέλουσι μάχην καταδύμεναι ἀνδρῶν,
Αἴσχεα δειδιότες καὶ ὀνείδεα πόλλ' ἅ μοι ἐστίν ;
Ὣς φάτο· τοὺς δ' ἤδη κατέχεν φυσίζοος αἶα
Ἐν Λακεδαίμονι αὖθι, φίλῃ ἐνὶ πατρίδι γαίῃ.

Dr. Hawtrey's version is thus given by Mr. Arnold :

Clearly the rest I behold of the dark-eyed sons of Achaia ;
Known to me well are the faces of all ; their names I remember.
Two, two only remain, whom I see not among the commanders,
Castor fleet in the car—Polydeukes, brave with the cestus—
Own dear brethren of mine—one parent loved us as infants.
Are they not here in the host, from the shores of lov'd Lacedæmon,
Or, though they came with the rest in ships that bound through the waters,
Dare they not enter the fight or stand in the Council of Heroes,
All for fear of the shame and the taunts my crime has awakened ?
So said she :—they long since in Earth's soft arms were reposing,
There in their own dear land, their father-land, Lacedæmon.

Now, I admit that there is a certain grace here even in the versification, and that for ten or twelve lines it is not an unpleasant kind of canter; but I doubt whether another dozen of the same would be agreeable, and I deny altogether that the metrical movement has any resemblance whatever to that of the Greek lines which we have just read. I should expect that the following translation in blank verse would give anybody who was not acquainted with the Greek measure a much better idea of what it is like to me :—

Yet still, though all the other Greeks I see
Whom I should know by person and by name,
Two chiefs I miss,—Castor, for horsemanship
Far-famed, and Pollux, matchless in the ring,—
My brethren : yea, one mother bare us all.
Came they not over from sweet Lacedæmon
In the sea-travelling ships ? Or are they loth,
Being here, to mix with the others in the field,
Fearing reproach and scorn because of me ?

> So spake she: knowing not that they long since,
> Lapped in the bosom of the teeming earth,
> In Lacedæmon lay, their native land.

I meant to confine myself to a protest against English hexameters, which I hold to be admirably adapted for a translation
of *Propria quæ maribus* and *As in præsenti*, and for nothing else.
But I will take the opportunity of adding a few words in favour
of an entirely different way of dealing with the *Iliad*—a way
which nobody seems to have thought of, though it offers a great
field for an enterprising genius.

To scholars " who possess at the same time with knowledge
of Greek adequate poetical taste and feeling," Mr. Arnold tells
us (p. 4), "no translation will seem of much worth compared
with the original." If this be so, is it judicious to attempt a
translation which shall aspire to present itself for comparison
with the original before that tribunal? If the true effect of
Homer cannot be reproduced in a translation, is it well that
anyone should take upon him a task which makes such reproduction "his indispensable business?" Is it not better that
those who wish to know what Homer is really like should be
recommended, as the shortest way, to learn Greek and read
him?

But though we cannot have Homer himself in English, there
is no reason why we should not have in English the story which
Homer told. Why should not the *Iliad* be made an English
book like the *Arabian Nights?* I want somebody to invite the
men and women, the boys and girls, now living in England, to
listen to an old story: and to tell them all about the quarrel
between Agamemnon and Achilles, and what came of it. He
may choose prose or verse, as he finds most convenient; he may
borrow from Homer as much as he pleases; he may leave out
whatever he cannot bring in with a good effect. But he must
address his audience in his own and their own language, in such
forms as may find easiest passage through their ears into their
hearts, and such cadences as are most agreeable to them.
Though his inspiration and his matter come from Homer, his
feeling, taste, and manner must be his own. Imitation he must

not think of.   He must consider himself rather as a rival than an imitator.   If he can tell any part of the story better than Homer, let him by all means do so; at all events, let him not deliberately prefer the worse effect to the better, in order to make it more *like* the effect which the original produces upon the mind of a Greek professor.   Pope did not trouble himself much with fidelity to the effect of Homer; but he would have made a much better poem of the *Iliad* if he had not attended to it at all.   As it is, it is in virtue of the freedom which he used in making it "a pretty poem but not Homer," that it still remains the only version of "the tale of Troy divine" which has obtained a popular audience in England.   Pope's genius, however, was not of the epic order; it was not a good subject for him.   But what if Tennyson had taken the story of the *Iliad* for his subject, and treated it, not in Homer's manner, but in his own?   I believe that England would have had an epic added to her literature as popular as *Waverley* and as great as *Paradise Lost*.   Is there no one among us with spirit for such an enterprise?

CORRECTIONS AND EXPLANATIONS: JUNE, 1862.

Concerning the merits and capabilities of the English hexameter as a representative of the movement of Homer, I wish to add a few words—but only in the way of explanation and correction.   The question, so far as I meant to meddle with it, has been fairly discussed, and may go to the jury as it is.   I wished only to remind scholars of the fact, so generally overlooked, that to the ear of a modern Englishman the effect of the metre which we call English hexameter, whether agreeable or not, is at any rate quite *different* from the effect of the classical metre *as we all hear and read it;* and therefore not a good representative of it: and my argument having been listened to with all the attention I could desire, I respectfully leave the decision with the people; promising for my own part, as one of that miscellaneous body, that if any one succeeds in translating the *Iliad* into such English hexameters as I can read with pleasure, I will read them, and exhorting others to do the same; though I must still be permitted to *hope* (even after reading Dr. Whewell's last remarks) that poets and scholars will refrain from an enterprise upon which I still think, for the reasons which I have already given, that their labour will be bestowed in vain.

But though both my conclusion and the reason it rests on still seem good to me, there was an error in the exposition of them, which I wish to acknowledge and correct; and there appears also to have been some misapprehension as to their scope and intention, which I wish to clear away.

The error is easily rectified; and if the notice taken of my argument by Mr. Munro in the appendix to his learned paper on the inscription at Cirta, and by Mr. Arnold in his *Last Words on Translating Homer*, should induce anybody to turn back to *Fraser's Magazine* of June, 1861, he will oblige me by introducing three corrections.

1st. After the word "metre" in the sixth line from the bottom of the first column of page 706, insert—" Of these groups of long and short syllables (which we commonly call *feet*), either the second or the third must be divided between two words— must be part in one word and part in another. This is the rule for what they call the *Cæsura.*"

2nd. For the note which now stands at the bottom of that page, substitute—" There are, however, several lines in Virgil in which the accents do coincide with the long syllables. See a paper read by Mr. Munro at the Cambridge Philosophical Society, Feb. 13, 1860, on a metrical inscription at Cirta, p. 16."

3rd. For "quantity," in the ninth line of the next paragraph, read "quantity *or cæsura;* " and in the tenth "quantity *and cæsura.*" *

Thus corrected, it will be found, I think, that the statement is accurate, and the argument will not be affected by the change.

In another statement, rather more important to the question

---

* In the reprint these corrections have, of course, been made.

at issue, of which Mr. Munro denies the accuracy, I cannot yet see that any correction is required. I said that verses in which the accent falls on every one of the six long syllables (that is, on the first syllable of every foot) are *rare* even in Homer; that if any one will read a few pages of the *Iliad*, as if he were *scanning* the verses, and count the lines which read naturally so, he will be satisfied of that fact; that nevertheless they do occur *now and then*. Mr. Munro says that "such verses, instead of being rare, are among the very commonest types of Homeric rhythm," and that he has "counted sixteen or seventeen of them between vv. 78 and 178 of the *Iliad*." I suppose he does not read Homer as I was taught to do. For certainly, in the first two hundred and fifteen lines of the *Iliad*, I could not when I wrote the remark, and cannot now upon a second trial, find more than five in which, as I should naturally read them, the accent—the predominant stress—falls upon the first syllable of each of the six feet. These are vv. 95, 121, 126, 173, 214. In every one of the others, if I want to mark the beginning of each foot by stress of voice, I am obliged in one place or another either to lay the accent on a syllable on which I should not naturally lay it, or to lay it more lightly than I should otherwise do upon the neighbouring syllable upon which it naturally falls. Now, when I am contrasting a metre in which this kind of verse occurs two or three times in every hundred with one in which it occurs, I suppose, at least ninety-five times in every hundred, I call it "rare"—a thing which occurs "now and then."

One point more there is, in which, though I am not prepared to offer a correction or to acknowledge an error, I wish to withdraw an assumption which, not knowing that it was disputable, I had adopted too hastily. I allude to the general question concerning the peculiarities of ancient Roman pronunciation, and the true relation between accent and quantity in the days when both (it seems) were essentially different from anything that has been known in the world for 1500 years. Upon this I can only say that, had I known there was a doubt, I should not have ventured an opinion. I had been told of the passage in Quintilian; had referred to it, and thought I understood it; and not knowing that there was a question among scholars as to the nature of the thing spoken of, had assumed that, Virgil's accent being placed exactly where we place it, his pronunciation was in that one respect like our own. This assumption I am quite ready to withdraw for further consideration, and to allow in the meantime that we know as little about Virgil's pronunciation in that particular as in others—that we know, in fact, nothing whatever about it.

I do not find, however, that these corrections and concessions at all affect the substance of my argument; and this leads me to the other branch of the explanation which I wish to offer.

The effect of Virgil's verse on the ear of Horace or Augustus, has nothing to do with the question as I handle it; except in so far as there may be reason for supposing that it was in some respects similar to the effect which it has upon *our* ears. At best, the resemblance must be very imperfect. That neither his metre nor his words can possibly affect the mind of a modern Englishman in the same way in which they affected the minds of his contemporaries,—that the poetical meanings which they had for them must have been very unlike the meanings they have for us,—is a conclusion too obvious to need enforcement. The finer effects of poetry depend upon the ideas which associate themselves with the words : and the ideas which associate themselves with the words of a dead language, laboriously acquired through grammars and dictionaries with a view to examination, *must be* so different from those associated with the words of a living language familiar from infancy and in daily use for all the common business of life, that they cannot be reasonably supposed to produce similar impressions on the imagination. Still less can we suppose that the rhythmical effect of Virgil's lines is the same for us as it was for them; for here not only the associations, but the sounds themselves in which the rhythm consists, are changed. We read them for our own pleasure in a way which we know to be very different from that in which they were meant to be read. Nay, if I understand Mr. Munro rightly, we cannot even conceive how they *were* meant to be read. The peculiar intellectual instinct which gave them all their meaning strangely departed from mankind 1500 years ago; and we know of it only as we know of a dog's

scent—by the acts which it prompted. "The old Greeks and
Romans (he tells us, p. 30) had an instinctive feeling for and
knowledge of *quantity* : upon which instinct depended the whole
force and meaning of their rhythmical measured verse." But in
the course of the third century "quantity perished"—perished
so completely from the earth that "it does not exist even
potentially in any modern language." No modern ear can
recognize it; we know it "only by the rules of prosody."
Consequently, "our English reading of Homer and Virgil has
in itself no meaning" (p. 31). How, then, do we put a meaning
into it? Thus. Upon the unmeaning sounds which we utter
with our lips and listen to with our ears, we "superinduce by a
mental process our acquired knowledge of the quantity and
rhythm;" that is to say, we call to mind that by the rule of the
metre this syllable must, in some inexplicable way, have been felt
by Virgil to be long, and that syllable to be short; and though we
cannot ourselves perceive that it is so, or understand how it could
be so, we take into consideration the fact that it was so. And the
result is, "all that wondrous harmony which we feel." The
quantity, upon an instinctive sense of which all the real harmony
depended, we cannot feel; but a harmony of some kind we
somehow do feel. Be it so. But since this harmony comes to
us by so very different a process, I can hardly be rash in concluding that it must be a very different kind of thing from that
which sounded in the ears of Virgil or Horace; and it is the
effect of the harmony as we feel it, not as they felt it, that we
talk of endeavouring to imitate in English.

Upon the question of historical fact,—the alleged existence in
ancient times of a natural instinct for the rules of prosody
(pp. 2, 3), which having been perfect in everybody from the days
of Homer to those of Plautus—as perfect in the swineherd as in
the poet—was lost by everybody before the end of the third
century,—I have nothing to say. I know nothing of the
evidence from which it is inferred, and I do not see how evidence
can exist which to me would seem satisfactory. Descriptions
may remain of the old Roman pronunciation, by grammarians
who had heard it; but who can assure me that they were
qualified to report what they heard? It is far from a common

accomplishment. How do I know that they refrained, until they had finished their description, from "superinducing upon the sounds they heard, their acquired knowledge,"—that they did not, by a mental process, hear with their eyes instead of their ears? There are hundreds of grammarians now in England who would tell me that *i* is a simple vowel, and *au* a diphthong; hundreds of scholars who would tell me that the first syllable in *niger*, as commonly pronounced, sounds short, the first syllable in *nigger*, long; though any clock that beats half seconds can tell them that the difference is exactly the other way. Think, if English were a dead language, what strange conclusions a scholar would be led to in trying to determine the pronunciation, with such data to perplex him. Mr. Munro himself, admitting that "two or more consonants take *longer time* in enunciating than one" (p. 33), declares in the same sentence (p. 32) that "neither his ear nor his reason recognizes any *real distinction of quantity*, except that which is produced by accentuated and unaccentuated syllables." If his paper survives the spoken language, and Lord Macaulay's New Zealander meets with it, what will he infer as to the pronunciation of ancient English? Two or more *consonants*, he will say, took longer time in enunciating than one. Yet in *syllables*, there was no real difference in *quantity*," except accent and no accent. How could this be? Was it that in a syllable involving two consonants the vowel was shortened in proportion to the increase of time taken in articulating the consonants? Or was it that the ancient English ear could not recognize differences of time in the act of enunciating consonants, but only in vowels; and that all vowels were pronounced in equal times? Or was it that by "quantity" they meant length measured in space, not in time, and reckoned a syllable long or short, according to the number of letters in it? The difficulties of the question would be insuperable, and a just conclusion hopeless.

Leaving the historical question, then, for scholars to debate at their leisure, I come back to the effect of the classical hexameter. upon the ear of a modern Englishman, about which we do know something, and to which I say that question is altogether irrelevant. For myself, at least, I positively declare that when

I speak of the effect of Virgil's verse, I speak of the effect which the sounds I utter make upon my own ear. And my case is, in fact, the very reverse of Mr. Munro's. For me, my English reading of Virgil *has* "in itself" a meaning; it is the rules of prosody (many of them) that have no meaning for me. That they had a meaning in connexion with the native pronunciation I do not doubt; but the pronunciation being changed, the principle is in many cases no longer applicable, and the meaning is gone. Words which, as spoken by Virgil, would have violated the law of the metre, accord with it as spoken by me; and a vast number of what we call false quantities may be committed without the least offence to any faculty which I possess, physical or intellectual. Take, for instance, *pater* and *mater;* both pronounced (as I was taught, absurdly enough, to pronounce them) like our English *waiter*. Can any one pretend that his *ear* is offended by hearing *pater* used when the verse requires a long syllable, or *mater* when it requires a short one? To us they are both *common*—admit of being pronounced either long or short, as we like; just as *patrem* was to Virgil himself; the mute followed by the liquid forming a combination which could at pleasure be uttered rapidly or dwelt on long, and being capable, therefore, when preceded by a short vowel, of any length which the verse required. If a modern reader feels any horror at seeing such a line as *Ipsa mater, media nimborum in nocte,* etc., it is not that the sound offends him, but that he knows there is a false quantity in it, and remembers the days when he would have been punished or laughed at for making a false quantity. Take, again, *itur* and *iter*. If "sic *itur* ad astra" sounds well, can it be said without absurdity that "Hic *iter* ad astra" sounds ill,—supposing the *i* to be pronounced long in both, as I was taught to pronounce it? Here to me the real false quantity would be committed in making the first syllable of *iter*, so pronounced, do duty for a *short* syllable. Our long *i* and *u* are both diphthongs; and so long by nature—that is, by the impossibility of articulating them rapidly—that we cannot put them in the short places without injuring the rhythm. A worse offence to my ear, and one which I have never been able to reconcile myself to, is the elision before words beginning with a vowel of syllables ending in *m*. With the Romans I suppose *m* represented a nasal *vowel*, which could not be sounded before another vowel without a hiatus : but with us there is no pretence for elision. The *quam* in " Tempore quan*quam* illo," etc., strikes my ear as a real false quantity—a combination inconsistent with the law of the metre ; and my only reason for acquiescing in it (so far as I do acquiesce), is that it accords with the written rule —just as my reason for objecting to *Ipsa mater* (so far as I do object) is only that it is against the written rule.

With me, therefore, however it may be with others, an acquired knowledge of the rules of prosody does *not* overrule the sense of hearing, or make me feel a wondrous harmony in sounds which are themselves unmetrical. Virgil's hexameters, as I read them, are no doubt very different and very inferior in melody to what they were as he read them. But it does not follow that the sound of them is not to me really beautiful—

> Tale tuum carmen nobis, divine poeta,
> Quale sopor fessis in gramine; quale per æstum
> Dulcis aquæ saliente sitim restinguere rivo.

In these there is a measure perfectly intelligible—an expectation of the ear delicately played with, a ground with fine changes, demanding no acquired knowledge to explain it to the ear, except a knowledge of the intention of the metre—the general law which governs it. And the result (in spite of five false quantities, which I confess with shame that I have always made in reading the lines, and never observed them till now—*tūum, sōpor, fessĭs, āquæ,* and *sĭtim*) is a sense of exquisite pleasure—the sort of pleasure which music gives. Mr. Munro would have me believe that an acquired knowledge of the rules of playing on the pianoforte might, by a mental process, be so superinduced upon the sense of the sounds actually emitted by an instrument false in every note, that to one who knew that the keys were rightly touched, even though he did not know what the sounds themselves *ought to be*, the result would be a feeling of " wondrous harmony." But I think he will hardly induce two musicians to make the experiment—one playing, the other reading and listening ; and yet the mental feat would be much easier to them than the analogous mental feat which he supposes to be unconsciously performed by all modern scholars; for the musicians have a clear conception of what the sounds *ought to be*, and if the instrument were silenced, could hear them in their minds: whereas the scholar only hears a jangle, and believes that the sound would be melodious if the instrument were rightly tuned, but has no conception whatever of the sort of sounds which the rightly-tuned instrument would make.

XII

"TWELFTH NIGHT" AT THE OLYMPIC THEATRE.*

———•◦•———

THE recent revival of *Twelfth Night* at the Olympic Theatre deserves special notice for two reasons. It is the first time in England that the difficulty of finding two actors sufficiently alike to be mistakable for each other has been met by the obvious expedient of making the same person play both parts: and it is the first opportunity we have had of seeing Miss Kate Terry in a part fine enough to test her capacity for acting "Shakespeare's women."

Though the experiment was tried under accidental disadvantages, which greatly impaired the general effect, and made the piece much less attractive than it deserves to be, the result was satisfactory on both points. It has been practically proved that in a plot which turns upon the perfect resemblance of two persons, actual identity need cause no confusion; and though we do not profess to be perfectly satisfied with Miss Kate Terry's performance, either in conception or execution, it has fully satisfied us of this—that nature has endowed her with all the gifts, both mental and corporeal, which are required for the task, and that there are very few of Shakespeare's women whom it does not lie within her power to act better than we of this generation have ever seen them acted. Hoping, therefore, that the play-going public will want to see more of her in such parts,—that so rare a chance may lead to the formation of a company qualified to support her in them,—and that the successful introduction of one novelty may make way for other much needed

* *Frazer's Magazine*, August, 1865.

improvements,—we propose to explain in some detail the points
in which her performance (though in all points highly interesting, graceful, and clever) was to us unsatisfactory.

But we will speak first of some defects in the arrangements
with which she is not personally concerned, except as suffering
from the effect of them in the general impression made by the
whole.

A company got together for the performance of the domestic
sensational prosaic drama upon which the Olympic has flourished
of late could not be expected to furnish a fit cast for *Twelfth
Night*—a play written for Burbage's company in its full strength,
and containing so many characters that require acting of the
highest order.   As far as the Olympic company is concerned, the
actors all deserve praise for the pains they took to do justice to
their several parts, and many of them for no inconsiderable
success.   But in considering the effect of the play itself, and its
capacities for popular attraction, it must not be forgotten that
the love-sick Duke is meant to be a man of the finest manners
and tastes :—

> Of great estate, of fresh and stainless youth,
> In voices well divulged, free, learn'd, and valiant,
> And in dimension and the shape of nature
> A gracious person :—*

Olivia to be a woman of dazzling beauty, high breeding, and
imperial manners :—Sir Toby, though a drunken reprobate, and
too fond of practical jokes, to be a gentleman of good birth, a
soldier, and a man of humour ; ready to fight with anybody,
though not wishing to hurt anybody ; ready also to take the
consequences without complaint or resentment when he is hurt
himself ; whose language, whenever he is tolerably sober, is that
of a well-bred man ; and who certainly did not end every
sentence with "haw! haw!" or carry his mouth in a perpetual
grin:—also that the Fool was not a merry, mischievous boy, but a
thoughtful man, something of a scholar, and full of music, whose
favourite songs were plaintive and pathetic.   The loss of these

---

* These lines, we observe, are left out in the acting, which is surely a great
mistake. As addressed by Olivia to Viola, they have a peculiar and pathetic
meaning, and it is strange that the mixed emotions which they must have excited
in her should not have been made one of the "points" in the play.

features puts the whole composition out of tune, and prevents the tragic and comic elements from combining. For in this, as in all Shakespeare's later comedies, the serious interest is allied, through the depth and tenderness of the sentiment, rather to tragedy than to comedy; and though the end is marriage and happiness ever after, the predominant impression is one of sadness rather than mirth—the sadness which accompanies a deep sense of beauty.

Perhaps these deficiencies could not have been avoided. But there was one part of the arrangement which had a very bad effect, and might certainly be corrected. The difficulty of representing on the stage a brother and a sister so like that they cannot be distinguished was not so great in Shakespeare's time as in ours. When women were acted by boys, two boys like enough for the purpose may have been procurable ; though even then it must have been hard to find two boy-actors of original genius, resembling each other in action, voice, and manner ; unless they were real twins, such as we occasionally meet with, and such as may possibly have been at this time in Burbage's company. In the present day we doubt whether all the theatres in London combined could produce a pair of actors qualified physically and morally to represent the two Antipholuses in the *Comedy of Errors*. But to find a *man* and a *woman* qualified to act Sebastian and Viola, and at the same time like enough to be mistaken for each other, is plainly impossible. The voice alone is fatal to the resemblance. In making the same person act both (a device which we are told has been long practised in Germany) there is no difficulty whatever until we come to the last scene ; for until the last scene they cannot by the nature of the case appear on the stage together. When they do, the difficulty does no doubt arise, and cannot be avoided. But that scene is never long ; it is at least *easier* to find an actress who can look and speak like another through one or two speeches than through several scenes of various emotion ; and even if she fails, the play is so nearly over that no great harm is done. But in dealing with this difficulty the managers of the Olympic have fallen, we think, into a great mistake ; and by making that concluding scene not merely imperfect, but incredible and ridiculous, have endangered the success of the whole experiment. We would readily excuse the representative of Sebastian for not speaking so well as Miss Kate Terry, but we cannot excuse her for not speaking at all. That a young gentleman, so spirited, so affectionate, so frank and bold, so ready and graceful in speech, as we have seen him in Miss Terry's admirable and almost fault-less rendering, should come before such a company in such circumstances and not have one word to say, is so very absurd that it produces a shock of disappointment sufficient to damp the effect of the whole piece; not to add, that it spoils the part of Viola herself, by obliging her to assume a prominence which is out of character and unbecoming. Surely Miss Terry might teach some one to deliver Sebastian's speeches well enough to leave her her own part in the scene of recognition. Perfect physical resemblance is comparatively unimportant; for play-goers are not used to be very exacting in such cases, and would readily accept a skilful "get up" as sufficient for the occasion. We can connive at some difference of features; but the total want of a tongue is too much for us. Until this defect is removed, it is vain to expect that the play will go off with triumph. A sense of disappointment coming upon an audience in the crisis of the last scene interrupts the current of sympathy, and deprives them of the power of hearty applause. And to this more than to anything else we attribute the fact that while the newspaper critics agreed in admiring and praising, the audience, though attentive and well pleased, saw the curtain fall night after night without any of the usual manifestations of delight.

With regard to Miss Terry's own performance—which is an event of higher importance, and may come hereafter to have a kind of classical interest—we cannot assent to what seems to be the general verdict of the critics,—namely, that it wanted nothing but *power*. We saw no want of power; we saw, on the contrary, unmistakable evidence that she has all the power which the part requires. And it was in fact from the remarkable skill and force with which she embodied her own conception, that we were enabled to see where the defect of her performance really lay. Following probably the traditions of the stage, which by successive corruptions have degraded this finest of all comedies almost into farce, she pitched all Viola's conversations with Olivia—which are as full of tender feeling as anything Shakespeare ever wrote—in far too light a key. So much so, that had we seen her in those scenes only, we should have doubted whether she had sufficient feeling for poetry, or sufficient sympathy with the deeper moods of poetic passion. But the scenes with the Duke prove beyond all doubt that she has no such defect; for when was deep and tender passion more touchingly expressed, or in a form more graceful and poetic? It cannot be therefore that she wanted power to express the same in the scenes with Olivia : she was trying to express something else. She did not give Viola credit for the depth and tenderness and delicacy, which to us are not less conspicuous in these scenes than in the other; and played them with a light and laughing heart. And it is not to be denied that she may cite in her justification some grave authorities. A charge has been made against Viola by at least two eminent critics, which if just would deprive her of all pretensions to those feminine attributes. In a note upon the scene in which she first appears, Dr. Johnson observes, " Viola seems to have formed a very deep design with very little premeditation. She is thrown by shipwreck on an unknown coast, hears that the prince is a bachelor, *and resolves to supplant the lady whom he courts.*" Hallam, following in his wake, says that "Viola would be more interesting if she had not, *indelicately as well as unfairly towards Olivia, determined to win the Duke's heart before she had seen him.*" And Miss Terry (though she tried to soften the effect by betraying an emotion at the mention of the Duke's name, which implied an attachment already formed, or at least a fancy already engaged) appears to have put the same construction upon the only passage by which this most injurious imputation can have been suggested. To us, however, the words convey no such meaning, but imply rather the very contrary. And the question is worth examining; for our conception of Viola's very nature, and with it the spirit of every scene in which she subsequently appears, and the complexion of the whole play, depends upon the answer.

How then stands the case? Viola has just escaped from shipwreck, having lost her twin brother—her only natural pro-

tector—and everything else except her purse with a little money
in it.   A beautiful, high-bred girl, alone in a strange country—
what is she to do?*   Where is she to lodge?   How to procure
food?   The captain and the sailors are kind and respectful, but
they are poor men, and have been wrecked as well as she.   But
she has sense and courage and character and accomplishments,
and addresses herself at once to meet the difficulty.   For a lady
of her birth and breeding, the court was the natural place to look
to for shelter and sympathy; and she asks who is governor.
Duke Orsino.   Orsino!   She remembered the name; she had
heard her father speak of him.   But "he was a bachelor then,"
she adds; thinking no doubt that if he were still a bachelor there
would be no female court; therefore no fit place for her.   Hearing that he was not married, but going to be, her next most
natural resource would be the lady he was going to marry—a
lady, it seemed, well suited to her case; for she also was an
orphan maid, mourning the recent loss of an only brother;† and
it was only on learning that there was no chance of obtaining
access to her, that she resolved to disguise her sex and seek
service at the court in the character of a page.   This would provide for her immediate necessity; and for her next step she
would wait till she saw her way.   There is not the shadow of a
reason for supposing that in wishing to serve either Olivia or the
Duke she had any other motive or design; the suggestion of
which is the more unjustifiable and unaccountable, because in
all her subsequent intercourse between them (though she had
then come to have a very deep and painful interest of her own in
the matter) she shows herself as fair and loyal, as unselfish, as

* *Cap.* This is Illyria, lady.
    Vio. And *what should I do* in Illyria?
        My brother! he is in Elysium.
† A virtuous maid, the daughter of a count,
    That died some twelve months since, then leaving her
    In the protection of his son, her brother,
    Who shortly also died; for whose dear love
    They say she hath abjured the company
    And sight of men.
    Vio. Oh, that I served that lady!
Surely it was not by accident that the wish followed so immediately upon the
report of a circumstance forming so natural a bond of sympathy.

tenderly considerate towards both, as it is possible for a woman to be.   Three days of confidential communication in so tender an argument as unrequited love had kindled indeed in her own breast a love which could not hope and did not ask for requital. But where are the traces of design, or intrigue, or endeavour to use opportunities for her own advantage?   Out of the experience of her own sad and hopeless passion she borrows imagery and eloquence to set forth her master's; and the sincerity with which she does it is proved by the effect.   How she might have been affected if the tenderness which her eloquence kindles in Olivia's hitherto unapproachable heart had turned it towards the Duke, Shakspeare only knows.   He spared her that trial.   But what she had to do she did with perfect loyalty and good faith; her own love—though restlessly struggling to utter itself—remaining to the last her own sad secret.

From overlooking or not appreciating the painful conflict between her office and her feelings, and the fine grace with which she manages it, Miss Terry seemed to us to miss many delicate touches of nature, for the exhibition of which her powers are well suited.   Nothing could be prettier or more proper than the assumed sauciness with which she forced herself upon Olivia, and *began* the conversation; but to keep it up to the end of the scene was surely a mistake.   The "skipping dialogue" is maintained only so long as others are present; as soon as the two are alone, it gives place first to seriousness and then to deep emotion:—

> *Ol.* Have you no more to say?
> *Vio.* Good madam, let me see your face.

Now why was Viola so anxious to see Olivia's face?   Not surely that she might make a pert remark or a cold criticism. She wanted to see the face that had so enchanted Orsino.   And when she does see it, what feelings does it excite?   Jealous dislike, or a desire to depreciate?   No: but earnest admiration of her beauty and deep sympathy with her lover, whose cause she immediately proceeds to plead as passionately as if it were her own.   Not another light word passes her lips.   And that her feeling towards Olivia herself was not less delicate and sympathetic, we may gather not only from her language during the

rest of the interview, but still more from a passage in the next
scene, which though it has puzzled many commentators, has
always appeared to us one of the finest touches in the play.
When Malvolio overtakes her with the ring which the Countess
pretended that she had left, her immediate answer is :—

> *She took the ring of me:* I'll none of it.

Now, as she had *not* left any ring, it has been thought that there
must be some mistake here, and that we should either read "*no*
ring" instead of "*the* ring;" or make an interrogative exclama-
tion of it (as Miss Terry did), "She took the ring of *me!*" But
it is plain from Malvolio's reply, "Come, sir, you peevishly
threw it to her," etc., that *he* understood her to mean that she
had left it. And so no doubt she did. For though taken quite
by surprise, and not knowing at first what it exactly meant, she
saw at once thus much,—that the message contained a secret of
some kind which had not been confided to the messenger ; and
with her quick wit and sympathetic delicacy suppressed the
surprise which might have betrayed it.

The messenger being gone, she proceeds to consider what
the meaning of it is. And it is in the soliloquy which follows
(though delivered with admirable spirit and skill) that Miss
Terry seemed to us to commit her gravest fault. Following
again the traditions of the stage—where "I am the man" is
commonly made the "point" of the speech—and forgetting how
sad Viola's heart was, and how forlorn her prospects—she
represented her as taking a light pleasure, as of gratified vanity,
in Olivia's mistake, and as rather enjoying the perplexity of the
situation ; for she made her exit with a laugh, musical enough
in itself, but terribly out of tune with the sentiment of the play.
According to Shakespeare, Viola's sense of the humour of the
situation is immediately lost in sympathy and sad reflection,
accompanied with a kind of self-reproach :—

> If it be so,—as 'tis—
> Poor lady, she were better love a dream.
> Disguise, I see thou art a wickedness, etc.

And most certainly it is with a sigh and not with a laugh, that
she gives up the attempt to see how it can all end :—

> What will become of this? as I am man,
> My state is desperate for my master's love.
> As I am woman,—now, alas, the day,
> What thriftless sighs shall poor Olivia breathe!
> Oh Time, thou must untangle this, not I;
> It is too hard a knot for me to untie!

And if further evidence were wanted of the gravity with which she regards the complication, we may find it in her subsequent interviews with Olivia, in which the light tone is entirely abandoned and exchanged for one of reserved, cold, and lofty, though not untender, reproof; meant to discourage hope without giving pain, and successful at least in the latter.

Another oversight, growing no doubt out of the same misconception, we observed in the beginning of the same scene, where Viola walking home (with too light a step, we thought, for one whose heart was so heavy-laden) is first overtaken by Malvolio. Here Miss Terry, after lightly answering his first question, turned immediately to walk on again as before. Now his question, "Were you not even now with the Countess Olivia?" implied that he had something to say; and Viola *must*, in common courtesy, have paused to hear what it was, unless she wanted to get away, for which there was no reason. This is a small thing; but small things help to give general impressions; and the impression produced by that slight action on one who did not know the plot, must have been either that Viola was very careless and thoughtless, or that she had some reason for being in a hurry to escape without further speech.

These are things which lie within the actress's own control; and if Miss Terry will but reconsider the original imputation against Viola, and acquit her of being a heartless schemer, planning to win the Duke and supplant Olivia before she had seen either of them, or knew how they stood affected towards each other, they will correct themselves. It will be self-evident that whatever is inconsistent with truth and tenderness of heart is impossible with Viola; and it will also follow naturally to speak the verse a little slower. For Viola, though very ready in apprehension, never *speaks* without pausing to think; and in her lightest and gayest moods (never very light or gay) cannot have spoken quick at any time.

That the humours of the duel-scene will ever be brought back
within the text of Shakespeare, and the limits of *becoming* mirth,
is more than we can hope. Managers can hardly be expected to
sacrifice a piece of farce, which always makes the audience very
merry; though Shakespeare has evidently taken pains to preserve
Viola from the ridiculous attitude in which it places her, and
she can never be seen as she was meant to be until it is reformed.
Miss Terry made the best of it, and acted it with great skill,
according to the directions in the stage copy. But if she will
carefully examine the original text, which contains no directions
except for the exits and entrances, she will find that the situation
gives scope for skill of a finer and subtler kind. Viola, it must
be remembered, has to sustain the part of a young gentleman,
who must not seem to be afraid of a drawn sword, or unused to
handle one. If she cannot contrive to avoid the fight handsomely,
the resource she looks too is not flight but confession—a confession of her disguise. "Pray God defend me," she says to
herself when it is coming to extremity, " a little thing would
make me"—not take to my heels—but " *tell them* how much I
lack of a man." How she would have done it we do not know;
but we may be sure that she would have known how to do it
gracefully and without loss of feminine dignity. But being a
person of great feminine (though not masculine) courage, of
remarkable composure and presence of mind and ready wit, she
reserves that for the last extremity; hoping by judgment,
gentleness, pacific bearing, and intervention of Providence, to
avoid the necessity of so inconvenient a disclosure. Of the
attempts to run away, and the dragging back and pushing on
by main force, it is not enough to say that there is no trace in
the original text; they are inconsistent with it. For up to the
very last, when there seemed to be no chance of escape left, the
only evidence she had given of the fear which she had such good
right to feel was " panting and looking pale." And even when
she is obliged to draw her sword, or prepare to draw it (for it is
doubtful whether Shakespeare intended to expose her to so severe
a trial as the actual crossing of weapons), her words are still
calm, and such as any gentleman might have used—"I do
assure you, 'tis against my will." Indeed, from the beginning

to the end of the adventure she neither does nor says anything
(her complexion and the beating of her heart excepted) that
would have misbecome a well-behaved, peaceful young gentleman,
who disliked to be drawn by a bully into a brawl. She acts
throughout with discretion, intelligence, and a collected judgment. When first warned of the danger, in terms meant to
inspire alarm in a man, she proposes to "return again into the
house, and desire some conduct of the lady—she is no fighter;
she has heard of some kind of men that put quarrels purposely
upon others to taste their valour; belike this is a man of that
quirk." When she finds that line of retreat cut off, not by being
forcibly held, but by Sir Toby's threat to make it a quarrel of
his own, she begs that she may at least "know of the knight
what her offence to him is; it is something of her negligence,
nothing of her purpose." When Fabian, staying by her, and
making it still impossible for her to get handsomely away, offers
to make her peace if he can, she takes the opportunity to repeat
her disavowal of a love for fighting, "I shall be much bound to
you for it: I am one that had rather go with Sir Priest than Sir
Knight: I care not who knows so much of my mettle." * But
she goes forward notwithstanding to the place where the danger
is; and there is not the slightest indication that she is either
pushed or pulled: so far, therefore, she has contrived to perform
her part without betraying more than had appeared before in
her countenance and behaviour: she "bore in her visage no
great presage of cruelty." And when it comes at last to a crisis,
in which she *must* either have disgraced her man's apparel or
betrayed her secret, the sudden appearance of Antonio rescues
her from the indignity; and drawing Sir Toby and Fabian out
of the way, enables her for the first time, with a simple, "Pray
sir, put up your sword, if you please," to settle the quarrel with
the principal for herself.

Now we submit that this struggle between woman's fear and

---

* The attempt at a swagger with which Miss Terry gave these words would
deserve all the praise it has received as an excellent piece of comic acting, if it were
not directly at variance with the words themselves. If Viola had professed that she
had rather go with Sir Knight than Sir Priest, it would have been in place. But
her anxiety was to put her pretensions to valour as *low* as, consistently with her
assumed character of a young gentleman wearing a sword, she possibly could.

woman's courage, wit, and self-respect,—gently, gracefully, bravely, and successfully carried through under very trying circumstances—is much finer comedy, as well as much more in harmony with the sentiment of the play, than the mere terrors and perplexities of a young woman frightened out of her wits at the idea of a naked sword,—though executed (as in this case it was) to perfection. The inward sinking of the heart may be made visible enough to the audience without any display of unseemly terror ; and Miss Terry's command of expression by play of countenance and action is so perfect, that an affectation of composure would be in no danger of being mistaken for an absence of fear.

We are aware that among the critics to whose judgment she will naturally look with most deference, there are many who will give very different advice. First impressions received early in life from a well-acted play are not easily removed or suspended for impartial reconsideration ; and those to whom the broader humours of the mock-duel, with Viola's ostentatious terrors, Fabian's shoulder applied from behind, and Sir Andrew's disappearance up the tree, are coeval with their first acquaintance with *Twelfth Night*, will hardly imagine what the play would be without them. Our own idea was formed from reading before we saw it on the stage ; and to us these humours have always been in the highest degree discordant and intolerable. But let Miss Terry take the case into her own consideration. The rare and peculiar merits which distinguish her acting are not such as she can have learned either from actors or critics. Her own feeling and imagination must have been her real tutors ; and it is to their decision we would refer her. Forgetting for awhile all that she may have seen or heard of other people's conceptions, let her conceive for herself the feelings of a tenderly-bred girl cast up from shipwreck on a strange coast, her affections all engrossed with grief for her lost brother, her wits all occupied in devising what to do ; and let her then accompany Viola through her various adventures, imagining what she must have felt in each situation, and how she must have spoken. She will feel, we think, in the first place, that a pretty and smiling consciousness of personal interest in the Duke's bachelor condition

is out of place in that sad and forlorn hour; not an hour for
vanity to take effect in a heart not disposed to vanity. She
will find her, on that first acquaintance, affectionate, gentle,
thoughtful, wise, pure, and brave; with manners that inspire
respect and tenderness in all she speaks to. On her next
appearance, after she has been listening for three days to the
Duke's eloquent description of his grief, she will find her changed
only in this—her heart has been smitten with a new affection,
apparently hopeless, and for which there seems to be no cure
but patience. It was nobody's fault. She has no complaint to
make, and she makes none; and patience does not fail her. But
though to the world she can still show a clear countenance and
a bright wit—never losing her dignity and grace of manner, her
quick intelligence, or her composure and self-possession—it must
not be forgotten that her days of mirth, if she ever had any,
are past, and that it is tragic business that is going on within.
Remembering this, Miss Terry will find no difficulty in following
all the changes of emotion in her interviews with Olivia, both
while she urges the Duke's suit, and while she rejects for herself
the passion she has involuntarily excited. We hope also that
she will feel—what Shakespeare plainly felt—that Viola must
not be exhibited in any attitude which is inconsistent with grace
and serious sympathy. And if on the next opportunity she will
try the experiment of playing the whole part according to this
conception and in this spirit, she may indeed disappoint some
" barren spectators " who came to laugh, but the effect of the
whole ought to be so beautiful and touching that we can hardly
imagine it not carrying the sympathies of the house with it; in
which case it may set a new fashion, and be the beginning of a
reform which will lead to the purification and regeneration of
our whole Shakesperian theatre.

XIII

THE "MERCHANT OF VENICE" AT THE PRINCE OF WALES'S THEATRE IN 1875.*

———◆———

THE decay of the legitimate drama has long been a subject of complaint; and if by the legitimate be meant the *poetic* drama, it must be admitted that fashion has not run strongly enough in that direction of late years to encourage managers to collect and train companies for the proper performance of it. A particular actor appears from time to time, and makes a name, by merit or otherwise, as representative of one of Shakespeare's great characters; and then a company of some kind is got together to support him. But it is long since we had a theatre that made the representation of the poetic drama its proper aim and business.

The immediate cause of this is not far to seek. The demand for the higher art is not sufficient to draw the supply; consequently the supply is not sufficient to encourage the demand. Playgoers do not ask for the great plays, because there is nobody to act them; managers do not procure people to act them, because playgoers do not ask for them. It is a difficulty which cannot be dealt with by way of precontract, for there is no way of engaging the public beforehand to supply full houses. The experiment must be made at the risk of the management, and the risk must be considerable. But it is all the more to be wished that when it is made, and made in a manner which deserves success, it should not fail for want of due information or appreciation on the part of the public. And here it is that the

* *Frazer's Magazine*, July, 1875.

Press has the power of doing both good and ill service. Though the concurrent applause of all the newspapers cannot make people take pleasure in a thing which does not amuse or interest them, it can make them go once to see it. Concurrent depreciation, on the other hand, by two or three will deter vast numbers from going at all, and so cut off the appeal which should lie from the judgment of the critic to the feeling of the audience. Thus it comes that the success of such adventures rests in great part with the theatrical columns of the daily Press; columns very unlike the *columnæ* that Horace speaks of, to which mediocrity was intolerable.

Through what we take to be nothing worse than thoughtlessness on the part of these invisible powers, a very praiseworthy experiment of the kind has lately fallen far short of the success it deserved, and is in danger of carrying with it in its fall a chance for the poetic drama which can hardly be expected to offer itself again. The managers of the Prince of Wales's Theatre having, by great care and skill, trained a company to act a certain class of popular plays (not of the poetic order) as well, perhaps, as they deserve to be acted, and thereby established for their house a well-merited reputation, were inspired with a laudable ambition to try the effect of the same care and skill in a higher region, and see whether one of Shakespeare's comedies could not be got up as perfectly, according to its kind, as *School* or *Society*. They chose a play which, though often acted, always pleasing, and containing one famous part, and one famous speech in another part, has never had justice done to it as a whole. They set it forth with scenery, costume, grouping, and general pictorial effect, equal to anything of the kind that has been produced in these times, when the arts of decoration have been so much studied. They took great pains both with the dialogue and the action, in all the parts, and in the minutest particulars. And though the best training for the Robertsonian drama leaves much to be learnt, and much also to be unlearnt, by an actor before he is fit for Shakespeare, they succeeded at least in inspiring every one of the company with a desire to do his best with the part assigned to him. More than all—because without some additional feature of special interest the best under such conditions would not, perhaps, have been good enough to make the *Merchant of Venice* attractive to a public which, if it will allow us to say so, requires " education " for the enjoyment of this kind of art no less than the players for the performance of it—they engaged for the principal part a lady ready furnished with all the qualities needed in it, who could show how "one of Shakespeare's women " may be and ought to be acted, and of whose performance it is not too much to say that it would of itself have gone far to supply that very " education " which both audience and actors stand so much in need of.

This being beyond all question the most important novelty and the great distinction of the enterprise, it might have been expected that judicious critics would try to make it conspicuous as a great event for playgoers, and a thing to be seen. And that they failed to do so is the more surprising because the merit of the performance, and even the singularity of its merit, appears to have been felt by them all. But unfortunately, while they agreed in distinguishing Miss Ellen Terry's Portia with exceptional praise, at once intelligent, discriminating, and unreserved, they agreed also in *beginning* their several notices with complaints of the unsatisfactory character and announcements of the imperfect success of the whole experiment, the effect of which must have been simply to warn people away ; and which have, in fact, resulted in the premature withdrawal of the piece before half the playgoing world have had a chance of seeing it. If the critics (who in these days of small theatres can make any play fail by calling it a failure, and give any play a chance of succeeding by calling it a success) had only begun by advising everybody to go and see Miss Terry in Portia—which was no more than the just inference from their own reports—they might have indulged themselves in what censures they pleased upon the rest, and done no harm. Those who went might have agreed with them or might have differed—all that *we* have happened to meet with did, in fact, differ with them widely and vehemently—but in either case they would have seen the play.

To us this premature withdrawal, though we cannot believe it to be final, seems an accident very much to be regretted, not only as tending to discourage a kind of enterprise which ought by all means to be encouraged, but because it will be difficult to find another part so well suited to the exercise of Miss Terry's peculiar gifts, and impossible to find another actress so well qualified to represent one of the most delightful of Shakespeare's female creations.

Mrs. Jameson, in attempting to classify the poet's women according to their characteristic qualities—as characters in which intellect and wit, passion and fancy, or the moral sentiments and affections, severally predominated—placed Portia among the women of intellect. But when we read her analysis of the character—one of the best things in a book which contains some of the best Shakesperian criticism that we possess—it becomes plain that a fourth class should have been provided for her—a class in which none of these qualities *predominated*, but all were equally developed; and if one was at any time more conspicuous than the rest, it was only because the accidents of the situation gave more occasion and scope for the exercise or exhibition of it. Suppose Portia's situation changed, and you feel at once that it would call up the appropriate feeling and be met in the appropriate attitude : for each of the enumerated qualities has its proper place in her nature, and is ready to answer the moment it is called upon. Even in the part which she has to play, bright, joyous, and happy as it is—a succession of fortunate adventures crowned with complete success —the occasional shadows which cross and threaten it are sufficient to draw out the virtues which she holds in reserve, and to reveal the latent capacities of her being ; giving certain assurance that tenderness, sweetness, modesty, affection, moral elevation, charity, self-denial, and magnanimity, are as inseparable from her nature as intellectual power and ready wit ; that she is capable of as much passion as is consistent with self-control, of as much imagination and fancy as can keep company with reason, of as much play of humour and sportive mischief as can be indulged without doing harm or giving pain. For though her lot is unusually free from strong contrasts of bright and dark, it is chequered with continual interchanges of light and shadow, which supply a succession of picturesque effects, and impart more real variety to her character than is to be found in

many of those which are made to pass through opposite
extremities of passion or fortune.

And if this variety of graces distinguishes the character of
Portia as designed by Shakespeare, it was not less the distinction of it as acted by Miss Terry. As she moved through the
changing scene, every new incident seemed to touch some new
feeling; and each change of feeling expressed itself by voice,
countenance, or gesture in a manner so lively and natural that
it was felt at once to be both true in itself and in harmony with
the rest. Everything that she had to do seemed to come
equally easy to her, and was done equally well; and the critic
who would undertake to define the limits within which her
power lies must be either very sagacious or very blind and deaf.
Putting aside the foolish prejudice which appropriates to a
particular character a particular type of face—which supposes,
for instance, that Lady Macbeth cannot be acted by a woman
whose face and figure cannot be made up into some kind of
resemblance to Mrs. Siddons—and remembering that where the
feeling is, any face can express it, if we ask ourselves what
forms of human feeling lie beyond the possible range of Miss
Terry's sympathetic conception, we find the question hard to
answer. We knew before that, within a certain range, she was
mistress of her art. We know now that her range is both wide
and high. The part of Portia is not a long one, but the memorable features in her performance of it make a long list. Remember
—we are sorry that we cannot now. say, observe—in the
scene where according to the new stage-arrangement she first
appeared, the reserved and stately courtesy with which she
received the Prince of Morocco, and explained to him the conditions of his venture; her momentary flutter of alarm as he
went to make his choice; her sudden relief, mixed with amusement, when he began by dismissing the leaden casket with
contempt; her conversation with Nerissa (properly her first
scene), half plaintive, half playful, in which she bemoaned her
fortune, and discussed the characters of the suitors—bringing
out every shade of humorous meaning in perfect relief, and yet
without the least coarseness or exaggeration; the delicate embarrassment of her first interview with Bassanio, when, in

desiring him to postpone his trial, she was betrayed into an avowal of her love; her deeper agitations of fear and hope as he deliberated over the caskets, and her outburst of passionate emotion when he concluded at last in favour of the right one; the sweet dignity with which she surrendered to him herself and all that was hers; her quick alarm at his change of counte- nance on reading Antonio's letter; her eager sympathy and impetuous resolution when she heard the contents; the hurried despatch of her letter to Bellario, writing and carrying on her conversation with Lorenzo at the same time (a novelty, by the way, required by the new scenic arrangements, but, as she handled it, a real improvement and enrichment of the text), and the bright promptitude of all her arrangements for departure,— all in the best blank verse, yet all so life-like; her perfect as- sumption of the manner and demeanour of the young and learned, and very gentlemanly, doctor of laws; the touching earnestness of her appeals to Shylock's better nature, as if desiring to save him from the penalty of his act by persuading him to forbear it; the silent accumulation of moral anger as he rejected each overture, and insisted upon pressing to extremity his legal advantage, till she seemed to feel for the moment a kind of scornful pleasure in offering him his own cup to drink; and at last, when, all serious business being happily over, she was at leisure to contemplate the situation, her infinite enjoy- ment of the humour of it—it would take a column to describe all that passed through her mind, and looked out of her eyes, as she said to Bassanio:

" I pray you *know me* when we meet again; "

the gaiety of heart which prompted her demand of the ring as a fee, and the abounding spirit of affectionate mischief with which she pursued the jest to its happy conclusion—all this, executed so perfectly as it was,—with a delivery of the words, whether verse and prose, so modulated that the ear was never for a moment weary; the action so delicately suited to the word and the word to the action; the meaning never missed and never obtruded; the modesty of nature never overstepped—implies, to our thinking, a degree of intelligence, imagination, feeling, humour, and taste, which (combined as it is with such perfect command of all the organs of expression) should suffice for the representation of *any* female character that is truly drawn by art from nature. And if, when such an artist appears, she may not act Shakespeare's women because the rest of the company have acquired a reputation for acting Robertson's men, who can wonder that the legitimate drama declines?

Every theatre in London has a public of its own, composed of those members of the general public who are attracted by the kind of entertainment in which it excels. The attraction held out by the Prince of Wales's has been what is called " pleasant comedy;" by which is meant correct imitations of the surface and slang of modern London life, with a careful setting of rooms and furniture and street landscapes very like the reality, and a careful avoidance of everything that appeals to the imagination or the heart. That a public brought together in the way of natural selection by a common taste for this kind of entertainment should find the *Merchant of Venice* less attractive, was to be expected. And though London contains other publics to which it was certain to prove much more attractive, and which would in due time have made up for secessions, time was required for the attraction to take effect upon them. They had to learn that there was something at the theatre worth seeing, and probably to alter domestic arrangements made on the assumption that there was not. But though this would be enough to account for a temporary falling-off in the attendance, it does not explain the chorus of depreciatory criticism with which the performance itself has been assailed, and which (there being so little apparent occasion for it) must be owing to some popular delusion with regard to the play itself. That in the representation at the Prince of Wales's Portia seemed for the first time a more interesting person than Shylock was a remark made by one of the critics, and made as much in derision of the whole perform-ance as in compliment to the exceptional merit of Miss E. Terry. Whether it was the first time that this has happened we cannot undertake to say, but if it was, it must be the first time that the play has been properly put upon the stage. For who that reads it as Shakespeare left it can doubt that this was *his* intention?

Those who know it only on the stage may doubt; for since the great tragic actors took up the part of Shylock the rest of the play (which was originally a comedy) has been sacrificed to it. The pruning-knife has been applied so freely to Bassanio (a part worthy of Charles Kemble in his prime) that no actor of eminence now takes it. The scenes at Belmont have been so handled that they might almost be left out without being missed. And though Portia has remained in possession of the chief actress in the company, she is associated in popular imagination chiefly with the elegant-extract speech in praise of mercy, which is remembered as the distinguishing feature of Mrs. Siddons' performance (and in that rather as a specimen of declamation than of true dramatic effect), and has never been reckoned among the great parts. In the case of Shylock, on the contrary, the admiration and sympathy properly due to the *actor*—generally the great tragedian of the day, and personally more interesting than all the rest of the company put together—have been transferred to himself; till we have come to regard one of the harshest pictures of malignity and depravity that Shakespeare ever exhibited in human shape as a kind of tragic hero, with something of the Miltonic Satan in him—

> The unconquerable will,
> And study of revenge, immortal hate,
> And courage never to submit or yield,
> And what is else not to be overcome.

Heroic qualities, which, joined with a feeling (belonging more to our own century than the sixteenth) that they are partly justified by provocation and hard usage and insults from baser natures, enable the actor to make his exit with an air of contemptuous superiority that imposes upon the audience, and brings them into a mood so sympathetic that if the end of the trial were the end of the play they would probably be quite satisfied, and care no more what becomes of Portia and the rest of her party. Indeed, we can remember long ago to have heard a good authority speak of the fifth act of the *Merchant of Venice* as an extraordinary instance of Shakespeare's inequality, all the interest having ended with the fourth; and extraordinary it would certainly be if the interest was meant to centre in Shylock.

But read the play as it was written, and imagine all the parts
acted equally well:—What title has Shylock to be the central
figure? There is nothing in him either good, or affecting, or
amusing, or terrible, or magnanimous. Passion there is, and
intellectual power; but it is passion of the meanest and most
malignant kind. There is no mystery about him. His first
soliloquy introduces him to us exactly as he is—a Jewish usurer,
who hates all Christians, but especially Christians who are
simple enough to lend money gratis; hates them because they
bring down the rate of usance, and means to be revenged when
he can. A chance offers itself at the moment. Antonio, a
gratuitous lender, who has often spoiled his bargains by redeem-
ing his debtors from forfeiture, wants to borrow money himself.
He offers it, under pretence of kindness, as a loan without
interest; but contrives, under cover of a jest, to engage the
borrower's life as security for the repayment of the principal.
There you have the whole case—the man, the motive, the design.
The hard words and indignities to his beard and gaberdine which
he has suffered in former disputes with Antonio are of small
account with him. Those he has always been content to let pass
with a shrug, and only remembers now for purposes of rhetoric.
But the delivery of debtors from forfeiture is an injury not to be
forgiven, and he deliberately resolves to kill him out of his way
if he has the chance. Who can suppose that Shakespeare would
have introduced *into a comedy* such a character as this, with
intent to make him an object either of admiration or pity, or
even of abhorrence? Is it not plain that, for purposes of
comedy, his proper fate is to be baffled and defeated, and then
dismissed with contempt? And so in the real play he is; for his
fate is no way tragical; and his punishment, while it is appropriate enough to satisfy the sense of justice, is not so heavy as to
cast a shadow inconsistent with merriment. One-half of his
goods is restored to him at Antonio's request; the other is to be
held in trust for his son-in-law, payable upon his own death; and
though the condition that he should "presently become a
Christian" may seem to us an inhuman and unnecessary
aggravation, we must remember that in those days a Christian
was a Christian, and that to the audience at the Globe it would

seem neither a punishment nor an indignity. Antonio meant it, we fancy, for a mercy; thinking that Shylock's soul, which he had some reason for supposing to be in a bad condition, would be the better for it.

The Shylock of the modern stage is said to have been invented and brought into fashion by Macklin in 1741. In the primitive times it was treated, no doubt, according to the description in the title-page of the *Comical History of the Merchant of Venice*, simply as "Shylock the Jew," whose "extreme cruelty towards the said merchant in cutting a just pound of his flesh" was advertised as one of the attractions. In the late revival, the restoration of Portia to her legitimate pre-eminence had the effect of reducing Shylock to his proper place. But the popular tradition of a century is not easily overcome, and its influence was traceable in the conception of the character. Mr. Coghlan, coming to his task with a reputation for success in the lightest and most modern comedy, has of course been reproved for aspiring to rise above it. It is the regular remark in all such cases. As it appeared to us, however, it was not the accomplishments of the light comedian so much as the example of the great tragedians, that really stood in his way. It betrayed him into an ambition to make too much of the part. His long pauses, his elaborate by-play, his exaggerated emphasis, were meant to make it impressive, and were in themselves skilful; but they did in fact make it slow and heavy, and combined with the tedious intervals between the acts (necessary, we suppose, for the arrangement of the scenery) to make the whole play drag. In addressing Antonio, he spoke of the insults he had received from him with an emphasis and angry bitterness which would have been very effective in the proper place, but were here against his meaning and inconsistent with his own game—which was to make Antonio believe that he was ready to forget all such things, and to deserve his love by friendly dealing. In the trial-scene he was so excessively deliberate in all his movements, so long in answering questions, so slow of delivery both in the set speeches and in the scornful retorts, that all the eagerness and impatience in pursuit of his prey which makes itself felt so strongly in reading appeared to have died out of him. A quicker movement all

through would have corrected the principal defects of the personation, and, whatever the critics might say, it would have had its
effect upon the audience. And if, at the same time, it had been
possible to shorten the intervals between the scenes, and restore
them to their proper order, the action would have been found to
be much lighter and livelier, and more harmonious. Shakespeare
was not troubled with complicated scenery. A room in Portia's
house at Belmont was easily changed into a street in Venice; and
a great part of his art in constructing plays so that they should
"please" consisted in the rapid interchange of short scenes. As
a series of pictorial illustrations, the scenic arrangements at the
Prince of Wales's cannot be too much praised. The living and
moving groups, as well as the painted scenes, formed a succession
of fine Venetian pictures. But it must be owned that the delays
which they involved interfered very materially with the enjoyment of the play.

But whatever improvements it admitted of, we must repeat
the expression of our regret that it has not proved attractive
enough to be continued; that the managers have had to fall
back again upon the humours of the club, the street, and the
drawing-room; and that the critics are all applauding them for
having so graciously submitted to "the judgment of the public,"
and by the simple expedient of substituting *Money* for the
Merchant of Venice, made their house once more "the home of
pleasant comedy."

For those who are ready to accept *Money* as the representative of pleasant comedy, its old attractions would probably have
been sufficient. But, in justice to the managers, and for the
encouragement of those who, like ourselves, have had enough of
such humours, it is right to add that it now appears with some
new attractions which will be more to their taste. Mrs. Ban-
croft's lively widow is a new thing, and a great improvement
upon the original type. And the heroine, who used to be a
somewhat doleful, sentimental, uninteresting piece of unhappy
virtue, reappears in Miss E. Terry as a true woman, full of
genuine feeling, and so natural in every tone and gesture that
(as a judicious critic has remarked) she makes the rest of the
piece unreal by contrast. This is indeed a new creation, worthy

of a permanent place among the classical figures of the poetic drama ; and though the passion is really tragic throughout, the authority of Lord Lytton will probably obtain leave for it to keep its place in pleasant comedy. We have been rather alarmed, however, by a remark which has been called forth by a still later exhibition of the same merits in a different subject. In a *comedietta*—very lively comedy from beginning to end—Miss Terry acted a young wife, and the remark was that she threw into her personation an amount of earnestness, pathos and real feeling, which, though very wonderful and admirable in itself, was perhaps hardly "suitable." It appears, therefore, that the *prestige* of this meritorious little theatre is in peril this way too. Is it beyond hope that, among so many rival candidates for popular attraction, some enterprising manager may train a company expressly for the exhibition of these very qualities, and establish for his house a *prestige* which can only be endangered by producing something for which they are *not* suitable.

XIV.

ON THE AUTHORSHIP OF THE PLAYS ATTRIBUTED TO SHAKESPEARE.*

———◦◦———

I HAVE read your book on the authorship of Shakespeare faithfully to the end, and if my report of the result is to be equally faithful, I must declare myself not only unconvinced, but undisturbed. To ask me to believe that the man who was accepted by all the people of his own time, to many of whom he was personally known, as the undoubted author of the best plays then going, was *not* the author of them—is like asking me to believe that Charles Dickens was not the author of "Pickwick." To ask me to believe that a man who was famous for a variety of other accomplishments, whose life was divided between public business, the practice of a laborious profession, and private study of the art of investigating the material laws of nature,—a man of large acquaintance, of note from early manhood, and one of the busiest men of his time—but who was never suspected of wasting time in writing poetry, and is not known to have written a single blank verse in all his life,—that this man was the author of fourteen comedies, ten historical plays, and eleven tragedies, exhibiting the greatest and the greatest variety of excellence that has been attained in that kind of composition,—is like asking me to believe that Lord Brougham was the author not only of Dickens' novels, but of Thackeray's also, and of Tennyson's poems besides. That the author of "Pickwick" was a man called Charles Dickens I know upon no better authority than that upon which I know that the author of Hamlet was a man called William Shake-

* From a letter to Professor Nathaniel Holmes, 15th February, 1867.

2 B

speare. And in what respect is the one more difficult to believe than the other? A boy born and bred like Charles Dickens was as unlikely *a priori* to become famous over Europe and America for a never-ending series of original stories, as a boy born and bred like William Shakespeare to become the author of the most wonderful series of dramas in the world. It is true that Shakespeare's gifts were higher and rarer; but the wonder is that *any* man should have possessed them, not that the man to whose lot they fell was the son of a poor man called John Shakespeare, and that he was christened William. That he was not a man otherwise known to the world is not strange at all. Nature's great lottery being open to everybody, the chances that the supreme prize will be drawn by an unknown man are as the numbers of the unknown to the known—millions to hundreds. It is not the famous man that becomes a great inventor; the great inventor becomes a famous man. Faraday was a bookbinder's apprentice, who in binding a copy of Mrs. Marcet's Conversations on Chemistry, was attracted to the study, got employed as an assistant to Sir Humphrey Davy—an assistant in so humble a capacity that wishing to make the acquaintance of some of the scientific men on the continent, he actually went with him to Geneva as his servant—and by his own genius, virtue, and industry, made himself the most famous man (probably) now living in England. Burns was a ploughman. Keats was a surgeon's apprentice. George Stephenson a lad employed in a colliery. Newton did not become Newton because he was sent to Cambridge; he was sent to Cambridge because he *was* Newton—because he had been endowed by nature with the singular gifts which made him Newton. But for the genius which nature gave them without any consideration of position or advantages, what would have been known of any one of these?

If Shakespeare was not trained as a scholar or a man of science, neither do the works attributed to him show traces of trained scholarship or scientific education. Given the *faculties* (which nature bestows as freely on the poor as on the rich), you will find that all the acquired knowledge, art, and dexterity which the Shakespearian plays imply, were easily attainable by a man

who was labouring in his vocation and had nothing else to do.
Or if you find this difficult to believe of such a man as you
assume Shakespeare to have been, try Bacon. Suppose Francis
Bacon, instead of being trained as a scholar, a statesman, and a
lawyer, and seeking his fortune from the patronage of the great,
had been turned loose into the world without means or friends,
and joined a company of players as the readiest resource for a
livelihood.   Do you doubt that he would soon have tried his
hand at writing a play? that he would have found out how to
write better plays than were then the fashion? that he would
have cultivated an art which he found profitable and prosperous,
and sought about for such knowledge as would help him in it,—
reading his Plutarch, and his Seneca, and his Hollinshead, and
all the novels and play-books that came in his way; studying
life and conversation by all the opportunities which his position
permitted; and generally seeking to enrich his thought with
observation?   Do not you think that Francis Bacon would have
been capable of learning in that way everything which there
is any reason to think the writer of the Shakespearian plays
knew? And if Francis Bacon could, why could not William
Shakespeare?

If therefore your theory involved no difficulties of its own—
if you merely proposed the substitution of one man for another
—I should still have asked why I should doubt the tradition;—
where was the difficulty which made the old story hard to
believe. I see none.   That which is *extraordinary* in the case,
and against which therefore there lies *primâ facie* some presumption, is that *any* man should possess such a combination
of faculties as must have met in the author of these plays. But
that is a difficulty which cannot be avoided.   There must have
been *somebody* in whom the requisite combination of faculties
did meet: for there the plays are: and by supposing that this
somebody was a man who at the same time possessed a combination of other faculties, themselves sufficient to make him an
extraordinary man too, you do not diminish the wonder but
increase it. Aristotle was an extraordinary man. Plato was
an extraordinary man. That two men each severally so extraordinary should have been living at the same time in the same

country, was a very extraordinary thing. But would it diminish the wonder to suppose the two to be one? So I say of Bacon and Shakespeare. That a human being possessed of the faculties necessary to make a Shakespeare should exist, is extraordinary. That a human being possessed of the faculties necessary to make a Bacon should exist, is extraordinary. That two such human beings should have been living in London at the same time was more extraordinary still. But that one man should have existed possessing the faculties and opportunities necessary to make *both*, would have been the most extraordinary thing of all.

You will not deny that tradition goes for *something*: that in the absence of any reason for doubting it, the concurrent and undisputed testimony to a fact of all who had the best means of knowing it, is a reason for believing it: or at least for thinking it more probable than any other given fact, not compatible with it, which is not so supported. On this ground alone, without inquiring further, I believe that the author of the plays published in 1623 was a man called William Shakespeare. It was believed by those who had the best means of knowing: and I know no reason for doubting it. The reasons for doubting which you suggest seem all to rest upon a latent assumption that William Shakespeare could not have possessed any remarkable faculties: a fact which would no doubt settle the question if it were established. But what should make me think so? It was not the opinion of anybody who was acquainted with him, so far as we know; and why was a man of that name less likely than another to possess remarkable faculties?

With one to whom the simple story as it comes presents no difficulty, you will not expect that the other considerations which you urge should have much weight. Resemblances both in thought and language are inevitable between writers nourished upon a common literature, addressing popular audiences in a common language, and surrounded by a common atmosphere of knowledge and opinion. But to me, I confess, the resemblances between Shakespeare and Bacon are not so striking as the differences. Strange as it seems that two such minds, both so vocal, should have existed within each other's hearing without mutually affecting each other, I find so few traces of any influence exercised by Shakespeare upon Bacon, that I have great doubt whether Bacon knew any more about him than Gladstone (probably) knows about Tom Taylor (in his dramatic capacity). Shakespeare may have derived a good deal from Bacon. He had no doubt read the Advancement of Learning and the first edition of the Essays, and most likely had frequently heard him speak in the Courts and the Star Chamber. But among all the parallelisms which you have collected with such industry to illustrate the identity of the writer, I have not observed one in which I should not have inferred from the difference of style a difference of hand. Great writers, especially being contemporary, have many features in common; but if they are really great writers they write naturally, and nature is always individual. I doubt whether there are five lines together to be found in Bacon which could be mistaken for Shakespeare, or five lines in Shakespeare which could be mistaken for Bacon, by one who was familiar with their several styles and practised in such observations. I was myself well read in Shakespeare before I began with Bacon; and I have been forced to cultivate what skill I have in distinguishing Bacon's style to a high degree; because in sifting the genuine from the spurious I had commonly nothing but the style to guide me. And to me, if it were proved that any one of the plays attributed to Shakespeare was really written by Bacon, not the least extraordinary thing about it would be the power which it would show in him of laying aside his individual peculiarities and assuming those of a different man.

If you ask me what I say to Bacon's own confession in the case of Richard II., I say that your inference is founded entirely upon a misconstruction of a relative pronoun. "About the same time I remember an answer of mine in a matter which had some affinity with my lord's cause, *which* though it grew from me went after about in others' names." I say that "which" means not the *matter* but the *answer*.* You make it

---

* Professor Holmes had assumed the "story of the first year of King Henry IV." (which was the matter in question) to be the Shakespearian play of Richard II.: and argued that, in saying that "*it* [namely the play] grew from him," Bacon

appear to refer to the "matter" only by inserting "and"
(p. 251, l. 8), which is not in the original: and if so there is an
end of your whole superstructure. When the queen asked him
whether there was not treason in Dr. Hayward's history of the
first year of Henry IV. he parried the question by an evasive
answer; which was quoted afterwards and ascribed in conversation to other people, but was really his own. Even if it were
possible to believe that the "matter" in question was the play
of Richard II., the only inference that could be drawn as to the
authorship is that the ostensible author was a doctor. But for
my part I can see nothing in it but a reference to Dr. Hayward's
historical tract.

These are my reasons for rejecting your theory. If you had
fixed upon anybody else rather than Bacon as the true author—
anybody of whom I knew nothing—I should have been scarcely
less incredulous; because I deny that a *primâ facie* case is made
out for questioning Shakespeare's title. But if there were any
reason for supposing that somebody else was the real author, I
think I am in a condition to say that, whoever it was, it was not
Bacon. The difficulties which such a supposition would involve
would be almost innumerable and altogether insurmountable.
But if what I have said does not excuse me from saying more,
what I might say more would be equally ineffectual.

I ought perhaps to apologize for speaking with such confidence on the question of style in a matter where my judgment
is opposed to yours. But you must remember that style is like
hand-writing—not easy to recognize at first, but unmistakable
when you are familiar enough with it. When some twenty-five
years ago I began the work of collating the manuscripts with the
printed copies, and plunged into a volume of miscellaneous
letters written in the beginning of the seventeenth century, I
could scarcely distinguish one hand from another, and it was
some time before I discovered which was Bacon's own. But
after a little of the close and continuous attention which collating and copying involves, I began to feel as if I could know it

confessed himself the real author. Mr. H. allows that he had misconstrued " which,"
and that this point of the confession must be given up, but remains otherwise
satisfied that Bacon *was* the author and that the queen knew it.

through all its varieties, from the stateliest Italian to the most sprawling black-letter, and almost swear to a semi-colon. And I am convinced that I could produce many cases in which the most expert palæographers and fac-similists would at the first view pronounce two hands different, yet find on examination that they were the same. Now it is the same with a man's manner of expressing himself. The unconscious gestures of the style, scarcely discernible at first, are scarcely mistakable after. The time may have been—I do not know—when I could have believed the style of Hamlet and of the Advancement of Learning to be the style of the same man: and the time may yet come when you will yourself wonder that you did not perceive the difference.

XV

ON A QUESTION CONCERNING A SUPPOSED SPECIMEN
OF SHAKESPEARE'S HANDWRITING.*

MR. RICHARD SIMPSON's note on this subject (4th S., viii. 1) has
not received so much attention from Shakespearian scholars as
I expected. If there is in the British Museum an entire dramatic
scene, filling three pages of fifty lines each, composed by Shakespeare when he was about twenty-five years old, *and written out
with his own hand*, it is a "new fact" of much more value than
all the new facts put together, which have caused from time to
time so much hot controversy of late years. As a curiosity it
would command a high price; but it is better than a curiosity.
To know what kind of hand Shakespeare wrote would often help
to discover what words he wrote. Is it possible that we have
here a sample, not only of his handwriting, but of his handwriting under the heat and impulse of composition? This is Mr.
Simpson's question; and though he does not pretend to offer
proof of the fact, he gives reasons for thinking it likely, which
certainly deserve serious consideration.

A play on the subject of the life and death of Sir Thomas
More, supposed on other grounds to have been the property of
the company of players to which Shakespeare belonged, and to
have been written about the year 1590, may still be read—all
but a scene or two—in the shape in which it was originally
submitted to the Master of the Revels for his license (Harl. MS.
7368). Large alterations have been made in it; whole scenes
have been added or rewritten. The rewritten scenes are found

* *Notes and Queries*, September 21, 1872.

on separate sheets of paper, and in different handwritings; and
being also very different in style, may be supposed to have been
contributed by their several authors in the state in which they
are. One of them shows so marked a superiority to the rest, in
every quality of dramatic composition, as to suggest the question: Who was there then living that could have written it?
Now it has always been supposed that one of Shakespeare's
employments, in the beginning of his theatrical career, was the
revision and adaptation to the stage of other men's compositions.
In this case the Master of the Revels had taken alarm at a scene
representing a popular insurrection, and ordered it to be struck
out. How it had been handled in the original copy we cannot
tell; for the leaf which contained it has been removed, and we
only know that it ended with the submission of the insurgents,
after a speech from More, concluding with a promise to intercede
for their pardon. From the closing sentence (top of page 30,
Dyce's edition), it may be inferred that this speech was in prose;
and if the argument was weakly handled—as from the rest of
the composition seems very likely—the young Shakespeare may
have been called in to mend and strengthen it. If the substituted scene was his answer to the call, no difficulty presents
itself for explanation; for, though a very good specimen of his
powers as a dramatic writer, we know that it was not beyond
them. But if it was not his, there must have been somebody
else then living who could write as well as he; and the difficulty
is to name him. These considerations are sufficient to make out
a case for inquiry, and the questions to be asked are two:—
1. Does the workmanship of this scene bear internal evidence
that Shakespeare was the workman? 2. Does the penmanship
bear internal evidence that the penman was the author?

The data for an answer to the first of these questions are
within the reach of most people who think the matter worth a
little trouble. The play has been printed by the Shakespeare
Society; and though the condition of the manuscript as to handwriting is imperfectly explained, every reader may judge for himself whether it contains any scene or scenes implying a different
and superior author to the rest, and how far they go to prove that
that author was Shakespeare. What he has to do is only to

read the whole play straight through with a free attention, and then to apply himself particularly to that part which begins near the top of p. 24 (Dyce's edition), and ends at the bottom of p. 29. If he finds nothing there but what might have been written by anybody, he need not trouble himself with any further inquiry; for the second question will have no interest for him. But if he finds in it, as I do, a stronger resemblance to the acknowledged works of Shakespeare's youth than to those of any other poet with whom he is acquainted, he will naturally wish to know whether the hand that wrote the lines belonged to the mind that invented them.

For this, as the case now stands, he must have recourse to the original manuscript—a condition which unfortunately excludes many persons otherwise well qualified to judge. For the manuscript can only be examined at the British Museum, and the character of the handwriting can only be understood by those who are familiar with the ordinary handwriting of the period. But those who are, and who can spare time for an attentive examination, will conclude, I think, that the penman was the author: for though the corrections are very few, they will see that those which do occur are not like corrections of mistakes made in copying, but like alterations introduced in the course of composition (see the lines quoted in note 2, p. 28). They will also see that it is a hand which answers to all we know about Shakespeare's. It agrees with his signature; which is a simple one, written in the ordinary character of the time, and exactly such a one as would be expected from the writer of this scene, if his name was William Shakspere, and he wrote it in the same way. It agrees with the tradition, that his first occupation was that of a "Noverint," a lawyer's copying clerk: for in that case he must have acquired in early youth a hand of that type, which, when he left copying and took to original composition, would naturally grow into such a hand as we have here. It agrees also with the report of his first editors, that they had "received from him scarcely a blot in his writings," he "flowed with such facility." And it shows more than one instance of a fault which has caused much trouble to his later editors—a fault incident to that very facility—the occasional omission of a word in the eagerness of composition. There are at least two places in which the metre halts, though no irregularity can have been intended (see p. 382, line 33 and p. 383, l. 2); doubtless from this cause. As for its appearance and character, that is a thing which can hardly be conveyed by description; but those who are possessed of Netherclift's "Handbook to Autographs" will find, in the auto-graph of Edmund Spenser, a hand a good deal like it; the letters are formed upon the same model, and there is some resemblance in the execution.

These, however, are mere opinions, not entitled to any authority. The point will never be settled unless people can see the evidence for themselves. And to bring it within reach of the generality of readers, I would suggest the publication in fac-simile of the whole scene in question; together with a line or two of each of the other hands contained in the manuscript (of which I make out five), by way of specimen, that the differences may be clearly shown. For Mr. Simpson takes both the scene im-mediately preceding (pp. 22-24), and the subsequent scenes from p. 39 to p. 53, to be in the same hand; whereas I take them to be certainly in another, as far at least as the twentieth line of p. 51, where a change occurs; the remainder of the dialogue having evidently been added by a different and very superior penman; though whether or not by the same who penned the insurrection scene, I should not like to say positively without taking the opinion of an expert. But any question which may arise on this point may be allowed to stand over. The inquiry will be much simpler if confined to the authorship and penman-ship of the insurrection scene; the handwriting of which, though of the ordinary type, is far from ordinary in character, but might be easily recognized wherever met with, and (with the help of the proposed fac-simile) identified.

If the question should prove interesting enough to call for a reprint of Dyce's edition of the whole play, it should be carefully collated: for, though generally very correct, I have noticed some errors and omissions.

NOTE.

The whole scene from which Mr. Simpson's *first* quotation is taken runs thus, in modern spelling.

Enter LINCOLN, DOLL, CLOWN, GEORGE BETTS, WILLIAMSON, others, and a SERGEANT-AT-ARMS.

Lincoln. Peace, hear me: He that will not see a red-herring at a Harry groat, butter at elevenpence a pound, meal at nine shillings a bushel, and beef at four nobles a stone, list to me.

George Betts. It will come to that pass if strangers be suffered. Mark him.

Lincoln. Our country is a great eating country. *Argo*, they eat more in our country than they do in their own.

Betts, Clown. By a halfpenny loaf a day, troy weight.

Lincoln. They bring in strange roots, which is merely to the undoing of poor prentices: for what's a sorry parsnip to a good heart?

Williamson. Trash, trash; they breed sore eyes; and 'tis enough to infect the city with the palsy.

Lincoln. Nay, it has infected it with the palsy: for these bastards of dung, as you know they grow in dung, have infected us, and it is our infection will make the city shake: which partly comes through the eating of parsnips.

Clown, Betts. True; and pumpions together.

Enter SERGEANT.

Sergeant. What say ye to the mercy of the king?
Do ye refuse it?

Lincoln. You would have us upon the hip, would you? No marry, do we not: we accept of the king's mercy, but we will show no mercy upon the strangers.

Sergeant. You are the simplest things that ever stood
In such a question.

Lincoln. How say ye now, prentices? prentices simple! Down with him!

All. Prentices simple! Prentices simple!

Enter The LORD MAYOR, SURREY, SHREWSBURY.

Mayor. Hold! in the King's name hold!

Surrey. Friends, masters, countrymen——

Mayor. Peace, ho, peace! I charge you keep the peace!

Shrewsbury. My masters, countrymen——

Williamson. The noble Earl of Shrewsbury, let's hear him.

George Betts. We'll hear the Earl of Surrey.

Lincoln. The Earl of Shrewsbury.

Betts. We'll hear both.

All. Both, both, both, both!

Lincoln. Peace, I say, peace! Are you men of wisdom, or what are you?

Surrey. What you will have them, but not men of wisdom.

All. We'll not hear my Lord of Surrey: no, no, no, no! Shrewsbury, Shrewsbury!

Moor. Whiles they are o'er the bank of their obedience,
Thus will they bear down all things.

Lincoln. Shrief Moor speaks. Shall we hear Shrief Moor speak?

Doll. Let's hear him: a keeps a plentiful shrievaltry, and a made my brother
Arthur Watchins Sergeant Safe's yeoman: let's hear Shrove Moor!

All. Shreve Moor, Moor, More, Shreve Moor!

Moor. Even by the rule you have among yourselves,
Command still audience.

All. Surrey, Surrey!

All. Moor, Moor!

Lincoln, Betts. Peace, peace, silence, peace!

Moor. You that have voice and credit with the number
Command them to a stillness.

Lincoln. A plague on them, they will not hold their peace;
The devil cannot rule them.

Moor. Then what a rough and riotous charge have you
To lead those that the devil cannot rule!—
Good masters, hear me speak.

Doll. Ay, by the Mass will we, Moor: thou art a good housekeeper, and I thank
thy good worship for my brother Arthur Watchins.

All. Peace, peace!

Moor. Look what you do offend you cry upon:
That is the peace. Not [one] of you here present,
Had there such fellows lived when you were babes
That could have kept [1] the peace as now you would,
The peace wherein you have till now grown up
Had been ta'en from you, and the bloody times
Could not have brought you to the state of men.
Alas, poor things, what is it you have got
Although we grant you get the thing you seek?

Betts. Marry, the removing of the strangers, which cannot choose but much
advantage the poor handicrafts of the city.

Moor. Grant them removed, and grant that this your noise
Hath chid down all the majesty of England.
Imagine that you see the wretched strangers,
Their babies at their backs and their poor luggage,
Plodding to the ports and coasts for transportation,
And that you sit as kings in your desires,
Authority quite silenced by your brawl,
And you in ruff of your opinions clothed;—
What had you got? I'll tell you: you had taught
How insolence and strong hand should prevail,
How order should be quelled; and by this pattern
Not one of you should live an aged man.
For other ruffians, as their fancies wrought,
With self-same hand, self-reasons, and self-right,
Would shark on you, and men like ravenous fishes
Would feed on one another.

---

[1] So the MS. as I read it. Dyce read it "topt."

Doll. Before God, that's as true as the gospel.

Lincoln. Nay, this is a sound fellow, I tell you : let's mark him.

Moor. Let me set up before your thoughts, good friends,
One supposition : which if you will mark
You shall perceive how horrible a shape
Your innovation bears. First, 'tis a sin
Which oft the Apostle did forewarn us of,
Urging obedience to authority.
And 'twere no error if I told you all
You were in arms against your [God himself.] [1]

All. Marry, God forbid that.

Moor. Nay, certainly you are.
For to the king God hath his office lent
Of dread, of justice, power and command,
Hath bid him rule and willed you to obey :
And to add ampler majesty to this,
He hath not only lent the king his figure,
His throne and sword, but given him his own name,
Called him a god on earth. What do you then,
Rising 'gainst him that God himself instals,
But rise 'gainst God ? . What do you to your souls
In doing this ? O desperate as you are,
Wash your foul minds with tears, and those same hands
That you like rebels lift against the peace,
Lift up for peace ; and your unreverent knees
Make them your feet to kneel to be forgiven.
Tell me but this : what rebel captain,
As mutinies are incident, by his name
Can still the rout ? Who will obey a traitor ?
Or how can well that proclamation sound
Where there is no addition but a rebel
To qualify a rebel ? You'll put down strangers,
Kill them, cut their throats, possess their houses,
And lead the majesty of law in liom
To slip him like a hound. Say now the king
(As he is clement if the offender mourn)
Should so much come too short of your great trespass
As but to banish you, whither would you go ?
What country by the nature of your error
Should give you harbour ? Go you to France or Flanders,
To any German province, to Spain or Portugal,
Nay, any where that not adheres to England,—
Why you must needs be strangers : would you be pleased
To find a nation of such barbarous temper
That breaking out in hideous violence
Would not afford you an abode on earth,
Whet their detested knives against your throats,
Spurn you like dogs, and like as if that God

---

[1] Dyce supplied the blank with " sovereign." The context seems to me to require " God."

Owed not nor made not you, nor that the elements
Were not all appropriate to your comforts [1]
But chartered unto them,—what would you think
To be thus used? This is the strangers' case;
And this your mountainish inhumanity.

    All. Faith a says true: let's do as we may be done by.

    Lincoln. We'll be ruled by you, Master Moor, if you'll stand our friend to procure our pardon.

    Moor. Submit you to these noble gentlemen,
Entreat their mediation to the king,
Give up yourself to form, obey the magistrate,
And there's no doubt that mercy may be found,
If you so seek.

    [From "Sir Thomas More, a play now first printed, edited by the Rev. Alexander Dyce. London: printed for the Shakespeare Society. 1844." pp. 24–29.]

The interpolated scene ends at the bottom of p. 29 of Dyce's edition. The three prose lines which follow at the top of page 30 appear to have been the conclusion of the same scene as originally written; and were meant, no doubt, to be struck out, along with the rest; which is lost; the leaf or leaves which contained it having been taken out when the new scene was pasted in.

But there is another scene which occurs further on, and forms part of the original MS. as it was sent to the licenser before any alterations were made in it, which shows that more hands than one had already been concerned in the composition. It cannot have been the work of the same person who composed the body of the play; and as a piece of dramatic blank verse written (see Dyce's preface) "about 1590 or perhaps a little earlier," is remarkable enough to be worth extracting. It will be found in its place at p. 75.

    Enter the Lady MOORE, her two daughters, and Master ROPER, as walking.

    Roper. Madame, what ayles yee for to looke so sad?

    Lady. Troth, sonne, I knowe not what; I am not sick,
And yet I am not well. I would be merie;
But somewhat lyes so heavie on my hart,
I cannot chuse but sigh. You are a scholler;
I pray ye, tell me, may one credit dreames?

    Roper. Why ask you that, dear madame?

    Lady. Because to-night I had the straungest dreame
That ere my sleep was troubled with. Me thought 'twas night,
And that the king and queene went on the Themes
In bardges to heare musique: my lord and I
Were in a little boate me thought,—Lord, Lord,
What straunge things live in slumbers!—and beeing neere,
We grapled to the bardge that bare the king.
But after many pleasing voyces spent
In that still mooving musique house, me thought
The violence of the streame did sever us

---

[1] So in the MS. There is something wrong in the line. A word omitted probably; or "all" written instead of "alike."

Quite from the golden fleet, and hurried us
Unto the bridge, which with unused horror
We entered at full tide: thence some slight shoote
Beeing caried by the waves, our boate stood still
Just opposite the Tower, and there it turnde
And turnde about, as when a whirle-poole sucks
The circkled waters: me thought that we both cryed
Till that we sunck; where arm in arm we dyed.

   Roper. Give no respect, deare madame, to fond dreames;
They are but slight illusions of the blood.

   Lady. Tell me not all are so; for often dreames
Are true diviners, either of good or ill:
I cannot be in quiet till I heare
How my lord fares.

   Roper (aside). Nor I.—Come hether, wife:
I will not fright thy mother, to interprete
The nature of a dreame; but trust me, sweete,
This night I have bin troubled with thy father
Beyond all thought.

   Roper's Wife.   Truely, and so have I:
Methought I sawe him heere in Chelsey churche
Standing upon the roodloft, now defacde;
And whilste he kneeld and prayd before the ymage,
It fell with him into the upper-quier,
Where my poore father lay all stainde in blood.

   Roper. Our dreams all meet in one conclusion,
Fatall, I feare.

   Lady. What's that you talke? I pray ye, let me knowe it.

   Roper's Wife. Nothing, good mother.

   Lady. This is your fashion still; I must know nothing.
Call Maister Catesbie; he shall straite to courte,
And see how my lord does: I shall not rest,
Until my hart leane panting on his breast.

XVI

THE DUTY OF ADVOCATES IN CRIMINAL TRIALS.*

———◆———

I.

WHY is it that when a criminal has a defence made for him
which the judge considers as an aggravation of his crime so
great that, if the law allowed it, he would give him hard labour
in addition to imprisonment, the lawyers through whom the
defence is made pass uncensured, as if they had merely done
their duty?

This question is suggested by a case tried last week at the
assizes in a country town. A young gentleman of twenty-three
was indicted for taking away from her father a girl of humble
birth under sixteen. He had induced her to leave her home
and go with him to a house of ill-fame, where he kept her for
some days, living with the inmates, till they were found there
by the defendant's father, who took his son home, and sent the
girl to the house of a relation. The defence was that he was
the seduced rather than the seducer; and the proof was, first,
that his *attentions* had been connived at by the parents in the
hope of entrapping him into a marriage (for it was not even pretended that they had connived at the *abduction*), and secondly
that she had gone willingly and remained without showing signs
of discontent. In support of the first allegation it does not
appear that any proof was offered. In support of the second,
women were produced who had seen the girl at the house in
question, and swore that she had drunk, laughed, and played
at cards, and lived comfortably with the defendant and the

* The *Examiner*, April, 1852.

2 c

inmates and visitors of the establishment, till the father came and took them away. On this point "a great body of evidence was adduced."

With all this the jury had of course nothing to do; the question for them being merely whether the father had connived at the abduction; which they found that he had *not*, and returned a verdict of guilty. It was for the judge to consider whether the evidence on the other point justified any mitigation of punishment. What said the judge? He "could not attach any credit to these creatures. It was repugnant to human nature that a girl brought up in habits of modesty, etc. It would have been far better if the defendant had offered her some compensation before the prosecution: but so far from doing so, he had to-day sought to *heap injury upon injury, by blasting her reputation as he had before ruined her virtue.* Such conduct deserved the utmost severity of punishment, and he *regretted that the law did not admit of his awarding him hard labour in addition to his term of imprisonment.*"

Such was the judge's opinion of the *defence* set up on behalf of the defendant. For setting up such a defence he deserved hard labour in a house of correction. Did the defendant then conduct his own case? No, it was conducted for him by a regular counsel. Who suggested it? Who got it up? Who procured these creatures of the brothel to bear what the judge believes to be *false* witness against a girl whom the law presumes to be helpless—the effect of which is to "heap injury upon injury" by "blasting her reputation?" Who endeavoured to persuade the jury that it was true? Will anybody believe that all this was done by the youth himself? Can anybody doubt that it was all done by professional advice, labour, and skill? And if, supposing it all the act of the defendant himself (who had at least the fear of punishment to plead in excuse) it was an additional crime that deserved the treadmill, what is to be said of those professional gentlemen whose act it really was, and who had no such excuse? what of the rules of a profession which allows such crimes to be committed as a matter of course? what of the judge himself, who in delivering so heavy a censure against the defendant, who was in all probability only a consenting party, passes by without a word of reproof, admonition, or regret, those whom he must have known to be the real originators and contrivers of it? It may be impossible to prevent these things from being done, but it must be possible, when they thus come to light, to make them infamous.

II.

WITH reference to the remarks which we made last week upon a criminal trial in which the judge denounced the defence as an aggravation of the crime, and yet found no fault with the professional advisers by whom it was got up, a correspondent asks what a barrister ought to do in such cases; and whether we are prepared to say that "no advocate should attempt to persuade a jury to believe that of which he is not himself satisfied."

If this question were advanced by way of objection to what we said, we should merely answer that at all events an advocate ought *not* to do that which was done in the case to which we refer (and which is done, we may add, in almost every case of seduction where the woman is the injured party), that is, to assist in a proceeding which adds a fresh injury to the injury already done. If a particular line of defence be one which the accused party is not justified in pursuing, it is also one which a lawyer cannot be justified in suggesting or advising or preparing or maintaining. With whom individually the responsibility rests, we leave the members of the profession to settle among themselves. We only contend that it rests among them. It is not the client, but his professional advisers, upon whom it depends whether a line of defence shall or shall not be taken. That the defence taken in this case was an *immoral* one; that the attempt to make it good, instead of "conducing to the ends of justice," was itself a new act of injustice, which deserved punishment; all this we take upon the authority of the judge himself. If he was wrong let it be said so. If the defence, however false and injurious in the particular case, was one of a class which cannot be generally proscribed without injury upon the whole to the cause of justice, let that be made out. If the attorney who got it up believed the story which his witnesses

told, or if the lawyers acted according to instructions which they
were not at liberty to disobey, let that be said. So the whole
guilt rests with the criminal, and the profession stands clear.

But as the matter stands, we must still say that the censure
which the judge directed against the defendant does in fact fall
upon the profession, and that they ought to be made to feel it.
A gross injury has been committed. It has been committed, if
not by the advice, at least with the consent and help of members
of a profession which aspires to be considered an honourable
one. Who they are, though it is not known to us, can be no
secret to their brethren, and yet they are not treated as if they
had done anything wrong. How should this be?

We do not however understand our correspondent as meaning
to dispute this position; but only as wishing to raise the larger
and more difficult question, which stands next in order, as to
the duty of an advocate. With regard to the defence of bad
cases, we have no hesitation in saying that we would *not* have
an advocate forbidden to argue in favour of the side which he
himself believes to be wrong. We do not want to assign to the
advocate the office of the judge. We believe that the true
interests of justice are best served, by having each side of the
case presented successively to the jury by a person whose special
duty it is to make *the most that can be fairly made* of the arguments on his own side. But what, it will be asked, is the most
that can be *fairly* made? Who shall say what is fair in an
argument, and what is unfair? To this we reply that though
no general rule can be laid down, and though many particular
cases will occur in which opinions will be divided, yet in a vast
number of cases, including all the gross ones, the common sense
and natural justice of mankind will settle the question by accla-
mation. As it is, there occur now and then abuses of advocacy
so extreme that even lawyers censure them as dishonourable,
and that censure it is which makes them rare. A thing which
is discountenanced by the profession to which a man belongs
he will not often do. We wish to see this power exercised far
more extensively and far more consistently than it is now; and
especially by the judges, who have the best means of understanding where fair-play ends and foul-play begins; under

whose eyes the iniquities are practised, and whose deliberate discountenance (which need only, one would think, be the natural expression of inward aversion) would have such great effect in checking them.   Sophistry and unfairness there will always be as long as there are parties ; but it may be reduced indefinitely both in quantity and quality.   Members of Parliament on both sides of the House are continually unfair and sophistical ; but would the most unscrupulous partisan in the House venture to use such liberties as a lawyer uses before the judge ?   The point of honour is as strong with barristers as with the rest of us.   What does any lawyer fear more than the doing what is unprofessional ?   Let it be considered *unprofessional* in an advocate to defend a cause by evidence of witnesses whom he has reason to believe perjúred, or by reasoning which he feels to be false ; and which he can therefore only make tell in his favour by confusing, misleading, and abusing the understandings of the jury.

XVII.

A QUESTION CONCERNING BOOKS PUBLISHED ON COMMISSION.

In a little book published in 1867 I tried to show that the payment of a percentage upon the receipts for copies sold was the form of agreement between authors and publishers most convenient for both parties. Among the daily and weekly critics who noticed the book, the only one that went into a discussion of the question was a writer in the *Spectator*, whose practical conclusion (though he wrote as an opponent and did not seem to be aware of it) was exactly and in all respects the same as my own.

But in proceeding to explain on behalf of the publishers why the share of the profits which they reserve for themselves is not more than their due—a charge by the way, made by other people, but not by me—he put it upon a ground which seems to me inconsistent with their treatment of books for which they are asked to risk nothing. According to him, their right to a share, which to the uninitiated may seem exorbitant, in the proceeds of all their publications rests upon this calculation :—In the case of new books by unknown authors so many fail to pay their expenses that a publisher who does not make sure of at least thirty per cent. upon his outlay in the case of those which do pay, will be in danger of bankruptcy. "The books which swim," he said, "must bear the loss of those which sink."

Be it so. He must calculate the chances for himself, and it is not for me, when asking for an advance of money on such doubtful security, to find fault with the terms upon which it is offered, otherwise than by refusing to accept them. But how if I offer to advance the money myself? If the risk of sinking in every such case be so great, such an arrangement must surely be for the publisher's advantage; publication by commission should be his favourite form of agreement, and with a view to his own interest he ought to make it as eligible as he can to all unknown authors who can afford it, by helping them to make it succeed; that is to make the printing cost as little and the book sell as fast as possible; for in that case it would be for their interest also.

Upon the *Spectator's* account of the matter, this inference seemed so inevitable, and the fact (if it were a fact) so well worth knowing, that I tried to call attention to it at the time in a letter to the editor; which, as I heard no more of it then, and as I still feel curious about the explanation, I take this opportunity of laying before other people. I am aware that there are *some* publishers who are glad to publish on commission books which they would not venture to publish at their own risk. But I have reason to believe that there are others who decline (or at any rate are *not* glad) to publish on commission any book which is not likely to have a sale large enough to repay its own cost. Though they are sure of a profit of ten per cent. upon that cost under any circumstances, with the chance of ten per cent. more upon the proceeds of all the copies they succeed in selling, the thing is not worth doing for the money. Authors who address a small number of readers scattered here and there about the land are thus left at a loss for convenient means of finding who they are and where; and for the benefit of the writers of books that are to be commercially unsuccessful—no inconsiderable body— those publishers who find it for their interest to do publishers' work on these conditions would find it worth while to advertise the fact.

To the Editor of the "Spectator."

18th March, 1867.

SIR,—I was very glad to see the remarks in your number for March 9 on "Authors and Publishers," because, if I understood them rightly, your practical conclusion is exactly the same as

mine : namely, that the fairest form of agreement between author
and publisher would be this :—For every copy that the publisher
shall sell, or if that be objected to, for every copy that he shall
sell above a certain number to be named beforehand, let him
agree to pay the author a fixed sum. This kind of agreement
you think would be readily accepted by the publishers. If it be
so, and if it be known that it is so, I have no more to say : for it
is exactly what I proposed, and all I proposed. If authors,
having the choice, do not prefer it to a share in the profits, I
think them unwise : but it is their own affair.

How far publishers are in the habit of undertaking, or authors
of asking them to undertake, the expense of publications which
are not likely to repay the outlay, I have no means of knowing.
I can only say for myself that no publisher ever incurred either
loss or risk of loss on my account. I never asked a publisher
to advance sixpence upon any literary adventure of mine, or to
pay sixpence for any help I have given him in any adventure of
his own.   There have been cases in which I have had something
to say which I wished to publish, and there have been cases in
which, finding a publisher engaged in an enterprise which I
wished to succeed, I have given the best help I could.   But
wherever he has undertaken the expense he has had all the
proceeds, and wherever I have retained any interest in the
proceeds, I have undergone all the expense.   If therefore he is
obliged to take thirty per cent. out of the gains of other men's
books, it is not to reimburse himself for anything he has lost by
mine.

But the price he demands for his services does not in my
opinion require any such justification.   In my opinion he may
fairly demand whatever he can fairly get.   I mean by " fairly,"
without fraud and without concealment.   If I could do any
service for *him* which he could not afford to forego, would I let
him have it for less than he could afford to give ?   Not I.   I
would screw him to the sticking place.   If I offer to do his work
for nothing, it is when I wish the work to be done to my own liking ;
and therefore to make it his interest to let me do it rather than
someone else whose work I might not like so well.   What I
objected and still object to in the general practice (for in my

own case, as I have said, I have no ground of complaint whatever) is not that he makes too good a 'bargain for himself, or
that he credits himself with ten per cent. upon all the money he
expends, or that he buys at trade prices and charges for what
he has bought at gentleman's prices, and so forth; but that he
does these things without letting it be known that he does them,
and so makes it impossible for the other party to know what the
bargain really is. Nay, if his friends and allies are to be
believed, he even resists and resents the attempt to investigate
the conditions of it. For when I try by the application of a
little arithmetic to find out what profit is made by each, and
how, they warn me to expect disastrous consequences; and the
fairest of inquiries into the practice of publishers is spoken of
for shortness as an attack upon the trade. But however that
may be, the adoption of the " royalty " plan would remove the
obscurity of the bargain without altering the substance of it.
The substance would be determined by the condition of the
market.

From what you say of the risks of the trade and the
chances of success and failure in books by unknown writers, and
the balance of obligations between author and publisher, I do
not distinctly gather on which side you suppose the chances to
be. But I fancy you would agree with those who think that
more books sink than swim ; and that when a publisher undertakes the publication of a work of which he knows nothing else,
he knows that it will *probably* be a losing bargain. This at any
rate is the opinion of some persons who profess to have had
means of judging. But if it be so, I cannot understand why in
such cases he does not decidedly prefer publishing by commission,
if he can ; the author taking all the expense and risk, and himself
receiving his percentage upon the sales, whether they reimburse
the author or not. Yet I have always been told that this
arrangement is considered a bad one for the author, because the
publishers do not like it, and not liking do not care to make the
best of it. Now, if they really prefer to pay the expenses themselves and take half the profits, it must surely be because they
expect not to lose by the bargain, but to gain; and to gain
something more than ten per cent. upon the sales (which the

commission secures to them) *plus* the interest of the money advanced, which you say pays ten per cent. where it is.   If on the contrary they really prefer the other arrangement where they can get it, and will take as much pains to promote the sale of a commission-book as of one published at half profits, it is a pity the fact is not known : for the class of books which are most likely to be the subject of such an arrangement, books which are wanted in the standard but not in the circulating library, is one of great value to literature ; and it is most desirable, if it be practicable, to relieve them from so heavy a tax as thirty per cent., added to the cost for the benefit of a middleman, whose services (it would seem, upon this supposition) can be secured for ten per cent. with conditions more agreeable to himself.—I am, etc.

XVIII.

ON SOME OVERSIGHTS IN RECENT HISTORIES.

ALLEGED CONFESSION OF INTENDED PIRACY BY SIR WALTER RALEGH.[*]

In one of the most original and valuable contributions to the biography of Sir Walter Ralegh which I have met with (*Edinburgh Review*, April, 1840),[†] the writer, in discussing the great question whether upon the failure of his last expedition to Guiana he had a deliberate intention to retrieve his fortune by piracy, produces two pieces of evidence as " settling the question." One is derived, through Mr. Tytler or Mr. Jardine, from the State-paper Office; the other directly, it would seem, from the British Museum. And certainly, as they stand in the Review, they have a very conclusive appearance. I had occasion, however, some time ago, while engaged in a different inquiry, to examine the original manuscripts in both cases; and I think I can show that in one of them the meaning has been misunderstood, and that in the other a circumstance has been overlooked which takes away the force of the evidence ; and that, instead of settling the question at issue, they do in fact leave it precisely where it was. I hope you will think a page or two of your Magazine properly employed in pointing out the error; the rather because it is one which would hardly be detected except by accident.

After arguing upon other grounds that "piracy was in

---

[*] *Gentleman's Magazine*, April, 1850.

[†] The article alluded to was written by Professor Napier, at that time editor of the *Edinburgh Review*. He long contemplated a new edition of the works of Raleigh.—Ed.

Ralegh's immediate view" (a point which I do not mean to dispute; for I think the appearances are very strong against him), the reviewer proceeds thus :—

"But there is further and conclusive evidence of the fact. It appears that at one of the meetings of the Commission appointed, after his return, to inquire into his conduct, he was examined upon this point, in presence of two óf his captains, and constrained *to make a confession which settles the question.* There is a minute of the proceedings of this Commission, in the handwriting of Sir Julius Cæsar, one of the body, which bears that, ' on being confronted with Captains St. Leger and Pennington, *he confessed that he proposed the taking of the Mexico fleet, if the mine failed.'* Mr. Tytler could not have been aware of this decisive admission, otherwise he would not have attempted to discredit the following remarkable anecdote, preserved in Sir Thomas Wilson's report of his conversations with Raleigh:—' This day,' says the spy, ' he told me what discourse he and my Lord Chancellor had had about the taking of the Plate fleet, *which he confessed he would have taken had he lighted upon it.* To which my Lord Chancellor said, " Why, you would have been a pirate ! " " Oh," quoth he, " did you ever know of any that were pirates for millions ? They only that work for small things are pirates." ' Looking to the character in which Wilson writes, and unacquainted with Raleigh's admission in presence of the Commissioners, Mr. Tytler represents the report of the former as more than suspicious; adding however, inconsistently enough, that ' the observation ascribed to Raleigh is characteristic.' If characteristic, does not that imply authenticity? The observation is indeed strongly stamped with Raleigh's mind and character ; and. *his intentions respecting the Plate fleet being otherwise certain,* we cannot for a moment doubt that it was truly reported." (pp. 87, 8.)

The original note from which this anecdote is taken (for it is not a *report*, but a *rough note* of the conversation ; an important distinction, as will appear presently,) may be seen in the State-paper Office, vol. 73, Domestic, fo. 304. It is in Sir T. Wilson's hand, and runs thus :—

"26 Sept. 1618. This day he fell of himself into discourse, in telling me what the lords asked him yesterday and what he answered ; and after told me how Secretary Winwood carried him twice to the French ambassador's Monsieur Marettz, to dispute with him about Sir John Fern's ship being taken in one of our ports after he had a commission from France to go to the Indies ; and what discourse he and my Lord Chancellor had about taking the Plate fleet, which he confessed he would have taken if he could have lighted on it right, and that when my Lord Chancellor said, ' Why then you would have been a pirate ! ' ' Oh,' quoth he, ' did you ever know of any that were pirates for millions ? They that mych for small things are pirates. I could have given 10,000 to this, and 10,000 to such an one, and 600,000 to the king, and secured enough besides.' "

---

* Brit. Mus. Lansdowne MSS. 142, fo. 412.

Now it is true that any one reading this note by itself, and not knowing or not considering the other circumstances of the case, might naturally suppose that this conversation with my Lord Chancellor was part of what had passed the day before in presence of the council. A little consideration should indeed have suggested that the thing was incredible. Whatever Ralegh may have *told* Sir Thomas Wilson that he had said, it is impossible to suppose that on such an occasion he really did make a *confession* so fatal, accompanied with a *profession* so audacious; and more impossible still to suppose that, *if* he did, the fact could have been left unnoticed in the king's "Declaration," which was put forth shortly after in justification of the execution. If the words admitted of no other explanation, one could only suppose either that they were falsely reported or that Sir Walter had been amusing himself by making a fool of Sir Thomas. But the truth is that this conversation (which Ralegh related to Wilson, you will observe, *after* he had told him what passed between him and the lords on the preceding day,) was not related as having taken place then, but long before. This is proved by a paper which may be seen at p. 314 of the same volume, and which is not a rough note, but the draft of a *collection* of all that Sir Thomas Wilson had elicited from Sir Walter Ralegh. It contains the following passage :—

"He hath always protested that he had never any purpose to hurt any of his Majesty's friends, neither Spaniard nor other; and yet now he confesseth that, *before he went*, having conference with some great lords his friends, who told him that they doubted he would be prizing if he could do it handsomely, 'Yea (saith he), if I can light right on the Plate fleet, you will think I were mad if I should refuse it;' to whom they answering, 'Why, then you will be a pirate!' 'Tush,' quoth he, 'my lord, did you ever hear of any that was counted a pirate for taking millions? They are poor mychers that are called in question for piracy, that are not able to make their peace with that they get. If I can catch the fleet I can give this man ten thousand, and that man ten thousand, and 600 thousand to the king, and yet keep enough for myself and all my company.'"

Now, if you bear in mind that this last is from the draft of a formal statement, meant, no doubt, for the king's information, whereas the other is only a loose note jotted hastily down at the time for the assistance of Sir Thomas's own memory, you will have no doubt that we have here the true explanation of the matter. It was *before Sir Walter set out on his expedition*, when he was newly set at liberty, and was making his preparations, that he had this curious conversation with Bacon, then Lord Keeper, now Lord Chancellor; and it is credible enough that in the gaiety of his spirits he may have talked at that time in that idle way; partly in mere jest, and partly, perhaps, by way of feeler. Such talk at such a time was characteristic of the man, and could only pass for nonsense. He may very likely have been reminded of it afterwards before the Council; but to quote it in support of a serious charge would have been absurd. This piece of evidence, therefore, whether urged as a direct proof, or only as corroborative, must in common reason and justice be set aside altogether, as having no real bearing on the point at issue.

But what shall we say of Sir Julius Cæsar's minute, which states that, being confronted before the Council with two of his captains, Sir Walter "confessed that he proposed the taking of the Mexican fleet, if the mine failed ? " In this there is nothing, on the face of it, difficult to believe ; he may not only have *proposed* such a thing to his captains on the voyage, but, being confronted with them afterwards, he may have been driven to confess that he did. To " propose," however, is not necessarily to "intend ; " and it is the intention with which we are concerned. Now it is stated in the king's "Declaration" that he made this admission; but it is added that he explained it away by saying, that " *he did it only to keep his men together ; *" that is to say, he admitted that he had *proposed*, but denied that he had *intended*, to take the Mexican fleet. In reply to another of the charges—that of having procured a French commission—he stood upon the same distinction.

" ' I urging him further,' says Sir T. Wilson, in a letter to the king, 21 Sept. 1618, 'that himself had said that he had a commission out of France, and that it was told at M. de Marettz table before his going hence, he said 'tis true that he *said* so ; for, saith he, when we found so ill success at S. Thome we fell to counsel about taking the Plate fleet or the Mexican fleet, at which, said some, what shall we be the better? for, when we come home, the king will have what we have gotten, and we shall be hanged. Then, quoth Rawley, you shall not need to fear that ; for I have a French commission, by which it is lawful to take any beyond the Canaries. And I have another, quoth Sir John Ferne, and by that we may go lie under Brest or Bell Ile, and with one part thereof satisfy France, and with another procure our peace with England. But he saith *he had no such commission; but spake it only to keep the fleet together, which else he found were apt to part and fall on pirating.'*" (S. P. O. Domestic, 1618.)

That the confession is important, and the explanation far from satisfactory, is not to be denied; but to urge it as an admission which "settles the question," and leaves no doubt as to his *intentions*, is manifestly unjust.

It may be urged indeed that the statement in Sir Julius Cæsar's minute is absolute, and not followed by any qualifying explanation; and this brings me to the circumstance which I have mentioned as having been overlooked. Sir Julius Cæsar's minute is written upon a single sheet, which has been folded up so as to contain eight narrow pages. They have [been taken in the order which the *folded* sheet naturally presented, but being now spread out and bound up in a folio volume the order is not easily discernible. Upon a careful examination however it will be found that they are all filled, and that the sentence cited by the reviewer is written *at the bottom of the last* (with the exception only of a single line of reference which appears to refer to something else), and I have little doubt that the notes were continued on another sheet, which has not been preserved. That the explanation therefore which is set forth in the "Declaration" does not appear in the minute, is an accident from which no fair inference can be drawn.

It is true that a table of contents is prefixed to the volume, drawn up apparently by Sir Julius himself: and that a description of this minute is entered there, without any intimation that it is incomplete. But this also is an accident from which nothing can be inferred. For it is evident that whoever inserted the description of it in that table had not looked to the end of the sheet, for it is described quite inaccurately as relating to Sir Walter's trial *at Winton*, which was in 1603. It so happens that the first column which meets the eye as it lies in the bound volume *does* relate to that trial; but the minute itself is of the proceedings before the commissioners in London in 1618; and gives an abstract of the formal charge made against Sir Walter, first by the Attorney and next by the Solicitor-General, for his conduct before, during, and after his voyage to Guiana, and of his answers. It is pity there is no more of it, for I do not doubt that it would have confirmed all the statements in the king's Declaration, which in all the parts where I have been able to test it by comparison with the original depositions is careful and accurate.

The true version of the conversation with Bacon about the taking of the Plate fleet may help us to the true explanation of another anecdote with which the reviewer confesses himself perplexed.

"Immediately after the death of Elizabeth (he says) a meeting took place at Whitehall of the chief public men then in London. . . . Aubrey . . . . ascribes to Raleigh a proposal not a little calculated to awaken curiosity; but to which neither Mr. Tytler nor Dr. Southey adverts—a proposal to pull down the monarchy and substitute a republic! Aubrey avers that this proposition was advanced by Raleigh at the above-mentioned meeting at Whitehall. 'Let us keep the staff in our own hands, and set up a commonwealth, and not remain subject to a needy and beggarly nation!'—were the astounding words he is represented to have there uttered. Dr. Warton might well consider this a very remarkable anecdote, if indeed it could be viewed as true. But it rests wholly on the authority of this credulous collector of historical gossip; and, though it partakes of Raleigh's bold, aspiring, and scheming disposition, the supposition of the possibility of establishing a republic at that time, and in the then state of England, is much too chimerical to allow us to imagine that it could be broached by a man of his understanding, and to such an assembly as that to which it was said to have been addressed." (p. 42.)

We have only to suppose that he said it *in jest*, and the wonder vanishes. Raleigh was a gay, bold talker, who cared very little for the impression he made upon his hearers; probably liked to astonish them. Compare the two anecdotes, and you will see at once the same man in both.

QUEEN ELIZABETH IN THE CAMP AT TILBURY.

(From the Notes to "A Conference of Pleasure," 1870.)

IN Mr. Motley's "History of the United Netherlands," vol. ii. p. 512, there is a passage relating to Queen Elizabeth's appearance at Tilbury, which tends indirectly and unintentionally to

throw undeserved discredit upon a very meritorious man.
" Great (he says) was the enthusiasm certainly of the English
people as the volunteers marched through London to the place
of rendezvous, and tremendous were the cheers when the brave
Queen rode on horseback along the lines of Tilbury. . . . 'It was
a pleasant sight,' *says that enthusiastic merchant-tailor John
Stow*, 'to behold the cheerful countenances, courageous words
and gestures of the soldiers as they marched to Tilbury, dancing,
leaping, wherever they came, as joyful at the news of the foe's
approach as if lusty giants were to run a race. And Bellona-like
did the Queen infuse a sacred spirit of loyalty, love, and resolution into every soldier of her army, who, ravished with their
sovereign's sight, prayed heartily that the Spaniards might land
quickly, and when they heard they were fled, began to lament.' "
This he gives as if it were an extract from Stow's Chronicle; and
then proceeds to remark that at the time of Elizabeth's appearance in the camp there was no longer any danger to be apprehended. " If a Spanish army had ever landed in England at all,
that event must have occurred on the 7th of August. . . . For
aught that Leicester, or Burghley, or Queen Elizabeth knew at
the time, the army of Farnese might, on Monday, have been
marching upon London. Now on that Monday morning the
army of Lord Hunsden was not assembled at all, and Leicester,
with but four thousand men under his command, was just commencing his camp at Tilbury. The ' Bellona-like' appearance
of the Queen on her white palfrey, with truncheon in hand,
addressing her troops in that magnificent burst of eloquence
which has so often been repeated, was not till eleven days afterwards, August $\frac{8}{18}$, not till the great Armada, shattered and tem-
pest-tossed, had been, a week long, dashing itself against the
cliffs of Norway and the Faröes on its forlorn retreat to Spain."
(p. 514.)

Had this passage not been given as a *quotation* from John
Stow himself, I should not have thought it worth noticing. If
the Queen had been in personal danger at Tilbury, she would
have had no right, except in a last extremity, to be there ; and it
was no fault of hers that a fine writer chose to compare her to
Bellona. But though Elizabeth's reputation is not concerned,

Stow's is; and if this be accepted as a specimen of the style of
his "Chronicle," it must materially affect the reputation of that
valuable work. The fact appears to be, that Mr. Motley, using
one of the later editions of Stow, "continued and augmented
with matters foreign and domestic, ancient and modern," by
Howes, and not remembering that additional matter may be
inserted in the middle of a book as well as at the end, assumed
that in quoting the description of a scene which occurred long
before Stow's death, he was quoting Stow himself. But this is
not so. The passage in question, the substance of it at least,
may be seen in Nichols's "Progresses of Queen Elizabeth," vol. ii.
p. 534; where it seems to be taken from an account in some contemporary tract, the title of which is not given, of the preparations for resisting the Spanish invasion. This account was
worked up by Howes, or some other unskilful redactor (for the
fragments are very badly pieced together), and interpolated into
the chronicle; but Stow's own account of the matter is in quite a
different style. In an old black-letter copy, published by himself,
and bringing the history up to the year 1592, the account of the
Queen's visit to the camp at Tilbury stands thus :—

" Now (as you have heard before) the campe in this meane
time, being kept at Tilbury in Essex, under the charge of the
erle of Leicester L. Steward, etc.; the 9 of August, hir
Majesty repaired thither, where al the whole campe being set in
order of battell, both horse and footemen, she passed through
every ranke of them, to their great comfort and rejoycing, and
was lodged that night and the night next following, in the house
of Master Edward Rich, a justice of that shire, in the parish of
Hornedon. On the next morrow, being the tenth of August,
hir majesty returning to the campe, beheld the same, they being
all trained in the best order that might be, and on the eleventh
of August returned to St. James', and shortely after the campe
was dissolved."

If too much was made of the matter, it was clearly not the
fault of John Stow. But though Mr. Motley may not have
exaggerated the danger that was past, I cannot but think that
he rather undervalues that which remained. On the tenth of
August, while the Queen was still at the camp, Sir Francis

Drake himself wrote thus to Sir Francis Walsingham :—" The Prince of Parma, I take him to be as a beare robbed of her whelps ; and no doubt but being so great a soldiour as he is, that he will presently, if he may, undertake some great matter, for his credit will stand nowe thereupon. . . . Wrytten with much haste, for that we are ready to set sayl to prevent the Duke of Parma this southerly wynd, if it please God, for truly my poor opinion is that we should have a great eye upon him.

August 10th, 1588.

" *Postscript.* Sithens the wryting herof, I have spoken with an Englishman which came from Dunkirk yesterday, who sayth, upon his life there is no fear of the fleet. Yet would I willingly see it ! " *

THE DAY AT ZUTPHEN.

(From the same.)

Tiis was the action of 22nd September, 1589, in which Sir Philip Sydney received his mortal wound ; and it is strange that Bacon in his " Considerations touching a War with Spain," where he is producing evidence to prove that " in all actions of war or arms, great and small, which have happened these many years, ever since Spain and England have had anything to debate one with the other, the English upon all encounters have perpetually come off with honour and with the better," should have forgotten to mention it. For whatever else may be said of it, there was never any which proved more signally the superiority of the English troops in an " encounter." The odds were in fact so great that it is difficult to understand either how so experienced a soldier as Sir John Norris (who was in command of the service and led the charge) could have risked an engagement on such conditions, or how so great a commander as the Prince of Parma could have failed to improve the opportunity to their utter destruction. " If you saw the ground," said the Earl of Leicester, writing to Walsingham a week after from the camp, " with the numbers of the enemy, and the advantage they had

* Wright's " Elizabeth and her Times," vol. ii., p. 389.

of the ground, you would marvel that even any one man escaped of our side." Yet what is certain is that 250 horse and 300 foot of the English attacked upwards of a thousand horse and two or three thousand foot of the Spanish, in a strong position and prepared to receive them, and after a hand-to-hand fight of an hour and a half, within short range of the enemy's muskets, drew off in good order, with the loss of only 18 horsemen and 22 footmen, and were not pursued.

The English reports are so much occupied with the personal exploits of the several knights in that fierce encounter, that they take no notice of the difficulty, and instead of supplying a satisfactory explanation, scarcely leave room for one. But in Grimestone's "History of the Netherlands," (a translation from John Francis Petit,) I find an account of the action, which, though the construction is in several places obscure, makes the conduct of it intelligible.

"The Prince of Parma fearing that the Earl of Leicester might do something against Zutphen . . . . went to Bunckloo, from whence he sent certain victuals into Zutphen, going himself in person with his vanguard; which the Earl of Leicester, knowing that the town was not yet fully victualled, he thought the next time they victualled it to set upon the convoy; whereunto he appointed Sir John Norris and Sir William Stanley, with certain foot, and others with some troops of horsemen. The 22nd of September, in the morning betimes, the Prince of Parma caused more victuals to be sent unto Zutphen with the same convoy of his vanguard as they had before; being 600 or 700 horse, and 2,000 pikes and musketeers. They staying in a strong place, by a village called Warnsvelt, half a mile from the town, and so let the carts and wagons pass along, which, being discovered by a troop of 30 horse, Sir John Norris, the Earl of Essex, the Lord Willoughby, Sir William Stanley, Sir Philip Sydney, Sir William Russell, and others, rode thither, with about 200 horse and 1,500 musketeers and pikes, *meeting with their enemies before they expected them, by reason it was then very misty;* they of the Prince of Parma's side, led by the Marquis of Guast [Vasto], upon their watchword given, began to shoot furiously out of their ambuscadoes, being a place of great advan-

tage, as if it had been a sconce: which they on the Earl of
Leicester's side manfully withstood, not any one once retiring
out of his place, to the no little amazement of the enemy, which
being past, *and the enemy not knowing how strong the Englishmen
were,* and perceiving them to advance, they sent out a cornet of
horse under the leading of Captain George Cressier, an Albanois,
which was presently overthrown, and the Captain himself taken
prisoner; after that they sent Count Hannibal Gonzaga with his
cornet of horse, the which was likewise valiantly charged, put to
rout, and part thereof slain, and he himself slain, or deadly
wounded; they pursued the rest close under their shot, where
the third cornet made show to come to charge them; but it
being likewise driven back, they parted one from the other, in
regard that the Prince of Parma began to send more men to
strengthen them . . . . whereupon the English, *not knowing how
strong the enemy was,* withdrew themselves unto their camp, and
so did the Prince of Parma unto his." (Lib. 13, p. 926.)

Except for a difference as to numbers (which shows that this
account did not come from the English side, for the numbers of
the Spanish convoy are diminished by about a third, and those of
the English infantry increased five-fold)—there is nothing here
inconsistent with the facts which come out in the letters of the
Earl of Leicester: namely, that the service committed to Sir
John Norris was only the interception of a convoy; that there
was no expectation of such a force coming with it, nor any
preparation for such an encounter; that the English troops,
advancing through a fog, came suddenly upon " an ambuscade "
of 3000 men, "the most muskets, the rest pikes;" that the
English horsemen being foremost "would not turn, but passed
through "—that is, as I understand it, passed through the fire
of the infantry—"and charged the Horsemen that flede (*sic*)
at the back of their Footemen "—that is, charged the cavalry,
which had withdrawn to leave the passage clear for the musketeers to fire—and that this charge was mainly assisted by
those principal noblemen and gentlemen, who having been staying by the Earl of Leicester in the mist, as soon as they knew
where the fighting was to be, " went on till they found Sir John
Norris; to whom " (adds the Earl) "I had committed this ser-

vice only to have impeached a convoy; but he, seeing these young fellows, indeed, led them to this charge, and all these joined in front together," etc. (Leycester Correspondence. Camd. Soc. p. 416.)   The expression "*went on till they found* Sir John Norris," coming as it does immediately after the mention of *the mist* in which they were staying, seems to imply rather that the mist continued than that it had dispersed.   And it is a circumstance of some importance.   Both Mr. Bruce and Mr. Motley represent it as suddenly clearing off.   "Suddenly," says Mr. Motley, "the fog, which had shrouded the scene so closely, rolled away like a curtain, and in the full light of an October morning, the English found themselves face to face with a compact body of more than three thousand men."   Now it may be that there is some contemporary authority for that picturesque incident, but I find no trace of it in any of the original English reports, and picturesque incidents, being easily imagined, require the more confirmation.   Unless there is very good authority for saying that the fog cleared away before the fight began, I shall believe that it took place while the fog was still thick enough to prevent either party from seeing more than what was immediately before them.   In that case, as soon as the foremost English horsemen came within sight of the Spanish musketeers, they would be fired upon, and would fall back upon the main body.   The gentlemen who were with Leicester, learning by the fire where the fight was to be, would make for the scene of action; and the whole 200, thus increased to 250, knowing the position but not the numbers of the enemy, would advance against those they saw.   The Spaniards, on their part, unable to guess the strength of the force that threatened them, would stand upon the defensive.   Failing to drive them off by their musketry, they would meet them with cavalry; and when three several companies had been sent against them, one after another, and each in its turn had been broken and overthrown by the impetuosity of the charge, they would be in no good condition to molest them in their retreat.   For by this time, whether the fog had dispersed or not, Norris had got near enough to form some idea of the strength of the body he was attacking, and to understand that without some very large reinforcements he could do no more.

Sir William Stanley also, with his 300 foot (which Parma supposed to be 3000), must have come to the same conclusion. And as reinforcements to the extent required were not forthcoming (no action on that scale having been contemplated), the best thing to be done was to get handsomely away. And the manner in which this was effected may fairly be counted among the felicities of the day. The account given in Stow's Chronicle seems to be the personal narrative of one who was present, and completes the history of the "day at Zutphen."

"All the time this skirmish was with these cornets"—that was the cavalry fight under Sir John Norris—"so our footemen were in fight with the enimie, and by fine force made them once again retire to their safetie. The enimie being retired to his strength, all our horse made a stand by the musket shot, which plaide on them sore, and braved the enimie, bidding him come foorth if he durst, but he would not; which Sir John Norris seeing, rode to his excellencie and bade him be merrie, for said he, you have had this day the honorablest day that ever you had, for a handful of your men have driven the enimie three times to retrait this one day. Further he willed his excellencie either to send for more strength, or else to sound the retrait; which last request he graunted, for that his strengthes were otherwise emploied, and so the retrait being sounded both by drumme and trumpet, our captaines came backe in good order, every man to his quarter, with great praise and honour." Stow, p. 1253.

But what became of the convoy of victuals about which all this dispute was? The old chroniclers say nothing of it, and the later historians tell strangely different stories. Mr. John Bruce—a writer habitually and studiously accurate—describing the result of the day according to the best English authorities as late as the year 1844, says, "The result was glorious. The enemy were driven from their position, *compelled to abandon their attempt to succour Zutphen*, and to retreat with great loss in killed and wounded." (Leicester Correspondence, p. 414, note.) Mr. Motley, writing in 1860, with the help of the best Spanish authorities, says, "The heroism which had been displayed was fruitless, except as a proof—and so Leicester wrote to the Palatine John Casimir—that the Spaniards were not invincible. Two thousand men now sallied from the Loor gate, under Verdugo and Tassis, to join the force under Vasto, and the English were forced to retreat. *The whole convoy was then carried into the city, and the Spaniards remained masters of the field.*"

The fact is, that of the two persons who should have known best, one says the one thing, the other says the other. Leicester, writing to Burghley, distinctly states that "notwithstanding all these troops, the Prince did not put in one waggon, save thirty which got in in the night,"—meaning, I suppose, the night before. The Prince, writing to the King of Spain, congratulates him upon the issue, seeing that they had completely succeeded in what they wanted to do. Leicester is not the best of witnesses, though his letters concerning this day's work are not written at all in the spirit of a man who is making a report in his own honour or justification; and Parma's evidence would have had more weight, if he had not in the same sentence pretended to have maintained the fight with few against many (*a la barba de tan buen numero con tanta poca gente*): a gratuitous misrepresentation which deprives his testimony on the other point of all value. But there is a better reason than the Prince's assertion of the fact for thinking that the waggons *did* get into Zutphen; which is, that we hear of no further fighting; and, without a fight, what could have prevented 3000 men (though reduced by the two or three hundred who may have been killed or disabled in the morning) from carrying them in after dinner? They were on the road, not above a mile off: * and it was never said that any of them were destroyed or carried away by the English.

---

* Warnsfeld, where the action took place, was "about an English mile from Zutphen." Motley, vol. i. p. 45.

XIX

TEACHING TO READ.[*]

THE late discussions at the London School Board on the best method of simplifying and shortening the process of teaching children to read, raised as they have been in the way of business by those who have the thing to do, can hardly fail to produce some good effect, unless the movers defeat their object by trying to do too much. If an attempt be made to introduce any change which would cause inconvenience, trouble, or offence to the multitudes who can read and write already, it will certainly fail. Old fashions go out and new come in—convenient or inconvenient as it may happen—but not upon the recommendation of Royal Commissions, or because they are likely to benefit another generation. In the mean time reading and writing are accomplishments too hardly acquired and too constantly in demand to be interfered with. All eyes, ears, fingers, and vocal organs would unite in indignant protest against any change of fashion which would make them less automatic, though it were but for a little while. To make the *Times* a little more difficult to read for a single day would be to raise a storm which the *Times* itself would hardly survive. If, on the other hand, an attempt be made to teach reading too curiously—to distinguish by letters all the minuter differences of speech, and require them to be learned—the lesson will be too hard for the learner. He will have too many things to remember ; he will learn it imperfectly ; a habit of reading without regard to the rules will soon destroy the connection in his mind between the rule and the practice, and in a

* *Nineteenth Century,* June, 1877.

short time he will be in as bad a condition as he is now; when,
however perfect he may be in his alphabet, he has still to learn
the relation between the letters and the spoken word by a separate act of memory in each case—each word being possibly, and
not improbably, an exception to the rule which ought apparently
to govern it.

Fortunately it is not necessary to encounter either of these
difficulties; for it is certainly possible, by a simple change in
the method of instruction—which nobody who can read already
need trouble himself with—which will task the learner's memory
much less severely than the present method—and which anybody
can easily try—to teach children to read books printed in the
ordinary way both faster and more pleasantly and more perfectly
than they are now taught.

I assume, of course, that the object is not to make them
either etymologists or mimics, but only to teach them to read
and write modern English as it is now spoken and written by
educated people. Now, though the sounds which good speakers
actually utter in speaking are innumerable, the sounds which
they *intend* to utter are limited in number and definite in form.
They correspond to certain definable positions of the vocal organs
of which the number (for English) is not more than forty-two.*
That with an alphabet containing forty-two letters, each letter
being understood to represent only one sound, and each sound
to be represented by only one letter, the proper pronunciation

---

* Though there is much difference of opinion as to the form in which these
sounds may be most conveniently represented, there is room for little or none as to
the sounds themselves which the representation of good modern English speech
requires to be known and discriminated. There are indeed some obscure, uncertain,
and almost indescribable modifications of these sounds which *introduce themselves*
unintentionally and unconsciously, and of which I shall say more presently. But any
alphabet which contains a distinct symbol for each sound in the following list will
be found capable of spelling any modern English word so as to show how it ought
to be spoken—in the opinion, of course, of the speller.

1. The long vowels heard in the words feel, fail, fah, fall, foal, fool.
2. The short vowels heard in the words knit, net, gnat, not, nut, foot.
3. The diphthongs heard in the words file, foil, foul, fow.
4. The sounds of *y* in yea, *w* in way, *wh* in whey, and *h* in hay; of the following
consonants, as ordinarily pronounced, *p, b, t, d, ch, j, k, g* (hard as in *go*), *f, v, s, z, l,
m, n, ng*; of the two sounds of *th* as in *thin* and as in *then*, of *sh* as in *rush* and as
in *rouge*, and of *r* as in *ear* and as in *ring*.

of any English word may be indicated intelligibly and with sufficient accuracy for all the ordinary purposes of speech, has been amply proved by practical trial in the special work of which I speak, the teaching of children to read. Several such alphabets have been proposed; but the one which is readiest for English use, and has also been best tested by actual work, is Mr. A. J. Ellis's, in which, the letters of the orthodox alphabet being used as far as possible for the same sounds which in the ordinary orthography they most frequently represent, any one who can read will find himself at home almost immediately—there being, in fact, more friends than strangers in the company. For him, to understand the notation and its rules thoroughly is the work of a few hours; and with a few days' reading he will find it as familiar as the one he has been used to. Any man who has made himself master of this alphabet is qualified to take a pupil; and if he wishes to teach a child to read, he has only to show him the letters, tell him the sound which belongs to each, explain to him how to make it, and remind him that whenever he sees that letter he is to make that sound, whenever he hears that sound he is to think of that letter.

So far all is as easy as A B C, and no easier. But when he has gone through the whole forty-two in this way, he will find himself in a very different condition from the boy we read of in "Pickwick," who, having mastered the orthodox twenty-six, thought he had gone through a great deal to learn very little. He will find that he has learned a great deal; no less, in fact, than all he need know in order to read correctly any word of one syllable. Take what monosyllable you please. Put the right letters in the right order, and tell him to make the sounds one after another, quickly, without pausing between. He will at once pronounce the word; he will not be able to help it. Before he advances to polysyllables he must learn one thing more, for the mark of accent must be introduced. He must be told that whenever he sees that particular mark over a letter, he must pronounce that syllable more strongly than the others, and he will then be able to pronounce correctly any word which may be shown to him, if it is correctly printed or written in those characters.

All this, however, is only by way of preparation; for we do

not propose to alter our alphabet or our orthography for him, and we must teach him to read our books. As soon, therefore, as he is perfect in the new (which I shall make bold to call the rational) alphabet—which, having no exceptions or irregularities to perplex his mind and burden his memory, he will not find difficult—he must be confronted with the orthodox or irrational alphabet, which he will have to work with in his generation. Then it will be found that the judicious arrangement of Mr. Ellis's notation, which made the transition from the old style to the new so easy for his master, will, for the like reason, make the transition from the new to the old easy for him. Take a list of words from any common spelling-book ; opposite to each in another column place the same word spelt according to the rational system : tell him that the word which is *pronounced* as in the second column is to be *written* as in the first. He will find the two so much alike that, in spite of the differences, he will easily recognize them as the same. He will see, almost without the help of the key, what the spelling-book words are meant for, and will be able to *read* them almost at once. But then will come the really hard part of his task, for he must still learn to *spell* them as they are spelt in the book ; and, having no principle to guide him, while such rules as he is troubled with are subject to so many exceptions that they give him no real help, he must do it by simple memory. He must endeavour to remember the letters which compose each word, and the order of them, and he must fix the impression in his mind by continually renewing it. In this respect, however, if he is no better off than the rest of us, neither is he worse off. It is by reading that we all learn to spell, and having once learned to read spelling-book English he will learn to spell by the same process, even without help, as fast as another—while under a judicious master his progress will be quickened by a simple exercise, the benefit of which will also be felt in other ways. If it be made one of his regular tasks to translate into the phonetic character sentences printed in the received orthography and (inversely) to translate into the received orthography sentences written in the phonetic, it will supply him with the very best kind of exercise both in spelling and pronunciation ; and when he is perfect in it who shall say that he has not been taught to read and write as well as the best of us?

It may be objected perhaps that, though he may have learned it at last, yet, having had so much more to learn by the way, he must have been longer about it. But that is a mistake. It is long since I happened to see any reports from phonetic teachers, but in the days of the *Phonetic News* I used to see many; and their tenor was uniform, to the effect that children who began with the phonetic could read and spell in the ordinary orthography both sooner and better than those who went by the old road. And this brings me to the practical question for the sake of which I have thought it worth while to call attention to these things, obvious as they must be to all who have considered the matter seriously. If this be so, and if, among the many schoolmasters whose business it now is to teach poor men's children to read, there are some who, believing that they can get through their work better and faster in this way, wish to be allowed to try it—is there any reason why they should be forbidden? If they fail, the harm done cannot be much; the worst would be that the time spent by some of the classes in learning how to pronounce their words has left them a little less forward in remembering how to spell them. If they succeed, the gain is substantial and not inconsiderable; for poor men cannot so well afford to keep their children at school longer than is necessary. Considered only as an experiment, it is surely worth the cost of trial; and the cost will be small, for everything is ready. I am told that the School Boards or schoolmasters are divided in opinion, some approving and some disapproving the proposed reform. So much the better. Let us have a match. Let the disapprovers with their twenty-six letters, and the approvers with their forty-two, try which can turn out the best spelling class (old style) within a given time; and if the forty-two carry it, let it be resolved that all teachers who find them useful shall be permitted to use them hereafter if they like. This would be all that is· necessary—perhaps all that is desirable—for the present. If the forty-two letters continue to prove their superiority by results, they may be trusted to take care of themselves, education being now a matter of business which will not consent to waste time and money for the convenience of etymologists whose objects are quite different, and whose means of pursuing them will not be in any way interfered with. The question which is sacred in the eyes of an etymologist is how a particular combination of letters came into use as the name of a particular thing. He follows its history back through all its recorded changes, and if he can trace it to some other combination of letters, supposed to represent a sound which was once used somewhere else as the name of the same thing (or some other), he is satisfied. With this the School Boards have nothing to do. Their business is to teach children the use of the language as it is, not to inquire into the series of changes through which it came to be what it is. But if they cannot help him in his work, neither do they threaten him with any hindrance. Some etymologists do indeed write as if a change in the orthography of the future would destroy all traces of the orthography of to-day—an apprehension which seems more strange in the mouth of an etymologist than of anybody else; for if each successive change in the state of a language must destroy the traces of the state which preceded, what becomes of the science of etymology? And if there is any stage in the progress of the English language in which the received orthography must be always ascertainable, it is surely the present. If all the world agreed to disuse it to-morrow, if not another book were printed in it, if ordinary readers lost the power of interpreting it, the etymologist would still find a perfect record of it in every book that has been printed within the last fifty years. Till every such book has been not only set aside but destroyed, the sacred record of the latest form of prephonetic orthography will be preserved intact for the learned. That part of our language of which every change does really "destroy the record" is the pronunciation. The most learned philologist of this generation does not know how his great-grandfather pronounced any single word. And it is satisfactory to think that, whatever be the fate of the present controversy, one result is secure—our posterity will, at any rate, have the means of knowing how English was *spoken* in the latter half of the nineteenth century, with a nearer approach to exactness than has ever been attainable by a third generation in any language. Of that the phoneticians of the present have already set down, for the benefit of etymologists of the future, a record which will remain.

But the registering of the sounds of the spoken language for scientific purposes is a collateral advantage which does not concern our immediate business, and must not be allowed to interfere with it. The forty-two symbols of Mr. Ellis's alphabet will serve to represent with sufficient accuracy all the sounds which a good speaker *intends* to utter. To represent all the sounds which are *actually* uttered in ordinary speech would require a great many more; and though scientific philology, seeking to determine the laws which govern the changes of pronunciation in different languages, requires to know and compare them in all their modifications, yet the simple art of correct pronunciation in a living language wants no more than practical directions for making them. Now it will be observed that, in the mouth of correct speakers with good articulation, all *accented* syllables have a determinate character of their own by which we can distinguish them from each other. Though each speaker sounds them somewhat differently, we all know which sound he means, and can reproduce our own variety of it in our own way. These are the forty-two sounds which form Mr. Ellis's alphabet. But who shall number or define the sounds of the *unaccented* syllables. They are indispensable constituents of every polysyllabic word, and of every combination of words into which unemphatic monosyllables enter; yet the most practised phoneticians cannot agree as to what they are or what vocal configurations they depend upon. How then are they to be represented on paper? and how are children to be taught to make them?

Now, though I should be very sorry to have to define or describe them, yet when I observe the conditions under which they present themselves, I think I see how they may be commanded. Ask a gentleman how he spells a word which he has just pronounced,—*circumstances* for instance,—distinguishing the several syllables in spelling-book fashion. He will say, ' c, i, r, *cir*; c, u, m, *cum,*—*cir-cum*; s, t, a, n, *stan*—*cir-cum-stan*; c, e, s, *ces*—*cir-cum-stan-ces.*' But when he uttered the word in conversation just before, there was only one of the four syllables to which he gave the same sound which he gives in spelling it. Try him with another, in which an unaccented comes before the accented syllable ; say, *committal; c, o, m, com ; m, i, t, mit—com-mit; t, a, l, tal—com-mit-tal.* When he pronounces the word without spelling it, you find that both the first and the last syllable have changed their character—*com* has almost turned into *cum*, and *tal* into *tul.* Now why is this ? He does not do it on purpose; he is not aware probably that he does it at all. He does it simply because it is the easiest way—because he could not do it otherwise without trouble. And this it is that suggests what I believe to be the true, exact, and sufficient direction for the formation of all these obscure and indescribable sounds, in all their varieties, as they are heard in the language of the best speakers. Each of them being in fact the nearest approach to the sound *aimed at* that can be made from the position into which the vocal organs have been brought by their last action, or have to bring themselves in order to be ready for the next, the practical direction for making it is to give to every syllable *as much* of its proper sound—of the sound you give it when you pronounce it by itself—as, without sacrificing the predominance of the accented syllable, *you conveniently can.* The best speakers are those who (subject to this last condition) preserve most of the characteristic sound in each case. It is a slovenly pronunciation which leaves it doubtful whether you said *cymbals* or *symbols.*

Even with accented syllables the same difficulty sometimes occurs, and is to be dealt with in the same way. When I say *"fair face,"* or *" bolt the door,"* I *mean* to give exactly the same sound to the *ai* and *a* in the first case, and to the *o* and *oo* in the second. The sounds I do give them are widely different. Yet it is not a case of obscurity, for the vowels into which the *ai* and the *oo* have transformed themselves are clearly and firmly enunciated, and in foreign languages, as well as in our own provincial dialects, hold a conspicuous place. But they are vowels which the English of the schools and the drawing-room does all it can to repudiate. They have no place in the alphabet or the spelling-book, and I doubt whether any polished English speaker ever utters either of them distinctly when he can avoid it. But here

again we have no need of additional letters; for the same necessity which causes the change of sound supplies an infallible
direction for making the change correctly. *Try* to prolong the
sound of *a* in the first case (*a* as heard in *face*), and of *o* in the
second (*o* as heard in *bolt*), until your tongue is in a position
to form an untrilled *r*: the required modification of the vowel
sound in both cases will be the inevitable result.*

I hold it certain, therefore, that with an alphabet of forty-two
letters sufficient directions may be given for pronouncing English
as correctly as it is usually pronounced in society, and with no
wider variations from the standard, if there be such a thing,
than are commonly heard wherever half-a-dozen Englishmen are
talking together in a drawing-room. The only difficulty which
appears to stand in the way is the choice of the particular
alphabet to be used and the rules for using it. Upon this it is
probable that opinions will differ. And yet, unless the several
teachers can agree to use the same in the same way, a great part
of the benefit will be lost; for the pupils of the several schools
will not have a common system upon which they can interchange
communications. And besides, though one of the rival systems
may be as good as another for the purpose of instruction in the
sounds; and, if they are all equally successful in shortening the
process of teaching to read common books, the *immediate* object
of them all is equally well answered;—it must not be supposed
that this is the only advantage which the pupils are to derive
from the course of instruction they will have to go through. It
must be remembered that all who learn the use of such a phonetic alphabet will possess for the rest of their lives an accomplishment of great value—so great, indeed, that it may be said
without any exaggeration to be coextensive with the value of
letters. They will be able to describe on paper by writing or

---

* Even if this be not, as I think it is, the most scientific direction for the production of the required sound in these cases, it has a collateral merit not to be
despised. It avoids in a vast number of cases the necessity of changing the vowels,
and so producing that strangeness of appearance which, besides offending scholars
(who seem to think it not only awkward but sinful), does really make the reform a
little more difficult. It is obvious that the liker to one another the words in the
two styles *look*, the more readily will they be recognized as the same, and therefore
that both the phonetic teacher will sooner be able to read easily in the new style,
and the phonetic pupil in the old; which is the end we aim at.

print the pronunciation of words, where it is impossible or inconvenient to impart it by speech, and the most ingenious manipulation of the sacred twenty-six, from A to Z, will fail to convey a notion of it. It is true that at first they will have it all to themselves, for their uninstructed elders and betters will not be able to profit by the information. But this will be only for a while. As soon as a knowledge of the phonetic characters becomes an indispensable part of general education, and is required by schools and colleges and Civil Service Commissioners (as it will be when its value comes to be generally understood), newspaper correspondents will be able to tell us what to *call* the people and the places about whom they are enlightening us; books of travels will be readable aloud without the interruption of a stumble and an apology at every proper name; missionaries will be able to give information which will be of use to comparative philologists about the languages of the countries in which they are labouring; we shall know whether another Captain Burnaby rides to Khiva or Kheva, and shall accompany another Commander Cameron with much greater comfort through regions that are now (because of the number of consonants without any vowel between which they require us to pronounce) not to be named. Of its uses in these ways I can speak confidently from personal experience; for I read the accounts of the Hungarian war of 1849 in the *Phonetic News*, where all the proper names were carefully spelt. But it is not merely in the foreign names which perplex us in English books that we shall feel the benefit; the foreign languages will be better and more easily learned, especially by those who aspire to teach themselves. The many scholars who have to learn these languages from books will be furnished with directions for the pronunciation that will serve them almost as well as a skilled teacher; and much better than an unskilled one, however good his own pronunciation may be. The latest reformation in the way of reading Latin and Greek may be circulated by post to all grammar schools. And in short, as soon as the accomplishment becomes as common as reading, it will be found that its uses are as various and as valuable as those of writing. Making it possible to hear by the eye (like a musician, who, having the benefit of a phonetic notation, hears the music as he reads it), it will extend the range of earshot both in time and space indefinitely. A man will be able to make his words heard in Australia with the next mail, and heard by the next ages as long as his book endureth. I know a poet who is happy in most things, but most unhappy in an apprehension that people who have not heard his poems read will never know how to read them. He will be able to stereotype the sounds, the quantities, the pauses, the intonations, the accents, and the emphases, for all the peoples in all the times. He will only have to publish a phonetic edition.

These results will depend upon the consistent use and the general acceptance of the alphabet which shall be chosen; and the very variety of the persons and causes that are interested in it will divide opinions and make the choice more difficult. It may be hoped, however, that if the reforming *teachers* keep to their own business and take counsel together,—leaving etymologists to invent a system of etymological orthography for themselves; foreign linguists to construct such alphabets as are easiest for *them* to work, as ours is easiest for us; making no attempt to convert or conciliate anti-reformers who regard the question as unworthy of serious consideration, and therefore have never considered it seriously; but applying themselves solely to find out the best method of teaching English boys and girls to read and write modern English for modern purposes—they will be able to agree upon one set of symbols and one set of rules to be used by all; and that such an alphabet, having the great advantage of being in possession of the field, will be strong enough to resist foolish changes, to entertain friendly suggestions, to test and adopt real improvements without breaking up, and to serve for the foundation of a system of phonetic notation, the powers and uses of which. may be gradually extended to meet all the requirements of the science of language.

PRINTED AT THE CAXTON PRESS, BECCLES.

www.ingramcontent.com/pod-product-compliance
Lightning Source LLC
Chambersburg PA
CBHW021332110726
47900CB00005B/1429